Visual artworks like Websites only gain with the addition of expertly created access features. Accessibility is value-adding.

Let's refuse to scrimp on **VISUAL SOPHISTICATION** in the name of accessibility. But let's refuse to compromise accessibility for visual sophistication, either.

This book, then, makes accessibility **LESS** of a **PAIN** in the **ARSE**.

BUILDING ACCESSIBLE WEBSITES

NEW RIDERS PUBLISHING

201 WEST 103rd STREET, INDIANAPOLIS, INDIANA 46290

AN IMPRINT OF PEARSON EDUCATION

BOSTON   INDIANAPOLIS   LONDON   NEW YORK   SAN FRANCISCO

BUILDING ACCESSIBLE WEBSITES

COPYRIGHT © JOE CLARK 2003

International Standard Book Number: 0-7357-1150-X
Library of Congress Catalog Card Number: 2001089177

Printed in the United States of America
First Printing: October 2002
06 05 04 03 02   7 6 5 4 3 2 1

Interpretation of the printing code: The rightmost double-digit number is
the year of the book's printing; the rightmost single-digit number is the
number of the book's printing. For example, the printing code 02-1 shows
that the first printing of the book occurred in 2002.

Publisher
David Dwyer

Associate Publisher
Stephanie Wall

Editor in Chief
Chris Nelson

Executive Editor
Steve Weiss

Production Manager
Gina Kanouse

Managing Editor
Sarah Kearns

Acquisitions Editor
Michael Nolan

Project Editor
Michael Thurston

Technical Editors
Curt Cloninger
Mark Pilgrim

Product Marketing Manager
Tammy Detrich

Publicity Manager
Susan Nixon

Manufacturing Coordinator
Jim Conway

Cover Designer
Matt Mahurin

Designer, Compositor
Marc Sullivan

Proofing
Moveable Inc.

Senior Indexer
Cheryl Lenser

Media Developer
Jay Payne

table of contents

A message from New Riders

As the reader of this book, you are our most important critic and commentator. We value your opinion, and we want to know what we're doing right, what we could do better, in what areas you'd like to see us publish, and any other words of wisdom you're willing to pass our way.

As Executive Editor at New Riders, I welcome your comments. You can fax, E-mail, or write me directly to let me know what you did or didn't like about this book — as well as what we can do to make our books better. When you write, please be sure to include this book's title, ISBN, and author, as well as your name and phone or fax number. I will carefully review your comments and share them with the authors and editors who worked on the book.

Please note that I cannot help you with technical problems related to the topic of this book, and that due to the high volume of E-mail I receive, I might not be able to reply to every message. Thanks.

— *Steve Weiss, Executive Editor*
steve.weiss@newriders.com
New Riders Publishing
201 West 103rd Street
Indianapolis, IN 46290 USA
(317) 581-4663 FAX

Visit our Website: www.newriders.com

On our Website, you'll find information about our other books, the authors we partner with, book updates and file downloads, promotions, discussion boards for online interaction with other users and with technology experts, and a calendar of trade shows and other professional events with which we'll be involved. We hope to see you around.

E-MAIL US FROM OUR WEBSITE

Go to newriders.com and click on the Contact Us link if you:

- Have comments or questions about this book.
- Want to report errors that you have found in this book.
- Have a book proposal or are interested in writing for New Riders.
- Would like us to send you one of our author kits.
- Are an expert in a computer topic or technology and are interested in being a reviewer or technical editor.
- Want to find a distributor for our titles in your area.
- Are an educator/instructor who wants to preview New Riders books for classroom use. In the body/comments area, include your name, school, department, address, phone number, office days/hours, text currently in use, and enrollment in your department, along with your request for either desk/examination copies or additional information.

tHe access manifesto

THE TRUE REASON TO DESIGN FOR ACCESSIBILITY is greed. Quite simply, I *want it all*, and so should you. Give us everything you've got. Give us everything there is to give.

Designers assume accessibility means a boring site, a myth borne out by oldschool accessibility advocates, whose hostility to visual appeal is barely suppressed. Neither camp has its head screwed on right. It's not *either–or*; it's *both–and*.

I want nothing less than spectacular graphic design, intelligent, well-tested usability, high-calibre writing with typography to match, top-flight photography and illustration, and resolute cleverness. I want standards compliance, with old, incompatible browsers left to die on the ice floes.

And while all this is happening, I want the highest practicable accessibility standards. I brook no compromises. Why should you?

I'll tell you where all this comes from. I respond strongly to visual stimuli *and to words*, an unusual combination. If you've read Howard Gardner's *Theory of Multiple Intelligences* (Basic Books, 1983), you'll be familiar with the idea that the human brain fires on a number of different cylinders, as it were, which explains why kids who are good in gym class are often lousy in math. Now, in my case the faculties are asymmetrical: I can write but I can't draw. Yet both words and pictures speak to me.

I go back over twenty years in accessibility, dating from a prophetic night at age 13 when I stumbled upon an open-captioned television program, *The Captioned ABC News*. Curiosity immediately took root about this newscast, with its heavily-edited visible words partially duplicating the news anchor's delivery. One detail grew significant: Why did the *W* in the captioning type-face stand higher than the other lower-case letters, and why were the quotation marks two little dots? Posing those questions to the actual captioners led me to discover typography and graphic design, which I have obsessed over, written about, and practiced ever since.

I love good TV, good cinema, good graphic design. I have a modest understanding of photography, and am a published photographer.

All these traits are inseparable. I cannot turn one faculty off while enjoying another. Accessible media, when very well done and when based on something worth looking at in the first place, will form a gestalt. Accessibility is *value-adding.*

I feel like I am missing out when I am forced to deal with inaccessible media. The communal sensory pleasures of watching films in first-run theatres are offset by the lack of beautiful captions and apt, well-delivered descriptions. I have been known to attend plays and subconsciously glance at the feet of the performers, expecting words to appear and disappointing myself when they don't. (Yet I have dreamed in captioning only twice. You'd think that would happen more often.)

Accessibility is value-adding.

True enough, some of us have a hard time taking in such a breadth of information when expressed through so many simultaneous channels. Among nondisabled people, baby boomers predominate in this category; they are one generation too old to have grown up with television, with computers, with foreground and background stimuli intermingling and swapping place. They will never *get* accessible media, nor should they be expected to, until of course their sight and hearing start to erode.

But this is how I look at it: I have high standards, and I know from direct, decades-long experience that beautiful visual artworks take on even greater appeal with the addition of expertly-created access features. You should have the same high standards and *you* should come to share that knowledge.

In this book, I refuse to advocate the unnecessary compromise of visual sophistication for accessibility. But I will not advocate the compromise of accessibility for visual sophistication, either. If you have to noticeably alter your layout to make it accessible, that's what I'll tell you to do. But if, as is nearly always the case, it is possible to provide accessibility with no visible alteration whatsover, I will tell you exactly how to do it.

It simply is not the case that appearance is more important than accessibility. Nor is it less important. Neither is it a question of "balancing" the two, as if they were incompatible. Zero-sum arithmetic is irrelevant here. Yes, you can design a site with a higher or a lower calibre of graphic design, and the entire edifice of Web accessibility as we know it is built around incremental compliance levels. You have lots of leeway. But despite what you have heard, appearance need not come at the wholesale expense of access, or vice-versa.

An objection will now come to mind. Even if we offer up every accessibility technique in the book, the experience of a disabled Website visitor simply cannot be the same as that of a nondisabled visitor. Those who advance this objection do so with the implication that they are telling us something new; it's supposed to be an airtight counterargument against *going to all that trouble*.

Well, newsflash, everyone: Blind people already know they're missing out on the full visual richness of the world, just as the deaf know they will never share in the world's wide-ranging auditory panoply. Telling us that people with sensory disabilities miss out on something is like complaining that vegetarians can't eat meat.

The limitations of disability are obviously built-in; are sometimes immutable but are, in any case, unlikely to change at any specific moment; are accepted by actual people with disabilities; and are barely worth talking about, let alone advancing as a justification for doing nothing. Why moon and gripe over what you cannot see or hear if accessible forms of representation are right there waiting to be used?

Equality is a misnomer. *Equivalency* is the goal. The only people who hold that disabled people's experiences must be on an absolute par with those of nondisabled people are *opponents* of accessibility. The real audience for accessibility features simply uses them; if well-executed, such access features are barely noticed. I speak very much from lived experience here. What gets noticed, what gets in the way, is *inaccessibility*, or, I suppose, inept or ill-executed accessibility.

< Accessibility puts the multi in media.

Nondisabled people view the media landscape and take it all in, and so do disabled people; the fact that the view and the media landscape might differ for each camp is neither here nor there. With access features, both camps are working at the top of their respective forms.

Besides, Web design is a form of *multimedia*. Adding access features brings truth to that word, or at least its first half. Just as even the crassest TV show becomes *way more multi* once you add captions and audio descriptions, even the crassest Websites turn into real multimedia with the rich textual and navigational redundancy this book teaches you to create. Accessibility puts the *multi* in *media*.

The only way to get what I want — which is everything at once: full-on design with full-on accessibility — is to teach you how to do the latter. I can't teach you to be a better designer or programmer, but I can and will teach you top-notch accessibility skills. As for the other half of my goal: Once you're finished with this book, it may be time to upgrade your design and programming skills to match your newfound mastery of accessibility.

This book is all about *raising the bar*.

1| HOW to read tHiS BOOK

THROUGHOUT THE BOOK, I ASSUME MY ESTEEMED READERS have basic knowledge of HTML, the markup language used to create Web pages. I really do mean basic: All you need to know is how to create the simplest text-only Web pages and you will be able to follow the examples I provide.

This book espouses standards compliance through and through. That means all the HTML in this book is actually XHTML Transitional, a current standard (or "recommendation") as of early 2001. If you're new to XHTML, don't worry about it: It *is* HTML, with a few modest modifications you can get the hang of more or less immediately.

I will spend a certain amount of time explaining old, nonstandard ways of doing things, and how browsers and devices that do not comply with standards (like the notorious hoary old cœlecanth of a browser known as Netscape 4) behave and misbehave, but I will spend as little time as possible documenting how to work around the quirks of nonstandard devices.

Code samples in this book are differentiated typographically. We use Signa as a typeface for the actual HTML or other code you'd use in development. (The Colophon at the back of the book tells you more about Signa, our other typographic choices, and computer-book typography in general.) If the idea of typing in those code samples seems daunting, remember that the entire text is available on the book's CD-ROM. Feel free to fire it up in your browser and copy and paste. Moreover, the CD-ROM files offer hyperlinks to references on the Web, including sources for quotations and facts – a more convenient method than publishing mile-long Web addresses that I know perfectly well you will not bother typing out.

Each chapter ends with Bottom-Line Accessibility Advice. Basic, Intermediate, and Advanced accessibility methods are identified as such. Note that certain dilemmas can be solved only with Intermediate or Advanced access techniques, but those are identified clearly.

Basic, Intermediate, and Advanced accessibility methods are provided.

I'll teach fundamental techniques before I teach how to apply them – philosophy first, technique second. That way, as future technologies, standards documents, and requirements come down the pike, you will be well suited to adapt your existing expertise to those new constraints.

I have adopted a resolutely international perspective throughout the book. I am not assuming anything about my readers save for basic ability in HTML; I certainly do not assume you are American, or that only American or English-language examples are appropriate. Case studies are drawn from around the world. Some examples aren't even in English; welcome to the global village.

I make no presumptions about whether you have or do not have a disability, or what method you're using to read this book. I've endeavoured to make the book understandable and pleasant if read in print or heard as speech.

Indeed, the audience for this book extends beyond the cohort of Web designers and programmers. If you are a site administrator or a department or facility manager (or a lawyer) who needs to know what is possible or readily achievable in making a site accessible, this book is for you. If you simply surf the Web and do not create Web pages yourself, you will learn more about the way accessible information is presented.

This book will teach you how to avoid elitism.

You will, I hope, find the book quite readable. I have this fantasy that *Building Accessible Websites* will be as enjoyable to read as a well-written cookbook. (What, you've never read a cookbook while reclining in bed, far removed from the kitchen?) Even though this book, indeed like a cookbook, provides instructions you could otherwise carry out, I hope the quality of the prose makes it attractive even when all you want to do is sit and read.

What this book will teach you

I wrote this book because it needed to be written. From the dawn of the Web, the combination of text and graphics in a visual interface, and the later excursions into sound and video, simply have not been available to everyone.

Of course, the Web isn't available to everyone, either. You need a computer and an Internet connection. In global terms, almost no one has one of those, let alone both. The Web is an elitist medium.

But two wrongs don't make a right. The Web may be elitist, but what is the justification for excluding people who do have a computer and a net connection on the basis of characteristics they cannot change? There's unavoidable elitism and there's the avoidable kind.

This book, then, will teach you how to avoid elitism.

You can still be an elitist after another fashion. You can produce Websites for any audience you want, even a rarefied group. But of course on the Web you cannot predict who your audience will really be. You may think that no one in your "target audience" could possibly require accessibility, but the Web is a pretty big place. Besides, unlikely combinations occur all the time.

Even if you think the content and approach of your site will – or should – appeal only to certain visitors, this book will teach you how to make sure you're not keeping people out for other reasons.

You can and will create, write, code, design any kind of Web page you like. For the record – and I'll be proving this over and over again – you can employ as many images, pictures, illustrations, and graphics as you wish and create designs of any graphic complexity. You can use advanced technologies, including multimedia, within certain limits. In all but the rarest cases, there will be no overt visual clues that your site is accessible or in any way different. (We won't be slapping big blue-and-white wheelchair logos all over your site.) People who don't require accessibility features rarely, if ever, even need to know they're there.

Quite apart from giving things up, you will add richness and layers of meaning to your site. Yes, there will be a cost in added complexity, but here is an advantage of this book: By presenting accessibility in three incremental levels (Basic, Intermediate, and Advanced, rather than an all-or-nothing approach), in the predominance of cases you will find a way to add accessibility to your work. Access, if only Basic-level, will no longer be a problem.

Quite apart from giving things up, you will add richness and layers of meaning to your site.

The three-step approach ensures that, no matter what your level of expertise (even a beginner) or budget (even none at all), you will be able to do something to improve your work. A judiciously-chosen, well-executed something genuinely is better than nothing. A haphazard, ill-informed something is, however, substantially worse than nothing, and I'll be going to some trouble to steer you clear of that.

Note, though, that this book will *not* teach you much about two specific topics: JavaScript and PDF. I cannot program worth beans in JavaScript and could not pretend to learn that skill well enough to teach JavaScript accessibility for this book. Adobe Portable Document Format documents were just beginning to be accessible to screen-reader users as I was writing this book, and indeed after beginning a chapter on PDF accessibility it became clear that the topic requires its own book. I apologize for letting readers down on these two topics, but I would prefer to do a good job on what I do know about rather than fake it on other issues.

All the existing resources for Web accessibility are either too terse or too verbose, offer too few examples or examples you'd never find in actual Websites, and don't pay enough attention to real-world use. This book will solve those problems once and for all, or at least until the next technical breakthrough comes along. And then, you'll have enough grounding in principle and technique to know what needs to be done, even if getting it done might still lie over the rainbow.

In short, I intend to make accessibility *less* of a *pain* in the *arse*.

2| WHY BOTHER?

LET'S RUN THROUGH SOME TYPICAL OBJECTIONS to providing accessibility, blowing them out of the water one after another. Then I'll give you a few reasons, some of them unexpected, why you actively should do it.

Accessibility myths

Access is poorly understood, and a range of myths has taken hold.

"Accessibility is expensive"

Yes, it is – for a large site and if you do it after the fact. Retrofitting always costs more, even at the level of adding a dimmer switch in your house. In all other cases, access may cost, but it is not necessarily expensive. In compensation, you gain a new audience. *<*

You need to know that your concern for cost is shared by everyone in all areas of the field of accessibility. Why? Accommodating people with disabilities usually costs *something*. Disabled people could be the only minority for whom equality costs money. It doesn't cost you extra not to discriminate *"equivalency" p. 3* against blacks or women.

It may cost you to accommodate religious practices in the workplace (for example, observant Jews who must leave work early on Fridays to be home before sundown), and pay-equity legislation may increase payroll costs for female-dominated occupations, but those are the exceptions.

In general, equality requires a change in attitudes, not a cash outlay. Disability is very often different. Automatic doors; sign-language interpreters; adaptive technology; attendant services; wheelchair-accessible housing, buses, and trains – they all cost money. In the field of employment, human-rights legislation and decisions by courts and tribunals have held that treating disabled and nondisabled employees exactly the same (which would in fact cost nothing) does not always constitute equality.

However, most accommodations in the workplace are low-cost. Here is some evidence:

- According to a report, Sears, Roebuck & Co. accommodated 436 U.S. employees from 1978 to 1992; accommodating 301 of them cost nothing at all, while only 13 employees' accommodations cost more than $1,000. The average cost per accommodation was $121.42.
- The Office of Disability Employment Policy's Job Accommodation Network, a unit of the U.S. Department of Labor, separately surveyed callers to its information line and found that 19% of callers incurred no cost to accommodate, 50% incurred $500 or less, and only 19% spent more than $1,000. A tiny 4% of callers could not identify a cost saving in carrying out the accommodation, and fully 25% of callers pegged the cost saving as between $20,001 and $100,000. A Labor report concludes: "Companies reported an average return of $28.69 in benefits for every dollar invested in making an accommodation."

Note that I am not attempting to snow you with magical claims that accessibility is free. It isn't.

In the same vein, accessible Web design is usually also cheap.

In the infamous Sydney Olympics case (described in detail in Appendix A, "Accessibility and the law"), the Sydney Organizing Committee for the Olympic Games purported that adding simple access features to its thousands of database-generated pages would cost $2.8 million in Australian dollars. No one with any real-world access experience, including the expert witnesses testifying in that case, believed or confirmed that figure. The expert witnesses did, however, concede that post-facto accessibility would cost the Committee tens of thousands above the existing project expenditures, a fact that is about as surprising as telling us night follows day.

On the other hand, building accessibility into the project from the word go would have added 2% to the cost, according to the experts. That figure could have been built into the original budget. You're still spending more money, but here you're planning for it. And that figure compares favourably with the billable staff hours – and expensive legal advice – associated with fighting a human-rights complaint.

Note that I am not attempting to snow you with magical claims that accessibility is free. It isn't. However, the graduated approach provided by this book makes access inexpensive, or at least reasonable in cost, for small, medium, and large Web projects – and for small, medium, and large Web shops. The cases in which accessibility is hugely expensive tend to limit themselves to Websites that are already expensive anyway. This book's access techniques scale with your project, your staff, and your own abilities.

In fact, Basic accessibility as described in this book is generally so cheap its cost can only be measured in pennies. If you think that typing the letter C costs twice as much in staff time as the letter c because you have to press the Shift key to do it, then you're pretty much the only kind of developer who will be able to pin a dollar value on Basic accessibility. If, on the other hand, you recognize that adding five alt texts of ten words each to a 50K Web page takes minutes and is about as taxing as typing out your name, address, and phone number, you may be persuaded that Basic accessibility isn't expensive after all.

Let's consider priorities. Developers think nothing of custom-coding JavaScript, ASP and other database back ends; designing graphics, including navigation buttons and rollovers; optimizing and slicing graphics for faster loading; creating animated GIFs; drawing custom page backgrounds, including dithered Web-safe colour combos; and writing complicated nested tables for precise page layout.

How many visitors do those tasks benefit? Most? Some? It doesn't matter how many. The fact is that the developers, and presumably the client, decided those activities were worth it – worth doing, worth the time, worth the money.

If you're willing to go to all that trouble, what's wrong with incorporating access techniques into your development cycle? Using this book's graduated approach, you will find an access technique your project budget can afford. You won't be able to use the cost argument ever again. You also gain a new audience, or at least you no longer antagonize part of your existing audience, as you'll see next.

"Accessibility serves too few people"

Accessibility is about accommodating minorities. So of course it serves small numbers – in each individual group. Add up the groups and suddenly the numbers aren't so small. But be mindful of the real people hiding behind small percentages. So-called minorities have a way of expanding as your site does: If 1% of your audience can't see graphics, and all of a sudden your site becomes popular and moves from 20,000 hits a month to two million, does the change from 200 to 20,000 affected users influence your opinion that "too few people" might benefit? Even with 200 affected users, can you justify ignoring the inexpensive Basic accessibility advice in this book?

Can't you readily imagine three city buses carrying a total of 200 passengers, none of whom can actually use your Website? The issue is a tad less abstract when you look at it that way, isn't it?

The available figures on numbers of people with disabilities online are sketchy at best.

- The American Foundation for the Blind estimates there are 900,000 visually-impaired computer users in the U.S. Note that computer use is not the same as Internet use even today.

marginalia: ✳ ＞

• A Harris poll released in June 2000 showed that 43% of U.S. adults with disabilities surveyed used the Internet and spent, on average, twice as long online as nondisabled adults. The specifics of the respondents' disabilities were not released; it is possible that many respondents required nothing special for Web accessibility.

marginalia: Really?

Figures with greater scientific credibility are rare and limited to the U.S., but they exist.

The Survey on Income and Program Participation (SIPP, 1999, carried out by the U.S. Department of Commerce, Economics and Statistics Administration, National Telecommunications and Information Administration) reported the following basic statistics on disability groups:

• 7,310,000 Americans had "vision problems"
(3.5% of the population)
• 6,961,000 Americans had "hearing problems" (3.3%)
• 6,272,000 Americans had "difficulty using hands" (3.0%)
• 2,945,000 Americans had a learning disability (1.4%)

marginalia: A Harris poll released in June 2000 showed that 43% of U.S. adults with disabilities surveyed used the Internet and spent, on average, twice as long online as nondisabled adults.

The number of people with certain disabilities and "access" to the Internet was also surveyed. What "access" means is ambiguous, though, by the researchers' own admission: It could simply mean a computer is in place in the home or workplace that can be connected to the Internet, or it could refer to active Internet use by the person in question. Even with this ambiguity, the figures are still helpful:

• 21.1% of people with "vision problems" had Internet access
(1,542,410 people)
• 27.2% of people with "hearing problems" (1,893,392)
• 22.5% of people with "difficulty using hands" (1,411,200)
• 42.2% of people with a learning disability (1,242,790)

marginalia: ?

By contrast, 56.7% of nondisabled people had Internet access. The disparity is considerable.

(Throughout this section, by the way, I'll omit statistics relating to disabilities that have no bearing on using the Web, like trouble with walking.)

A University of California, San Francisco study from the year 2000 uses a broader definition of disability ("work" disability, which, for this topic, does not break down *specific* disability categories, like blindness or deafness). In that study, "[o]nly one-tenth (10%) of people with disabilities connect to the Internet, compared to almost four-tenths (38%) of those without disabilities .... Of the 21 million Americans with work disabilities... only two million ever use the Internet."

This same study also finds very low usage rates of adaptive technology other than white canes: "A very small number of people (3% of blind persons and 0.1% of those with low vision) specifically [mention using adapted] computer equipment." It is likely that many low-vision people do not need adaptive technology, but these numbers are still surprisingly low. (Adaptive technology is described in detail in Chapter 3, "How do disabled people use computers?")

But let's approach this quantitative objection qualitatively. To use the old terminology from modems, the Web is about *feature negotiation*. You program a Web page and my browser attempts to render it, and there are many provisos. But if you publish a print brochure or shoot a TV commercial, you can be quite sure every reader or viewer has the same experience, disability notwithstanding. That isn't true online. A page using anything other than 1994-era plain-Jane HTML will look noticeably different in different browsers. In effect, the Web forces developers to accept multiple fragmented audiences.

Indeed, you're dealing with two audiences: The technical device (the browser) and the person at its controls. Large shops working on large sites will pull their hair out trying to make layouts work more or less similarly in Explorer and Netscape. In so doing, they acknowledge the diversity of the audience.

The claim that access serves too few rests on the assumption that it serves only a few disabled people, chiefly the blind and visually-impaired. And here we need to expand our discussion to the real world. Web developers are visual people. It is hard for them to imagine being blind. With rare exceptions, they don't know any blind people, and haven't even exchanged E-mail with a visually-impaired person.

Underlying all this is a very human kind of fear: To imagine your site as experienced by a blind person is to imagine you are blind yourself. You would have a hard time finding more than a handful of sighted people in the history of the world who willingly wished to become blind. The fear of blindness is natural and understandable. It is also quite irrelevant, and it is something you have to get over.

Disability advocates point out that any nondisabled person could become disabled at a future time. While this veiled threat–cum–guilt trip is obviously true, it is unlikely to happen to any specific Web designer or developer. You are not adapting your Website for a nightmarish hypothetical future in which you yourself cannot see. You're doing it because, deep down, you accept that the Web is attractive to people who aren't exactly like you. It's a mature, worldly approach, one that comes with education and practice, both of which this book will provide.

> *You're doing it because, deep down, you accept that the Web is attractive to people who aren't exactly like you.*

> *Not so of the aged, however*

"Accessibility is too hard"

In all honesty, some forms of accessibility are exceedingly difficult – captioning, subtitling, dubbing, and audio description (described in Chapter 13, "Multimedia") are so complicated that, save for short one-off applications, only experts in the field should attempt them, and even they flub it a lot of the time.

Still, making Websites usable by disabled visitors is generally straight-forward even for beginner Web developers. Only a couple of access tags, like longdesc and a few dealing with HTML tables, are head-scratchers. But they aren't included in the Basic level of accessibility you'll learn from these pages. Intermediate and Advanced access levels are the sort of thing that only intermediate and advanced developers would attempt for pages of intermediate to advanced complexity, and for them even the obscure and difficult access tags aren't necessarily all that obscure or difficult. These *are* the guru developers, after all.

The complaint that accessibility is difficult camouflages another complaint: No one teaches accessibility in an understandable way. It is no surprise, then, that accessibility is hard to understand and unfamiliar. And that's quite a fair complaint, actually. Bookstore shelves groan under the weight of JavaScript, Python, ASP, SQL, Oracle, and HTML programming books, among dozens of other well-covered topics, but accessibility remains obscure and unexplained. This book attempts to do it right, explaining not only how to make online media accessible, but why.

Bookstore shelves groan under the weight of JavaScript, Python, ASP, SQL, Oracle, and HTML programming books, among dozens of other well-covered topics, but accessibility remains obscure and unexplained.

"The Web is visual"

If the canonical reason to make a Website accessible is to make it usable by a blind person, just what is a blind person going to get out of a Website? With rare exceptions, the Web is a visual medium, right?

Well, so are TV and the movies, and studies have repeatedly shown that blind and visually-impaired people have the same basic desire to watch TV and film. Blind and sighted viewers even have similar tastes in film and TV programming. The blind live in the same world as the sighted. Both groups understand that the Web is a useful medium of information, entertainment, communication, and community.

(Television, film, and home video are already being made accessible to blind viewers, by the way, through audio description. It isn't a theoretical issue. Chapter 13, "Multimedia," explains it for you.)

There's a pragmatic reason, rooted in technological history, why visually-impaired people are into the Web: The blind are avid computer users. Back in the days of DOS and the earliest Macintosh systems, a number of mom-and-pop vendors had already invented screen readers, screen magnifiers, Braille displays and keyboards, and other adaptive technology that made computers usable by someone with limited vision. When the Web came along, it was merely a question of updating the adaptive technology, though the level of complexity involved in making DOS accessible is nothing compared to a graphical user interface.

"Accessible sites work on any device"

Well, this is a common enough misconception, but it isn't generally true. The claim here is that an accessible site can adapt itself automatically to devices like personal digital assistants and Internet refrigerators and anything else with a smaller screen than a typical computer with its graphical Web browser (or at least with a screen that is, say, monochrome or unable to display graphics).

Uncommonly advanced "non-browser devices" can in fact understand well-authored HTML pages and turn them into something readable. If you take precautions like adding text equivalents to all images, these well-behaved non-browser devices may indeed not make a complete mishmash of an HTML page.

But that says nothing about the page's usability. It is atypical for the devices in question to understand tables, for example, and even if they do, they may not have the screen real estate to lay them out properly. Using a Web page with these devices then becomes a matter of serial access – reading and using one table cell at a time. As we will see in due course, the dozens and dozens of navigation links (whether plain text, graphics, or a combination) commonly used in commercial Websites all pile up in serial-access mode.

You may be faced, then, with screenful after screenful of navigation links on your PalmPilot, all of which must be tediously downloaded and scrolled past. Yes, your machine may have succeeded in loading the page, and the content may be more or less comprehensible, but is it really usable? Probably not – an issue this book will return to.

Moreover, non-browser devices never seem able to handle accessibility features that aren't even particularly advanced, like titles on nearly everything, longdescriptions on images, or iframes. Merely as examples, Blazer 2.0, a Web browser from Handspring that runs on Palm OS, understands images but not imagemaps; EudoraWeb 2.0, another browser for Palm OS, does not understand images or imagemaps (or tables, rendering table-based layouts questionable).

Could I also point out that non-browser devices (typically PDAs) may be perfectly usable by, say, deaf people, but that blind/visually-impaired and mobility-impaired people find them hard to use? Just how accessible are these things then?

The few devices (few in North America, at least) that use Wireless Markup Language are really in a separate universe from the non-browser devices discussed here for the simple reason that WML is not HTML, and WML is at best tangentially part of the Web.

The most that can be said about non-browser devices is this: If you use valid HTML (which naturally includes text equivalents for images), you stand the best chance of making a page that is readable, perhaps inconveniently so,

If anything, shopping in the real world – in meatspace – is enough of a bother that shopping in cyberspace becomes particularly attractive for the blind consumer.

on a non-browser device. Accessibility is incidental, if not an outright accident, in this case.

"It's not our market"

If you're not interested in making your pages accessible because you think the main audience is blind people and blind people just aren't your market, the question to ask yourself is: Are you sure?

It is self-evident that some products and services are intrinsically inaccessible to blind and visually-impaired people – military service, for example, or driving schools. On the other hand, blind people have friends and relatives. If you're a low-vision person and your nephew is considering joining the army, you may wish to check the relevant Website to learn what he's getting into, or to double-check a few facts he found on that site. Is it really true that the blind person is not your customer in such a case? Does the concept of "customer" relate strictly to lone individuals? If so, what about word-of-mouth?

This reasoning is particularly dangerous at E-commerce sites. For the canonical accessibility audience (blind and visually-impaired people), getting around town and navigating inside retail stores are real barriers. Shopping online assists in independence: You can find out about a sweater or a book or a refrigerator without having to ask a sales clerk to guide you to the right section of the store and to explain the range of options available and exactly how they differ.

If anything, shopping in the real world – in meatspace – is enough of a bother that shopping in cyberspace becomes particularly attractive for the blind consumer. In effect, online retailers can claim a new audience that traditional retailers, who are nominally the competitors of online stores, could reach only with difficulty.

Actually, there are a couple of unspoken undercurrents in the objection that visitors who require accessibility aren't the desirable market. There's the feeling of discomfort and ignorance in contemplating a group with a disability you yourself may fear. There's also the classist assumption that, for example, blind people are too poor to deserve access to your site. As with so many stereotypes, there's a grain of truth at work there: As a group, blind and visually-impaired people are underemployed and rarely are high-wage earners.

The U.S. SIPP survey aforementioned found that, among people with disabilities (though not necessarily only those disabilities relevant to Internet use), income distributions were as follows:

- 10.4% of people with disabilities whose family incomes were less than $25,000 had Internet access (compared with 23.1% of nondisabled people)
- 23.8% with incomes of $25,000 to $49,999 (nondisabled: 35.0%)

> The unpalatable truth is that a Website developed without due regard to minimal accessibility is a slap in the face to an entire category of people.

same is true for people w/ limited mobility, or who can't drive themselves to stores, etc

- 34.2% with incomes of $50,000 to $74,999 (nondisabled: 49.6%)
- 51.3% with incomes $75,000 and above (nondisabled: 62.0%)

The University of California, San Francisco study aforementioned found that people with work disabilities (again, a broad definition) used the Internet less often than nondisabled people. Only 5% of people with work disabilities with low incomes (less than $20,000 a year) used the Internet; the figure was 17% for people with work disabilities with higher incomes. (On this question, the study had only two categories – below $20,000 and above.)

But let's approach this from an ethical angle, which, you'll note, I am at pains to avoid in this book. If it were technically possible to create a Website that excluded Jews, women, Albertans, or men over 60, would you do it? Even if that were the unintended effect, once alerted to it, would you leave it in place? The unpalatable truth is that a Website developed without due regard to minimal accessibility is a slap in the face to an entire category of people. History is replete with insults applied to categories of people.

In most cases, accessibility is required due to a characteristic the audience cannot change. I doubt you would countenance racism, sexism, or anti-Semitism on your Website. Ask yourself if you really want to be complicit in a similar social ill.

> The basic legal principle of accommodating a person who requires accessibility provisions is exactly the same in the U.S., Canada, the U.K., Australia, and elsewhere.

Reasons to do it

Now that I've exploded some myths and provided counterarguments for typical excuses, here are a few active reasons to provide accessibility.

It's the law

Antidiscrimination legislation in most Western nations, including the U.S., Canada, Australia, and the U.K., forbids discrimination or unequal treatment on the basis of disability. In most cases, accommodation is actively required: You have no legal basis to sit around and wait for someone to request accommodation or to file a complaint alleging discrimination or unequal treatment.

Are you legally required to provide an accessible Website? The answer is often a clear yes. At time of writing, I was able to find only one court or tribunal ruling that specifically addresses accessibility of Websites. In the year 2000, Bruce Maguire, a blind person in Australia, filed a complaint with the Human Rights and Equal Opportunity Commission alleging that the inaccessibility of the Website of the Sydney Organizing Committee for the Olympic Games constituted discrimination on the basis of disability. He won.

If you aren't a resident of Australia, you mustn't think the Maguire decision has no bearing on your country. When it comes to disability, antidiscrimination laws are broadly comparable in countries that have them. The basic legal principle of accommodating a person who requires accessibility provisions is exactly the same in the U.S., Canada, the U.K., Australia, and elsewhere. Human-rights law is international by definition (think of the war-crimes tribunal in The Hague), and precedents need not be drawn from within a country. Quite simply, the Maguire case constitutes a *worldwide* precedent.

The legal issues are clear-cut enough that a single blind person could take on the mighty Olympic "movement" and win. (The whole case is documented, and explained in layperson's terms, in Appendix A, "Accessibility and the law.")

In the U.S., the Americans with Disabilities Act unequivocally does apply to Websites. At press time, no complaints or lawsuits had been filed under the ADA. Moreover, for U.S. government agencies, so-called Section 508 regulations require accessibility of Websites and a great many other areas. Again, no complaints had been filed at time of writing.

In Canada, no complaints have been filed under legislation covering federally-regulated industries, which encompasses Websites. However, the Canadian Human Rights Tribunal did rule in 2000 that an absence of captioning on a television network constituted discrimination on the basis of disability. (Similar rulings were brought down in unrelated cases in Australia. There are many provisos in the Australian cases, but the effect is the same.)

The parallel here is not exact: Television is not the Web, but both are media, and captioning is one means of making the medium of television accessible. The parallel, however, doesn't *need* to be exact. We have various means of making the Web accessible (including, as it turns out, captioning). A complaint lodged on the grounds that a Website failed to provide accessibility is likely to be well-grounded.

Unless you worked for the Sydney Organizing Committee for the Olympic Games, which in any event had been legally dissolved by the time this book was published, there is next to no chance at all that you would have been served with a human-rights complaint or a lawsuit over your inaccessible Website. Plainly, it is unlikely in the extreme that such a complaint would be served on you. Do not use that as an excuse to avoid accessibility.

Are there limits to legal requirements? Yes. Human-rights legislation, including the Americans with Disabilities Act, provides a number of exemptions; of particular relevance here is "undue burden" or "undue hardship." Simply put, an entity is not required to provide accommodation if that provision would materially endanger the entity or alter its fundamental purpose.

In general, that exemption has been interpreted to mean "the accommodation would cost so much it would bankrupt the company – or nearly so." Even if that condition holds, you may be required to find another way to provide accommodation that you *can* afford.

In the case of Websites, a small business may not be required to caption and describe online video, for example, if the cost might endanger the company's ability to pay for the entire site itself. That doesn't mean you are legally entitled to post online video with no access features whatsoever. Providing separate transcripts may be deemed appropriate accommodation under applicable laws.

Or a stock-photo agency may not be required to write long descriptions for tens of thousands of online photographs; to do so might alter the fundamental nature of the business. But that says nothing about adding accessibility to the general navigation and all aspects of the site *other than* the differences among the photographs available for purchase.

To reiterate this point: While there are limited exceptions to legal requirements, there is no blanket exemption.

Another arrow in your quiver

You used to be able to get away with writing easy HTML version 1.0 in designing Websites. Then you had to learn tables and frames. But aren't text-only pages boring? To add graphics, didn't you need to learn Photoshop? Then JavaScript, then Java applets, then database back ends (what kind? Oracle? SQL? ASP?). Suddenly these were bigger and bigger projects, so you became a project manager. You had to wrangle text and images, verbally camouflaged as "content"; some jobs demanded PHP, others Perl, so you learned both. Browser-compatibility work went on forever, and still does. (Curse you, Netscape 4!) Stylesheets cascaded into your workday. Content management, the dark art. Usability and information architecture. The wireless Internet.

Not everyone in the biz needs to know every skill. But you can't get by with a single skill anymore. In particular, if you are a Web programmer or a Web designer, you already boast a constellation of skills – HTML *and* JavaScript *and* Flash *and* basic usability, for example.

Accessibility, quite simply, is the next skill you have to learn. Due to its cross-disciplinary nature, if you know HTML or JavaScript or usability, even in small doses, you are already equipped to expand your repertoire of talents.

You have, in effect, another paragraph to add to your résumé.

You also have to know what you don't know. Even if you do not wish to learn accessibility techniques well enough to do the work yourself, if you know the lay of the land you'll be able to manage someone who does the actual coding, write an accurate job spec for a client, or at least sound halfway knowledgeable in a pitch meeting.

An inaccessible Website tells visitors with disabilities "You have no business being interested in our site."

At top, an extensive breadcrumb trail from Yahoo España. Below, three examples of Easter-egg-like hidden richness (from top to bottom): iCab on Macintosh shows you accesskey assignments; Internet Explorer on Macintosh and Mozilla provides pop-up tooltips (in two different presentation styles) for arbitrary text and for links with title attributes set.

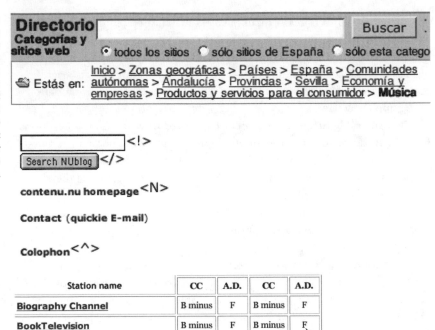

10.11

After finding life too short to look up all the previously-described **Hollywood movies** without description on DVD, I did it anyway.

Hollywood MoPixed movies without description on DVD

10.08

Posted.

Redundancy

A founding principle of accessibility is providing alternatives – "When there's an image, also give us text," that sort of thing. It's a form of beneficial redundancy.

Experienced Web designers already code for redundancy. Think of a typical commercial Website. How does a visitor get around?

- Major links on the page, like tabs or graphical buttons ("navbars").
- The same navigation, in text-only links, at page bottom (itself a minor accessibility feature).
- A search box. And a separate advanced search box.
- Breadcrumb navigation: You are here: Home > Services > Web Design > Portfolio.

Take another example: Feedback. It is commonplace for sites to offer all of the following: A free-standing form that visitors can fill out to contact the site's owners; individual contact E-mail addresses; and the owners' postal address and fax and phone numbers. Nowadays sites offer discussion forums and/or set up entire Weblogs to which you are invited to contribute.

Redundancy, then, is a required practice in commercial Web design. Accessibility provides merely another form of redundancy.

Richness

Remember when the JavaScript rollover was invented? As you passed the mouse cursor over a graphic image, the image changed. Maybe the type turned red. Maybe a little ferret or a canary popped up over the link. Maybe an entire new picture, one-third the size of the whole browser window, flashed into being alongside the link.

Initially dismissed by lapsed purists like me, rollovers are now such an accepted practice that standard software creates them for you automatically; the concept has spread to the a:hover pseudoclass in cascading stylesheets; and the technique has spawned progeny in the form of DHTML menus.

Standards compliance is a form of programming maturity.

A page with rollovers, or any of its related interface elements, is a richer page. It's not quite "interactive" (though the twits from marketing would be the first to claim so), but rollovers hide little pockets of delight throughout a page like Easter eggs.

Speaking of which, I am honour-bound here to include a phenomenon I do not really *get*. Geeks and laypeople love to spend hours hunting down *Easter eggs* — cute messages and pictures hidden in software that appear when you take some obscure action, like selecting the Open command from the File menu with three modifier keys held down.

Easter eggs are fun and harmless and add an unexpected layer beneath the straitlaced surface of boring old software. The phenomenon is responsible for much of the appeal of movies on DVD: Don't you feel cheated when a disc does not provide director commentary, deleted scenes, the movie trailer, Web links, and a video game based on the film? (Some DVDs include actual Easter eggs in the computer sense.)

For the developer, accessibility follows in this tradition. An accessible page provides pop-up balloons, secret alternative functions available only with a special key sequence, and unexpected variations that you unlock only when a page is spoken rather than displayed. With these features, you turn your entire accessible site into an Easter-egg hunt.

It's worth more when you flip it

This rationale may seem a bit crass, but not every rationale need be high-minded. A Website built according to accessibility principles — better yet, a Website that conforms to published specifications like the Web Accessibility

Initiative's Web Content Accessibility Guidelines or U.S. government Section 508 requirements — has greater value than an inaccessible site. It becomes one of the many attributes to which you can attach a price should you wish to sell your site; ready-made accessibility represents work the buyer does not have to do. This advantage does admittedly assume the buyer is engaged in due diligence on the topic of accessibility, but nothing stops you from bringing it up yourself.

Standards compliance

As I write this book in 2001–2002, a trend is sweeping the ranks of elite Web developers: Absolute standards compliance.

For half a decade we have put up with nonstandard extensions to World Wide Web Consortium HTML standards — blink, marquee, margin attributes on the body tag. What's much worse, we've put up with browsers and authoring tools that cannot render or produce standards-compliant code.

The days of hacking out ad hoc solutions to standards incompatibilities — the days, in other words, of doing anything special at all to accommodate the quirks of Netscape 4 or FrontPage or their ilk — are drawing to a close, at least if the trend toward absolute standards compliance is any indication. A chief advantage of standards compliance is the realization of the long-cherished goal known as "write once, read anywhere." Instead of coding four different versions of a page (for Netscape and Internet Explorer on Windows and Macintosh, respectively — a real-life example), you write one page according to spec and each device displays the page accurately. Some differences, like the specific appearance of fonts, will remain, but designs should be flexible enough not to be broken by such details.

The "read anywhere" side of the argument has hitherto restricted itself to visual display in browsers, if only because Web designers are visualists. Yet if you truly believe in this philosophy, you need to accept that "anywhere" really means "anywhere," including a screen reader, a printout, a Braille display, or a text-only variation, all of which can be produced by a visitor's browser or device without a stitch of extra effort on your part if and only if you code to standards. (It's true that adding access-specific tags is an extra effort, but not all pages require them.) Adapted variations of your page will come into being with little or no foreknowledge or involvement on your part. You will have given the world not merely a page that looks and acts analogously in whatever visual browsers you think are important but one that works with devices you cannot even test by yourself.

Standards compliance is a form of programming maturity. Perhaps it is time to grow up a little. You, esteemed reader, will have a conflict to resolve if you want to produce accessible Websites but still work around the quirks of noncompliance. One of them has to go.

Social maturity

To design for accessibility requires you to design for people who aren't exactly like you. That's true whether you, the designer or programmer, are or are not disabled yourself. Even if you act like it's 1996 and you design pages "best viewed in Netscape Navigator," people will defy your expectations and view your page in whatever browser or device they feel like using.

Of course, the norm these days is to design for multiple browsers. But do you run multiple browsers yourself? Do you do your actual day-to-day surfing in more than one browser? (I do, but I'm unusual.) You're already designing for people not like you. The distinction? They're using a different browser. A disabled visitor using adaptive technology, or using no such technology but relying on correct design and coding, falls into the same category.

One limited exception comes to mind – an Intranet where the number of users is small, you know absolutely all of them personally, and you are perfectly sure that none of them has a disability or ever will. Even so, designing to standards will save you time, and you might as well build in free Basic accessibility while you're at it.

Further, I work from the premise that you would never presume to limit what your visitor can and cannot learn from your site. An inaccessible Website, in effect, tells visitors with relevant disabilities to get lost: "You have no business being interested in our site."

The sophistication advantage

To sum up these related "soft" arguments for accessibility, then: Once you learn accessible design techniques, you heighten your sophistication, and may then stand taller in the saddle. "You mean you don't know about accessibility?" you may archly ask your inferiors, rolling your eyes and sharing a knowing grin with your compadres.

3| HOW DO DISABLED PEOPLE USE COMPUTERS?

ACCESSIBILITY ADVOCATES AND NONDISABLED PEOPLE can both be wrong at the same time. Or if not wrong, misinformed or misguided. Case in point: Terminology.

We have decades of history of stigmatizing terms used for people with disabilities. *Crip* and *gimp* were seen as disparaging for decades (and still are in many usages), but have been slowly reclaimed by disability activists. *Handicap* really does derive from "hand in cap," which we would now describe as a "disempowering" mental image. *Deaf and dumb* technically means *deaf and mute*, which would be OK if the phrase weren't misunderstood to mean *deaf and stupid* and if deaf people were all unable to speak, which is hardly the case.

In any event, disabled people and their advocates (I suppose I would fall into the same category) have spent years raising the consciousness of average people so that outdated and stereotyped terminology might fall by the way-side. But unfortunately, a certain overcorrection has taken place.

Handicapped was replaced by *disabled*, a value-neutral term that is and should be widely used. But then we were told a phrase like *disabled person* could never be used; we were to say *person with a disability* in order to "put the person first." (Up with people!) Well, maybe. Forcing people to use some maladroit, saccharine, ill-gotten catchphrase instead of plain words seems like a cure that's worse than the disease. (We are also told not to use constructs like "the deaf" or "the disabled" for similarly weak reasons.)

And of course many readers will be familiar with querulous but well-meaning ninnies, overconcerned with "offending" anyone, who love to suggest nauseating euphemisms like *handicapable* or my personal favourite, *physically challenged*. ("Challenged"? Meaning disabled people merely have to try *a bit harder*? Someone in a wheelchair merely has a bigger "challenge" in climbing stairs than a nondisabled person? If that person tries really, really hard, his or her "challenge" will disappear?)

Neither are disabled people "differently abled." A person who cannot hear or see or walk clearly does have abilities "different" from a nondisabled person's, and in accessible Web development we may in fact create "different" or analogous forms, but nonetheless, the term doesn't tell us much. *Differently abled* seems to apply more to zoology, where, say, raccoons can climb trees but dogs can't, or kookaburras can fly while ostriches cannot. Those animals are all *differently abled* when compared across species, but they aren't *missing an ability* that other members of their species typically have, which is actually the case when considering human disability. It's not as though disabled and non-disabled people merely hold different portfolios of abilities that are equal in number or capacity, like maintaining a diverse envelope of stocks and bonds.

Shall we cut the crap, folks?

Now, then. There actually *are* salient differences in meaning among the various terms used to describe disability groups. Some examples follow.

Deaf, hard-of-hearing, hearing-impaired

Everyone with significantly impaired hearing is *deaf* in a generic sense. But someone with a lower degree of impairment may be more accurately called *hard-of-hearing*. *Hearing-impaired* is a more medical-sounding term that not many people voluntarily use to describe themselves.

Deaf people tend to have the least hearing (and "culturally Deaf" people issue eye-rolling demands to capitalize the D); they are the most apt to use whatever sign language or language is native to their region. (American Sign Language isn't the only one in the world; yes, they are real languages; no, if you know one of them, you can't understand any other; no, you don't have to be deaf to be fluent in, or a "native speaker" of, a sign language.)

Deaf people are most apt to attend segregated deaf-only schools or classrooms, though "mainstreaming" of disabled students (including them in nondisabled classrooms) has been an ongoing trend for 30 years. There tends to be such a thing as a "deaf community" in any given city, state, or province.

Hard-of-hearing people tend to have a greater degree of usable hearing than deaf (or Deaf) people. They can often speak intelligibly (more often than deaf people, at least), and are more apt not to have attended a school for the deaf. If they received special education for deaf students, it was more likely in the oral tradition (teaching lipreading and use of residual speech rather than sign language). Many hard-of-hearing people deny categorically that they are in any way different from hearing people. There is much less cohesiveness among hard-of-hearing people; it is difficult indeed to find a genuine "hard-of-hearing community."

The term used to refer to someone with no auditory disability is *hearing*.

Most deaf, hard-of-hearing, or hearing-impaired people either now have or used to have some actual hearing. In addition, a *late-deafened* person lost his or her hearing in adulthood or at least after completely learning a spoken language. Having been hearing people for many years, late-deafened persons tend to have the best understanding and production of spoken language (which comes up in discussions of reading level of television captioning, for example).

Whenever you have the time or space, it is generally preferable to refer generically to *deaf and hard-of-hearing people*. It's more inclusive and acknowledges that deaf and hard-of-hearing people actually are different. But it isn't wrong to use the single term *deaf*. In a long text like this book, you can mix and match according to the sense you require.

Blind, visually-impaired, low-vision

Everyone with significantly impaired vision is *blind* in a generic sense. But someone with a lower degree of impairment may be more accurately called *visually-impaired*. A low-vision person is not significantly different from a visually-impaired person, but the former term is preferred by some.

Blind people are most apt to have attended a school for the blind, though the same mainstreaming trend affects blind students. Not many people with any kind of visual impairment read Braille – estimates run as low as 10%. Visual impairment is largely a condition of age; there are not that many very young blind or visually-impaired people.

As in the previous case, when you can swing it, a phrase like *blind and visually-impaired* is most inclusive and correct, but in a pinch *blind* will do.

Mobility-impaired

A bit of a tricky group to discuss as far as this book is concerned. When you think of a disabled person, I'd wager that the first image that pops to mind is a *person in a wheelchair*. But *wheelchair users* are not a group that's entirely relevant to accessible Web design. Instead, people with *mobility impairments* have difficulty moving one or more parts of the body. Where Web design is concerned, a mobility impairment that affects use of a computer or device (chiefly a disability involving the hands and/or arms) is really the only relevant disability. Some of those people may also be wheelchair users (for example, quadriplegics).

Learning-disabled

Learning disabilities affect the perception, processing, understanding, and reception of information and other stimuli. Dyslexia is the most famous learning disability (it causes confusion in reading and a few other tasks), but there are many others. "Learning" per se is not always the issue; the last time you stepped foot in a classroom may have been 40 years ago, yet you may nonetheless have a learning disability.

You may also run across the term *cognitive disabilities*, where *cognitive* refers to the functions of the brain ("the mental process of knowing, including aspects such as awareness, perception, reasoning, and judgement").

What about mental retardation? It's not the same as a learning disability, and the phrase *mentally retarded* is somewhat stigmatized. (Actually, the worst term I've run across is "trainably mentally handicapped." How'd you like people calling you *that*?) Yet the suggested substitute, *developmental disability*, is too bafflingly vague. (Development? Like development of the fetus? Like not walking till you're three and a half years old?) At a conference I attended, a researcher in the field tended to use both terms together, as *mentally retarded/developmentally disabled*, a mouthful that is often contracted to MR/DD. I'm mentioning the issue because, if you develop educational Websites, you may be required to accommodate learning-disabled students (not very easy) and MR/DD students, too, the latter being even more difficult.

Adaptive technology

Here's a related term that comes up in the field of accessibility of computer hardware specifically: *Adaptive technology* is any implement that modifies existing hardware or software for use by a disabled person. It doesn't have to be anything special — an off-the-shelf trackball can constitute adaptive technology. Screen readers and magnifiers are two examples of adaptive technology relevant to Web development.

So how do disabled people use computers?

Now that you know a bit more about disability in general, the obvious question becomes: How do disabled people use computers?

A typical nondisabled person (is that you?) does not have many — or any — disabled friends. This is understandable: Despite the insinuations of cheerily multicultural advertising, it's difficult to expand your social sphere outside your own group. Think of that smug expression "It's a black thing. You wouldn't understand." And even after decades of feminism, how many men have female friends?

Anyway, even if you did have a friend with a disability, what can your friend teach you about other disabilities?

On the whole, then, you probably aren't exactly conversant with the ways in which people with disabilities use computers. There's no shame in that. Let's start with the basic issues. The "correct" thinking holds that disability is never the problem; it's barriers in the outside world, including barriers of attitude, that are the problem. This is a bit *de trop*, in my experience. Here in the real world, the general issue of accommodating people with disabilities does relate to the specific disability and to what the person is trying to do.

A (somewhat high-end and luxurious) refreshable Braille display from Tieman. Note the single line of Braille cells, each of which features a control button on top. These and the other keys – at top left and right and on the front of the unit – work with a screen reader or other software to position the cursor, control reading speed and options, and the like. Braille displays aren't all as complex as this, but for an advanced computer user, like a systems administrator or programmer, the range of controls makes up for the inability to view the screen. A blind person using a Braille display this advanced will also probably use voice output via a screen reader, many of which can drive voice and Braille simultaneously. A deaf-blind person may use a computer exclusively through Braille display and keyboard. (You're meant to rest the computer keyboard, or an entire laptop computer, on the rear half of the display.)

One cannot separate the two.

In this case, the question to ask is: Is your disability severe enough to affect your use of a computer?

In some cases, the answer is a clear no. A single-leg amputee, for example, has no barriers at all to using a computer. But other disability groups do face barriers:

- If you're blind or visually-impaired, how do you read and interpret the text, graphics, menus, dialogue boxes, and other visual details on-screen? How do you read the legends on the keyboard? How do you read software documentation? What about multimedia?
- If you're deaf or hard-of-hearing, how will alert sounds (like error beeps) actually manage to alert you? How do you benefit from soundtracks found in multimedia?
- If you have a mobility impairment that prevents you from moving the mouse or typing on a keyboard, what do you do?
- If you have a learning disability like dyslexia, just how do you read and decipher all that colourful text onscreen?

It's actually not too complicated: Some disabled computer users do nothing different from nondisabled people, while others (indeed, for some disabilities, the majority) require so-called adaptive or assistive technology – hardware or software that eliminates barriers to using a computer. In the olden days (like the era of the Apple II, when adaptive technology first blossomed as a consumer-level industry), adaptive technology was klugey and homemade; a lot of it looked like warmed-over Heathkit experiments. Now, though, after two decades of development and maturity, adaptive technology is generally quite sophisticated and impressive – or, to apply the highest praise the geek crowd could possibly confer, *cool*.

Here is a guide to disability groups and the relevant adaptive technology.

Mobility impairment

The requirements of someone who cannot readily type or use a mouse (or press a switch, or engage any other hardware interface) are the easiest for accessibility neophytes to understand. Why? Because the adaptive technology they use generally takes the form of alternative keyboards and mice, and hardware of that sort makes for tidy photographs. You can immediately see the necessary modifications, if not actually understand every detail of their operation.

Text is not a feature of Websites; it is a primitive, a fundamental and unalterable component

For the purposes of this book, "mobility-impaired" people have trouble using the hardware of their computers rather than understanding or interpreting information.

So what's the solution? There are actually tons of options; only some have a bearing on writing accessible Websites, but as in every sphere of understanding, you need to know more than the bare minimum to be considered civilised.

Keyboard guards and overlays: A sheet of thick plastic with holes lets you guide your fingers to just the right key. Useful if you have cerebral palsy or a tremor that makes you depress more than one key at a time, or if too many errant keystrokes precede or follow a correct keypress.

Slow keys and onscreen keyboards: Software can automatically discard keystrokes typed in too quick a sequence, and can show you a picture of a keyboard that you can actuate with a switch or a mouse. (The really good onscreen keyboards predict the words you're trying to type, and the next word or phrase after that. It's surprisingly efficient.)

Replacement mice: Everything from foot pedals to gigantic trackballs are used as direct mouse surrogates. An ordinary off-the-shelf trackball can be a good adaptive technology for some people.

Switches and scanning software: If you can take one action reliably (blinking an eye, flexing your wrist, jostling your knee, or, in the best-known case, sipping and puffing on a straw), then you can actuate an on/off switch. Since computers are binary devices, that's all the ability you need. While still laborious, switch access is now much less so than, say, back in the mid-1980s, when quadriplegics' use of sip-and-puff switches began to be covered as a human-interest story in newspapers. (Just as people seem to know the phrase "carpal-tunnel syndrome" but nothing about repetitive-strain injuries in general, the use of personal computers by blowing on a straw seems to be a fact widely known in the absence of other disability knowledge.) Note, though, that the days of sip-and-puff switches are largely behind us. In the 21st century, "switch access" may still rely on a single on/off signal, but hardware switches are now more sophisticated (requiring, say, a simple head nudge). Software now does a better job of interpreting and predicting the intent behind that signal: Your onscreen keyboard may divide and subdivide itself into quadrants for you until the right letter appears under your cursor, and also predict the words you wish to type.

How does this adaptive technology relate to accessible Web design? Page navigation becomes the big issue. If you the Website visitor are using particularly primitive adaptive technology (or none at all – some disabled people are too poor, or too proud and stubborn, to modify their machines), you may be stuck pressing the Tab key repeatedly to move from link to link, from link to image, from field to image, and every other combination within a Web page. If your site loads up three dozen (or a hundred, or 200) navigational links in a left-hand table cell, a visitor with this disability has to tab through them one at a time.

Just how long would *you* put up with that, if you don't already? Fortunately, there are solutions – usually not great and often not really enough, but solutions nonetheless. I'll get to those in Chapter 8, "Navigation."

Hearing impairment

The access requirements of deaf and hard-of-hearing people are quite modest given that, even in a post-Napster demimonde, computers are largely silent devices that communicate visually. You can, for example, simply turn the alert-sound volume to zero, which might cause the menubar to flash as a replacement for an audible beep.

Adaptive technology? There really isn't any. A hard-of-hearing person may use amplified headphones or a particularly high-powered speaker, but those are off-the-shelf additions with no bearing on Web design or programming.

Visual impairment

Of all the disabilities affected by computer use, visual impairment is the most significant. As we have seen with devices varying as widely as the Palm (and the Newton – remember the Newton?) and a range of tablet computers and Internet refrigerators and whatnot, in real-world use *a computer is mostly a display*. And if you can't see a display, how do you use a computer?

Well, if you have a relatively modest visual impairment, all you may need is screen magnification. You can blow up the size of text, menubars, icons, and everything else to any necessary size. (That really means everything else. Your whole system, including menubars, has to be made accessible, not just the text in a single window in a browser.) Software designed just for this purpose can also scroll text horizontally for you within a window of fixed position, alter foreground and background colours, and turn the mouse cursor into a moving magnifying glass.

(Don't underestimate the issue of screen colours. Many visually-impaired people find dark text on a brilliant white background unbearable. Such settings are quite easy to change for Websites, as we'll see in Chapter 9, "Type and colour," but it's a process of trial and error, and if you, as a Web author, don't code your pages properly, your text might just disappear altogether!)

If you're blind enough that you can't really see a monitor, you need something called a *screen reader* – a program that reads aloud onscreen text, menus, icons, and the like.

(They're not called "talking browsers," "text readers," or "speech browsers." There's one and only one generic term for the technology: Screen reader. Having made this categorical declaration, I note that there *are* programs that do nothing but provide voice output for Web browsers to the exclusion of all other software on a computer, like IBM Home Page Reader and pwWebSpeak, and I suppose we could call those talking browsers, but I am eliding that distinction for the purposes of this book.)

Screen readers don't simply spit out a monotonous sequential verbal itemization of a Web page. Developed in the late 1970s on character-mode platforms like Apple II and MS-DOS, screen readers have evolved out of view of the rest of the computer industry, like some form of underground dance music beloved by recherché klub kidz worldwide but unknown to their parents. Screen readers are sophisticated enough to use multiple voices and (limited) sound effects to interpret Websites. It's quite commonplace to listen to screen-reader speech at speeds no human being, not even an auctioneer, could produce. At 300 words a minute (twice the speed of a vibrant human conversation), you can zip through even a verbose Web page pretty efficiently, though that is no excuse for you to produce verbose Web pages.

One crucial fact to understand about screen readers, though: They're run from the keyboard. The mouse is still usable but in practice is not used. A mouse requires hand-eye coördination, and a blind person is missing half of that. Accordingly, anything you design that seems to require a mouse also has to work without one.

Another curious factoid: Some totally-blind people don't bother installing a monitor at all. (Computers can often run "headless.")

A deaf-blind person will rely exclusively on a Braille display: Nylon or metal pins controlled by software protrude upward through a grid, forming the cells used in Braille writing. Characters are replaced ("refreshed") either automatically at intervals or after you press a switch. Typical Braille displays reveal two to four lines of text, but truly gigantic displays, almost equivalent to the 80-character-by-24-row screens of MS-DOS, can also be found, at prices rivaling the equivalent weight in platinum.

While a few blind people rely on Braille displays alone, without screen readers, of more interest are the few super-elite blind people who use a Braille display in tandem with a screen reader. One such use: The screen reader speaks onscreen text and interface elements, while the Braille display gives system and status-line messages. Practical for blind computer programmers especially.

Since the canonical group served by Web accessibility is indeed the blind and visually-impaired, the bulk of this book is devoted to documenting how to accommodate them.

Learning disabilities

Without a doubt the most neglected disability group online, and, not coincidentally, the very hardest to accommodate, learning-disabled Web surfers face frustrating barriers.

The issue here is comprehension of visible language in the broadest sense. Words are the biggest problem, one that is ostensibly alleviated by providing pictures and sounds. Yet even pictures and sounds may cause confusion, particularly if all the above are provided simultaneously. (I specifically advocate watching, listening, and reading simultaneously in Chapter 13, "Multimedia," but that may be unsuitable for a section of this population.)

However, the essence of the Web is text. Almost no Websites lack text altogether, and that cohort tends to cluster around all-Flash experimentation (like Praystation.com); while the Web is the delivery mechanism for such experiments, it is debatable whether they actually are Websites at all rather than online cinema.

Text is not a *feature* of Websites; it is a *primitive*, a fundamental and unalterable component.

An existing requirement of the Web Accessibility Initiative's Web Content Accessibility Guidelines (No. 14, "Ensure that documents are clear and simple so they may be more easily understood") makes a feeble and inconsequential effort at solving the inaccessibility of textual Websites for people who cannot read well. Checkpoint 14.1 tells us: "Use the clearest and simplest language appropriate for a site's content." Nowhere does this guideline explain how you will afford an editor for your site, or how you or that editor will know in specific how to write so that learning-disabled people can understand you. Are there proven techniques? And if so, how do they apply to the tens of thousands of topics discussed online?

As I write this book, the Web Accessibility Initiative is actively considering an update to its Web Content Accessibility Guidelines that would require all Web authors — everywhere and without exception — to add images or other "non-text content" to their Websites if they wish their sites to be certified as complying with the WCAG. Essentially every concept would require an illustration, irrespective of these undeniable facts:

- Some concepts cannot be illustrated. (Remember the parlour game on *The Simpsons* in which the Simpsons' neighbours, the Van Houtens, are asked to illustrate "dignity"? Luanne Van Houten actually does it, but we never see the actual drawing, rather proving the point. I hope it is not bathetic to suggest the WAI learn from cartoons.)
- Many Web authors are not professional illustrators; many do not own illustration software.
- The requirement discriminates against other disabled groups: How do blind Webmasters draw pictures?
- Similarly, each added image or multimedia file requires an equivalent (like an alt text or captioning). The addition of images implies the addition of more text, a tautology and a source of frustration for blind visitors.
- Image and multimedia files cause page sizes, hence download times, to balloon, in turn harming usability.
- The requirement naïvely assumes that all Websites are custom-created and continuously overseen by expert human beings; many Websites, like discussion fora and mailing-list archives, are autogenerated by software. Many pages at the World Wide Web Consortium's own site, W3.org, fall into this category. How do we illustrate them?
- There is no proof that illustrations will be as effective at guaranteeing comprehension for the learning-disabled as, say, alt texts are for the blind.

It is not at all clear that this proposed requirement will actually be ratified by the World Wide Web Consortium; it faces strong and reasoned opposition from people like me. The needs of learning-disabled Web visitors and everyone else with a mental impairment are real; they're also ill-understood by Web designers and by Web-accessibility experts both.

Still, the proposed cure is worse than the disease. It is apparent that there is no practical way to make textual Websites genuinely accessible to people who cannot read well. Q.E.D.

So what are the real options? They don't have a lot to do with your work as a designer or developer. The use of adaptive technology in accommodating learning disabilities is relatively uncommon, but the big surprise is how applicable the gear intended for the blind can be. Dyslexic kids and adults often find speech output useful, though usually at far slower speeds than blind users are accustomed to. Screen magnification is helpful. There's certain limited evidence (included on this book's CD-ROM) that audio description helps kids with dyslexia concentrate. Long descriptions, used for blind access to Websites, may work the same way, but there is no research on that topic.

There is no plan of action available to you in order to accommodate learning-disabled visitors in the way that plans of action are available for other disability groups, however contingent and fractured those latter plans might be. There are no simple coding or programming practices – or even complex practices, for that matter – in which you can engage to accommodate this group.

We are left with the knowledge that our sites *are* inaccessible to a known group with next to nothing we can do about it. However antithetical that may seem at first blush, in fact it responds to the real world. Recall that antidiscrimination legislation includes exemptions for undue hardship or burden. Recall also that some features of the physical world cannot be made accessible without destroying or fundamentally altering them – antique streetcars, for example, or the ancient pyramids. On all counts, these are unavoidable exceptions which we have no choice but to live with.

4| WHat is meDia access?

THE WEB IS MERELY THE LATEST MEDIUM REQUIRING ACCESSIBILITY. Work has gone on for generations on improving the accessibility of other media of communication and of the physical world.

Some Web-access techniques stand on the shoulders of ancestors in "old media" like books, film, and television. Conversely, some access techniques from so-called old media are directly applicable online (typically only for multimedia). Just as you need to know more about disability than might seem immediately relevant to the Web, you need to expand your understanding of *media access*. The techniques and technologies behind media access are hard to understand, obscure, and poorly documented. It's difficult, for example, to learn about captioning, or audio description, or dubbing, or subtitling.

Here is a quickie introduction to the various techniques and technologies in use to make media of information accessible to people with disabilities and others. We'll start out with a basic definition.

What is accessibility?

Accessibility involves making allowances for characteristics a person cannot readily change.

It's a simple, sweeping definition. Practical examples of its application to Websites:

- A deaf person cannot stop being deaf when confronted with a soundtrack.
- A blind person cannot stop being blind when confronted with visible words and images.
- A learning-disabled person cannot reset the functions of the brain when confronted with the same.

- A person with a mobility impairment cannot suddenly begin to move when confronted with a navigation task.
- A unilingual anglophone cannot suddenly understand French when confronted with that language.

Old-media accessibility

Let's learn a little about the means of making old media like film and television accessible.

Access for the blind and visually-impaired

The relevant technique is *audio description*: Narration, read out loud by a human being (or, in the future, by voice synthesis), that succinctly explains visual details not apparent from the audio alone. Audio description takes a movie, for example, and talks you through it. A narrator tells you everything that's happening onscreen that you can't figure out just from the soundtrack.

That's a rather dry definition. Audio description (A.D.) is actually an advanced literary form that traces its origins to live theatre. True enough, akin to the practice of reading print books aloud for the benefit of the blind, for centuries sighted people have sat alongside their blind friends at theatrical performances and filled in the blanks with spoken descriptions. Experiments in providing descriptions for TV date back thirty years. But audio description as a practice, with its own norms and a name unto itself, began in 1981 with the work of Cody and Margaret Pfanstiehl in the suburbs of Washington, D.C. The Pfanstiehls introduced the first regularly-scheduled description of live theatre.

A year later, the Pfanstiehls began work with Barry Cronin and PBS in the United States. (I am obliged to mention that PBS is the Public Broadcasting Service, a television network.) Years of demonstration projects ensued, leading to the founding of the Descriptive Video Service (DVS) at WGBH-TV in Boston. Audio description has been a feature of American television – albeit in a very limited way – since 1988.

Theatrical audio description is available in many countries – Spain, England, New Zealand, and beyond – and A.D. on television can be found, albeit rarely, in Canada, Germany, the U.S., the U.K., and Australia. If you can watch North American–standard NTSC home videos, have a look at DVS's line of Hollywood movies and PBS specials with always-audible descriptions. The Royal National Institute for the Blind (RNIB) in the U.K. offers a similar line of described home videos in PAL format (and in some cases, DVS and RNIB have both described the same films). You can also watch a tiny handful of Region 1 and 2 DVDs with audio description, although an interface problem comes up: Since you need to manipulate an onscreen menu to turn audio description on, just how do you do that if you're blind?

It's also possible to describe first-run movies, and it is being done today, though even more rarely than on television; the predominant service provider is the Descriptive Video Service, whose DVS Theatrical system is an adjunct to Rear Window captioning explored in the next section.

Wordwatch

It's important to get the terminology right. Audio description is often misnamed:

- *Video description* (more than video can be described; the technique started in live theatre, remember)
- *Descriptive Video* (a registered service mark of WGBH Educational Foundation)
- *Auditory description* (an early favourite of the World Wide Web Consortium, the only entity anywhere that uses the term, which oVers the disadvantages of pretense and an extra syllable, and no advantages at all)
- *Audio captioning* and a range of other abominations

It must be pointed out, however, that the Federal Communications Commission in the U.S. has more or less adopted the term "video description," while the Canadian Radio-television and Telecommunications Commission, the broadcasting regulator in Canada, seems to think that "audio description" and "described video" are two different things, which they are not. These broadcasting regulators, with their government imprimatur, have unfortunately muddied the terminological waters. I suggest you act smarter than these bureaucrats and stick to the only generic term, "audio description."

Access for the deaf and hard-of-hearing

The technique of record is *captioning*: Rendering of speech and other audible information *in the written language of the audio.* Usually *closed*: Captions are encoded or invisible and must be decoded or made visible. Some captions are *open* and can't be turned off (and indeed, that's how captions started out in the 1970s, when I first started watching them and before closed-captioning systems were invented).

Previously, to watch closed captioning you had to use a separate decoder connected to your television. (I still own one.) Caption decoders are built into televisions now. Nearly all TV sets sold in North America come so equipped (U.S. law requires it; split manufacturing runs for Canada are rare, so Canadians buy the same sets). So do a majority of sets in Europe, according to all indications, though there is no legal requirement. Built-in caption decoders are much less common a feature in Australia.

Television isn't the only medium that can be and is captioned. Theatrical motion pictures can be open-captioned; it's still being done, but prints and screenings are virtually impossible to find, and even after more than twenty years, I have watched but a single open-captioned film in a movie theatre. (And that one was Liar, Liar with Jim Carrey!) In 2001, after a human-rights complaint alleging discrimination on the basis of disability, certain Australian cinema owners agreed to exhibit open-captioned films several times a week – a first in the English-speaking world.

A sexier technology is the Rear Window system devised by a team of inventors centred at WGBH, which actually allows first-run movies to be closed-captioned. A large display sits on the back wall of the auditorium on which captions are displayed in mirror-image. You the viewer attach a semi-transparent plexiglas panel on a long stalk to the arm of your chair; place the panel in a comfortable position, possibly overlapping the bottom edge of the movie screen; and watch the reflected right-reading captions and the movie together. Only a tiny handful of cinemas use Rear Window, a number that is unlikely to grow significantly due to cost and resistance; this closed captioning of first-run movies will remain rare.

Note that subtitling is not the same as captioning. Despite their seeming similarity, captioning and subtitling have very little in common.

- Captions are intended for deaf and hard-of-hearing audiences. The assumed audience for subtitling is hearing people who do not understand the language of dialogue.
- Captions move to denote who is speaking; subtitles are almost always set at bottom centre.
- Captions can explicitly state the speaker's name:
  Helmut Kohl (translated):
  [MARTIN]
  >> Announcer:
- Captions notate sound effects and other dramatically significant audio. Subtitles assume you can hear the phone ringing, the footsteps outside the door, a thunderclap.
- Subtitles are typically open; in fact, subtitles were almost always open in all media for decades until DVDs, with their selectable subtitle tracks, came along. Captions are usually closed.
- Captions are in the same language as the audio. Subtitles are a translation.
- Subtitles also translate onscreen type in another language, e.g., a sign tacked to a door, a computer monitor display, a newspaper headline, opening and closing credits.
- Subtitles never mention the source language. A film with dialogue in multiple languages will feature continuous subtitles that never indicate that the source language has changed. (Or only dialogue in

one language will be subtitled – for example, *Life Is Beautiful*, where only the Italian is subtitled, not the German.)

- Captions tend to render dialogue even in a foreign language, transliterate the dialogue, or state that the character is speaking a different language.
- Captions ideally render all utterances. Subtitles do not bother to duplicate some verbal forms, e.g., proper names uttered in isolation ("Jacques!"), words repeated ("Help! Help! Help!"), song lyrics, phrases or utterances in the target language, or phrases the worldly hearing audience is expected to know ("Danke schön").
- Captions render tone and manner of voice where necessary:
  (whispering)
  [BRITISH ACCENT]
  [Vincent, Narrating]
  (imitating Katharine Hepburn)
- A subtitled program can be captioned (subtitles first, captions later). Captioned programs aren't subtitled after captioning.

WORLDWIDE CAPTIONING

Captioning is available in dozens of nations worldwide. In television, two broad technical standards are in use:

- Line 21 in the U.S., Canada, Japan, and a few other countries using the NTSC television standard
- World System Teletext in countries using the PAL and SÉCAM standards

The systems are incompatible (then again, so are the telecasts), though it's possible to translate caption files between them. Only North American Line 21 captions are readily recorded on home videotapes, and for nearly 20 years closed-captioned home videos have been the norm with larger studios. You simply play the same tape everyone else plays with your decoder turned on, and captions appear. (The same applies to TV broadcasts you tape yourself.)

It is possible to record World System Teletext captions on a tape, but there is no standard, easy, foolproof way to do so; it doesn't just happen automatically on a standard VHS VCR as it does with Line 21. In this case, sometimes you need a special VCR that converts closed captions to open. A variation of the Line 21 system (called Line 22, confusingly) was introduced in Europe and Australia specifically for home-video captioning. In those countries, then, you need two different and incompatible decoders. It is rare to find a television or VCR that includes both decoders, so if you want the full captioning experience you end up buying a set-top decoder.

A note on the U.K. lexicon: While Canadians, Australians, and Americans can keep captioning and subtitling straight, our dear British friends employ the worst possible terminology. *Captioning*, as far as they are concerned, is "subtitling," while *subtitling* is also "subtitling." (A *caption*, in British vernacular, is any kind of onscreen graphic, like the name of a city written out onscreen during a news report.) It then becomes possible to subtitle a subtitled program, or subtitle a captioned program. British correspondents tell me, in a manifestly false claim, that it is impossible to confuse subtitling and subtitling in their grand nation. Yet this is not a case of using different words for the same concept (as *lift/elevator* or *boot/trunk*); here we are using the same word for similar but readily-confusable concepts. Because the two techniques are not at all the same or interchangeable, I'll call *captioning* "captioning" and *subtitling* "subtitling" in this book, and so should you.

Language accessibility

Two old-media techniques are in use in this domain:

- *Dubbing:* Replacing vocal tracks with vocal tracks in another language.
- *Subtitling:* Translating speech (and, in specific limited cases, onscreen type) into one or more written languages added to the image.

> I like to refer to captioning, audio description, subtitling, and dubbing as the Big Four access techniques.

In online multimedia, you may be confronted with adapting a segment of video more than one way. Recall that dubbed programs can be and are captioned, as are subtitled programs; I've seen it myself. (Remember, subtitles fail to render a lot of sounds and don't tell you who's speaking, information a deaf viewer needs.) Both types of programs can be described. To describe a subtitled program, the subtitles are read out loud and typically *enacted* – using a delivery more akin to a dubbing actor's than the newsreader-like pseudo-objective delivery of normal descriptions.

Applicability to the Web

I like to refer to captioning, audio description, subtitling, and dubbing as the Big Four access techniques. Web accessibility, the subject of this entire book, is the fifth. This quintet clusters in the way the four fingers and single thumb of a hand do – all of them interrelated if not interchangeable.

Similarly, in the way that a thumb is a finger as well as a thumb, Web accessibility occupies two categories at once. Whenever you're dealing with online video, and often when dealing with audio, the Big Four are relevant to Web access for the simple reason that online video is video, full stop. Now, audio is a more complicated matter, and those complications are explored in Chapter 13, "Multimedia."

Additionally, longdescription of still images on the Web is cognate with the practice of audio description of film and video.

5 | tHe structure of accessible pages

ACCESSIBLE WEB AUTHORING RELIES ON STANDARDS. HTML accessibility tags are defined in standards (actually "recommendations") issued by the World Wide Web Consortium (the W3C or W3). If you want the accessibility provisions of your pages to function predictably and reliably, you must work with the standards, not against them.

In other words, forget about coding special workarounds for Netscape 4. Forget marquee and other nonstandard HTML tags embraced and extended by Microsoft or "innovated" by Netscape. Forget anything that isn't in the spec. Forget it all, even if your favourite browser relies on it.

"But-but-but!" you sputter. "I run a commercial Website with ten million hits a month. We do a browser sniff for Windows and Mac versions of Explorer and Netscape because we can't get our standard design to look the same in all four. Are you saying I have a choice between what I'm doing now and accessibility?"

Um, yes.

Quite bluntly, none of us should be made to suffer for the longtime failure of browser makers to conform to W3C standards. (Really, I'm talking about Netscape, but Microsoft cannot play the angel here, either.) We all deserve better.

The decision by developers to code around the incompatibilities of existing browsers has had certain consequences, among them the fact that such incompatibility has to come to an end someday. If you want your pages to function with accessible coding, that day is today. You have enjoyed a lengthy crime spree, but I hear the handcuffs jingling.

There are now enough browsers available with reasonable standards compliance that real-world sites can finally get away with coding to those standards. It's the only way to *assure* accessibility.

You have enjoyed a lengthy crime spree, but I hear the handcuffs jingling.

Goals

In this chapter:
- We'll learn the basic structure of HTML documents.
- We'll understand the need to declare document types and validate HTML documents.
- We'll take our first look at the Web Content Accessibility Guidelines.

Leave yesterday behind

What happens to Netscape 4 users? Pages won't look so hot for them. Big deal. Absolute visual equivalence was always a pipe dream in any case.

Let's recap the *reality* of the World Wide Web:
- You have no way of predicting the conditions under which your site is viewed. Even with absolutely equivalent computer platform, connection speed, and browser on your part and a visitor's, you cannot predict so much as *the size of the user's monitor*, or indeed if the user has one at all.
- You have never had absolute control over the appearance of your pages. (No, not even by using graphics, and text rendered as graphics. Ever heard of different screen resolutions and colour gamuts? How about black-and-white displays?)
- As a corollary to the foregoing, coding for access merely enlarges the existing truth about Web design: You have no hope of dictating the pixel-level appearance of your page. There may be no visual display at all, or your visitors may require huge fonts that throw your layout out of whack.

The sooner you grasp the reality that you are not designing for print, where you *can* oversee every single dot on a page, the sooner you will succeed *as a Web designer*, let alone as a contributor to an accessible Web.

If you've done any kind of reading on Web design or if you've simply looked at the same pages on different computers, you know that ironclad visual control is unattainable. Don't cling to a myth, and don't try to tell us your myths are real. No one's ever seen a unicorn, either.

A question that comes to mind, of course, is "What about people stuck with Netscape 4? Aren't they a disadvantaged minority who are rendered functionally disabled by their out-of-date equipment?" True enough, but the parallel with, say, a blind person using adaptive technology like a screen reader is not quite apt. Netscape 4 in particular will actively sabotage standards-compliant coding – everything from table cells to alt texts. Designers and developers do not bear sole responsibility for accessibility; the site visitor must come to the table with something resembling functional equipment. In that vein, when adaptive technology like a screen reader ignores or misinterprets fully legal HTML, site authors can quite reasonably consider themselves blameless; they too have come to the table with functional equipment in the form of standards-compliant HTML coding.

Nonetheless, it is true that people stuck using broken or outdated equipment like Netscape 4 (because, for example, it is the standard at the company they work for or the school they attend) genuinely are *stuck*. But that is not a problem designers and developers should be expected to solve. If anything, hewing to strict standards compliance acts as an inducement to get rid of outdated equipment.

Frankly, it causes less harm to sentence users of nonstandard equipment to nonstandard Web experiences than to hold back the adoption of standards that benefit everyone else, including the disabled. Standards-compliant devices behave in a more or less standard way. Other devices do not.

Now, it is in fact true that you can plop a few access tags (particularly those found in Basic accessibility as documented in this book) into a maelstrom of nonstandard HTML and be reasonably assured of a modicum of improved accessibility. But it's not reliable (try reading title texts in Netscape 4), and it's also too complex to maintain. Instead, I will teach you strictly legal, up-to-the-minute techniques using XHTML and cascading stylesheets. In some cases, incorrect or absent interpretation of access tags causes incompatibilities, but that tends to limit itself to the same outdated browsers I recommend you no longer coddle.

An example, mentioned in passing above, is the provision of graphic images' alt texts as pop-up tooltips in version 4 of Netscape Navigator and Internet Explorer – a categorical, open-and-shut violation of W3C standards, which hold that alt is a replacement, not an addition ("Several non-textual elements... let authors specify alternate text to serve as content when the element cannot be rendered normally"). Yet if you provide alts anyway, these same misbehaving browsers work correctly when image-loading is deactivated *and*, moreover, alts work properly in every other browser, too.

What about "old" browsers like Lynx? Indeed, Lynx is the only example anyone ever cites, because there are very few text-only browsers in the world today and Lynx is the giant squid flailing about in a very small pond. (Other text-only or "console" browsers are WannaBe, Links, and W3M.) Ironically, these programs do a very admirable job of interpreting standard HTML. (Working under severe limitations can force higher quality.) An accessible HTML page remains accessible for these browsers.

> Frankly, it causes less harm to sentence users of nonstandard equipment to nonstandard Web experiences than to hold back the adoption of standards that benefit everyone else, including the disabled.

Basic page structure

You have to abide by only a few ironclad rules in structuring HTML pages. They're dead-simple. You can save them in templates in your authoring program, or set up your own stationery, or simply drag and drop the codes. Let's cover a couple of features you must use to assure accessibility.

Start off with DOCTYPE

You will probably be familiar with the basic structure of an HTML document. Leaving out a great many details, it looks like this:

```
< html >
< head >< /head >
< body >< /body >
< /html >
```

But a certain code goes in front of all that, the DOCTYPE. This *document-type declaration* informs the browser or device what kind of page it's dealing with. It sits at the very top of an HTML file, before anything else (and with no carriage returns or spaces preceding it).

While there are a range of DOCTYPEs available for different levels of HTML (that is, HTML 4 as distinct from XHTML), the options for XHTML 1.0 DOCTYPEs you are most likely to use are as follows:

```
< !DOCTYPE html PUBLIC "-//W3C//DTD XHTML 1.0 Strict//EN"
"http://www.w3.org/TR/xhtml1/DTD/xhtml1-strict.dtd" >
```
XHTML 1.0 *Strict* – If you're super-hardcore and write XHTML that includes no elements tolerated in the olden days whatsoever, use this DOCTYPE.

```
< !DOCTYPE html PUBLIC "-//W3C//DTD XHTML 1.0 Transitional//EN"
"http://www.w3.org/TR/xhtml1/DTD/xhtml1-transitional.dtd" >
```
XHTML 1.0 *Transitional* – You'll be using this DOCTYPE most of the time. It permits certain old-fashioned "presentational" elements, as explained below.

```
< !DOCTYPE html PUBLIC "-//W3C//DTD XHTML 1.0 Frameset//EN"
"http://www.w3.org/TR/xhtml1/DTD/xhtml1-frameset.dtd" >
```
XHTML 1.0 *Frameset* – Identical in effect to the Transitional DOCTYPE; choose this one if you also use frames.

Some details must be mentioned, if only *en passant*.

- XHTML 1.1 DOCTYPEs are also available, but XHTML 1.1 is newer (dating from May 2001, halfway through the writing of this book), hence is used by fewer developers; 1.1, moreover, is stricter even than XHTML 1.0 Strict.
- For all XHTML variants, the W3C specification recommends including an Extensible Markup Language or XML declaration in front of the DOCTYPE, which, for HTML documents written in Roman-alphabet languages, will typically be ‹?xml version="1.0" encoding="UTF-8"?›. The presence or absence of this declaration, which pertains to the encoding of characters used on that Web page, does not alter our discussion here, and in any event it is known to be incompatible even with very new browsers.
- The URL in the DOCTYPE is technically optional for XHTML documents and mandatory for XHTML documents; browsers may behave differently if you do or do not include it. This too does not alter our discussion here.

What does it all mean?

Let's start with a quick history lesson. While HTML has been tarted up considerably since its earliest days, its fundamental purpose is to mark up the *structure* of a document, not its appearance. "Presentational" elements, like B for bold, have been discouraged but tolerated. (Everyone has a presentational element they love to hate. blink and marquee — the element that makes text march across the screen like a cavalcade of ants — are infamous villains. I personally cannot stand u. We invented italics for a reason, and underlining has special purposes online. Indeed, later I'll show you some accessibility applications for underlining.)

Meanwhile, "structural" elements (like ‹strong›‹/strong›, whose contents may indeed be displayed using bold type) are the preferred approach. Accessibility elements are structural, to a greater or lesser degree, though as elsewhere in HTML discourse, "structural" is as porous a concept as "presentational."

Getting back to DOCTYPE: Someday all browsers and devices will read the DOCTYPE and vary their interpretation of the subsequent code. At time of writing, only Mozilla (hence also Netscape 6 and 7), Internet Explorer for Macintosh version 5 and later, and Windows IE 6 perform this so-called DOCTYPE-switching, but it provides an augury of the future.

If your document uses a Strict DOCTYPE (any Strict declaration at all — older HTML 4-level DOCTYPEs work fine), then, for example, Explorer 5 for Macintosh interprets HTML and stylesheets with commensurate strictness. One example from Tantek Çelik, a leading Microsoft browser developer: "Strict interpretation causes a strict treatment of the [Cascading Stylesheets] box model, whereas non-strict interpretation causes a backward-compatible (i.e., Windows IE 4–compatible) interpretation." Another example from Çelik: Unitless dimensions, which are "rejected in Strict mode as illegal values – with the exception of line-height, which specifically allows a unitless value [with] a particular meaning."

It is not improper to use a Transitional declaration. In certain cases, you may require Strict-level control over stylesheets, but it's generally unnecessary, and nothing says that all the pages within your site have to use the same DOCTYPE. You can mix and match as appropriate.

There is another reason to declare your document type: You must do so in order to prove your document is correct or *valid* HTML. To *validate* a document means to check it for errors, and, at time of writing, there is only one official validator, located at the W3C's own Website (validator.w3.org). Since there are so many variants of HTML and XHTML, the validator, which is nothing more than a software program, must be told up front which reference standard to use. The DOCYTPE does exactly that. If you want to write pages that are true, valid HTML, you must use a DOCTYPE or your page won't validate.

There are a few unofficial validators: HTMLHelp.com/tools/validator/ is one.

Language

While this may contradict whatever passes for conventional wisdom in the accessibility demimonde, making your site work in some other language really does constitute accessibility. (When you visit a Website, you can't change the languages you understand, can you? Aren't you functionally disabled if the site you want is in Dutch and you don't read a word of it?)

I've elected to keep this book focused on disability-related accessibility, but there's one language detail you cannot ignore. It is a ramification of an accessibility requirement that forces you to declare a change in natural language in your document.

What's a natural language? It's a human language, as distinct from a computer language like C++, Pascal, or PostScript. Natural languages are not necessarily spoken; indeed, essentially all the language available on Websites is written, though sign languages are also natural languages.

Why do you have to declare a change of language? Because adaptive technology can theoretically alter its interpretation of a document – by switching Braille standards or using a new voice dictionary, for example. If you specify that a passage in your document is actually written in French, a screen reader able to interpret and enunciate French won't attempt to read the text as fractured English.

There's an implication here that you must respect. To mark a *change* in language, the *original* language must have been specified. Otherwise what are you changing *from*?

It's easy to do. Just add a language attribute to the html tag in the head element. Whatever else ends up in your ‹html›‹/html› element, add lang="en", as in these examples:

- ‹html lang="en"›
- ‹html lang="en" xmlns="http://www.w3.org/1999/xhtml"›

As elsewhere in HTML, order of attributes in a tag does not matter. There is a wrinkle: In one of the very few differences between XHTML 1.0 and 1.1, if you wish to use the latter you must write xml:lang="*languagecode*" in all tags where you would once have used lang="*languagecode*". It is not wrong to use both in XHTML documents (and is in fact recommended), but it *is* wrong in HTML 4.

Putting all this advice together, then, the best language declaration to use in XHTML 1.0 is:

‹html lang="en" xml:lang="en" xmlns="http://www.w3.org/1999/xhtml"›

The en code, as you have probably gleaned, means English. You are under no obligation to write Web pages in English. You may produce French or Icelandic or Spanish pages in your day-to-day work, or for special localization projects. All you need to do is match the language you're using with the appropriate language code, a full listing of which is given in Appendix B, "Language codes." Use whatever code applies to the language a visitor will encounter and read. Possible sources of confusion:

- HTML itself is based on English, an immutable fact that has nothing to do with the human language you're using.
- If you're bilingual, you may write a page with English-language text and Spanish-language HTML comments visible only to you and your team and whoever Views Source. Set the language to English in that case. It is the *visitor's* experience that counts.
- If the page does nothing but give the visitor a choice of which language the *rest* of the site should use or is in any other way bilingual or multilingual, there is no legal way in HTML to indicate that the page is multilingual.

Now, the actual requirement in the Web Content Accessibility Guidelines states: "Clearly identify changes in the natural language of a document's text and any text equivalents (e.g., captions)." To do so, merely add lang="*languagecode*" or xml:lang="*languagecode*" to whatever tag structurally encloses the foreign-language text. Typically, you will use ‹p›‹/p›, ‹div›‹/div›, ‹blockquote›‹/blockquote›, and ‹span›‹/span›.

- A separate paragraph in, say, German embedded in an otherwise-English-language Web page could use ‹p lang="de"›‹/p›. A block quotation (‹blockquote›‹/blockquote›) can take a lang="*languagecode*" attribute as readily as anything else can, and might well be a better option if you're excerpting a full paragraph.

- A couple of words in French sitting inside a sentence can use `<span lang="fr"></span>` or, if you want to be pluperfect, `<cite lang="fr"></cite>` (since you are actually citing the French terms).
- A significant, multi-paragraph section of your Web page could sit inside `<div lang="`*`languagecode`*`"></div>`. This `<div></div>` element can of course be nested within other `<div></div>` elements.

Do not use this technique to indicate foreign-language proper names save for extremely rare cases. A man named Simon Robert who is in fact Swiss and not British may wish to mark his name as `<span lang="fr-ch">`Simon Robert `</span>` in the hopes (possibly vain) of triggering a French pronunciation in a screen reader. But these cases are rather quite unlikely to come up in day-to-day Web design.

There is no convention for the use of language codes to indicate the language of multimedia. Technically, you can add `lang="`*`languagecode`*`"` to an enormous range of HTML elements; it is possible, therefore, to add `lang="`*`languagecode`*`"` to, say, the object but not the embed element (both of which are discussed in greater length in Chapter 13, "Multimedia").

If your page includes a link that opens a new document that in turn contains the multimedia file, you may use the `hreflang="`*`languagecode`*`"` attribute on the `<a></a>` element to indicate the language of the *destination*.

Quickie review

Set up templates for all future documents to include a DOCTYPE and a language attribute on the `<html></html>` element.

There. That was the easy part.

The Web Content Accessibility Guidelines

In exploring Web accessibility, one quickly learns that all roads lead to the WAI, the Web Accessibility Initiative of the World Wide Web Consortium.

The WAI, founded in 1997 and headed, at time of writing, by Judy Brewer, describes its purpose as follows: "The World Wide Web Consortium's... commitment to lead the Web to its full potential includes promoting a high degree of usability for people with disabilities. WAI, in coordination with organizations around the world, pursues accessibility of the Web through five primary areas of work: Technology, guidelines, tools, education and outreach, and research and development."

Everyone working in Web accessibility swims in a pool filled a bucket at a time by the WAI. The entire base of widespread understanding, knowledge, and scholarship on Web access can be traced to the WAI, including this book, which nonetheless diverges from the gospel in limited ways.

In your role as a Web designer or developer, your interest will focus on the WAI's Web Content Accessibility Guidelines (WCAG), which explain how to write HTML and other authoring languages accessibly.

If you've ever tried to actually read and comprehend the WCAG, I can understand why you ended up buying this book. Reading a dictionary from back to front is a more pleasant experience than plodding through pretty much any document the WAI has ever produced, including the WCAG.

The Guidelines are too vague and too detailed all at once; ask for the moon, without giving you a rocket to get you there or even instructions on how to build one; and are unusably long and meandering.

Worse, the WCAG are written with no discernible authorial voice – no doubt under the guise of "objectivity," but leaving the impression that the words were strung together by a committee of Brussels functionaries.

The Web Content Accessibility Guidelines, then, while constituting the gospel of whatever endeavour that Web accessibility hopes or pretends to be, are unworkable in practice.

Yet you – and I – are forced to become fluent in the Guidelines nonetheless. They represent our *environment*.

The best I can hope for is that this book becomes a kind of companion volume, like an interpretation of the gospel. You can and will consult the inscrutable source text from time to time, but I hope you will learn more in these pages.

1, 2, 3; A, AA, AAA

This book teaches a phased approach to accessibility, with Basic, Intermediate, and Advanced steps applicable to most tasks in Web design and programming.

On the surface, the WCAG take the same approach, offering three priority levels in Web content accessibility. Priority 1 techniques are the highest; authors "must" do them. You "should" use Priority 2 techniques and "may" use Priority 3s.

Having already given us a three-tier classification system, the WAI proceeds to give us another one: Level A, AA, and AAA compliance. If your site meets the requirements of a particular accessibility level by fulfilling all requirements for Priority 1, 2, or 3, you have the right to mark your site as meeting a corresponding level of access. From the actual guidelines:

- Level A: All Priority 1 checkpoints are satisfied
- Level AA: All Priority 1 and 2 checkpoints are satisfied
- Level AAA: All Priority 1, 2, and 3 checkpoints are satisfied

As it turns out, Basic access as described in this book usually corresponds to Level A, and Intermediate and Advanced access to Levels AA and AAA, respectively, but the correspondence is not exactly one-to-one. In particular, the WCAG's expectations for multimedia access are unrealistic for all but the very largest Web conglomerates, and even for those entities the cost escalates quickly.

At times, this book explicitly counsels you to defy the Web Content Accessibility Guidelines, but only with very good reason and under strictly limited circumstances. In other words, I give you a defence, which might disappear if circumstances change (e.g., your budget increases or access technology improves).

In order to demonstrate the confusion and complexity that typify our environment, let's look at the checklists for Priority 1, 2, and 3 accessibility. In the w3c's grand tradition, the document from which these items are adapted is entitled "Checklist of Checkpoints for Web Content Accessibility Guidelines 1.0." A checklist of checkpoints? How is that different from a checklist? (Isn't that like saying your wall is covered by a bookshelf of books of pages of words?)

I'm giving these "checkpoints" to you up front, before any concepts are explained, to give you an idea of the lay of the landscape. What follows is the level of explication everyone working in this environment has had to put up with.

Priority 1 requirements for Level A compliance

General

- Provide a text equivalent for every non-text element (e.g., via alt, longdesc, or in element content). This includes: Images, graphical representations of text (including symbols), imagemap regions, animations (e.g., animated GIFs), applets and programmatic objects, ASCII art, frames, scripts, images used as list bullets, spacers, graphical buttons, sounds (played with or without user interaction), stand-alone audio files, audio tracks of video, and video.
- Ensure that all information conveyed with colour is also available without colour, for example from context or markup.
- Clearly identify changes in the natural language of a document's text and any text equivalents (e.g., captions).
- Organize documents so they may be read without stylesheets. For example, when an HTML document is rendered without associated stylesheets, it must still be possible to read the document.
- Ensure that equivalents for dynamic content are updated when the dynamic content changes.
- Until user agents allow users to control flickering, avoid causing the screen to flicker.

- Use the clearest and simplest language appropriate for a site's content.
- And if you use images and imagemaps:
  - Provide redundant text links for each active region of a server-side imagemap.
  - Provide client-side imagemaps instead of server-side imagemaps except where the regions cannot be defined with an available geometric shape.
- And if you use tables:
  - For data tables, identify row and column headers.
  - For data tables that have two or more logical levels of row or column headers, use markup to associate data cells and header cells.
- And if you use frames: Title each frame to facilitate frame identification and navigation.
- And if you use applets and scripts: Ensure that pages are usable when scripts, applets, or other programmatic objects are turned off or not supported. If this is not possible, provide equivalent information on an alternative accessible page.
- And if you use multimedia:
  - Until user agents can automatically read aloud the text equivalent of a visual track, provide an [audio] description of the important information of the visual track of a multimedia presentation.
  - For any time-based multimedia presentation (e.g., a movie or animation), synchronize equivalent alternatives (e.g., captions or [audio] descriptions of the visual track) with the presentation.
- And if all else fails: If, after best efforts, you cannot create an accessible page, provide a link to an alternative page that uses W3C technologies, is accessible, has equivalent information (or functionality), and is updated as often as the inaccessible (original) page.

Priority 2 requirements for Level AA compliance

- General
  - Ensure that foreground and background colour combinations provide sufficient contrast when viewed by someone having colour deficits or when viewed on a black and white screen.
  - When an appropriate markup language exists, use markup rather than images to convey information.
  - Create documents that validate to published formal grammars.
  - Use stylesheets to control layout and presentation.
  - Use relative rather than absolute units in markup language attribute values and stylesheet property values.
  - Use header elements to convey document structure and use them according to specification.

- Mark up lists and list items properly.
- Mark up quotations. Do not use quotation markup for formatting effects such as [indention].
- Ensure that dynamic content is accessible or provide an alternative presentation or page.
- Until user agents allow users to control blinking, avoid causing content to blink (i.e., change presentation at a regular rate, such as turning on and off).
- Until user agents provide the ability to stop the refresh, do not create periodically auto-refreshing pages.
- Until user agents provide the ability to stop auto-redirect, do not use markup to redirect pages automatically. Instead, configure the server to perform redirects.
- Until user agents allow users to turn off spawned windows, do not cause pop-ups or other windows to appear and do not change the current window without informing the user.
- Use W3C technologies when they are available and appropriate for a task, and use the latest versions when supported.
- Avoid deprecated features of W3C technologies.
- Divide large blocks of information into more manageable groups where natural and appropriate.
- Clearly identify the target of each link.
- Provide metadata to add semantic information to pages and sites.
- Provide information about the general layout of a site (e.g., a site map or table of contents).
- Use navigation mechanisms in a consistent manner.
- And if you use tables:
  - Do not use tables for layout unless the table makes sense when linearized. Otherwise, if the table does not make sense, provide an alternative equivalent (which may be a linearized version).
  - If a table is used for layout, do not use any structural markup for the purpose of visual formatting.
- And if you use frames: Describe the purpose of frames and how frames relate to each other if it is not obvious by frame titles alone.
- And if you use forms:
  - Until user agents support explicit associations between labels and form controls, for all form controls with implicitly associated labels, ensure that the label is properly positioned.
  - Associate labels explicitly with their controls.
- And if you use applets and scripts:
  - For scripts and applets, ensure that event handlers are input device–independent.

- Until user agents allow users to freeze moving content, avoid movement in pages.
- Make programmatic elements such as scripts and applets directly accessible or compatible with assistive technologies.
- Ensure that any element that has its own interface can be operated in a device-independent manner.
- For scripts, specify logical event handlers rather than device-dependent event handlers.

PRIORITY 3 REQUIREMENTS FOR LEVEL AAA COMPLIANCE

- General
  - Specify the expansion of each abbreviation or acronym in a document where it first occurs.
  - Identify the primary natural language of a document.
  - Create a logical tab order through links, form controls, and objects.
  - Provide keyboard shortcuts to important links (including those in client-side imagemaps), form controls, and groups of form controls.
  - Until user agents (including assistive technologies) render adjacent links distinctly, include non-link, printable characters (surrounded by spaces) between adjacent links.
  - Provide information so that users may receive documents according to their preferences (e.g., language, content type, etc.).
  - Provide navigation bars to highlight and give access to the navigation mechanism.
  - Group related links, identify the group (for user agents), and, until user agents do so, provide a way to bypass the group.
  - If search functions are provided, enable different types of searches for different skill levels and preferences.
  - Place distinguishing information at the beginning of headings, paragraphs, lists, etc.
  - Provide information about document collections (i.e., documents comprising multiple pages).
  - Provide a means to skip over multi-line ASCII art.
  - Supplement text with graphic or auditory presentations where they will facilitate comprehension of the page.
  - Create a style of presentation that is consistent across pages.
- And if you use images and imagemaps: Until user agents render text equivalents for client-side imagemap links, provide redundant text links for each active region of a client-side imagemap.
- And if you use tables:
  - Provide summaries for tables.
  - Provide abbreviations for header labels.

- Until user agents (including assistive technologies) render side-by-side text correctly, provide a linear text alternative (on the current page or some other) for all tables that lay out text in parallel, word-wrapped columns.
- And if you use forms: Until user agents handle empty controls correctly, include default, place-holding characters in edit boxes and text areas.

As you can see, a range of topics, some of them only tangentially related, are grouped within each level. True enough, the checkpoints provide links to further explanations of what is demanded of you, but you should not expect to actually understand all the descriptions and effortlessly put them into effect.

Level A/AA/AAA compliance is something you'll have to wrap your mind around, and in certain cases (e.g., U.S. government agencies), you will, on paper, be required to certify such compliance exactly as prescribed in the Guidelines. You may find that impossible to do. Just as some buildings and vehicles can never be made wheelchair-accessible without unreasonable and extraordinary measures, some features of Websites will remain inaccessible without similarly unreasonable and extraordinary measures. This does not constitute a blanket exemption; circumstances can change, and you are still required to do everything *else* in your program of improving accessibility. But the Web Content Accessibility Guidelines make few allowances for circumstances, let alone changing circumstances.

Here in the real world, you may simply live with failure to meet certain specific and highly-qualified details of the letter of the WAI's unrealistic and overblown standards. That says nothing about the real-world accessibility of your site.

Nonetheless, this book builds up your understanding of concepts and techniques in its own way. Though I do not cover every detail, at the end of the process, you'll be able to look at the Priority 1 through 3 and Level A through AAA requirements and, in most cases, know immediately what to do to meet them. You will also know when and under what circumstances you will *not* meet the requirements.

You will know enough at that point to be able to make sense of the mishmash of topics found in the compliance guidelines.

Certification

I devote an entire chapter (Chapter 14, "Certification and testing") to certifying accessibility. It's not cut-and-dried. And that is the problem.

In evaluating accessibility in the physical world (in "meatspace"), a specification may call for a doorway 100 centimetres wide for wheelchair access. Your tape measure will tell in an instant if you comply or not. It may be somewhat involved to widen the doorway if it's too narrow, and it may be impossible in rare cases, but the plan of action is predictable and reproducible.

Yet in cyberspace, every Website is slightly different. It's possible to meet the letter of a requirement without meeting the spirit. For example, using the filename for an alt text on an image is technically legal, since you have in fact provided an alt, but the function of the alternative text is thwarted. (If you couldn't see or use graphic images, is a replacement like spacer.GIF of any use to you whatsoever? Especially if you're using a screen reader and have to listen to the words "spacer dot gee eye eff" over and over again?)

More pressingly, accessibility requires design decisions. The Web Content Accessibility Guidelines force such decisions, as does practical work on actual Websites. To reconsider the previous example, you may code an appropriate alt, but if you leave off titles and longdescriptions (documented in Chapter 6, "The image problem"), do you jeopardize your accessibility certification?

If you use the most minimal coding for HTML tables with no access tags or attributes, are you engaged in wrongdoing? If you provide a small text-only variant for an extravagant Flash animation, have you merely met the letter of the law and not the spirit?

In all these cases, the answer is "Quite possibly yes." In building access-ible Websites, you will be forced to make design decisions with no objective proof that your choices are defensible. But the whole point of the exercise is that *objective proof* is occasionally unattainable and unrealistic. And in general, such issues as these come up only in advanced cases. With this book as your guide and with a little practice, you will be able to make the right kind of defence of your accessibility choices – a combined functional and design defence.

Bobby

A little knowledge is dangerous, and that maxim comes into play in two ways online.

Ever heard of Bobby? It's a free online accessibility validator formerly offered by CAST, the Center for Applied Special Technology (cast.org/bobby/). In August 2002, Bobby was "acquired" by a firm called Watchfire (bobby. watchfire.com). Run your site through Bobby and it lists your accessibility failings (anything that violates Priority 1).

What is the problem, exactly? Well, there are two.
- Web designers with passing knowledge of accessibility think "If my site passes Bobby, I'm OK."
- Bobby itself, being nothing but software, is too stupid to actually look at your site and understand what you *meant* to do or *ought* to have done.

Easy example? Running an early version of the New Riders Website, newriders.com, through the Bobby validator elicited a sequence of clear-cut

Priority 1 errors (all pertaining to alt texts, easily cleaned up) and a litany of errors that more or less mean "I can't tell what you were really doing or if you've actually made a mistake, but here's an error message just in case":

- If this is a data table (not used for layout only), identify headers for the table rows and columns.
- If an image conveys important information beyond what is in its alternative text, provide an extended description.
- If a table has two or more rows or columns that serve as headers, use structural markup to identify their hierarchy and relationship.
- If you use colour to convey information, make sure the information is also represented another way.

Then Bobby simply nags at you:

- The following 4 item(s) [sic] are not triggered by any specific feature on your page, but are still important for accessibility and are required for Bobby Approved status.
  - Use the simplest and most straightforward language that is possible.
  - If ASCII art is present, consider substituting it with an accessible image.
  - Identify any changes in the document's language.
  - If you can't make a page accessible, construct an alternate accessible version.

What we have here is a computer program that threatens to withhold its certification badge (of dubious value in any case) if you didn't write clearly enough. How does it know the difference, exactly? You probably get enough of that kind of bellyaching at home. Do you also need it at work?

My advice is simple: Do not use Bobby. Do not rely on software as dumb as a dromedary to evaluate accessibility.

An environment desperate for an upgrade

You now know how muddled the "environment" in which we work actually is. Starting now, you and I are going to hack out a kind of *quality upgrade* for Web accessibility.

Separate pages are not equal

Let's put a myth to rest right here and now. There is no real benefit to setting up – either manually or through a content-management system that autogenerates pages on demand – a regular page and a so-called "accessible" page. Here, "accessible" usually means "text-only."

Now, this is not the same as self-reconfiguring pages that respond to the visitor's preferences, as described in Chapter 15, "Future dreams." Nor does it really have anything to do with separate printable pages (which very often

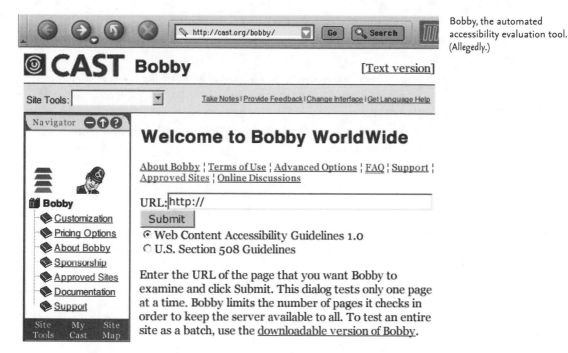

Bobby, the automated
accessibility evaluation tool.
(Allegedly.)

are functionally equivalent to text-only pages), which in any case can be
generated by a media="print" stylesheet and nothing more.

Separate "accessible" pages are wrong in principle because they cause
segregation. You've got your back-of-the-bus page for those disabled people
and your regular page up front for the real people. Nearly any Website
imaginable can be made accessible *enough* within itself that an allegedly
superior separate page isn't necessary.

And anyway, a text-only page simply does not carry the same information
as a regular page. Graphics, typography, colour schemes, and page design *are*
information. Moreover, not every person with a disability benefits from a
text-only page, a case in point being learning-disabled people who get
bogged down in masses of continuous text.

And do untrained but well-intentioned designers out there really have any
idea what an "accessible" page would be *other* than a text-only page? What
does it really mean?

Answer: Nothing.

The bottom line is that separate is not equal.

Bottom-Line Accessibility Advice

Basic, Intermediate, and Advanced accessibility

- Include a DOCTYPE on every single page and a language code on each html tag.
- Write only standards-compliant HTML, and validate your pages to prove it.

6| tHe image ProBLem

ONLINE IMAGERY IS A CORE CONCERN IN ACCESSIBILITY. And that includes more than just photographs. On the Web, images are used for logos, navigation instruments (like "forward" and "back" or "next" and "previous" arrows), form buttons and labels, and for text itself (as *pictures of text*, with text saved as a bitmapped image rather than selectable characters). We find information graphics online – everything from spreadsheet-like graphs and charts to flowcharts to sewing patterns to musical scores.

And if visitors to your site cannot see, or if their browsers do not show graphics, they face a barrier in understanding those images.

The good news is that minimal access to imagery is ridiculously simple to achieve, while an intermediate level of access is not very much harder. The highest degree of accessible imagery is admittedly complex and harder to implement, but it is nonetheless a skill you can acquire. In this chapter, you'll learn how to use alt, title, and longdesc to make any image barrier-free.

Goals

In this chapter:
- We'll learn three levels of accessibility for uncomplicated image types.
- We'll work through a list of complicated image types and come up with ways to make them accessible.
- We'll discourage the use of a few well-intentioned but counter productive accessibility methods.

More than half the battle

The importance of making absolutely all the images on your Website accessible cannot be underestimated. This simple action alone gets you more than halfway toward an accessible site. You have to do it *correctly*, but even if you skip every other accessibility step, your sites immediately become fundamentally accessible.

The basics

Note: If you're already familiar with basic HTML, you can skip this section.

With uncommon exceptions, Web pages include *text* right within the page but merely *refer* to graphics. When you open a page in your browser, the page directly contains its own text. On the other hand, any graphics that appear in your browser are actually called up *separately* by the page. You've probably seen this yourself: The text of a page loads, but the browser status line tells you it is "fetching image" of such-and-such a name.

While it's not the only way to do so, images are almost always called up using the img element. Here's a typical (inaccessible) example:

```
< img src="sunset.gif" width="400" height="300" border="0"/>
```

The parts are:
- src ("source") is the filename. I'm using an easy example here, but the filename can be any URL anywhere – from a subdirectory on your hard drive, from another server in the same domain, or from a separate site altogether.
- width and height are measured in pixels. These attributes are not mandatory, but they speed up display because the browser knows how large an onscreen display area to reserve.
- border describes the visible border around the image, in pixels. A border of zero is invisible or nonexistent; most of the time, a border is visually undesirable.

In this inaccessible example:
- The browser will dutifully load the image if the file named sunset.gif is actually available, but if you can't see the image, it is of no help to you.
- If you've turned image-loading off, you'll see a placeholder graphic, if that.
- A text-only browser like Lynx will display only a placeholder – in the Lynx case, [INLINE] or the image filename.
- A screen-reader program cannot look at the image, understand it, and turn it into words. You need a text equivalent for the image to be accessible.

You have three levels of text equivalent at your disposal: alt, title, and longdesc.

Your first course of action

You do the greatest good with the easiest access technique: alt. A part of the HTML standard since HTML 2.0 (way back in 1992!), alt simply means "alternate" — a text alternative for your image.

Write an alt text by summing up your image in a few words. Include it right in the img element, like so:

```
< img src="sunset.gif" width="400" height="300" border="0" alt="Sunset over Darling Harbour" / >
```

The attributes can appear in any order, and alt doesn't have to be last. The alt text can be read and used in the following circumstances:

- A screen reader can read the text aloud or send it to a Braille display.
- A graphical browser with image-loading turned on that nonetheless cannot find the image file will display the alt text. (This happens even on well-funded commercial sites; I run across an example about once a month in recreational surfing.) Since the alt text sits inside the img element, it is loaded with the main page; even if the browser cannot find the graphic, it already knows the contents of the alt text and can display it.
- A graphical browser with image-loading turned off will display the alt text.
- Theoretically, alt texts can be indexed by search engines, but this is not much of a reason to use them.

Keep the alt text short. There is no set limit on the length of an alt text, but as we shall see shortly, a very long alt may not be fully displayed when image-loading is turned off or when the browser cannot locate the image file. By convention, limit alt texts to 1,024 characters (1 K) or less.

When it comes to writing the actual text, remember that alt takes the place of the graphic. Tell us what the picture *is* or *represents* or sum up its function, but don't tell us that it's a picture. I'll give you actual examples in a moment, but steer clear of writing a sort of meta–alt text, like "Picture of sunset over Darling Harbour" or "Picture of company logo."

Examples to avoid

Do not use the image filename, and don't let your authoring program substitute a filename automatically for you; it's better to leave an alt text blank or leave it out altogether than to foist a filename on your unsuspecting visitors. (How would you like to see the word "spacer.gif" ten times on one page? Isn't it even worse to hear your computer utter the phrase "spacer.gif" ten times on one page?)

An alt text must embody the essence of the information provided by the graphic. It's a replacement, after all. Do not load up alt texts with marketing propaganda, as in this most banal case, alt="check out our sponsor!"

If an image is a thumbnail link to a larger version of itself, by all means say so in the alt text. But you have to add that information to the rest of the alt text, which must nonetheless fully explain the function or purpose of the graphic. Here we know the image showed product 9000a, that we can get a bigger picture by "clicking" this one, and that one of the two images was 14 K in size. Thanks for clearing that up. You don't even know what the product is from the alt text provided. Something along the lines of alt="Fleur-de-Sel de Camargue (click for larger image)" would do nicely here.

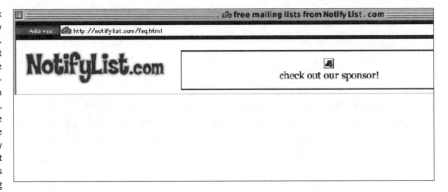

Also be sure not to accidentally leave in an authoring program's reminders: Merely in the course of recreational Web-surfing while writing this book, I found more than one site with alt texts reading "short description of image."

Further, do not get cute. I know of an adult site – contain your *pro forma* surprise, please; it's Nightcharm.com – that uses "lubricating" as the alt text for a simple, G-rated photograph of the site owner. (Should we call this photo a "headshot"?) I guess that's supposed to be some kind of tremendously droll synonym for "loading image."

On that topic, do not act as though alt texts function as placeholders while graphics load; do not, in other words, use alt="Loading image" or anything similar. Nor should you fill an alt text with advertising slogans of any kind. (Alternate texts for ads are discussed later in this chapter.)

Include an alt for absolutely every img without exception. An alt is required for every graphic in HTML 4 and XHTML. (The requirement reads: "The alt attribute must be specified for the img and <area></area> elements.") An img without an alt will cause your page to flunk when passed through a validator. For most of us, skipping an alt here and there was a way of life for years, and this new strictness is a bit of a pain at first. Then again, every authoring tool prompts you for an alt, and if you're typing out code by hand, adding a single tag is not exactly onerous.

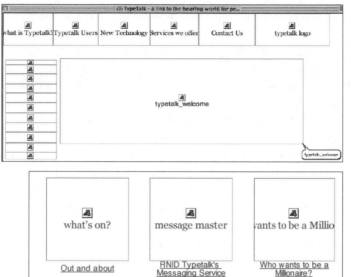

The whole point of this book is to help make all Websites accessible, within certain minor limits. It is nonetheless true that any disability-related site has to offer unimpeachable accessibility. In this example, the Website of the Typetalk relay service in the U.K. (www.Typetalk.org) shows a litany of inaccessibilities. Note the unhelpful alt texts based on filenames, like typetalk_welcome. (In this example, the browser used to capture the image, Macintosh Internet Explorer, errantly pops up a tooltip containing the alt text.)

The argument, by the way, that a relay service is used by deaf people and not the blind is beside the point, and is blown out of the water anyway by the fact that deaf-blind people use relay services, too.

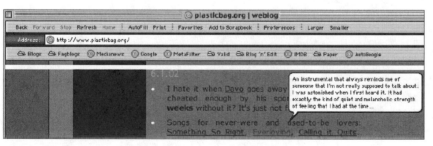

There is no predetermined length limit to title text; even quite lengthy paragraphs can and will be displayed, as in this example. The convention I suggest is to keep to 1 K of text or less.

The next step up the ladder

You can add another attribute on the img element to improve accessibility: title.

Although it is not widely known, in fact the title attribute can be applied to virtually anything in HTML. Further, the purpose and function of title are quite broad (you might say vague): The actual World Wide Web Consortium definition reads "This attribute offers advisory information about the element for which it is set." In other words, anything goes.

You've probably run across titles without even knowing it. If you use a graphical browser, you may have witnessed a "tooltip," or small pop-up windoid, appear when you hover your mouse over an image, a link, or even a chunk of text. The windoid shows the text of the title attribute. Unfortunately, some versions of Netscape 4 and certain early Internet Explorer versions also display a tooltip for alt text, a phenomenon World Wide Web Consortium guidelines do not authorize; conversely, W3C guidelines do not require that title be displayed any particular way (or at all: Netscape 4 ignores it, and such behaviour is legal). Accordingly, it is also legal for iCab on Macintosh and Opera on several platforms to display title text in a status bar, as they in fact do.

In image accessibility, you can use the title attribute to load up an img element with helpful but optional details; to expand on an alt; to warn about unusual browser behaviours; and to have a little fun. Using the markup ‹img src="sunset.gif" width="400" height="300" border="0" alt="Sunset over Darling Harbour" /› as an example, you could add one of the following titles:

- title="Darling Harbour, Sydney, October 2000, Olympic cleanup underway"
- title="Darling Harbour Sunset. Click for larger image (800x400)"
- title="Darling Harbour. Got rid of the Americans, but not their garbage"
- title="Darling Harbour Sunset. Full-size version opens in new window"

As you'll see later, title falls between alt and longdesc in degree of descriptiveness: alt gives you minimal, absolutely essential information; title adds useful information and can add flavour; longdesc (to be examined shortly) provides for rich, expressive documentation of a visual image.

You don't have to be dry and uptight in writing title texts. In fact, feel free to add some verve. If you're presenting a photo album (of a vacation, a conference, a day in the life), you can use an alt to describe the basic setup of a photograph and title to explain the photo's significance in the big picture, as it were.

- alt="Cabot Trail, Monday"
  title="When I was growing up, everyone visited the Cabot Trail but us. I would have been too young to appreciate it anyway"
- alt="Cusack, Oscars 97"
  title="John was ROBBED AGAIN at the Oscars, not even getting NOMINATED for Grosse Pointe"
- alt="Medical examiner"
  title="The medical examiner, John Butt, inside Hangar B, where he spent three months identifying victims"
- alt="Left ventricle"
  title="I had bypass surgery in 1994, but this is from my double bypass in 1997. Here Dr. Otinsky prepares to insert a shunt"

What do you do when you don't have anything special to add to your alt text? Adding a title is optional. There's no harm in making the title text identical to alt. I recommend consistency in coding: If you use title anywhere on a page, use it everywhere on that page. If you can write an alt and a title that are respectively different for three out of four images on a page, for the remaining image the alt and title can be the same. The result is a page that provides title text for *all* images rather than some of them. If you opt to provide only alts for an entire page, stick with that.

If you hate titles, by the way, you can suppress their display in graphical browsers by using title="" (empty title, analogous to empty alt, coming up shortly). To be thorough, you'd have to add it to every image on the page. Worth your while? I doubt it.

However, if alt and title have the same text, enclose the title in brackets [ ] like so: alt="Sunday picnic" title="[Sunday picnic]". That way you will know for sure which of the two otherwise-identical texts your browser or device may be displaying. We wouldn't have to bother with this if Netscape and Microsoft had not defied the HTML specification and popped up alt texts as browser tooltips. (To reiterate, *alternate* texts are replacements, not additions.) It does no harm to write all your title texts this way if you wish.

Here in the real world, individual pages are upgraded faster than entire sites. If only a few of your pages have titles while the rest (mostly older pages) do not, it is not something to worry about. Consistency within a page is more readily achievable and more important.

I can think of one rather unusual exception: Drop caps, as described later, do not need a title, and it may be viable to code a graphic acting as a drop cap as the only img element on a page without a title even if the other images do have them.

Compatibility

Screen readers have access to titles and may read them out loud if the user requests it. I may be describing an idealized case here, since occasional reports I've seen hold that certain screen-reader versions under certain conditions cannot read titles. Even if that is true, it is not your problem as a Web designer or developer; we have to expect software manufacturers to provide support for basic HTML.

- Lynx, the leading text-only browser, displays titles if and only if the image is also a link or imagemap; press L or l for List of links.
- No version of Netscape Navigator or Communicator ever displayed title text before Netscape 6; that version, and any Mozilla build current with the release of this book, both pop up a tooltip for titles.
- iCab on Macintosh and Opera on several platforms display title text on a status line.

- I have never seen a version of Internet Explorer on either Macintosh or Windows platforms that did *not* display a tooltip for any kind of title anywhere on a page, including titles on images.

As you'll see throughout this book, you can slap a title on virtually anything in HTML. In fact, the only tags where it is apparently illegal to include title are:

- ‹html›‹/html›
- ‹head›‹/head›
- base
- meta
- ‹script›‹/script›
- ‹title›‹/title› (inside ‹head›‹/head›)
- basefont ("deprecated" in XHTML anyway; use stylesheets instead)
- param (inside ‹applet›‹/applet› and ‹object›‹/object›)

Waxing poetic: Long descriptions

When alt and title are insufficient to embody the visual qualities of an image in words, HTML offers an access feature at a higher level of complexity: longdesc.

A longdesc is a *long description* of an image. How long? The sky's the limit. longdesc is meant for pictures worth more than a thousand words (or 1,024 characters). The aim is to use any length of description necessary to impart the details of the graphic. It would not be remiss to hope that a long description conjures an image – *the* image – in the mind's eye, an analogy that holds true even for the totally blind.

Unlike alt and title, which are included in the img element and are always available for rendering in a browser or screen reader, a longdesc is a separate file. You would normally write write a valid (albeit small) HTML file for each longdesc. Your browser or screen reader has to support longdesc, and very few do.

Here's how you add the longdesc attribute to an img element:

```
‹img src="sunset.gif" width="400" height="300" border="0"
title="Darling Harbour, Sydney, October 2000, Olympic cleanup underway"
alt="Sunset over Darling Harbour" longdesc="sunset-LD.html" /›
```

The naming convention I suggest is to use the same filename as the image file plus the characters -LD; remove the extension used for image files (.gif, .JPG, .png, or any other) and replace it with whatever extension you use for HTML files. Since a longdesc is an HTML file, it uses the same filename structure as all your other HTML files. If you use .html or .htm as a filename extension for other files, stay consistent. Preserve any hyphens, underscores, and extended characters in the original image filenames.

This way, in alphabetical file listings in your operating system, the graphic file and the longdesc will be right next to each other; the use of capitals in -LD makes the longdesc files easier to spot, and, if you're consistent in your file naming, you can search for and manipulate all longdesc files easily. Another advantage: The character sequence -LD is not likely to come up very often in filenames – certainly not when followed by .html or .htm. Example filename pairs:

- src="photo6.gif" and longdesc="photo6-LD.html"
- src="map-europe_2.JPG" and longdesc="map-europe_2-LD.htm"
- src="S%8Bo%20Paulo%206.jpg" and longdesc="S%8Bo%20Paulo%206-LD.html" (where S%8Bo%20Paulo%206 is the character encoding for *São Paulo 6*, complete with accent and space characters)

Use fully-qualified directory addressing in your URLs if necessary. Should you keep longdesc files in the same directory as images? Probably. I suspect the only likely reason to keep them separate is to make allowances for the day when you will run batch operations on, say, every graphic or every long-description file. But I'm sure your software is clever enough to manipulate only files of a certain type; they're readily differentiated by filename and extension, and of course by type and creator codes, MIME type, or whatever other metadata your system stores for every file. In any event, the following examples are equivalent save for file structure:

- src="/img/png/cavernosum-6.PNG" and longdesc="/img/png/cavernosum-6-LD.html" (same directory)
- src="/img/png/cavernosum-6.PNG" and longdesc="/longdesc/cavernosum-6-LD.html" (different directories)

File structure

What does a longdesc file look like? Like any other HTML file. But you might as well keep it small. Now is the time to write the simplest, plainest text-only page. You want nothing to stand in the way of reading the long description; we're already loading a separate file here, which takes a certain time to do, so we might as well make the longdesc file as compact as possible.

```
<!DOCTYPE html PUBLIC "-//W3C//DTD XHTML 1.0 Transitional//EN"
"http://www.w3.org/TR/xhtml1/DTD/xhtml1-transitional.dtd">
<html xmlns="http://www.w3.org/1999/xhtml" xml:lang="en" lang="en">
<head>
<title>Long description for sunset.gif</title>
</head>
<body>
```

```
<p>At dusk, the sun&#8217;s rays turn the wispy clouds over Darling Harbour,
Sydney, brilliant orange and red. A ferry, distantly visible, crosses the harbour from
right to left. The deserted remnants of the Sydney 2000 Olympic rowing facilities
are visible in the far distance. A small clump of people, some with cameras
strapped around their necks, stand at the right of the picture peering and snap-
ping photographs.</p>

<p>Back to the <a href="photoalbum.html#sunset" title="Photo album">photo
album</a>.</p>
</body>
</html>
```

Let's consider the structure of the file.

- As is recommended practice (see Chapter 5, "The structure of accessible pages"), use a DOCTYPE definition so the browser or screen reader will know which level of HTML you've employed.
- All HTML files begin with <html>, require a <head> (in which you can include a <title> and other elements), and move on to <body>. I recommend a consistent scheme for entitling your longdesc files (i.e., the text inside the <title></title> elements): "Long description for *filename*" is short and to the point.
- In the body itself, write the long description. Use any accessible and legal HTML features you want (including, in this example, non-ASCII punctuation like ’ for an apostrophe), though it might be a tad recursive to use images.

Links back to the original

The last paragraph in the above example is a nice touch that isn't strictly necessary but will be helpful in real-world usage. In it, I've added a link back to the previous document just *past* the point where the graphic image occurs. The visitor can simply keep on reading from that point. I used a page anchor – the characters after the # in the <a></a> link. Different circumstances may warrant different usage.

- If the source page, as in the case of a photo album, shows the image by itself with little or no additional text, just give a plain link back to the page.
- If you're dealing with a longer source document that includes intermingled graphics and text, add an anchor to the text immediately following the graphic you are describing. In this case, place <a name="sunset"></a> around the first few words of the subsequent text. (Example: <a name="sunset">When evening came</a>, we headed off to Darlinghurst for a quick bite.) Other naming techniques (like adding name

and/or id to the `<p></p>` element surrounding the text) are sometimes viable, but browser support varies.

- If your page uses frames, I have no foolproof method to offer. I suppose placing an anchor link inside the frame that contains the image being described is the obvious course of action, but coding the URL of a specific frame may cause only that frame to load in the browser. (A number of JavaScript techniques − all of them, as the saying goes, beyond the scope of this book − are available to ensure that surrounding frames are reloaded whenever a browser requests only a single frame. This does tend to work at cross-purposes to your visitors' ability to load a single frame in the first place.) Or it may suffice to use the URL of the page enclosing the entire frameset, with appropriate added anchor. I can only counsel experimentation and debugging in sites that use frames.

- If your site uses a content-management system that assigns a filename only when source code is uploaded or saved, you will not know the filename to which to append the anchor link until the original file is uploaded − in the example above, you may know that you're using an anchor called sunset but not that the filename is photoalbum.html. In practice, this is not much of an impediment, since you're surely going to perfect the main page first and work on long descriptions later.

How to write descriptions

If your background is in computer programming, you may find it intimidating to write concise, evocative descriptions of pictorial imagery. If you're a visual designer, prose is not likely your forte. (If it were, you'd be a writer, not a designer.) Even if you have a lot of writing experience, you still won't find it very easy. Because it isn't. Writing descriptions, however, is a skill that becomes less difficult with exposure and experience.

Exposure, however, remains a problem. There are very few examples of longdescs on the Web today, meaning there are few models to emulate. I can, however, provide rules of thumb that will guide you on what to mention and how. With experience you will develop your own style.

- The cardinal rule of description is "Describe what you see."
- To get you in the right frame of mind, imagine you're talking on the phone to one of your good friends. It's one of those phone calls where you're just shooting the breeze. Imagine you've casually mentioned that you have just gotten your photos back from the developer, or you're working on a portfolio downloaded from your digital camera. Now imagine telling your friend you especially like this certain picture. "Oh?" your friend asks. "What's it look like?" "Well, it's a picture of..." A picture of what? The way you'd finish that sentence is pretty much the way you'll write a description.

- Here's another approach: What words would you use to describe the photo to clearly distinguish it from another photo – from *every other* photo there is? Does it show a person, as opposed to an airplane? Is it an indoor or an outdoor photo? Daytime or nighttime? Is it actually a line drawing rather than a photograph? Are there mountains in the photo, or a canoe on a lake?

- With personal image collections, it can be quite helpful to explain nice little details about how the photo came about, particularly if the text of the original page mentions it. You could add, for example, "Jim still has his cast on at this point; it came off the next day." That kind of folksy tone is unlikely to be appropriate in a business site, for example, but, as with the fun you can have with the title attribute, a colourful writing style can jazz up an otherwise dry description, actually fulfilling the goal of rendering the essence of the image in words.

- Mention the point of view or position of the camera or observer, if implicitly: "A black Labrador retriever sniffs the beach sand nearby. Farther down the road, an elderly man leans over and waves a leash."

- Definitely mention colours. All blind and visually-impaired people understand the social significance of colour: Everyone knows red is the colour of blood and connotes passion; the sky is blue, and blue is peaceful; green, the colour of grass, represents nature. Brown eyes are common, blue eyes unusual, green or grey eyes very unusual. Keep in mind that most blind people either now have or used to have some usable vision; even people blind from birth have a conversational understanding of colour.

- Point out details that would be unexpected based on common knowledge of the visual world.
  - "On top of Marge's head sits a two-and-a-half-foot-tall column of blue hair with a rounded tip. Her eyelashes are prominent and she wears a blue dress, round earrings, and a choker with big white stones. Like all the Simpsons, her hands have four fingers, and her skin colour is dull yellow."
  - "Salif Keita sings into a microphone onstage, his backup band playing drums, guitars, and congas behind him. Keita and his band are all black guys, but Keita is also albino, with very pale, pinkish skin and translucent hair and eyebrows."

- There's no such thing as a graphic with nothing to describe.
  - An image in which not much seems to be going on – a simple snapshot of a person, for example – gives you the opportunity to describe what the person looks like. Tall or short? Curly brown hair, long blond hair, shaved head, reddish sideburns? Make-up? Flannel shirt, leather jacket, silk blouse, striped tie, tuxedo? How would you describe the facial expression?

- If the graphic is a drawing of an object, what does the object look like? If it's a guitar, is it acoustic or electric? What colour? Tell us the shape of the guitar. If it's a bass guitar, say so, and maybe mention how few strings there are. Is it plugged into an amplifier? (If a cord is plugged into the guitar but you can't see the amplifier, the answer is no: "A patch cord is plugged into the guitar's jack.")
  - If the photo shows Nick poking his head out from behind a palm tree, what does a palm tree look like? How tall is it? What do the leaves and trunk look like? (Feel free to make a comparison: "Unlike pine trees, with branches nearly all the way up the trunk, palm trees concentrate their long, rubbery leaves at the very top.")
- Use tight, evocative adjectives phrases: "long, furry tail with two matted brown burdock burrs near the tip"; "bright-red earphones half the size of a grapefruit"; "navy-blue cargo pants, with Velcro-flapped pockets on the sides of both legs and an elastic waistband"; "hundreds of wide concrete steps lead to the massive wooden doors two storeys up"; "low-hanging, dull-grey clouds almost touch the church spire in the near distance."
- You don't have to include every single detail (like how many flowers are in a vase), but exceptions should be mentioned: "The vase holds a few dozen roses, all red except for a single yellow one in the centre."

Browser complications

While there isn't a browser you could name that doesn't support alt, and most modern browsers support title, at time of writing there's virtually no support whatsoever for longdesc. Even screen readers generally ignore the attribute altogether. It's an issue of chicken vs. egg: Browsers and devices have to support longdesc before developers use it consistently, while makers of browsers and devices are in no hurry to support longdesc until it is in wider actual use. Even so, given that longdesc is *intended* for blind and visually-impaired visitors and has been part of HTML 4 since late 1999, it is scandalous that every screen reader updated *since* that time does *not* directly support longdesc.

In fact, only iCab, the Macintosh graphical browser; Mozilla and Netscape 6 on all platforms; and the Jaws screen reader (version 4.01 and later) all have access to longdesc.

To view a long description:
- In iCab, Control-click on an image. In the resulting contextual menu, look for Description under the Image submenu. iCab will open a new window displaying the longdesc file.
- In Mozilla and Netscape 6, bring up a contextual menu for an image (by right-clicking or Control-clicking, or whatever technique your

operating system requires). Select Properties. The link to the long description will appear.

So-called standards-compliant browsers, like Internet Explorer 5 for Macintosh and Explorer 6 for Windows, allegedly support longdesc, but do so merely by passing on the presence of longdesc to some unspecified separate program (i.e., they pass it on through the DOM, or document object model).

It is certainly open to question why graphical browsers should provide an interface that lets sighted users read a longdesc at all. Unlike the summary attribute on <table></table>, which the World Wide Web Consortium specifically states is limited to "user agents rendering to non-visual media such as speech and Braille," the W3C makes no recommendations on limiting access to longdesc. That in itself is sufficient reason to make it available to all users. I can, however, see a few other reasons:

- Standards compliance: If browser makers want us to believe they take compliance with HTML standards seriously, they cannot pick and choose which features to support. That, of course, is exactly what they do at present, but the practice is to be discouraged.
- Testing: Providing even a hidden interface for longdesc lets developers test their accessible pages.

D-links

To get around these incompatibilities, well-meaning experts (most prominently, the Web Accessibility Initiative itself and the WGBH Educational Foundation) have promoted the use of D-links — the use of the letter D for Description (rendered any way you want to write it — D, [d], [D], D., d., whatever) as a visible, explicit link to the long description of the image.

The idea is that you will somehow figure out a way to place a tag like <a href="*imagename*-LD.html" title="Long description of image">D.</a> somewhere alongside your actual image. This link works exactly the way longdesc itself does and points to the exact same file.

It's a noble idea, really. But unless your software creates them automatically for you, don't bother. Reasons:

- I promised at the outset of this book that I would advise you to make visible alterations to your layout only if necessary. Here it is not necessary; we have the longdesc attribute for this task.
- D-links look awful.
- It is often difficult or impossible to associate them unambiguously with the graphic they refer to. (Don't believe me? Think of a photo gallery with three rows of five photographs. Just where do you add the Ds?)
- The fact that longdesc is poorly supported is not really your fault, or even your concern. A great many accessibility features of HTML are

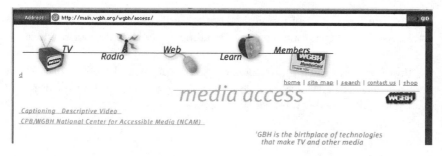

God love 'em, but our friends at WGBH Educational Foundation still seem to believe that a D-link (seen at lower left), which leads to a text description of the appearance of the entire page, actually has value to a blind visitor. In practice, D-links needlessly clutter the layout of a page and sidestep the main issue: Access to information rather than graphic design.

poorly supported, even by adaptive technology. But there are virtually *no* access features that are entirely unsupported. There's always *some* population out there that can use what you code, including long descriptions. If it is incumbent on you the designer or developer to code according to standards, it is even more incumbent on makers of browsers and adaptive technology to *support* those standards. To solve the dilemma of chicken and egg, somebody's got to volunteer to be one of them.

- If, on the other hand, the use of longdesc caused actual bugs or catastrophic failures (the way <object></object> does in some versions of Netscape 4), then a case could be made against its use. But there are no such bugs or failures. It's either supported or it's not. Nothing undesirable happens in either case.

- While I do not *strictly* adhere to the usability dictum "Make link texts self-explanatory," I do feel that links along the lines of <a>Click here!</a> are trite, stick out like a sore thumb from the surrounding text, and don't give us enough information to figure out where we will end up once we "click" the link. I would place D-links in this same category, but much worse: A page with three or four D-links, all of which look the same and differ only by the href URL, is just asking you to make mistakes. (Which D goes where? Which D goes with which image?)

- If including longdesc on the img element adds a wee bit of extra work (excluding the task of writing the description file itself, which you'd always be doing anyway), the D-link technique requires essentially double that effort. You will end up using the longdesc attribute anyway *and also* set up an entirely separate hyperlink, with careful attention paid to URL and positioning. It ain't worth it.

I do know of one software package that can create D-links automatically — PopChart [D] by Corda (corda.com/d/), which automatically summarizes numerical charts and graphs, produces a long description using longdesc, *and* sets up a D-link. If you like that package, use it.

Also, the University of Toronto's A-Prompt utility (described in Chapter 14, "Certification and testing"; available online at APrompt.ca) can produce D-links for you.

If, in some imagined future, DreamWeaver, GoLive, and the like all automatically create D-links, you could use those, too. But D-links remain pug-ugly, and entering D-links by hand simply is not worth it.

Page descriptions

Similarly, well-meaning access advocates have suggested using a D-link to describe *the overall appearance of a page*. I see this advice as a form of displaced liberal guilt of the sort William Hurt exhibited in *Children of a Lesser God*, in which his character, James Leeds, suddenly feels guilty about playing LP records because his girlfriend, Marlee Matlin as Sarah Norman, is deaf. Funnily enough, this guilt trip never hit him during all the years he was a teacher at a school for the deaf. In any event, Sarah rightly tells him to stuff it. The fact that she cannot hear says nothing about the fact that he can. Use what you've got. If you can enjoy music, go ahead; you should not be impeded by the fact that someone else cannot (and in this case cannot be accommodated, since LP records, unlike music videos, cannot be captioned).

I suppose it is possible that some blind or visually-impaired person here or there might be interested in the specific graphic-arts details of your page layout, but just what does that add? Page descriptions are in no way comparable to audio or text descriptions of artworks like paintings, photographs, plays, television programs, and films, where appearance cannot be separated from enjoyment, meaning, and understanding. Online, we go to considerable lengths to do just that. Stylesheets separate presentation from structure, for example. The bulk of the techniques explained in this book make it possible to use Websites without one of the five human senses.

I assume, at this point in your understanding of Web accessibility, it will not hurt your feelings to be told that the specific appearance of your site is not really important; while we will not sacrifice appearance for accessibility unless we have to, it remains true that your site's *meaning* is important, not its appearance.

And anyway, how would you link to such a description? I guess we're supposed to double up page descriptions and image descriptions on those ill-advised D-links. So does the D-link refer to the nice big central graphic or to the whole page?

Here is an example page description from WGBH.org:

Five selectable images appear at the top of the page. From left to right they read: "Television," "Radio," "Web," "Learn" and "Members." Below is the WGBH logo, the words "media access," and "GBH is the birthplace of technologies that make TV and other media more

accessible to disabled people." Additional selectable images are
"CPB/WGBH National Center for Accessible Media (NCAM),"
"Descriptive Video" and "Captioning."

Most of the phrases in quotation marks above are live hyperlinks in the
original. Accessible images (including imagemaps) would give the blind
visitor *direct* access to each of those items on the original page in question.
How many levels of abstraction are we dealing with here? Do we want the
page itself accessible, or do we want a description of the page accessible?

Don't waste your time with page descriptions. They're a misguided idea
and are not worth the trouble.

Problem cases

As you build Websites, you'll find a range of image types that present a few
problems. How do you summarize problem graphics like these?

Before delving into an excruciating degree of detail, I will provide an
overriding principle: Be specific. Do *not* give us something generic, like "Ad"
or "Bullet" or "Arrow."

Advertising

Graphical advertisements are a big enough issue to warrant their own
section. Ordinary GIF and JPEG images used as advertising are not difficult to
make accessible.

- By far the most important task: Keep marketing propaganda *out* of the
  alt text. Cut, as they say, the crap. Give us *the bullet*: Use a concise, self-
  explanatory alt text that explains the benefit or purpose of the ad.
  Imagine you are transforming your visual ad into a slogan used as a
  sponsorship credit on a television program. How would you sum up
  the *message* of the advertisement? Or imagine you are boiling down the
  advertisement to a classified ad where you pay by the word. What is
  the irreducible minimum message?
- Do not bother attempting to epitomize the visual appearance of the ad.
  Remember, the alt text encodes the *function* of a graphic. With animated
  GIFs, it is better to pretend the GIF is static rather than animated and
  treat the ad no differently from others.
- Include the word "Advertisement" (in brackets or parentheses) somewhere in the alt text. Such a disclaimer is not required on all Websites
  for the *visual* manifestation of an ad, but then it isn't always necessary;
  as in newspapers, a disclaimer, if not used in all cases, is used where
  an ad may be mistaken for editorial copy or illustration. But alt texts
  are not visual, except inasmuch as they can be seen in graphical
  browsers under certain unusual circumstances. You must imagine the

screen-reader or Braille-display user whose experience of a Website is one of subtly-differentiated text streams. A blind or visually-impaired visitor cannot determine at a glance that your ad actually *is* an ad because, of course, such a visitor cannot necessarily cast a glance. I would use alt="(Advertisement)" or alt="[Advertisement]" followed by a space and the rest of the copy.

- Sponsor advertisements are used somewhat differently from banner ads. You can still click them and visit the actual sponsor, but the approach is usually more low-key. We often see a column of sponsor logos labeled as such (e.g., "Please visit our sponsors"). It would not hurt to use (Sponsor) or [Sponsor] inside your alt rather than (Advertisement) or [Advertisement].
- Do not use "Click here!" or any conceivable variant of it inside an alt or title! We know that it's an advertisement already (you marked it as such after reading the preceding advice), and we'll "click" if we feel like it.
- You can add whatever brief, tightly-written marketing copy you wish inside title. I'm leaving this intentionally vague; my overriding concern is that you keep marketing copy *out* of the alt text. I suppose the advice I could give is "Boil down the marketing pitch from the site to which the ad links into a couple of sentences and add them in a title."
- Text-only ads, as seen on Google.com and Metafilter.com, self-evidently do not need any kind of special markup *unless* they include little images here and there, as with pictures of text reading "Textad information." Use an alt text (alt="Textad information"), possibly also a title.

Copious examples are provided in the section entitled "Special 'Advertising' Supplement." Have a look at those.

Multimedia advertising

Now, then. The current scourge, as I write this, is the use of Flash and other animations in advertising, as though by annoying us even more we will somehow finally give in and buy the damned product. If you use the ‹object›‹/object› element to mark up the Flash advertisement, you can include alternative texts and images right inside the element, a technique described at length in Chapter 13, "Multimedia." You have no such options with the embed element. Accordingly, if you want to build an accessible Website, don't use anything inside embed.

This advice will of course be unworkable if you are required to make your site function in Netscape 4, which tends to choke on the ‹object›‹/object› element, or if your client simply demands to use Flash. Something's got to give. I know perfectly well what will give in most cases, but you must acknowledge that it is my job to tell you the right way to do it even if I expect you actually will not.

THE IFRAME SOLUTION

The little-known ‹iframe›‹/iframe› element lets you set up a frame that floats "inline" (hence iframe) within your page. We should really add "iframe" as a generic term to our Web vocabularies alongside "frame," since in some ways iframes are much more useful and are a far better idea than frames per se.

If you include an animated advertisement in an ‹iframe›‹/iframe› element (used, for example, at NYTimes.com), you have ample opportunity to provide a wide range of equivalents. A generic but valid ‹iframe›‹/iframe› tag, this time for a Saab car advertisement, resembles the following (though many other attributes are available):

```
‹iframe src="95ad.html" longdesc="95ad-LD.html" width="160" height="600"
title="3.9% APR on all new 9-5 sedans and wagons till November 2002"›
‹/iframe›
```

Now, the source here (src) is typically an entire, self-contained HTML document, which in practical use will include a Flash movie or some other desperate and overwrought attempt to get the visitor's attention. You can include a title, as with essentially every other HTML element. But ‹iframe›‹/iframe› directly supports longdesc the way img does. I would strongly encourage using it.

What is little known is the fact that, rather like ‹object›‹/object›, everything you place between ‹iframe› and ‹/iframe› is the alternate markup for any device that cannot understand or display the src file.

You thus have the best of all possible worlds:

- You may use absolutely any form of presentation whatsoever in the iframe's src.
- ‹iframe›‹/iframe› itself carries intermediate and advanced access features (title and longdesc).
- You have essentially unlimited space to provide multiple forms of accessible alternative content directly between ‹iframe› and ‹/iframe›.

An iframe-based advertisement (in this case, without animation). The fact that the ad is encoded in an iframe is not visually apparent here (as it need not be), and indeed NYTimes.com serves different HTML based on browser type (a "browser sniff"); your browser might not even use an iframe to serve this same advertisement.

In the previous example:

- The iframe src could link to a Flash animation documenting the glories of the Saab 9⁵ sedan and wagon.
- You could fill in title and longdesc.
- You may use a QuickTime movie (with captions and descriptions if you want), and/or a GIF or JPEG still image with standard alternative texts, and any length of hyperlinked, styled, rich body copy within the full-fledged HTML document contained inside the ‹iframe›‹/iframe› element.

Everybody's happy. It's a pretty good system. And yes, I quite insist you go to all this trouble. Iframe-based advertising is a lot of work already; it has the highest production values of any advertising form regularly encountered online (well, apart from self-contained sites that do nothing but advertise) and amounts to coding a whole other Website just to sell something. Budgets are generally quite high. As such, in the terminology used by this book, iframes are an advanced-level construct. Advanced HTML requires advanced accessibility. In any event, the accessible alternatives suggested here are inexpensive to create – particularly if you stick to still images and marked-up text.

Long descriptions

I will suggest you go ahead and use long descriptions in advertisements if you wish. I just hope you will use that facility for its intended purpose – to elucidate the visual appearance of an image, not to directly sell something. In the iframe example, the longdesc would explain what the advertisement looks like; ‹iframe›‹/iframe› content would try to sell you the car.

Pop-ups and pop-unders

Pop-up advertising windows (that sit, by definition, on top of the window you really want to read) are actually less egregious than pop-under windows for a screen-reader user, but both of them cause undue complication.

- Nondisabled visitors have to get rid of a pop-up ad before reading the actual desired window it obscures. This takes half a second, but is annoying.
- Blind visitors cannot glance at the screen and instantly understand that a windoid has popped up. A screen reader may dutifully alter focus to the frontmost window, which in this case is an advertisement.
- Accordingly, you absolutely must follow my instructions here and use an alt text that includes the word "Advertisement" in some form. title is virtually mandatory here just to make what's going on understand-able. Long descriptions are certainly not wrong. A screen-reader user will figure out that a new window has appeared; that part you cannot

control or even assist with. What you must not do is make it difficult to figure out *what the window is*.

- Pop-under ads are a bother for nondisabled surfers because they get in the way *later:* They sneak up on you when you're trying to clear away unwanted windows. A screen-reader user is not disadvantaged at all in this context. Everyone is equally inconvenienced, *if and only if* the window content is accessible.
- A low-vision person may well be able to figure out what's going on with pop-up and pop-under windows without assistive technology. alt and title are still useful for this group.
- A person with a learning disability like dyslexia may well be *especially* confused by the plethora of windows, with their attendant colour and possible animation, alongside standard "content" pages with their own text, graphics, and/or animation. I doubt you particularly care about this group, particularly since the only way to accommodate them with pop-up and pop-under ads is to cease their use.

See "Spawned windows" later in this chapter.

accesskey values

The accesskey attribute, used to assign a keystroke to various elements, is exhaustively explained in Chapter 8, "Navigation." It is not helpful to list the accesskey value inside an image alt text. accesskey helps mobility-impaired people more than blind people, and most mobility-impaired visitors will not have access to the alt text. The issue of making accesskey values actually understandable and usable to visitors is not easy in the first place, but this is the wrong way to do it. (See Chapter 8, "Navigation.")

Animated GIFs

Use an alt that reflects the most representative frame – possibly the last (alt="Children on the ferris wheel"). Your title can mention the animation: title="Kids enjoy a full revolution of the ferris wheel". A longdesc can describe the complete animation.

Arrows

Arrows, when displayed in text sizes, are a bit of a bother online because they are small and hard to work with. HTML actually contains character entities for arrows in four directions –

- ← or ← for left arrow
- ↑ or ↑ for up arrow
- → or → for right arrow
- ↓ or ↓ for down arrow

– but they are poorly supported. Knowing this, designers resort to little images instead. Your alternative text can use the HTML entities if you are brave, or you can swallow your pride and use ASCII-art-style equivalents, alt="<-" for left arrow and alt="->" for right arrow. Or you could just use less-than and greater-than signs.

ASCII art

If you're an oldschool Usenet geek or an hepcat and like to make pictures out of printable characters, you must add a [Skip] link before the ASCII art. Otherwise screen readers will dutifully pronounce every damned letter. And we don't *want* that. (See Chapter 8, "Navigation.")

Background graphics and patterns

Page or table backgrounds do not need an alt text; it's not part of the HTML standard. Do not even attempt it.

Borders, rules, and other meaningless graphics

Any graphic that actually means nothing requires alt="". Examples include borders (including images jimmied together to form tabbed navbars); rules; images of rounded corners used to make a rectangular box look nicer; and repetitions of either meaningless or meaningful graphics (if your page features five occurrences of the same logo, handle the first one appropriately and make the rest of them disappear with alt=""). This is admittedly one of the tougher judgement calls to make, and you have to be ruthless with yourself. If heard in voice through a screen reader, in all honesty, do you *need to know* that particular graphic exists?

Bullets

Some Web designers use little graphics in place of true typographic bullets in itemized lists. My first advice is: Don't! True to this book's espousal of full standards compliance, you should mark up lists as lists – in this case, unordered lists <ul></ul>. Just as you should use a heading code (<h1></h1> through <h6></h6>) rather than piling up a sequence of font tags to *simulate* the large type commonly used for headings, you should not code a sequence of paragraphs preceded by bullets that will typographically masquerade as a list.

Using cascading stylesheets, you may specify the appearance of unordered lists. Let's consider the case where you the designer are *not* using an image as a bullet but are relying on the browser's built-in list rendering. Stylesheets give you three options for visible bullets: disc (canonically, a filled bullet), circle (an outline bullet), and square (a filled square). You may write a stylesheet declaration of this sort:

```
ul { list-style-type: disc }
```

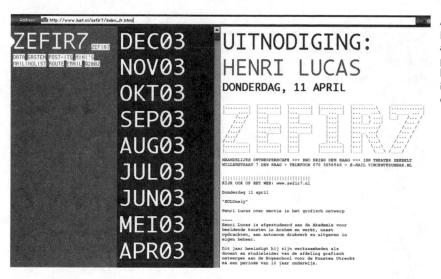

ASCII art requires a visible [Skip] link (using an ordinary a href="#anchorname" tag) to pass over the ASCII characters lest they all be spoken out loud in strict, maddening linear order.

Typically, graphical browsers default to the equivalent of list-style-type: disc anyway, but it does not hurt to declare it explicitly, and it is a good idea for other reasons to be described momentarily.

If you want or need to use a decorative image bullet in your lists, cascading stylesheets make it possible. Use a style declaration along these lines:

    ul { list-style-image: url(image-URL) }

According to Håkon Wium Lie and Bert Bos's book *Cascading Style Sheets: Designing for the Web* (Addison-Wesley Longman, 1997), "If for some reason the browser is unable to download or display the image, it will use the list-style-type again." Hence, to combine visual appearance, safety backup in case of a graphical-bullet file that cannot be located, *and* accessibility, use a style declaration like so:

    ul { list-style-image: url(*image-URL*); list-style-type: disc }

Or you may combine the declarations –

    ul { list-style: url(*image-URL*) disc }

– which tells the browser to use the *image-URL* file by preference and a filled circle if necessary.

Even if you're using list-style-image, the list retains its HTML structure as a list and can be read by adaptive technology. One notes that the HTML specification lacks any means whatsoever of assigning an alt text to the bullet replacement image, which surely is a failing, though one we can do nothing about. Also, paradoxically, you may use list-style-image with ordered lists

Cutesy little graphic images masquerading as list bullets (as in this example) should be used only as a last resort and only through correct stylesheet declarations along the lines of ul { list-style: url(*image-URL*) disc }.

‹ol›‹/ol›, which makes no sense at all. (Why order list items if they are not actually enumerated?)

If you absolutely must misbehave and engage in what I feel should be legally prohibited behaviour by using cutesy bullet-like characters in standard paragraphs, you are obliged to use an alt text. (You are so obliged with every img element, as you know well enough by now.)

Here you want the alt text to refer to the function of the graphical bullet, not its appearance. By convention, the alt text for graphical bullets is alt="*" (asterisk). If an asterisk is hard to type on your keyboard, use alt="*" or alt="*".

You could experiment with encoding the actual bullet character, using alt="•" or alt="•". Newer browsers will display the bullet character if the graphical bullet is unavailable, but screen readers may read out the word "bull" or the number "8,226." Under no circumstances should you use alt="[Bullet]", alt="CIRCLE", or anything that attempts to describe the looks of the graphical bullet, like alt="A small, 3D, spherical, red bullet" (an actual example). alt texts encode *function* or *purpose*, not appearance.

Think about it: If you're not loading graphics, instead of a tidy surrogate for a real bullet (the asterisk:*), you're stuck with a whole word like "bullet." A screen reader will actually read the word aloud, getting in the way of the structure of the itemized list.

Charts and graphs

I don't have a lot of good news when it comes to charts and graphs that attempt to bring graphical form to numerical data. It is difficult to make the case that such illustrations cannot be rendered in text; most of the time they *derive* from numbers, which *are* text. But we use illustrations to make the numbers *more understandable*. We are undoing that process by rendering charts and graphs in words even if that is necessary for anyone who cannot see the illustration to understand it at all.

However, like packing, unpacking, and repacking a suitcase, once some numbers are rendered graphically, it is not always easy or straightforward to re-render that graphic in numbers (and words).

The first-level approach is pretty obvious: Use alt to tell us what the chart or graph is.

- alt="HIV incidence among males 18 to 34, 1996"
- alt="Sulfur emissions by state"
- alt="Litres of water per capita (Africa)"

Do *not*, as ever, give us anything generic, like alt="Chart" or alt="(graph)".

The only really useful advice I have for you is to load up the title attribute with the important or salient information the illustration is supposed to impart. In many cases, this will be impossible; the chart or graph attempts to visually impart many streams of interrelated data that resist distillation to a few words. But in a surprising number of other cases, the graph or chart is used to communicate a central idea, and you will usually be able to sum that up in a sentence or two inside a title:

- title="13.6% spike in MSM cohort vs. 11.5% average spike"
- title="Overall reductions, strongest in Ohio (down 3.6%) and Indiana (3.3%)"
- title="Max: Republic of Congo (298,963); min: Tunisia (439)"

What about long description? Charts and graphs are in many ways the canonical use for longdesc. But as we'll see in Chapter 11, "Stylesheets," what the pie-in-the-sky working groups at the Web Accessibility Initiative think is possible and what is actually usable in the real world are two separate universes. An actual WAI example (with an original error in URL corrected):

```
< img src="sales97.gif" alt="Sales for 1997" longdesc="sales97.html" >
```

In sales97.html: A chart showing how sales in 1997 progressed. The chart is a bar chart showing percentage increases in sales by month. Sales in January were up 10% from December 1996, sales in February dropped 3%....

Apart from its clumsy repetitiveness, note that the authors conveniently avoid the dirty work of listing every single month's sales through the mechanism of an ellipsis. The Web Accessibility Initiative cannot even be bothered giving us a full example showing all the work they want the rest of the world to do.

Charts and graphs by definition resist encapsulation in words. This example – a logarithmic chart of stock-market performance – gives the impression of being summed up in the subsequent text paragraph, but in fact the graph still shows much more data than a hundred-word text block. Among other things, logarithmic relationships are intrinsically graphical; we use log charts because we need to visualize unreadable masses of numbers.

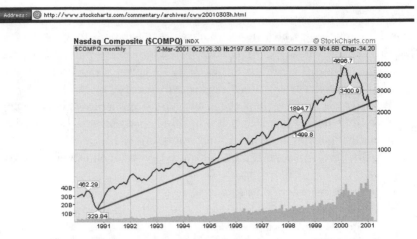

As this 11-year logarithmic chart shows, the Nasdaq composite recently broke through a very significant trendline that stretched back to the recession of 1990. The trendline was established in January of 1995 and confirmed in 1998 when it provided support in the wake of the Asian currency meltdown. The trendline was violated convincingly when the Composite moved below 2200 last week. The demise of such a long term support mechanism without any kind of struggle suggests one of two things - 1.) **All** of the forces that powered the Nasdaq's rise during the 1990's are well and truly gone **OR** 2.) Investors have over-reacted to the current downturn in the fortunes of technology companies. Let's look at some more charts to see which conclusion is more likely.

In an even more complicated case, the numerical data set accompanying the graph is an inseparable part of the illustration. Do you think you could sum all this up in words, even given unlimited space?

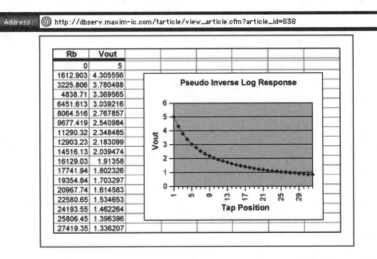

Excel spreadsheet for Pseudo Inverse Log Response (ZIP, 8K)

Figure 3. Pseudo inverse-logarithmic response circuit and spreadsheet

If you feel like being super-extra-thorough, yes, of course you may use longdesc to describe, in ravishing detail, the numerical or other factual and data underpinnings of your chart or graph. Just keep in mind that the typical "user" here will be stuck listening to all that data in sequence, or reading it via Braille display. To set it all up properly, you will have to use accessible table markup, a task so daunting it takes up nearly an entire chapter (10, "Tables and frames").

As discussed elsewhere in this chapter, PopChart [D] by Corda (corda.com/d/), which automatically summarizes numerical charts and graphs, can produce a long description using longdesc and set up a D-link.

Relatively uncomplicated charts and graphs can be handled with long description, but there are practical limits.

Comix

Comic strips – to use the hipster orthography, comix – are another of those seeming dealbreaker graphical forms that appear to be impossible to make accessible. In fact, it's not hard: Just use the same techniques you would adopt in writing long descriptions. In fact, you can write out the setting and dialogue in a longdesc, through alts and titles, through imagemap area declarations, or any combination. In this example from Doonesbury, map coordinates are faked, but the approach works fine.

```
<img src="http://images.ucomics.com/images/doonesbury/strip/dailydose/images/
todays.gif" border="0"
alt="Today's strip" title="[Today's strip]"
longdesc="todays-LD.html" usemap="#todaysmap" />

<map name="todaysmap" id="todaysmap">

<area shape="rect" coords="0,0,100,250" href="nohref"
alt="Zonker and BD regard Ground Zero. ZONKER: Wow... so this is it. BD: Yup..."
title="Zonker and BD regard Ground Zero. ZONKER: Wow... so this is it. BD:
Yup..." />

<area shape="rect" coords="101,251,200,500" href="nohref"
alt="BD: I feel privileged to be serving here. Most of the guys got reassigned,
but I've been here the whole time, battling looters!"
title="BD: I feel privileged to be serving here. Most of the guys got reassigned,
but I've been here the whole time, battling looters!" />

<area shape="rect" coords="202,502,300,750" href="nohref"
alt="ZONKER: Uh... battling looters? Really?"
title="ZONKER: Uh... battling looters? Really?" />

<area shape="rect" coords="303,753,400,850" href="nohref"
alt="BD: OK, eating donuts. But people know – you loot here, you're going
```

```
DOWN!"
title="BD: OK, eating donuts. But people know – you loot here, you're going
DOWN!" />


</map>
```

No, it's not all that easy to read due to the absence of linebreaks in alt and title, but it's passable.

Then you can make a separate longdesc file if you wish, named todays-LD.html:

```
<!DOCTYPE html PUBLIC "-//W3C//DTD XHTML 1.0 Transitional//EN"
"http://www.w3.org/TR/xhtml1/DTD/xhtml1-transitional.dtd">
<html xmlns="http://www.w3.org/1999/xhtml" lang="en">
<head>
<title>Today's strip</title>
</head>
<body>

<p class="scene">
Zonker and BD regard Ground Zero.
</p>

<p class="dialogue">
<span class="zonker">ZONKER</span>: Wow... so this is it.
</p>

<p>
<span class="bd">BD</span>: Yup...
</p>

<p>
<span class="bd">BD</span>: I feel privileged to be serving here. Most of the
guys got reassigned, but I've been here the whole time, battling looters!
</p>

<p>
<span class="zonker">ZONKER</span>: Uh... battling looters? Really?
</p>

<p>
<span class="bd">BD</span>: OK, eating donuts. But people know – you loot
here, you're going <em>down</em>!
```

```
    </p>

    </body></html>
```

(Consistent with the advice given in Chapter 11, "Stylesheets," and Chapter 13, "Multimedia," I've used style declarations to mark up scene-setting and character dialogue. Optional but helpful.)

Moreover, if you're handy with XML, you can make use of Jason McIntosh's ComicsML set of document type definitions, available at jmac.org/projects/comics_ml/.

Company logos

Opinion is mixed on the right approach to a company logo. Here I'm referring to a decorative or identification logo that is not a link: It's present just for "branding," as the marketing types say. You can use alt="*Company name*" or alt="*Company name* logo". For example, alt="Kwik-E-Mart" or alt="Kwik-E-Mart logo". For a screen-reader user, there is modest added value in knowing that the item is a logo; there is no downside to including that single word.

Exploded, X-ray, phantom, or cutaway drawings

If, like me, you believe the best thing about cars is not in fact driving them but gazing in agape fascination at cutaway drawings of them, are *you* ever in for a disappointment in Web accessibility. As with charts and maps, the richness of visual information in what are variously known as exploded, X-ray, phantom, or cutaway drawings cannot be conveniently recapitulated in words. Generically, you could use alt="Cutaway drawing of firefighter boot" or equivalent. If you're actually concerned with one *detail* of the illustration, you can point that out: alt="Cutaway drawings show concealed tether anchorages (1997 model) and visible anchorages (2002 model)".

Graduated ratings schemes

If you use a thermometer, graduated color rankings, a rectangle that fills with colour to denote a proportion of a possible rating, or a fixed-size graphic whose colour *changes* in direct proportion to a rating assigned to it, use something simple like alt="Ratings bar" plus a plain text of the actual rating. RottenTomatoes.com and Metacritic.com use such systems, and handle them properly.

Now, if you're a proud designer and you deliberately set up your page so that ratings are an analogue visual presentation only (just a partially-filled graduated rectangle with no associated number), this may be another case where you have to visibly modify your content. You *must* be able to articulate the graduated ratings allotment in words. If you aren't doing that already, you're going to have to start.

Exploded diagrams are usually too visually rich to lend themselves to epitomization in a simple alt text. You may be stuck using alt="Cutaway drawing: HAIX® Construction". If you intend for one specific component to be the focus of attention, go with that: alt="Stainless-steel midsole, flexible, puncture-resistant".

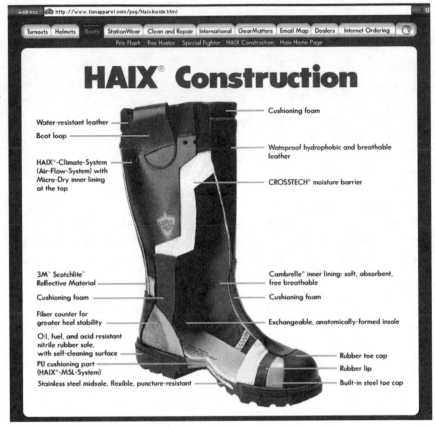

A more sophisticated approach: Add the actual rating value in the alt text, as alt="Rating: 86%". You may or many not have a sophisticated enough back-end system to autogenerate such alt text. Then again, if your system can autogenerate the plain text I asked for in the preceding paragraph, why can't it do the same in alt text?

The text equivalent of your visible rating allocation doesn't have to be numeric. alt="Warm"/"Hot"/"Cold"/"Tepid" are imaginable possibilities. If your ratings system is somewhat cutesy (like a pink teddy bear with a ribbon in its "hair" who smiles or frowns her ratings), you are certainly entitled to come up with equivalently cutesy words: alt="Blossom the Wonder Bear frowns with horror!"/"Blossom the Wonder Bear smiles quietly to herself!"/"Blossom the Wonder Bear gazes impassively!"

Hitcounters

You can download little pseudoprograms that count how many hits your page has received and display the number. Only a few are accessible through the alt attribute. The right way to do it is to produce an alt that renders the

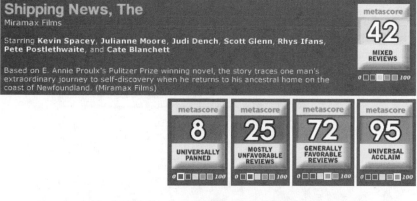

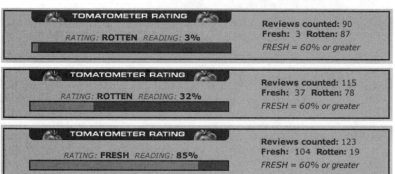

Graduated rating systems reminiscent of a thermometer (with results given as a quasi-analogue reading along a bar, optionally including colour changes) need to be translated into actual words. An inaccessible Website can afford to be wishy-washy and vague by providing an unadorned analogue graduated rating; an accessible Website must provide a text equivalent that more or less forces you to assign a word or number to the rating. Examples: alt="Rating: 95%: Universal Acclaim" (as in the Metacritic.com example); alt="Rating: Rotten. Reading: 35" (as in the RottenTomatoes.com example). Creativity in Web accessibility is encouraged, so you can, in fact, fudge a little: alt="Ehh"; alt="[Shrug]".

actual number, either by stitching together a set of img files with alts (alt="3" alt="3" alt="7" alt="9") or intelligently reading the number and serving up a single text (alt="3379"). Under battle conditions, we can live with alt="Hitcounter". (alt="" would be wrong because a hitcounter is not a spacer or some other meaningless image.)

Only a few hitcounters *can* be accessible in the first place. Why? The code you use on your little homepage to produce one might actually be a Java applet that cannot be made accessible as easily as adding an alt to an img. (Java accessibility is one of the few topics I do not cover in this book. As explained early on, I know nothing about JavaScript and was not willing to fake it.)

Anyway, I mailed the owner of each and every English-language site in the Open Directory Project's listing of hitcounter providers asking if their hitcounters were accessible in any way at all, even with alt="Hitcounter" or equivalent. Look at these sites for at least halfway-accessible hitcounters: Web-Stat.com, PageNetPets.com, and Freecounts.com.

Maps are yet another graphical genre that, by definition, resists being boiled down to words. In this weather-map example, would you prefer to scan about twenty lines of text to find your forecast (written out in words), or would you prefer to glance at your city's location and take in everything in a single glance? (Text-only weather forecasts are, of course, possible, but they are not equivalent to a map.)

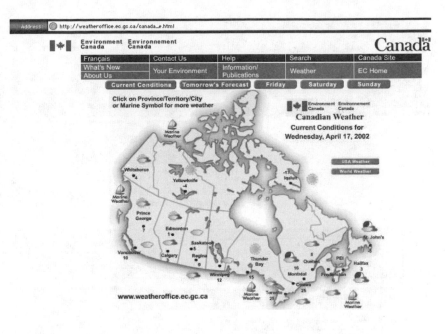

This topographical map uses 3D contours and false coloration to impart information. Care to sum that up in an alt text? I think not.

this website and website links, or, as hardcopy posters, slides, and Web-CDs.

Products such as field trips, study guides, and theme-related background material and references will be featured on the website as they are developed.

Topographic relief or digital elevation model of the Oak Ridges Moraine (1) with a view from west, near the Niagara Escarpment, to the east.

Identical alt and subsequent words

If the alt text of an image would duplicate words that immediately precede or follow the image, you may use an empty alt text. A typical example of this is an About Us page that shows little thumbnail photos of staff next to their names:

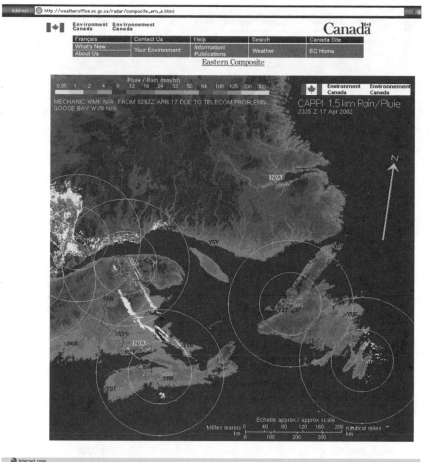

A combined weather/geographical map provides an even denser array of information (shading, colour, concentric range markings, airport designations, dates, and more) that could never reasonably be epitomized even in long passages of text. That's why we draw pictures.

```
<img src="ian.JPG" />Ian
```

It is redundant and serves no accessibility purpose to write out the full alt (and indeed title) of the image using the same words that immediately follow:

```
<img src="ian.JPG" alt="Ian Northcote-Smith, shop steward, Local 217" title="[Ian
Northcote-Smith, shop steward, Local 217]" />Ian Northcote-Smith, shop
steward, Local 217
```

It might be better to do something like this:

- ```
  <img src="ian.JPG" alt="" title="" />Ian Northcote-Smith, shop steward,
  ```
  Local 217
  (empty alt and title)
- ```
  <img src="ian.JPG" alt="" title="Shop steward, Local 217" />Ian Northcote-
  ```
  Smith, shop steward, Local 217
  (empty alt, but a bit of detail in title)

Indicating outline hierarchies is quite a bother online; designers have understandably resorted to wee graphic files. Accessibility options are not fantastic here. Vertical and horizontal lines are best embodied in alt="|" and alt="--"; it may be necessary to add (folder) in this edited example's alt texts to differentiate folders from files.

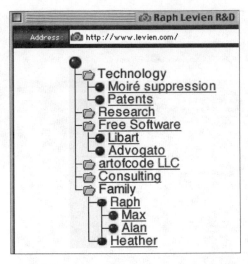

- <img src="ian.JPG" alt="" title="Shop steward, Local 217" />Ian Northcote-Smith

  (loading up extraneous information in title)

This approach is by no means wrong, and is, moreover, morally defensible under the Web Content Accessibility Guidelines. Checkpoint 1.1 says "Provide a text equivalent for every non-text element (e.g., via alt, longdesc, or in element content)." The "element content" bit refers to a case like <iframe></iframe> or <object></object> that can encompass alternative forms within themselves, but surely the same principle holds here: An img element (which cannot encompass anything or have "element content" because it is not paired) that sits right next to clear text that says exactly what an alt text would say has to be considered a valid text equivalent. If alt="" can be a correct text equivalent (it can), then alt="" followed by readable words has to be, too.

Images as links

Users of adaptive technology can tell what's a link and what isn't. It is generally redundant to preface an alt text with words like "Link to" ("Link to portfolio," "Link to résumé"). Merely write an alt text as though the image weren't a link.

Long alts

There is no official size limit to an alt text, but convention holds that 1,024 characters (1 K) should be the maximum. In some browsers and under certain circumstances (e.g., Netscape 4, *encore et toujours*), a full alt text may not

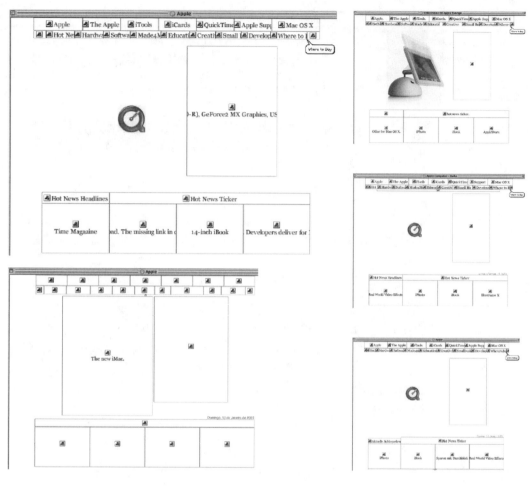

be visually displayed, or may not be displayed at all. Some other such circumstances:

- The alt text is wider than the graphic. Netscape is often too stupid to wrap lines inside a graphic placeholder. (iCab on Macintosh attempts to show the alt in full on the status line if it is too wide for the allotted space.)
- No size was specified for the graphic. An alt may not appear at all. In Explorer version 4 and later under Windows, you can set preferences to display a full alt text in every case, though even then the browser will not necessarily show an alt text if it cannot fit inside the bounding box no matter how its text is wrapped.
- Fonts are huge. If a visitor uses very large type sizes, even a few words may not fit in the bounding box. That's why system-wide adaptive technology that magnifies everything is better than dialing up extra-

Apple.com (the U.S. English main site) seems to handle its alt texts more or less adequately. But what happens to local Apple sites in Sweden, Italy, and Germany? They get the same English-language alt texts! (Sure, some product names don't need to be translated, but advertising copy certainly does.) It could be worse: Brazil (lower left) mostly loses its alt texts altogether.

A graphical drop cap, something of an unwelcome, superfluous, and inaccessible legacy from print typography.

Address: http://www.nytimes.com/learning/general/featured_articles/010411wednesday.html

Student Connections
News Summaries
Daily News Quiz
Letters to the Editor
Crossword Puzzle
Ask a Reporter

Teacher Connections
Daily Lesson Plan
Lesson Plan Archive
Education News
NIE Teacher Resources
Subscribe to the Times

Parent Connections
Conversation Starters
Discussion Topics
Product Reviews
Vacation Donation Plan
Educational Products

On this Day in History
Resources on the

Quebec Journal: A Chain-Link Fence Rankles an Old Walled City

By ANTHONY DePALMA

GO TO LESSON PLAN

Knowledge Tools

Turn Vocabulary On: Link words to the Merriam-Webster Collegiate® Dictionary.

Turn Geography On: Link countries and states to the Merriam-Webster Atlas®

QUEBEC, April 5 — Separation has always been entwined in the raison d'être of this beguiling bit of France, a walled city perched on a towering promontory and defined by the limits of geography, language and politics.

The French built forts to keep out the British, then the British erected their own walls here to keep out the upstart Americans. More recently, separatists have made Quebec their ideological bastion, at times banning even the sight of a Canadian flag as they battled to win independence.

Robert J. Galbraith for The New York Times

Workers building part of a six-mile security barrier for the 34-nation

big type; it's likely that any visitor who can't read a full alt text because fonts are too big is not actually visually-impaired but simply finds the body copy on the site too small.

Maps

Maps — not HTML imagemaps; maps in the conventional sense, as geographical maps, blueprints, floorplans, and the like — have remained an unsolved access mystery for decades. Blind people cannot see them, and Braille or raised or tactile maps are very rare and somewhat unwieldy; people with learning disabilities may find the density of lines, colours, and words incomprehensible. Some efforts have been made in using the accessible Scalable Vector Graphics (SVG) format to produce maps. Such efforts tend to do little more than crash this author's browser. I must wearily conclude that typical maps cannot really be made accessible to the blind. A map of Europe that sighted readers are intended to use for general, undirected reference (i.e., "Look anywhere you want on this map for whatever information you're looking for") will probably be inaccessible until some sexy new technology

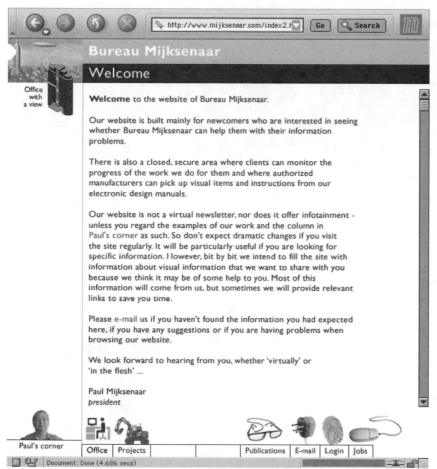

Because international wayfinding consultants are extremely artistique people, nothing but a picture of text set in pristine Gill Sans type will do. And the blind? Well, they're not our market, really, are they? (In fairness, picture-of-text blocks even as large as this can be made passably accessible.)

comes along to solve the problem. Even in these cases, though, you must use markup along these lines:

- alt="Map of Europe"
- alt="Australia (geographical)"
- alt="Map of the World (Mercator projection)"
- alt="Map: Nunavut"
- alt="Two views of Germany before division" title="Map shows East and West Germany in 1955 (left) and 1985 (right)"

This isn't anything remotely like making the information in the map accessible, but you can't just leave the img tag empty, now, can you?

Would it be unfair to suggest that if you're going to go to all the trouble to save your pristine advertising copy as a GIF that it *actually make sense*? (What happens if you want to fix it later?)

Nut Hammer

nuts!

Here is a nutcracker which can be used by all people. A hammer, a polished bowl made of stainless steel and an effective shock absorber made of rubber.

Put the nut in the bowl. An easy blow with the hammer, then is that nut cracked. Say then good-bye to the old-fashioned nutcracker. The hammer handle? It is made of walnut. Of course.

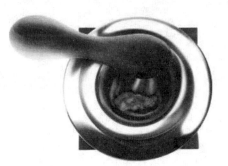

On the other hand, more focused and topic-specific maps – like a map showing you where a small country like Malta or Andorra is in comparison to a larger known country – can be made reasonably accessible through alt and title:

- alt="Malta is an island directly south of Italy in the Mediterranean Sea"
- alt="Map of Andorra, France, and Spain" title="Andorra is nestled between France to the north and Spain to the south and east"

Now, what if your geographical or other map is also an imagemap? (For example, a map of districts of a city used to look up restaurant inspection records – an actual example here in Toronto.) Use standard imagemap accessibility techniques, and pat yourself on the back for having gone to all that trouble.

Mismatched languages

If you run a multilingual site or one with many variations in different languages, text equivalents must be translated. Some exceptions come to mind – product names and trademarks; phrases borrowed from some other language (alt="Big Brother" can be appropriate even in a French-language site if that is the name of the French-language show) – but they are unusual. Failure to translate text equivalents – alt, title, and longdesc, of course, but also content within ‹object›‹/object› and ‹iframe›‹/iframe› tags, for example – is an amateur error committed all the time by the world's biggest, richest, smartest, and very often most American companies. Don't let this happen to you.

Organizational and genealogical charts and flowcharts

Any organization whose hierarchy is extensive enough to require an actual chart probably has a hierarchy that cannot be adequately conveyed in words. As with charts and graphs generally, there's a reason we're using illustration, and the reason is we would spend the rest of our lives writing out relationships that can be immediately apprehended, in all their complexity, through a visual illustration.

The same applies to flowcharts, whether for an industrial process or information architecture or anything else. (See Jesse James Garrett's "visual vocabulary" of IA iconography at JJG.net/ia/visvocab/.)

Outlines and hierarchies

The visual structure of an outline (e.g., topic threads in Usenet or another discussion forum) is rather difficult to make accessible. How do designers approach this problem in general? Commonly, designers attempt to show the levels of discussion hierarchy through indention: First post at flush left, first reply indented slightly, reply to that reply indented further. There are other indention styles, but the pattern is essentially identical.

These indentions are indicated by more than mere whitespace. Typically, we see little icons, like horizontal and vertical lines, to explicitly indicate the hierarchy.

If you're using ordinary HTML text, like vertical bars and dashes of whatever sort, to create the outline structure, there is no accessibility problem because you aren't using images, though there is something of a usability problem because a screen reader will dutifully read out text like |---- as "bar dash dash dash dash." Consider using styled HTML lists instead. This is not a vastly superior approach, I must admit.

If you're using little *images* of arrows and vertical and horizontal lines (properly called "rules"), there is no obvious alternative to duplicating the appearance of the lines with alt texts containing vertical-bar and hyphen characters – alt="|", alt="-". I suppose you could use em dashes, namely alt="—" (imperfectly supported by browsers) or alt="—" (well supported, even by Netscape 4), but that may be over the top. Usenet old-timers will be aware that underscores and equal signs were also used to simulate horizontal lines, but I would tend not to use alt="_" or alt="=". We should stick to the convention that horizontal lines are approximated by hyphens.

I've never seen a case where the designer uses customized sets of images showing horizontal or vertical rules of specific lengths – one image file for single-character width, a second image file two characters wide, and so on. Instead, designers place uniformly-sized graphics next to each other to create a cumulative visual appearance. Of course, this means a number of identical alt texts sit alongside each other, which is a bother to deal with via adaptive technology. Each image may trigger a discrete audible rendering, one after another after another. A sequence like alt="|" alt="-" alt="-" alt="-" alt="->" may be read as "image bar image dash image dash image dash image dash greater than."

There is a very slight theoretical advantage to using customized images of specific lengths because then you're dealing with a single alt text even if it contains exactly the text of all the individual alt texts put together. Thus alt="|---->" may simply be read as "image bar dash dash dash dash greater than." Not hugely better, but slightly so. Of course, this approach essentially requires you to program logic into your system that will substitute specific graphic files for each level of hierarchy, but on the other hand your system is *already* keeping track of the levels of hierarchy and substituting *multiples* of graphic files. If it is possible to put this option into practice, give it a try. Frankly, I expect you will be first in the world to do so.

Phonetics and mathematics

There is no practical way to make phonetic symbols or mathematical notation accessible. There does technically exist an XML-derived markup language for mathematics, MathML (see W3.org/Math/), which is *quite* poorly supported. In old media, there is such a thing as Braille for mathematics. I suspect more blind people interested in mathematics read Braille math than rely on MathML to understand online math. It's rarely a good idea to reinvent the wheel; MathML exists and can be perfectly accessible to browsers and devices that understand it, but that is indeed the problem because so very few browsers and devices actually *do* understand it. Mozilla allegedly understands MathML, but in practice does not in my testing. And even if we had a Web browser that understood MathML, would a screen reader or other adaptive technology be able to turn the math into voice? (It's hard enough for a nondisabled person to read math aloud in an unambiguous and understandable way.)

I suspect it will be some years before online math presentations become genuinely accessible. My sole recommendation is to use MathML where necessary. If you must include a math equation as a GIF (as a picture of text), you have a few options for alternate text. If the equation is lengthy or you just can't be bothered, you can simply name the equation: alt="Quadratic formula", which probably works better in the real world than .alt="(&minusb &plusminus; sqrt(b^2 − 4ac))/2a" If the formula is short, you can try typing it out in text: alt="E=mc^2". It becomes a tad ridiculous, however, in short order, and you end up using spreadsheet-like functions that are themselves abbreviations or symbols.

Phonetic symbols – that is, International Phonetic Alphabet (IPA) or the many half-arsed variants used in American dictionaries – have no genuinely viable online presentation in the first place. Only professional linguists and lexicographers have phonetic fonts installed on their systems, and character mapping becomes a serious issue, so it isn't sufficient to use whatever Unicode character entities may exist because they will almost never end up being rendered or presented correctly. If you use pictures of text, you are then stuck with the problem of writing a comprehensible alt text, which you essentially cannot do because *that's why we invented phonetic alphabets* – to avoid writing "high back unrounded vowel" or "voiced pharyngeal fricative" for the rest of our lives. Nor can you epitomize IPA symbols in truly understand-able ASCII text, though linguistics mailing lists do give it the old college try.

Photocomix

I am again using the hipster orthography. Comix made entirely of photo-graphs are a bit of an acquired taste and are rather rare even in the print medium. But for a visitor who cannot see the photographs, the fact that they are indeed photographs may be irrelevant. Treat the page exactly as if it were composed of drawn or illustrated images.

Certainly a case can be made that photocomix are different from the expected norm, and that's the sort of thing I've suggested you notate. So here's a nice additional touch: Surround the photo layout in a div tag that explains the content is in fact photographic: div title="(All images photographic, not hand-drawn)".

Pictures of text

Some designers set words in type using Photoshop or moral equivalent and save those words as graphic images (*pictures of text*). Sighted visitors can read them; screen readers and browsers that don't display graphics cannot. In these cases, an alt and a title must be provided.

For small amounts of text (typically, text rendered as graphics is used for navigation buttons), enter the complete text into alt; you can add explanatory details to title if you wish. (Example: alt="Contact" title="Contact information, job listings, and feedback page".) Accessibility purists may hate this entire approach, but I simply do not see any harm whatsoever in limited bits of text rendered as graphics since it is dead simple to make those graphics accessible. I use pictures of text myself.

If you use a graphic image as a drop cap at the outset of a paragraph, use the tiniest alt text possible – give us nothing but the character rendered by the drop cap, like alt="C". If your drop cap is actually a sentence or a phrase (e.g., a dateline) or a couple of characters, include those verbatim, but a drop sentence or drop phrase of this sort barely resides in the same category as a true drop cap.

You may wish to emulate the case of the original graphic for verisimilitude: If a dateline on a news article reads "REGINA" in uppercase in the graphic, use alt="REGINA". If the word I is used, you may wish to include a space or non-breaking space ( ) in the alt text to signify it is a separate word: alt="I " or even alt="I ".

If your drop cap includes a visible quotation mark, encode it inside the alt using either " or " (for a tacky neutral quotation mark) or a numeric or literal entity, like “ or “ for " or ‘ or ‘ for '.

Understand, though, that screen-reader users will be inconvenienced by the use of a drop cap. It simply breaks up a word. The following do not have the same effect:

- The word B*read*
- The sequence ‹img src="B.gif" height="40" width="27" border="0" alt="B"›read

Quite obviously, adaptive technology cannot read the latter example as a full word because it consists of an image followed by a series of letters. The visitor will end up hearing something like "bee reed" (keeping in mind that "read" has two pronunciations), and indeed there may be some other audible signal that an image has been encountered, producing an audible sequence like "[Click] bee reed" or "image bee reed."

A visitor with a Braille display may be much less inconvenienced; the sequence may be rendered as "b read," which is not great but not so bad, either.

Don't use a title on a drop cap, unless, I suppose, it's more of a drop sentence or a drop phrase. A title on a one- or two-character drop cap is gilding the lily; alt already fully explicates the function of the graphic.

Extensive text rendered as graphics is another story. Using graphic images to typeset large blocks of text is a miserable idea. For large blocks of text, experiment with either filling alt and title with the verbatim text or summarizing the text briefly in alt and listing it verbatim in title. longdesc is at best marginally useful here since it is poorly supported and requires you to load a whole new page. The best approach is to slice up your graphic with its extensive text into subgraphics with more manageable quantities, providing hestar.com/NASApp/cs/ContentServer?pagename=thestar/Layout/Article_Type1&c=Article&cid=101∤

Atanarjuat (The Fast Runner)

Innovative Inuit movie thrills, chills and uplifts

Peter Howell
Movie Critic

Atanarjuat (The Fast Runner)
AA
Starring Natar Ungalaaq, Peter-Henry
Arnatsiaq, Lucy Tulugarjuk and Sylvia
Ivalu. Directed by Zacharias Kunuk.
At major theatres.
★★★★

---

alt and title for each.

There is no need for an exact match between the image blocks and the text used in alts. You can create convenient rectangular slices even if you split a sentence in half. You can place the text of the whole sentence in one of the two alt texts and/or titles. A reasonable correspondence is in order, but you don't have to make the visible picture of text and the computer-readable alternative text exactly the same — as long as, when all alternate texts are read, they correspond exactly to the text available in pictures.

Another option, one that is legal in HTML but rather oddball, is to use the area element typically found in the creation of imagemaps. In that typical case, you associate URLs with specific regions through an href="URL" attribute. But it is possible to associate an explicit lack of URL with a specific region using nohref="nohref"; that region can simultaneously carry an alt and a title. (This technique, when employed at all, is normally used to carve a hole or link-free region out of an imagemap.)

In this way, you can use a large single image divided into an imagemap that will pass through multiple alt and title texts to a browser or device — not that it's worth the trouble in the first place. In the following example, we will attempt to render the following mass of text (an actual example taken from Descartes.com) as a GIF image:

> In response to globalized trade and increased competition, organiza-
> tions have chained together processes for faster times to market and
> lower customer costs. This new business model is built from:
> • Supply-chains
> • Logistics-chains
> • Demand-chains
> • Value-chains
> • Customer-chains
> • Even Profit-chains!

Rating stars can carry an alternative text for each individual star or as a group (often preferable for readability, especially when half-stars are awarded).

A selection of graphical search and login buttons – all from Swedish TV sites (coincidence, surely?!).

The bottom four examples come from sibling sites owned by the same conglomerate; note the slight graphic differences even there.

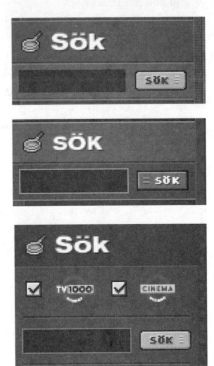

Descartes calls them nChains, where the "n" means whatever the organization wants it to mean. To be competitive, organizations need to more effectively manage their nChains by managing events and critical moments between trading partners. This is a complex process – hundreds of different trading partners, with different ways of communicating and data formats. Only a network can effectively, privately and securely handle it. Our collaborative network helps organizations manage their business processes to their plan, while identifying and proactively handling the divergent off-plan events. It's called nChain Event Management.

Note the complexity of the task, and how ill-suited the use of text rendered as graphics really is. As in the pure-text rendering above, the copy cries out for multiple paragraphs and an unordered list, all of which is easy to do in HTML, easy to visually simulate in a graphic, but next to impossible to duplicate using alt and title. I'm hoping this example, taken from the real Web, will prove so unpalatable that you will never attempt to render this much text as a graphic image.

On with the show. In the HTML syntax below, all numerical values are simulations and will not actually work. You will get the idea nonetheless, I'm sure.

```
< img src="../images/nchain.gif" width="400" height="500" border="0"
alt="nChain Event Management" title="What are nChains?"
usemap="#nChainmap" />


< map name="nChainmap" >


< area shape="rect" coords="31,266,188,294" nohref="nohref"
alt="In response to globalized trade and increased competition, organizations
have chained together processes for faster times to market and lower customer
costs. This new business model is built from:"
title="In response to globalized trade and increased competition, organizations
have chained together processes for faster times to market and lower customer
costs. This new business model is built from:" >


< area shape="rect" coords="31,295,188,322" nohref="nohref"
alt="Supply-chains | Logistics-chains | Demand-chains | Value-chains | Customer-
chains | Even Profit-chains!"
title="Supply-chains | Logistics-chains | Demand-chains | Value-chains |
Customer-chains | Even Profit-chains!" />


< area shape="rect" coords="31,323,188,350" nohref="nohref"
alt="Descartes calls them nChains, where the "n" means whatever the
organization wants it to mean. To be competitive, organizations need to more
effectively manage their nChains by managing events and critical moments
between trading partners."
title="Descartes calls them nChains, where the "n" means whatever the
organization wants it to mean. To be competitive, organizations need to more
```

```
effectively manage their nChains by managing events and critical moments
between trading partners." />

< area shape="rect" coords="31,351,188,378" nohref="nohref"
alt="This is a complex process – hundreds of different trading partners, with
different ways of communicating and data formats. Only a network can
effectively, privately and securely handle it."
title="This is a complex process – hundreds of different trading partners, with
different ways of communicating and data formats. Only a network can
effectively, privately and securely handle it." />

< area shape="rect" coords="31,379,188,406" nohref="nohref"
alt="Our collaborative network helps organizations manage their business
processes to their plan, while identifying and proactively handling the divergent
off-plan events. It's called nChain Event Management."
title="Our collaborative network helps organizations manage their business
processes to their plan, while identifying and proactively handling the divergent
off-plan events. It's called nChain Event Management." />

</map >
```

Note that I had to fake the unordered list by stringing its components in a
phrase divided by vertical bars – one of many strikes against this technique.
Frankly, the whole exercise of rendering extensive text as graphics is so much
trouble I don't know why anyone would bother. Styled HTML text is quicker,
easier, and more accessible for long segments of copy. Use it.

Stylesheets give you considerable control over the appearance of text; the
use of actual fonts on the visitor's computer may make for a better appearance anyway (antialiasing will likely be turned on); text rendered as bitmaps
is invisible to search engines and enormously difficult to update. (What if
you misspell a word? Or at least mistype one?)

Porn

I'm not exactly in a position to ignore "adult" Websites since I do in fact
have my own personal favourites. For all navigational, design, and identity
graphics, there is no alteration in accessibility practice. For the actual
photographs and illustrations of interest, I advocate treating the page like a
portfolio site (see advice for that application). I suppose this advice applies
mainly to commercial sites.

If you're running a ratings site of the "Am I Hot or Not?" variety
(HotorNot.com) but more explicit – two examples are RateaRod.com and
RateaRear.com – then the alt text for submitted photos may end up being
inane and/or annoying, like alt="Rate this member!" Porn cannot always be

taken seriously. Accessible porn may end up being even slightly more ridiculous.

Now, if your porn page carries on a kind of narrative (either in a photo-comix style or in a sequence of written segments and pictures), you are in for a tough slog. You have to make the narrative work comprehensibly in text alternatives (I would certainly use title and longdesc at this point); if the page is a mix of paragraphs and pictures, you have to avoid repeating yourself in text equivalents for the images. In essence, if you select a photograph because it communicates something that words cannot, or if you are setting up an antiphonious relationship between words and pictures, you're going to have to devise a way to make everything work in words.

(If you think this is extraneous, please don't. In a survey of attitudes and responses to audio description of TV and video, the American Foundation for the Blind found that some respondents would indeed like to watch audio-described X-rated films. In one poll as part of this single survey, 9% of respondents voiced that preference; in another poll, 22%. Men wanted described adult films more often than women. The mind fairly boggles as to how this would actually be done, but the desire is there. And certain broad-casters in the United Kingdom are required to audio-describe a portion of their programming; "adult" programming is not, in fact, exempt, so all this may actually come to pass!)

Portfolios, stock photos, clip art, typefaces

What if you are an artist showing off your portfolio of photography, graphic design, illustration, sculpture, Web design, or anything else?

What if your company is in the business of selling stock photos or clip art or typefaces – or anything else graphical?

In extreme cases – like the near-duopoly of American stock-photo agencies, Corbis and Getty Images – designers and programmers are faced with making hundreds of thousands of images accessible. This constitutes undue hardship under any sane interpretation.

However: A site with a few dozen or even a hundred or so images can be made quite accessible, and even the extreme cases have certain options.

In all these cases, you can simply use something like the following for all sample images:

- alt="Sample photo"
- alt="Sample"
- alt="*Font name* sample" (for typeface showings)

This Yahoo sign-in screen uses a picture of text – in this case, a picture of a secret passcode you are intended to read and retype. The picture lacks an underlying structure in order to thwart spammers. It is not particularly easy to remedy this accessibility barrier, but it can be done with creative use of randomized alt texts.

2. Select View Preferences

By default, sort my files by [name ⬍] in [ascending ⬍] order.

3. Enter Confirmation Code

946849

Type the 6-digit number above into this box: [   ]

Note: This step is required to ensure quality of service.

[Submit]

Rudimentary. Possibly even undesirable in a strict interpretation of accessibility. But far better than an image with no alternate text at all. Any content-management system worth its fees should be able to automatically populate such quasi-generic alt texts through the images of a site. It may be practicable to insert them only when they are called up from the database rather than methodically thrashing through the database and adding them in advance.

Now, if, upon sober and realistic self-evaluation, you know perfectly well that you do not have *so* many sample images that you can't do them justice, I encourage you to use more specific and descriptive alts, titles, and longdescs. After reading this chapter, you already know how to write them. It merely becomes an issue of slogging through all the available files. And when you add new samples, *always* include accessibility.

As in other facets of making sites accessible, you can phase in retrofitting of this sort. You can work on one page a week, in decreasing order of popularity according to your Web server logs. Or you could convert all your most popular pages immediately and pick away at the rest according to a schedule. (Do keep to a schedule, otherwise you will procrastinate and nothing will get done.)

In every case, make *all* images on a page accessible. If, for example, your three most popular images are spread across three separate pages, then you must retrofit those entire pages to make them accessible. That should come as no surprise by this point.

If you really feel you cannot make your many portfolio or sample images accessible, understand that you will incur my scorn, which will in turn be leavened if you make very sure that every *other* part of *all* your pages is accessible. This is not particularly difficult to do given that typical portfolio sites are created with page templates; when pages are handrolled, they are usually so few in number that fixing them by hand cannot be considered an undue burden.

Long descriptions are clearly applicable to portfolios and samples, but the labour involved is a deterrent.

Font samples are a special case, I think, due to the many levels of speci-

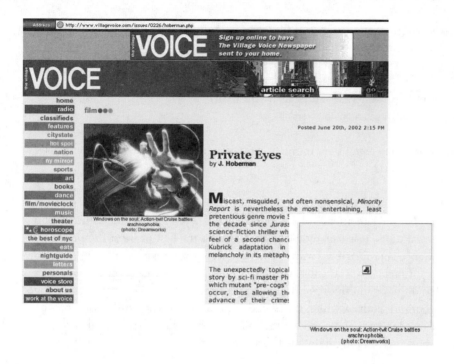

A case in which an image can legitimately use alt="" is a newspaper site offering a photo and an immediately-adjacent caption. Even with an empty alt text, the function and meaning of the image are clear. An absent alt, however, is not allowed, and that is what this example actually uses.

ficity at work (typeface family and variant; differentiation from other fonts; individual characters). For complete alphabet showings, alt="**Font name sample**" is quite functional. When comparing one font to another, say so:

> alt="Univers vs. Helvetica" title="Univers (top) has a point on its lowercase t. Helvetica (bottom) does not". When giving closeups of individual characters, tell us as much: alt="New Century Schoolbook Q".

Rating stars

If your site reviews cultural works or anything else and uses the rating-star system of the print world, you have a few options:

- alt="[Star]"
- alt="*" (or the usual character entities for the asterisk, alt="*" or alt="*")
- alt="[Rating star]"

I suppose I am being slightly inconsistent here given that I am suggesting you use brackets in your alt text. I tend to advocate that practice only for titles when alt and title have the same text. My reasoning here is that a rating star is one step removed in abstraction from an asterisk used as a genuine asterisk or a bullet. I suppose this is not an airtight case.

The best way to do it? Reprogram your system so that you use individual graphic files for each level of rating: A one-star film uses a single graphic showing one star, a five-star film uses a single separate graphic showing five stars, a three-and-a-half-star film has its own graphic, and so on. Then use equally specific alt texts:

- alt="One star"
- alt="5 stars" (use numerals if you wish)
- alt="Three and a half stars"

Or, if you're using stars in the first place, why not just use asterisk characters in plain text?

Repeated graphics

Another judgement call: If a page (not a site, a *page*) shows the same graphic several times, it is usually wisest to deal with the first or most important instance appropriately (with a descriptive alt text or with alt="") and treat the rest of them as extraneous (with alt=""). The same advice applies to graphics that differ by unimportant details – for example, blue logo at top, green logo at bottom, both of which are intended to mean the same thing, or a picture-of-text logotype at top giving the full name of your site and another logotype at bottom reducing the name to an acronym.

Rollovers

All states of a rollover must be accessible. While editing this very chapter (actually, while procrastinating *before* editing this very chapter), by pure chance I happened upon a page at Doonesbury.com in which all of the following were true:

- Even with graphics-loading turned on, the top-of-page banner ad was missing. The server could not find the image file.
- That banner had no alt text.
- The *rollover* for that banner could not be found either, but it *had* an alt, which, brilliantly enough, merely read "Click here to find out more!"

(Wow!)

It was thus possible to cause an alt text to appear and disappear by moving the mouse onto and off the rectangle that, through incompetence or error, failed to display an advertisement.

How's *that* for stupid?

Every image requires an alt text. "Every" really means "every," including rollover states.

Rules and dividing lines

HTML offers an element for horizontal rules, ‹ hr /›, which you can format in varying thicknesses and colours using cascading stylesheets. Since ‹ hr /› is an actual element, use it in preference to any other technique; adaptive technol-

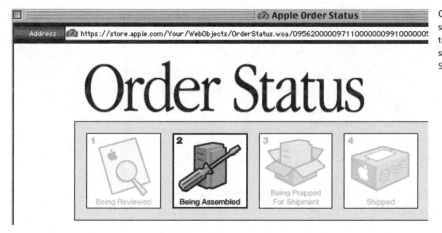

Graphical renderings of the status of a process require a text equivalent for the current step in the process, as alt="Order Status: Being Assembled".

ogy can read the presence of the rule and interpret it properly. (Don't let anyone tell you horizontal rules provide no structure. Of course they do. Once you hit a ‹hr /› element, you suddenly have a dividing line between Before and After or Above and Below.)

If you really must, you may use graphic images for horizontal or vertical rules – usually done for a "better" appearance. For horizontal rules, use alt="–" so it will resemble a horizontal line in a graphical browser and be read as a line in a screen reader. Limit yourself to two or maybe three hyphens; don't just hold down the hyphen key on the keyboard and fill up the full width of your editing program's text window.

There seems to be an issue of scale among alt="-", alt="–", and alt="—-". I suppose you could selectively deploy each of those depending on the width of the horizontal rule you are attempting to encode.

Vertical lines have a different structural intent, usually encoded in HTML tables or frames and rendered by default in graphical browsers. Let the tables or frames embody that structure (see Chapter 10, "Tables and frames"); it is possible, with a great deal of fiddling, to control the display of table and other borders via stylesheets.

Otherwise, use alt="" for other vertical rules. If you look critically at vertical rules as used on real-world Websites, they are generally optional; some other structural cue (like columns, as expressed in all-stylesheet layouts or table cells) will nearly always remain in place even if you remove the rule. Frankly, most vertical rules added to a page through the img element have no meaning unto themselves.

Don't use a title or longdesc. Exception: If your page is all *about* rules (if you're giving them away in the form of graphic files, for example, or teaching designers how to use them), then use alt, title, and, if absolutely necessary, longdesc to explain the visual differences between the graphics.

Search and login fields

If you use a graphical button next to a type-in textarea in your search function – you know, the kind that says "Go" or "OK" in a picture of text – obviously that image needs an alt text. There are certain peculiarities with button types that are documented in Chapter 12, "Forms and interaction."

Secret passcodes

To thwart spammers and the like, some sites provide secret passcode numbers (they're almost always numbers) in graphical images. You are expected to look at the number, understand it, and retype it into a certain field. This practice *relies* on inaccessibility – on the fact that images are not machine-readable. It's got to go. It isn't sufficient to provide a little message saying "If you are unable to view this passcode, send E-mail to technical support." That isn't equivalent access, and it is quite simple for a spammer to simply dispatch an automated E-mail reading "I'm legally blind and I can't access your site. Can you give me the passcode in clear text?"

On the other hand, the solution I offer, while only marginally more resistant to misuse, at least qualifies as an accessibility provision: Split the passcode up into one image per digit and give the *name* of the digit in the alt text:

```
< img src="num207.gif" alt="three" />
< img src="a318.gif" alt="seven" />
< img src="hur_1.gif" alt="nine" />
< img src="num207.gif" alt="three" />
< img src="l33t.GIF" alt="five" />
```

(You could also use numerals inside the alt text.)

The alt text is of course computer-readable, leaving you open to spam. But reasonable security provisions are provided here: You can store large numbers of identical numerical images with different and unpredictable filenames and serve them up randomly. A spambot would have to spider your site at unfeasible length in order to learn them all, requiring too much programming time for many penny-ante spammers. If you set up your Web server's file permissions to prohibit mass downloading of entire folders, a spammer would also be unable to read in all your digit image files and develop a database to crack this system.

For numerical passcodes, you can also save alt texts that represent variable lengths of digits: You could render 37935 as "three seven nine-thirty-five," "thirty-seven thousand nine hundred thirty-five," "thirty-seven nine thirty-five," or any other combination.

For alphabetic passcodes, I have no solution. I suppose you could write the names of letters phonetically (ay, be or bee, see, dee, eff, gee or jee, aitch, eye, jay, kay, el, em, en, oh, pee, kyoo, are, es or ess, tee, you, vee, doubleyou, eks, why, zed or zee), but let's not turn Web accessibility into the delirious mutterings of the Katzenjammer Kids.

Self-captioning photos

A newspaper site may run an editorial photo whose caption or cutline fully explains the contents of the photo. In those cases, it is redundant to use anything beyond a basic alt text: alt="John and Joan Cusack" is sufficient when the photo cutline, marked up as an ordinary paragraph or table cell, reads: "Knockout brother-and-sister one-two punch John and Joan Cusack pose for photographers on the runway outside the Dorothy Chandler Auditorium. John Cusack's feature comedy, *Grosse Pointe Blank*, was shut out of this year's Academy Awards."

Sliced graphics

Authoring programs let you divvy up a large image into an interlocking jigsaw of smaller rectangular slices. Less is more here. Select a single slice that will epitomize the entire image. Use alt="" for every slice but that one, which you will treat differently.

If you were viewing the page under difficult conditions and could load only one slice to understand the meaning of the entire graphic, which would it be? Take *that* image and give it a full descriptive alt and title (even a longdesc, if desired) that describe *the whole assemblage of all slices*. The Chosen Slice is a proxy for the entire image.

If you are tempted to strew marketing slogans in every alt text but for the Chosen One, don't; the alternative text has to be genuinely related to the image. Nothing, save for the constraints of good taste, stops you from doing that with titles. By the way, I suppose it is possible that a very complex sliced graphic could require more than one slice with full alt and other text equivalents, but don't overdo it.

Spacers

Because it is so difficult to control horizontal and vertical spacing in Web pages (yes, it's still difficult even with stylesheets), a standby technique designers rely on is the use of very thin graphics files to provide the appearance of spacing on a page. They're usually saved as transparent GIFs (or in rare cases, as the same colour as the background) and thus appear invisible – as they should, given that they're meant to represent space. Nonetheless, as graphics, they require alt texts, and there's only one option here: alt="". Yes, an empty alt text.

Why not just leave the alt text out? Because then your visitor will be faced with the filename, either visually or audibly. With alt="", a graphical browser that can't load the image will show nothing but a placeholder. (If the designer included height and width attributes, the browser might end up showing the right amount of space.) A screen reader will skip the image completely or will, at worst, indicate an image is present; I suppose it is hypothetically possible that this might confuse the blind visitor, but you will have gone to some length to avoid *actual* as opposed to hypothetical confusion.

For the purposes of this book, incidentally, alt="" will nonetheless be considered an alt text. Using an empty alt text can be and is appropriate in img elements; omitting an alt text is never permitted. (It's akin to the distinction between having no money in a bank account and having no bank account at all.)

In using empty alts, an issue comes up: Placeholder icons. I have never met a graphical browser yet – and I've been using them since the first versions of Mosaic and Netscape version 0.9 – that did *not* use a little placeholder icon to represent a missing image. But in my experience, browsers use that same icon for all the following cases:

- No alt
- alt="" (empty)
- alt=" " (space – indeed, any number of spaces)
- alt=" " (non-breaking space – indeed, any number of them)

The only difference I could find is vertical positioning of the visible manifestation of the placeholder icon (the little X in a red box, for example) within the space allocated for the image, which is too subtle to notice most of the time.

If you're testing your pages with graphics loading turned off, you may be misled by the appearance of placeholder icons. You may be tempted to conclude that those graphics lack alt texts. That is not necessarily true; you need to examine the source code. It follows, then, that when evaluating the accessibility of other people's work, you cannot rely on the appearance of a site in a graphical browser with image-loading turned off. Even perfectly legal techniques like alt="" have essentially the same appearance as illegal techniques like missing alt texts. Consequently, do not fire off angry E-mails to site authors accusing them of foisting images without alt texts on an unsuspecting public purely on the basis of a site's appearance with image-loading turned off.

Spawned windows

Just as a general principle, warn all visitors when a new window will open.

If an image that is also a link opens in a new window (by adding target="_blank" to the <a></a> element), then warn us in advance: alt="Sunrise at Darling Harbour (larger image opens in new window)". Depending on your personal style, it is not impermissible to use a title instead to explain that the link opens in a new window.

Status bars

Similar to graduated ratings indicators, a graphical status bar that indicates where you are located in a process through imagery must be translated into plain text. alt="Your order status: Being assembled" is sufficient. A title or long description could explain all the possible steps. Really, what you're interested in is where you sit now, not what the entire range of options might be.

Thumbnails

It's good practice to provide bite-sized versions of large photographs and graphics. As seen in online photo galleries and albums, thumbnails are very often links to full-sized illustrations, making them another example of images-as-links. Write an alt text that sums up the image *and* tells you it's a link to a larger version, as with alt="Sunrise at Darling Harbour (link to larger image)" or alt="Sunrise at Darling Harbour. Click for full-sized version".

Web bugs

Late in the previous century, a quasi-sinister new technique emerged to track the loading of Web pages. A minuscule graphic, like a single-pixel GIF, triggers a cookie that is sent back to another server (usually an advertiser's or an advertising broker's). As a BBC report explained, "The HTML code hidden in the image can request additional information from that computer or the past visits to that site. The Web bugs can mine information about who owns the site you are surfing from as well as details about your computer such as what data is held in the Windows registry [if applicable]." Is it fair to speculate that designers with no ethical qualms about including Web bugs are not all that concerned with standards compliance or accessibility? Nonetheless, if you are somehow required to make such a page accessible, treat the Web bug as a spacer image and use alt="".

Webcams

Webcam software isn't smart enough to be accessible. Ideally, you should be able to attach alts to images transmitted at different times of the day: alt="Me at my desk"; alt="I'm away at lunch". In an ideal world, you could link a different alt to every frame, but that would be above and beyond the call of duty.

Until Webcam software wakes up to accessibility, if you have any ability to rewrite the coding inserted by the Webcam software, use an alt and a title; longdesc may be rather too much to hope for. Engage the same rules as ever: alt sums up the function, title tells you more, and longdesc attempts to document the full appearance of the image, which in this case could describe the kind of Webcam image a visitor would see. For example, alt="Daily Webcam" title="Webcam is on all day while I'm at my desk".

A long description could run like this:

My Webcam runs all day when I'm at my desk – a typical cubicle here at Wonderworks in Fredericton. I have a black Æron chair (an ergonomic chair with nylon netting for upholstery) and a flatscreen PC on my desk. If you see a pale blur in the image, that's me — I've got blond hair and fair skin and I tend to wear a white T-shirt to work unless we're meeting a client or something. I also have a Webcam ‹a href="http://www.nbnet.nb.ca/ bruceg/cam/" title="Webcam at my personal site"›at home‹/a›.

If your Webcam software lets you hack its code to include an alt and/or title, do it. If not, then your Webcam could be the only image on your page that is inaccessible. I suppose the options then are to live with it (antithetical to the purpose of the exercise), switch software (requiring the nontrivial task of chasing down an accessible alternative), or pestering software makers until they upgrade the program.

What about Scalable Vector Graphics?

In 2001, the World Wide Web Consortium ratified a "recommendation" on Scalable Vector Graphics or SVG, a Flash-like graphics format that includes a raft of features for accessibility. SVG objects can include a range of text and other equivalents. You may be wondering why I'm not documenting this raft of features. Simple: As with JavaScript and PDF, I know essentially nothing about SVG, and I won't pretend to be able to learn it quickly enough to do a proper job in this book.

More importantly, support for SVG in real-world devices, even something as simple as the browser that ships with a nondisabled person's brand-new computer, is so poor as to be essentially nonexistent. For the time being, SVG is vapourware.

Bottom-Line Accessibility Advice

Basic accessibility

Use alt texts on absolutely every image without exception.

Intermediate accessibility

Add titles to images in increments no smaller than a page: Either all graphics on a page contain titles or none.

Advanced accessibility

Write long descriptions for the rather more intricate images.

Special "Advertising" Supplement

BEHOLD A RANGE OF REAL-WORLD ADVERTISEMENTS — banner ads, annoying pop-ups, the lot — with suggested alt and title texts provided. Notice how many of them are straight transliterations of words already visible in the ad? That's because online advertising does not work, and advertisers have given up any pretense of "art"; you the visitor are already so apt to overlook online ads that advertisers can hardly risk putting up something that's not self-explanatory. As you'll see here, it's generally quite obvious what text to enter into alt and title. Note that some texts are given twice — once in HTML-compliant escaped character encoding and once in human-readable accented characters for convenience.

alt="[Ilmoitus] Sisustuksellinen Vuoropuhelu"

alt="[Ilmoitus] Ryijy tuo läämpöä talveen"

alt="[Ilmoitus] Ryijy tuo lämpöä talveen"

alt="[Ilmoitus] Unien mystinen talo: Villa Sarastus"

alt="[Ilmoitus] Illallinen Kansainväliseen tyyliin"

alt="[Ilmoitus] Illallinen Kansainväliseen tyyliin"

title="Hanselin toimitusjohtajan Kristiina Illin"

alt="(Advertisement) JetUSA.com"

title="America’s Photopolymer Specialists"

alt="[Advertisement] Lotus KM Solutions"

Embody the message of the ad in the alternative text; don't try to describe the imagery.

alt="(Pubblicità) Scarica gli appunti su Studenti.it"

alt="(Pubblicità) Scarica gli appunti su Studenti.it"

Make no attempt to mimic the fake interface elements.

alt="[Advertisement] Sugar Larry: Powered by righteous anger"

In cutesy, ambiguous text ads like these, tell us where we're going or who the sponsor is (here, Sugar Larry).

alt="(Pubblicità) Tosinvest: La riabilitazione comincia così"

alt="(Pubblicità) Tosinvest: La riabilitazione comincia così"

Another animated GIF. Use all the available text from every frame.

Íslandssími C

Höldum jól fram í apríl

Ókeypis GSM símtöl í kjarnaáskrift til 31. mars

Kjarnaáskrift Íslandssíma

alt="ÍSLANDSSÍMI – Kjarnaáskrift Íslandssíma – Höldum jól fram í apríl"

alt="ÍSLANDSSÍMI – Kjarnaáskrift Íslandssíma – Höldum jól fram í apríl"

title="Ókeypis GSM símtöl í kjarnaáskrift til 31. mars"

title="Ókeypis GSM símtöl í kjarnaáskrift til 31. mars"

In an animated GIF, write an equivalent for all states. Text equivalents rewritten here in order of serial interpretation, not presentation.

alt="(Publicidade) Warner: Promoção Super Preço"

alt="(Publicidade) Warner: Promoção Super Preço"

alt="[Advertisement] Pontiac Sunfire: Drive away without paying. SunfireDeals.com"

alt="[Ilmoitus] Sonera: Make things click"

title="Ethän anna tasoitusta?"

title="Ethän anna tasoitusta?"

A strange bilingual case. Here I've split the sexier English slogan into the alt text and hived off the rather less sexy Finnish into the title.

alt="(AD) Orbitz: Most Low Fares"

title="The world’s leading airlines bring you the most low fares. Try a search! Great rates on air, hotel & car"

alt="[Publicidade] Catho Online"

title="8 diferenciais para
você incluir agora o seu
currículo na Catho Online!"

title="*8 diferenciais para você
incluir agora o seu currículo na
Catho Online!*"

With this much copy, a
longdescription may be in order.

alt="[Ad] Circuit City: Holiday
2001. Give them gifts
they’ll treasure –
and maybe even lend you!"

alt="*[Ad] Circuit City: Holiday
2001. Give them gifts they'll
treasure – and maybe even lend
you!*"

title="With our Holiday Gift Guide,
you can buy the hottest products
for everybody on your list. And
with Express Pickup, you can pick
up your order immediately,
avoiding ALL shipping costs! Only
available at CircuitCity.com"

advertisement

advertisement

alt="(Advert) ING Savings
Maximiser: Earn 4.50% p.a. | ING
Direct: straight forward"

title="No bank fees. No min.
deposit. No fixed term. Open a
Savings Maximiser and receive 2
free movie tickets!"

It may be wise to include the
company slogan or catchphrase
within the alt text. A case like
this, with frankly excessive copy,
brings into focus the inconvenience of text equivalents. Memo
to copywriters: Write shorter.

7| text and links

TEXT IS THE MOST ACCESSIBLE DATA FORMAT THERE IS. The preponderance of "content" in Websites worldwide is, in fact, text.

Any browser can read plain HTML text, and can at least muddle through even the most convoluted HTML text – e.g., text interspersed with inline images; text in table cells; text marked up with unwise formatting codes like `<u></u>` and `<blink></blink>`; text structured with the relatively advanced accessibility codes described in this chapter. Modern browsers even take a stab at rendering characters you may not understand (like Japanese, or even the many symbols – "pi" characters, to use the old typographic terminology – available in HTML).

You would have to search high and wide to find any kind of adaptive technology that doesn't understand and manipulate text. It stands to reason: HTML and its accessibility codes are expressed in text.

There are, however, many subtle wrinkles involved in accessible text design – and one big myth. First, though, a definition.

Goals

In this chapter:

- We'll adopt a specific definition of text.
- We'll understand the importance of sticking to the admittedly boring and limited World Wide Web Consortium official structural markup.
- We'll learn about a few access-specific HTML elements.
- We'll document the quirks of marking up quotations, and learn stylesheet variations for those.
- We'll disabuse a myth about the value of text-only Websites.

What is text?

In building Websites, we consider text to be any series of recognized characters expressed in a form readable by computers.

Note that comprehension is not part of the definition. Neither, for that matter, is a human being at the receiving end. The issue is computer manipulability, a necessary prerequisite for accessibility.

This definition excludes "text" that is rendered as bitmapped graphics that the human eye can interpret as letters, characters, symbols, or words (as a *picture of text*) but with no underlying representation. If I press the e key on my computer, I produce a code for that letter (an underlying structure) and, in nearly all cases, a visual representation of it. If I fire up Photoshop and type an e in a certain font, size, and colour and save that combination as a GIF file, all I have produced is a visual representation with no underlying structure.

And remember, adaptive technology relies on structure. A picture of text is essentially invisible or nonexistent to technologies like screen readers and Braille displays. It also disappears entirely when graphics loading is turned off in a graphical browser. For the purpose of our discussion, a picture of text is more picture than text.

Now, as we saw in Chapter 6, "The image problem," it is easy to produce multiple text equivalents for any kind of graphic, so pictures of text are not necessarily inaccessible. This chapter explains how to make *text as defined here* accessible.

Basic facts

Note: If you're already familiar with HTML basics, you can skip this section.
As you likely know, Websites written in the Roman-alphabet languages typically found online are coded in the rudimentary character set known as US-ASCII, the latter term being a quaint acronym for American Standard Code for Information Interchange. ("Quaint" because, like EPS, VHS, and both meanings of ABS, the expansion of the acronym is either forgotten or irrelevant or both.)

The issue of character sets is convoluted. For our purposes, all you need to keep in mind is that the HTML files that cause Websites to come into being in most Western languages are typed with a rudimentary set of characters. Most relevantly, no accented letters are present, as are relatively few punctuation marks.

So how do we refer to accented letters, exotic punctuation, and anything else beyond US-ASCII? By taking advantage of the fact that computers and computer scientists love to number things. Tens of thousands of characters of every description have already been numbered, in some cases several different times in several different *encoding* schemes, all of which may someday be subsumed under the big tent of Unicode, which seeks to categorize nearly every differentiable character in human writing systems.

These numbering systems are sometimes incompatible, meaning that the use of a character number from one system may not work on a certain browser or platform. HTML may permit any and all representations from various numbering schemes. This complication, however, can sometimes be avoided: Many characters in HTML also have names made up of letters.

In HTML, you can refer to and invoke characters by their number or name. Both the numeric and alphabetic character representations are called *entities*, with the latter specifically known as literal or named entities. Of course, this quickly threatens to become a circular argument: We may dress them up in a buzzword of "entities," but we're still using characters to refer to *other* characters, so where do you draw the line?

To tell the browser or other device that we are referring to another character rather than using those numbers or names for their own sake, we *encode* or *escape* these characters by surrounding numeric entities with ampersand-octothorpe and semicolon, or &#___;. Literal or named entities use the appropriate name surrounded by ampersand-semicolon, or &___;. Example: The symbol for pounds sterling, £, has the name pound and the number 163. To use that character in an HTML document, type either £ or £.

(If you ever need an ampersand for its traditional uses, type the ampersand's HTML name: &. Don't worry about semicolons used in their traditional way; they're always mirrored by unencoded ampersands in character entities and are not misinterpreted by browsers or devices.)

A cottage industry has developed online to document the thousands of available characters and the many available encodings. Visibone.com sells a printed card that's quite useful.

Character encodings

Ideally, your server, if correctly configured, will transmit the character encoding used in a document inside an HTTP header. It is nonetheless considered good authoring practice for you to declare character encoding yourself within a Web page.

Browsers and devices behave unpredictably if your Web pages do not declare whatever character encoding they use. All you need to do is add the following declaration inside the head element of your page:

```
<meta http-equiv="content-type" content="text/html; charset=iso-8859-1" />
```

Don't create any pages without a declared character encoding. Add it to your page templates, or just copy and paste or drag and drop.

That declaration is consistent with the advice of this chapter; the ISO 8859-1 character set encompasses US-ASCII. Experts in multilingual Web design will voice the objection that authors can actually use any of numerous character encodings in their Web pages, making it possible to type, for example, accented characters directly into HTML code as long as you declare the correct character encoding. (An attribute like content="text/html; charset=iso-8859-2" lets you write directly in Polish, for example.)

I have assumed that typical readers will find the US-ASCII character set and 8859-1 declaration sufficient. For readers who already know how to use alternate character encodings, the bulk of this chapter's advice is unaffected.

Headers and tabbing

What's the best way to keep your text accessible? Use proper markup.

Yes, I know, how tedious and unsexy. You didn't buy this book to be told to use ‹p›‹/p› to mark up your paragraphs. Well, the truth hurts: Strict by-the-book HTML is all but universally readable.

Web designers will gnash their teeth at the prospect of a lifetime of header-tag monogamy. Can you imagine using ‹h1›‹/h1› through ‹h6›‹/h6› to describe heading text for the rest of your life?

You may *have* to imagine it. Screen readers and Braille displays churn through a Web page *serially* or *sequentially*, not randomly.

How do sighted people read Web pages? In general, they ignore what isn't interesting and focus on what is. The decision on what is and is not of interest is made quite literally in the blink of an eye.

Skipping entire regions of a Web page is so automatic for sighted people that it has contributed to the economic decline of the commercial Web. The phenomenon of *banner blindness* is well documented: People with even a modicum of online experience do not so much as bother looking at banner ads, and indeed they sometimes fail to notice anything that merely resembles a banner ad but is in fact a navigation or "content" element. Among other reasons, banner blindness explains why almost no one selects and follows a banner ad.

Banner blindness has an upside: It creates an instant visual sophistication that enables a sighted visitor to locate the useful components of a page, like the search box, headlines, and body copy, and focus on them right away. True enough, this facility is not foolproof, and substandard information architecture can cause even sophisticated Web users to sit there scanning a page for seconds or minutes trying to figure out what's what, but the fact remains that *random* access to Web pages is the norm for sighted people.

A screen-reader user has no such luxury. A screen reader provides a form of *serial* access to a Web page: You hear or read items one after another in sequence. You cannot instantaneously jump from one part of the screen

The decision on what is and is not of interest is made quite literally in the blink of an eye.

to another, as you can with the naked eye. Now, there *are* ways to speed navigation in a page, but the fundamental process is one of sequential travel from one item to the next.

What constitutes an item? HTML structural constructs occupy the highest level of abstraction, including headings formatted in hx elements; unordered, ordered, and definition lists; images; tables and frames; and of course paragraphs and links.

At the rudimentary level, the Tab key is what skips the cursor from item to item. Nondisabled visitors can already do that on nearly any Web page with certain browsers, including Internet Explorer on both Mac and Windows; the concept is taken to the max with screen readers, which provide a panoply of keyboard commands for page navigation. The Tab key barely scratches the surface.

Through accessible HTML (the tabindex attribute, discussed in Chapter 8, "Navigation"), you can provide pit stops along the way as one tabs through a document, but even if you do not take that step, navigating through a Web page more or less means tabbing from item to item.

Styled headings

Screen readers and the like let you select the order in which you'd like to tab through elements, but the fundaments lie in HTML. The Web Content Accessibility Guidelines tell us to use heading elements in strict numerical order — ‹h1›‹/h1›, then, if necessary, ‹h2›‹/h2› through ‹h6›‹/h6› in that sequence. That dictum suits androids and Vulcans quite well, but here in the real world you can skip intervening levels and you don't have to start at ‹h1›‹/h1›. I am telling you that you can defy the WCAG in this limited way. You must not, however, use heading elements in anything but ascending order.

If you design a page whose headings are marked up with presentational attributes — even legal or tolerated HTML like the ‹big›‹/big› element or an align="center" attribute on a paragraph element — it may be apparent to sighted visitors that the text is meant as a heading, but there is no reliable way for a screen reader to select that header in sequence. Adaptive technology relies on structure, remember. h means heading. ‹big›‹/big› and ‹center›‹/center› mean big and centred.

Plain heading elements have a murky reputation in large part due to clumsy handling by browsers. There is no credible reason why an unadorned ‹h1›‹/h1› should be displayed in flush-left 28-point bold type by default in a graphical browser, but that's the sort of typographic atrocity we've put up with since the earliest days of Mosaic, which I specifically remember.

Such type is just too big. In print typography, size increments are small: "Display" or headline type typically runs in steps of 14, 16, 18, 20, 22 or 24, and 24 or 28 point, and there is no necessity for boldface.

Moreover, graphical browsers overlook the structure implied by indention. (Not "indentation." The word is *indention*.) Heading elements are either all flush-left or all centred. Lynx, the text-only browser, centres ‹h1›‹/h1› text, runs ‹h2›‹/h2› text at the left margin, and indents remaining successive hx levels.

Accordingly, visual sophisticates have been insulted over the years by the default appearance of heading elements. Hurt feelings can be assuaged with stylesheets.

Generic text tags

HTML comes equipped with a surprising range of "phrase elements" or tags to mark up text – *way* more than ‹strong›‹/strong› or ‹i›‹/i› or whatever else we keep reading about over and over again in intro-to-HTML courses.

The problem? Practically nobody uses them. There may be good reason for this: Too many of the available tags are suited to computer scientists and pretty much no one else.

> Accordingly, visual sophisticates have been insulted over the years by the default appearance of heading elements.

Let's run through the list. As usual, naughty presentational tags are excluded.

- ‹abbr›‹/abbr› and ‹acronym›‹/acronym›, for abbreviations and acronyms. Important enough to warrant their own section, "Access tags," coming up shortly.
- ‹em›‹/em› for emphasis of any sort other than the special case of citations. How this differs from ‹strong›‹/strong› has never been entirely clear. Here's the entirety of the W3C's advice in this regard: "em: Indicates emphasis. strong: Indicates stronger emphasis." Thanks for clearing that up. In differentiating the two, I often permit myself the following forbidden presentationalist thought:
Use ‹strong›‹/strong› for anything whose rendering in a bold font you could put up with, since that's what graphical browsers have used since time immemorial. Use ‹em›‹/em› for everything else, except...
- ‹cite›‹/cite› for "citations," meaning titles (of books, films, plays, television programs, court cases, possibly even ships) and words and phrases quoted for themselves. It must be reiterated that citations are not interchangeable with ‹em›‹/em› for general emphasis.
- The oddball computer-science quintet:
  - ‹code›‹/code›, for computer code; ‹var›‹/var›, for variables, like the numbers 1 through 6 in the hx elements; and ‹kbd›‹/kbd›, to represent text typed at a keyboard. Such elements are used extensively in a book like this, but rarely at an E-commerce site or pretty much anywhere else on the Web, really.
  - ‹dfn›‹/dfn› for definitions. Note that this element applies to the term being defined and not the text of the definition.

- ‹samp›‹/samp› for "samples" — of output from a computer program, for example. The idea of small, discrete samples of output that need to be marked up as such harkens back to 1980-era Radio Shack TRS-80 computers programmed in BASIC. Hats off to you if you can figure out an appropriate real-world use for this one.

Of this list, the elements you will use in day-to-day life are ‹em›‹/em›, ‹strong›‹/strong›, and ‹cite›‹/cite›. If you find yourself needing the Albert Einstein set of elements for definitions, samples, and the like, you may wish to set up stylesheets so they won't all end up rendered in too-small Courier type, which does seem to be the default in every graphical browser you could name. You will cause no lessening of accessibility using stylesheets and will improve the appearance of your sites.

For completeness, I'll mention two more text elements, though they're unrelated to accessibility: ‹ins›‹/ins› for inserted text and ‹del›‹/del› for deleted text. They're reasonably well-supported, and indeed you find ‹del›‹/del› in common use at E-commerce sites to strike out old prices in favour of the *new, low!* price.

Accessibility-specific elements

HTML 4.0 introduced a pair of sometimes-troublesome conjoined twins, ‹abbr›‹/abbr› and ‹acronym›‹/acronym›, for abbreviations and acronyms. You may wonder why anyone bothered: Aren't abbreviations and acronyms already discernible? Abbreviations tend to end in a period; acronyms tend to be written in capitals.

Screen readers, however, are too stupid to figure out those nuances. Sentences can end in periods; if a screen reader encounters an abbreviation also terminating in a period, does it indicate the end of the sentence? Capital letters are used for many purposes, and all-caps acronyms can be found in all-caps text ("VAT INCREASE PROPOSED").

Also, let's not be presumptuous about language diversity. Many languages (and some national English variants) do not use periods in abbreviations. Some acronyms (even in English) use upper- and lower-case. Some languages lack a concept of case entirely but nonetheless use rules for creating abbreviations.

At first blush, the use of ‹abbr›‹/abbr› and ‹acronym›‹/acronym› is straightforward. Just surround the abbreviation or acronym with the element, and type the full expansion inside the title="" attribute:

- ‹acronym title="not in my backyard"›NIMBY‹/acronym›
- ‹abbr title="continued"›cont'd‹/abbr›

If you're switching languages for some reason — if, for example, you are writing a section in a book on foreign-language acronyms (and you *know* how often that task comes up) – you can add a lang="" xml:lang="" attribute. Don't bother if the language of the text (as declared in the document's ‹head›‹/head›) and of the acronym or abbreviation are the same.

- ‹abbr lang="de" xml:lang="de" title="Hauptbahnhof"›Hbf‹/abbr›
- ‹acronym title="societate per azioni" lang="it" xml:lang="it"›SpA‹/acronym›

Do you really have to use these tags for every abbreviation or acronym, no matter how well-known? Technically, yes: The Web Accessibility Initiative Web Content Accessibility Guidelines tell us to "[s]pecify the expansion of each abbreviation or acronym in a document where it first occurs."

But in reality, sometimes the expansion, as in the case of EPS and both meanings of ABS, is irrelevant. Does anyone really care anymore that a fax is a facsimile?

Legal company designations, like ‹acronym title="societate per azioni" lang="it" xml:lang="it"›SpA‹/acronym› cited above, are a good example. They tend to be read as irreducible units whether or not every letter is articulated. Rules vary: In English, "Inc." is read out as "incorporated" or "ink," but either way everyone knows it is a legal company designation. Whether or not people know how "Inc." varies from "Ltd.," "PLC," or any other designation is irrelevant from an accessibility standpoint.

Many abbreviations are so well-known, and so unlikely to trip up a screen reader, that using the "required" tags seems like gilding the lily. An example given in a WAI resource document actually marks up the acronym *WWW*, rather proving my point.

The unwritten intent of the Web Content Accessibility Guidelines is to mark up unfamiliar or ambiguous acronyms and abbreviations. And yes, you only have to do it the first time it appears in a document. If you're doing a search-and-replace, however, having decided it is easier to bang out the plain text of an article about EPS graphics and bolt on the access tags later, you might as well replace all occurrences at once. What with search engines, browser Find functions (letting you locate any text on a page), and your own possible use of anchor elements for navigating within a page, you cannot be sure that people will read from the very beginning. And what if the first instance of an abbreviation or acronym comes up at word 300 of a thousand-word document? Should we have to go hunting for the first instance merely because we started reading at word 700 and you've used the access element only once?

The ‹abbr›‹/abbr› and ‹acronym›‹/acronym› elements are, moreover, an imperfect guarantee of accurate voicing by screen readers. It's not really their fault. There is no guarantee that a screen reader will pronounce an abbreviation or acronym more accurately merely because it is marked up as such, if only because pronunciations are unpredictable. You should use them anyway; while they are imperfect, they are generally quite functional.

The unwritten intent of the Web Content Accessibility Guidelines is to mark up unfamiliar or ambiguous acronyms and abbreviations.

Some exceptions come to mind. Don't use the elements for initialed proper names: Composer J.S. Bach is J.S. Bach and not <acronym title="Johann Sebastian">J.S.</acronym> Bach. (Writing "J.S. Bach" is more than sufficient to differentiate him from C.P.E., J.C., or W.F. Bach.) Don't use the elements even if you write initialed proper names without periods and they form possible words: Architect IM Pei is IM Pei and not <acronym title="Ieoh Ming">IM</acronym> Pei.

Units of measure should be exempted. Even imperial units like pounds, with the Latinate abbreviation *lbs.*, are well enough understood to be left alone. (Screen readers ship with pronunciation exception dictionaries. A common abbreviation like *lbs.* will likely be pronounced correctly. If not, you the user can add it to your custom dictionary.)

Metric symbols are a trickier case, since they are in fact symbols and not abbreviations. While this is something of a legalistic distinction in cases like *kg* (kilograms) or *kWh* (kilowatt-hours) that tend to be pronounced letter-by-letter or in their full expansion, we nevertheless find single-letter symbols like *m* (metres) or *a* (years: *a* for *annum*) whose pronunciation is ambiguous. Rare combinations, like *am* for attometres, pose the same problem.

But it is a problem that the brute-force remedies of <abbr></abbr> and <acronym></acronym> elements cannot solve. There is no element in HTML for ambiguously-pronounced units of measure. It must also be pointed out that nondisabled people reading printed text may have to stop and think for a moment to decode an ambiguous metric symbol, too. In this case, a screen-reader user may not be significantly worse off than a nondisabled person.

Merely on the face of it, the definitions of the <abbr></abbr> and <acronym></acronym> elements preclude using them for symbols of any kind. Just use the symbol by itself, properly escaped as a numeric or literal entity. Don't write <abbr title="pounds sterling">£</abbr> or <abbr title="plus or minus">±</abbr>.

(So what do you do if a symbol combines a character outside of the US-ASCII set alongside one that is from that set, as in °C? Best leave it alone. If <abbr></abbr> and <acronym></acronym> are too hamfisted to handle attometres, how can we expect them to handle degrees Celsius?)

BROWSER SUPPORT

Support for <abbr></abbr> and <acronym></acronym> elements in real-world browsers is not fantastic. A case could be made that graphical browsers shouldn't have to support <abbr></abbr> and <acronym></acronym> at all given that they're intended for adaptive technology, but they're useful enough to nondisabled people that some kind of interface to their underlying title="" attribute is in order. Besides, some browsers already provide visual support.

- Some versions of Internet Explorer on Mac and Windows pop up a tooltip when you hover the mouse over an item coded with `<abbr></abbr>` and `<acronym></acronym>`.
- Macintosh IE 5 attempts to render all acronyms in small capitals (indistinguishable from all-caps rendering for all-caps acronyms, but not all acronyms are written that way); Mac IE 5 does nothing special to indicate abbreviations.
- Some Windows versions render `<acronym></acronym>` but not `<abbr></abbr>`. Windows IE 4 truncated the `<acronym></acronym>` text, down to the first word.
- Netscape 4 provides no interface for the title="" attribute on `<abbr></abbr>` and `<acronym></acronym>`. Netscape 6 and later and Mozilla show a tooltip for both. The latter displays both properties using dotted underlines — by far the most sophisticated approach extant.
- iCab on Macintosh — well-behaved as ever with advanced HTML — underlines `<abbr></abbr>` and `<acronym></acronym>` text and reveals the title="" attribute in the status line, and actually changes the hover cursor to remind you to look there.
- Lynx does nothing special for `<abbr></abbr>` and `<acronym></acronym>`.

STYLESHEET ISSUES

If you accept the premise that `<abbr></abbr>` and `<acronym></acronym>` provide accessibility, in a catholic sense, to anyone who cares to learn the expansion of an abbreviation or acronym with or without the use of adaptive technology, you might as well make users of graphical browsers aware that `<abbr></abbr>` and `<acronym></acronym>` are actually available.

A quick and dirty way to do so is to set up a stylesheet that underlines `<abbr></abbr>` and `<acronym></acronym>` text. Are you aghast? Aghast that I would counsel the use of the typographic abomination known as underlining? Especially since we also use underlines for links, and a certain Danish-American usability "super-expert" has declared that designers should never make links confusable with anything else?

Well, bollocks. Selecting links in graphical browsers is a multi-stage process with feedback all the way.

- If you use a mouse, you spot something that looks like a link and move the cursor onto it. Your cursor image changes, usually to a hand with an extended index finger. You click the link and you're all set.
- If you use the keyboard, in typical interfaces tabbing from one item to another causes the item or link with "focus" to be outlined. You don't have to go hunting for links; every link will be selected in turn. You can, of course, spot something that looks like a link and keep tabbing until you highlight it. Then press Return and you're all set.

Let's envisage the worst-case scenario: Underlining ‹abbr›‹/abbr› and ‹acronym›‹/acronym› text causes everyone to mistake the text for links. When you hover the cursor over the text, there is no change to a link cursor. The cursor may *otherwise* change (as in iCab's case), but not to a link cursor. If you're using keyboard access, you'll skip the ‹abbr›‹/abbr› or ‹acronym› ‹/acronym› because it isn't a link.

What's the problem?

Short answer: There isn't one. Indeed, there are advantages. Underlining abbreviations and acronyms makes them noticeable and invites visitors to poke at them, causing the desired tooltip to appear. The prime disadvantage is æsthetic, but we're already underlining links hither and yon, so the waters are already muddied.

How do you do it? Add this to your stylesheet:

```
abbr, acronym { text-decoration: underline }
```

What we really need is a different kind of underlining, like dotted underlines, to denote metadata of this sort. Mozilla and Netscape 6 and later do just that, and it's quite attractive. (If you use a stylesheet like the one just mentioned, those browsers will render a dotted underline *and* a continuous one, double-underlining your abbreviation or acronym.

And you can actually do that in a stylesheet:

```
abbr, acronym { border-bottom: 1px dotted gray }
```

Looks very nice.

Even rarer cases

It is incumbent on me to point out that we do find the occasional term written in capitals or otherwise resembling an acronym that actually is not. Is KISS an acronym or a clownish, superannuated rock embarrassment? The Macintosh file format PICT is not an acronym – and not much of an abbreviation, either. The spy game is replete with oddball acronym–abbreviation amalgams, none of which I particularly understand or will bother to define but which make for a fun list: ACINT, ACOUSTINT, COMINT, ELECTRO-OPTINT, FISINT, HUMINT, IMINT, IRINT, LASINT, MASINT, NUCINT, OSINT, RADINT, RF/EMPINT, RINT, SIGINT, TELINT. None of the examples in this paragraph require HTML accessibility tags as far as I'm concerned.

Also, the Web itself has spawned a rash of abbreviations taking alpha-numeric form – e.g., the unholy conjoined twins favoured by marketing poseurs, B2B/B2C (business-to-business and -consumer); P2P (peer-to-peer); i18n (internationalization) and l10n (localization). Certainly those last two deserve proper ‹abbr›‹/abbr› markup in any document a layperson is likely to read.

Small capitals deserve their own discussion. Some typographic style guides advise typesetting uppercase acronyms and any other sequence of capitals in small caps. Ostensibly, full-height capital letters are too conspicuous. I have never subscribed to this style, which, in my opinion, only ever works for acronyms that are pronounceable words, like NORAD.

Out in the real world of print typography, it is still too difficult to use *true* small-caps typefaces to set such passages; ignorant designers, or those with no other option, merely use full capitals a point or two smaller in size, which end up looking too light and spindly. Two methods are in use: Typing text and applying a Small Caps character attribute, or typing text and manually resizing it.

In any event, when such documents are "repurposed" for the Web (surely the most disagreeable word ever coined in the English language), invariably the small-cap styling is lost. A chief miscreant here is HTML export from Quark Xpress, a decidedly antitypographical program that practically begs a designer to use fake small caps.

The problem? If, somewhere along the copy chain, the acronym had been typed in *lower case* or mixed case and merely *styled* as small caps, unless extraordinary measures are taken that word will be exported to HTML *in the original lower case or mixed case.*

In the following example – from Playbackmag.com, quite real, and a textbook example of a worst-case scenario – the nonacronym CODCO is written in full capitals (it's the KISS-like name of a defunct comedy group). MOW, meaning movie of the week, is rendered both correctly and incorrectly, most egregiously in the plural ("mows" – as in "Dad mows the lawn every couple of weeks"?). YTV and CBC (both TV networks) and U.S. are incorrectly written in lower case, while CBS comes through all right. The phrase "delayed cbs mow" is particularly rich. Note also the lack of heading markup on "MOW Power to them" and the absence of anything resembling italics (not ‹cite›‹/cite›, not ‹em›‹/em›, not even ‹i›‹/i›) throughout. And if anyone's keeping score, Kirstie Alley spells her name thus.

> Their CODCO days are over, but the talented Greg Malone and Tommy Sexton are back at the cbc, this time to do the musical MOW for the Mother Corp., Adult Children of Alcoholics. Malone and Sexton are writing and starring in the movie. They have enlisted Paul Brown (I Love a Man in Uniform) to produce. The project was scheduled to shoot this month but has been delayed.
> MOW Power to them
> Power Pictures is cranking out the mows in association with Hearst Entertainment. And Then There Was One is a movie starring Amy Madigan and Dennis Boutsikaris for Lifetime in the u.s. Angela

Bromstad is producing and David Jones is directing. Executive producer is Freyda Rothstein and supervising producer is Julian Marks.

CBS is getting David's Mother, an mow starring Kirsty Alley that's being serviced here. Director is Robert Allan Ackerman and producer is Bob Randall. Jennifer Allward is executive producing and supervising producer is Julian Marks. Production on David's Mother starts Sept. 15.

The delayed cbs mow Ultimate Betrayal is back on track with director and executive producer Donald Wrye. The shoot is scheduled to begin Sept. 27. Producer is Julian Marks. Ultimate Betrayal stars Marlo Thomas, Ally Sheedy and Mel Harris.

As the outdated, gender-specific saying goes, "Men, don't let this happen to you." In cases like these, it is arguably less important to ensure that abbreviations and acronyms are marked up in their respective HTML tags than to ensure that the damned things come through in their proper case.

If you wish to retain the small-caps appearance, a stylesheet like the following will work:

```
abbr, acronym { font-size: smaller; letter-spacing: .1em; text-transform:
uppercase }
```

which you may combine with my previous advice to yield:

```
abbr, acronym { font-size: smaller; letter-spacing: .1em; text-transform:
uppercase; text-decoration: underline }
```

In this example:

- font-size: smaller works better than listing a specific point size. Type used for ‹abbr›‹/abbr› and ‹acronym›‹/acronym› will remain smaller when viewed in a graphical browser at at any zoom level.
- letter-spacing: .1em adds a tiny bit of space between the letters, which admittedly may be too subtle for onscreen display given that the smallest unit of measurement is a pixel and pixels are usually enormously bigger than one-tenth of an em.
- text-transform: uppercase ensures all-caps rendering. This can be undesirable in rare cases, like government ministry abbreviations (MoH, DoD).

In CSS level 3, there does exist a small-caps attribute, which sometimes works:

```
abbr, acronym { font-variant: small-caps }
```

Quotations and making editing obvious

Back in our halcyon youth, when we ran red lights in our Camaros (or Minis, or Renault 5s, as culturally appropriate), we unabashedly deployed an element called BLOCKQUOTE to indent snippets of text.

We are now all grown up and have various mortgages and certificates of equivalent-to-spouse status weighing us down, and we are sober enough to recognize that the ‹blockquote›‹/blockquote› element, as it is now known in the minusculist orthography of XHTML, is reserved for quoting blocks of text. We feel shame for having pressed it into unnatural service in the early days of our dalliance with the Web.

We know, moreover, that indenting a section of text is as simple as adding style="margin-left: 2em" or something along those lines to whatever element we're using, like ‹p›‹/p›.

But how many of us know that blockquotes have a new younger sibling, and have added a piercing in a place not immediately obvious to outsiders? Start with the new feature added to ‹blockquote›‹/blockquote›. In XHTML, you are now encouraged to cite the URL of the document from which you are quoting. This of course presumes you're quoting from a document that's actually online.

The syntax is pretty simple: ‹blockquote cite=""›‹/blockquote›. Just dump in whatever URL is appropriate between the quotation marks. Typical examples will look like this:

- ‹blockquote cite="http://www.newsbytes.com/pubNews/00/156859.html"›
- ‹blockquote cite="ftp://ftp.dcita.gov.au/pub/digitaltv/caption/acc_ap_b.doc"› (you may use any valid file URL, even one that leads to a Microsoft Word document on an FTP site, though the practical usability of such a link is questionable)
- ‹blockquote cite="http://www.aftonbladet.se/vss/nyheter/story/0,2789,101786,00.html"›

Browser support for this feature is terrible. Only iCab, Mozilla, and Netscape 6 and later give you access to the citation.

Now for the little sibling. XHTML provides structured markup for quotations used within paragraphs or in any similar block-level structure. Just wrap the quotation in ‹q› and ‹/q›. Simple? Yes. If for some reason you wish to cite another Web page as the source of your quotation, you can add cite="", like so:

> ‹q cite="http://www.newsbytes.com/pubNews/00/156859.html"›*Various quoted words*‹/q›

The ‹q›‹/q› element allegedly makes it easier for adaptive technology to isolate quotations from the surrounding text. Since the element offers readily-differentiated open and closed states, then yes, it is true that computer software can figure things out more easily. Yet it is spectacularly rare to find a case in which the start or finish of a quotation marked up with simple quotation marks is ambiguous.

Using ‹q›‹/q› has certain heavily-qualified advantages in multilingual text: You can drop a French quotation into an English paragraph and, if you declare the quotation's language using the lang="" attribute, a device might use proper French quotation marks rather than English. The sentence –

> He was laying on the charm, telling me I had "a certain
> ‹q lang="fr"›*je ne sais quoi*‹/q›"

– might be rendered thus:

> He was laying on the charm, telling me I had "a certain
> «*je ne sais quoi*»"

But of course this would be improper typography in any context other than language teaching: The dominant language is the language of the paragraph, not the quotation, and its rules for quoting text prevail.

Moreover, current graphical browsers use double neutral quotation marks to render ‹q›‹/q›, if they render it at all, and several do not, like Netscape 4. A failure to indicate quotations, through lack of support of a "correct" HTML element, is arguably worse than simply using neutral quotation marks. Not all English-speaking countries use double quotation marks as their first choice. Proper typographer's quotation marks, as preferred in the English language, are easily used:

- left double (opening) quotation mark ("): “ or “
- right double (closing) quotation mark ("): ” or ”
- left single (opening) quotation mark ('): ‘ or ‘
- right single (closing) quotation mark or apostrophe ('): ’ or ’

If you're writing in Latin-alphabet languages other than English (I suppose this applies to Greek and Cyrillic-alphabet languages as well), you will need language-specific quotation marks. Working on the assumption you know which character to use in the respective language but do not know how to encode it, here are nearly all the available options:

- Left double (opening) *guillemet* («): « or «
  - Do not use two less-thans, <<
- Right double (closing) *guillemet* (»): » or »
  - Do not use two greater-thans, >>
  - Note that the numeric references are not successive – compare « and »
- Left single (opening) *guillemet* (‹): ‹ or ‹
- Right single (closing) *guillemet* (›): › or ›

· Both poorly supported, but also rarely used
- Left single (opening) "low-9" quotation mark (‚): ‚ or ‚
  · Absolutely *not* a comma
  · To close this quotation mark, use left single (opening) quotation mark ('): ‘ or ‘
- Left double (opening) "low-9" quotation mark („): „ or „
  · Literal reference here does not follow the pattern of the single "low-9" variant – compare ‚ and „
  · To close this quotation mark, use left double (opening) quotation mark ("): “ or “

The numeric entities, at least for English-language characters, are very well-supported, even in Netscape 4, and are unique, hence entirely unambiguous, save for the double application of ’ or ’ as apostrophe or closing single quotation mark. But that ambiguity is built into English. True, ‹q›‹/q› can remedy that extremely modest and rarely-encountered confusion, but that's hardly a persuasive advantage.

In Cascading Stylesheets Level 2, there is a way to control the quotation-mark characters used to surround ‹q›‹/q› text. Use this declaration:

q {quotes: '\201C' '\201D' '\2018' '\2019'}

Real-world testing shows one must use the Unicode hexadecimal escaped character sequences, which are so complicated and extraneous I have avoided talking about them so far.

In the declaration, you must list, in order, the high-level opening, high-level closing, low-level opening, and low-level closing quotation marks. Hardly worth the bother. You can vary the declaration by language, should you use multilingual text, using q:lang(*languagecode*), as q:lang(en) for English or q:lang(fr) for French. I don't see how this is really worth the bother, either.

Use ‹q›‹/q› if you want. It won't hurt – most of the time. But it's not significantly better than neutral quotation marks and is generally inferior to typographer's quotation marks.

Text and learning disability

And I will briefly mention a large topic: A person with a learning disability may be particularly stymied by a text-only page. Reading extended text is a common problem for this group. A page with mixed text and graphics will not necessarily be genuinely accessible to this group but may be less inaccessible. As ever, it remains virtually impossible to *really* accommodate the learning-disabled on the Web where nearly every page contains something to be read. That may indeed never change no matter how hard people wish it would.

...only a tiny few access techniques require an overt visual form at all, and in the majority of cases you can provide a fully-accessible page with no changes to your layout whatsoever.

Links

I'm splitting the discussion of accessibility of links into two parts. In Chapter 8, "Navigation," you'll learn about the sexy accesskey and tabindex attributes. But for now, there are two very simple guidelines.

If you want to be thorough, don't run two consecutive text links together without a printable character between them. Some early screen readers will enunciate the pair of links as one link, and for users of graphical browsers it is next to impossible to tell that adjacent words are different links. Webloggers love the effect produced by four or five separate consecutive links related to the same concept, but it's inaccessible.

On the other hand, the case can be made that users of old screen readers really should upgrade; even consecutive links are actually perfectly discernible in the underlying HTML: The sequence `<a></a> <a></a> <a></a>` is quite self-evidently a set of three self-contained hyperlinks.

In any event, which printed character should you use to separate links? In a navigation bar or some other region of text whose entire *raison d'être* is a set of links, a vertical bar (|) will do. (The character is sometimes hard to find on foreign-language keyboards. You can always use | or |.)

For a better typographic appearance, an en dash (– or –) is very nice and is supported in every browser I've ever seen (using the numeric entity, at least – Netscape 4 chokes on the literal entity, to no one's surprise). The pilcrow or paragraph symbol ¶ (¶ or ¶) has its merits. Note that some screen readers have not yet been upgraded to understand every HTML character and may skip over these escaped entities. The goal of separating adjacent links will nonetheless be met.

> But nobody authorized you to give us nothing but text in the name of accessibility

The big myth

At the outset of this chapter, I warned of one big myth in the accessibility of text. It's this: The most accessible sites are text-only.

It is not true. Maybe in 1996, sure, but adaptive technology and HTML have advanced a bit since then. Everything you find on the Web that isn't text – images, multimedia, Flash – can be made at least partially accessible, and in the most common case, GIF and JPEG images, something broadly approaching full accessibility is possible. As I continue to emphasize in this book, only a tiny few access techniques require an overt visual form at all, and in the majority of cases you can provide a fully-accessible page with no changes to your layout whatsoever. Remember, we want beauty *and* accessibility.

Text-only parallel sites are to be discouraged. They're too easily neglected. They assume you're more disabled than you may actually be, and that you are alone: Providing text-only pages as the accessible form of your site assumes that disabled visitors have no use for visual appearance or structure, require something "separate," and will never look at your pages accompanied by nondisabled people. What, you've never been to a business meeting? Blind people don't have sighted family members? You've never had friends over and noodled around online?

A case can actually be made that custom-generated, media-dependent pages enhance accessibility. Stylesheets make provision for this in the aural, braille, and tty media types, among others. In Chapter 15, "Future dreams," I discuss the options for automatic transformation of Web pages for optimized use with a screen reader. Yet these are not the same as stripping out all the pictures and typographic formatting from your site and calling what you did accessibility.

Sure enough, the separation of style and content espoused by advocates of cascading stylesheets shares many goals with text-only pages. Or seemingly so. But you can't run stylesheets without HTML markup. And that's really what people imagine when visualizing a text-only page: Stripping out not only the markup for images, layout, and typography, but every other fragment of markup, too. Goodbye, ‹h1›! Goodbye, everything, in fact – the entire World Wide Web turned into a mass of Readme files. But that sort of thing is *de trop*. It throws out the baby with the bathwater.

Moreover, masses of uninterrupted, unadorned text are confusing to learning-disabled people. Your "accessible" text-only page may be less accessible than your illustrated *real* page to this hard-to-accommodate group.

Text is the most accessible data format there is. But nobody authorized you to give us *nothing but text* in the name of accessibility. And after reading this book, you will know better than to try.

Bottom-Line Accessibility Advice

Basic, Intermediate, and Advanced accessibility

- Declare the character encoding of all documents.
- Use structural rather than presentational text elements, including headings.
- When revising old documents and producing new documents, use ‹abbr›‹/abbr› and ‹acronym›‹/acronym› to mark up abbreviations and acronyms that would be unfamiliar to a typical visitor.
- Mark up block quotations with ‹blockquote›‹/blockquote›, but do not use that element for other purposes.

8| navigation

WEB DESIGNERS, INFORMATION ARCHITECTS, USABILITY EXPERTS (or, as I like to call them, "usabilitistas") – everybody's got an opinion on navigation, the simple act of getting around on the Web. I will bite my tongue and attempt to remain descriptive rather than prescriptive in this chapter, which will teach you how to make the navigation systems we find in real Websites accessible.

If making images accessible is more than half the battle (as claimed in Chapter 6, "The image problem"), accessible navigation takes care of another disproportionate chunk. Since the Web is a system of interconnections, the fact that navigation systems on commercial sites are so often based on graphic images means that making the images accessible usually makes the navigation accessible right away.

All your navigation has to be accessible. Getting to that point with old-school HTML is often clumsy, while the use of newfangled HTML that was defined specifically for accessibility brings up incompatibilities. The coding process of accessible navigation, if not the actual result, is quite often un-beautiful and adds another level of complexity. But we're all grownups here. We deal with unbeautiful HTML every day of the week (our coding is seldom as compact and elegant as something like $E=mc^2$, is it?), and you knew all along that accessibility added new wrinkles.

Philosophy lesson

I suppose this is as good a time as any to broach the intractable philosophical distinction between usability and accessibility. Certainly, thousands of Gitanes have suffered smouldering deaths as bands of intellectuals, wearing *dramatic* rectangular eyeglasses and sporting just the right handbags and mock turtle-necks, spend countless hours debating the fine gradations of difference between one discipline and the other. (Can you imagine being stuck at the adjoining table, forced to listen?)

What, then, is usability? It is the practice of designing Websites so visitors can do what they wish without undue impediment. (Some impediments are necessary, like typing in personal identification numbers to look at your bank statement. Other impediments, like indulgent Flash intros, are rather quite unnecessary.) You can see a clear kinship between usability and accessibility, given that we are trying to lessen the effects of the impediment of disability. Usability is a good predictor of accessibility, since usable sites are put together by intelligent, thoughtful people (not necessarily paid experts), and that is exactly the group that pays heed to access without being pushed and prodded. But we should not expect a one-to-one relationship. Usable sites can be inaccessible (e.g., an E-commerce site where every navigation button is an image without a text equivalent). Conversely, accessible sites can be unusable – e.g., Jakob Nielsen's Alertbox.com, which is so outlandishly undesigned as to make it hard to find anything, not to mention dozens or hundreds of pages at the World Wide Web Consortium itself, where we similarly drown in accessible data.

The scales of usability and accessibility, while kindred spirits, are not fully interdependent. There is no genuinely predictable cause and effect between them.

Further, we are forced to expand our conception of usability here. Is your site fully and conveniently usable by sighted people but an exercise in tedium for the blind?

If so, is it still "usable"?

There's only one realm where usability *noticeably* suffers at the hand of accessibility (and vice-versa), and that is navigation. This is one of the rare instances where you may have to add a visible indicator to your pages to make them accessible.

Goals

In this chapter:
- We'll understand the inconvenience of typical Website navigation mechanisms for mobility-impaired people.
- We'll explore ways of skipping over unwanted parts of a page and skipping directly to other parts.

The basics

Note: If you're already familiar with basic HTML, you can skip this section.
On the Web, you can zip from page to page ("external" navigation) or from point to point within a page ("internal" navigation).

You already know how to skip from one page to another: You use a hyperlink of the form `<a href="http://www.example.com" title="Example.com homepage"></a>`. (I've added the optional but helpful title metadata.) Your external address can be another file on the same site (as in `<a href="/news2001.asp title="2001 News Roundup"></a>`); it is "external" as viewed from the vantage point of the *current page*.

You can, of course, link to other URL types, including FTP sites (via ftp://ftp.example.com address encoding), E-mail links (via mailto:address@example.com encoding), and a few others that rarely come up. (Remember gopher://?)

Within-page or internal links, on the other hand, rely on *named anchors*. You must decide in advance the location where your visitors will end up and give it a name (or, in XHTML, an id, or sometimes both) that begins with a letter. The destination is otherwise known as the *anchor*. Whenever you think of anchors, think of destinations.

The name and id attributes are known as *fragment identifiers* and are unreasonably complicated for such a simple concept. We'll learn the intricacies in two steps – by focusing first on destinations and then on the links used to send visitors to those destinations.

Coding the destination

The HTML syntax to mark the destination looks confusingly similar to an actual hyperlink: Surround all or part of the destination with `<a>` and `</a>`. But you must use a different attribute on the element: Instead of href, use name and/or id to identify the anchor.

Why must you use "name and/or id"? Because name is oldschool HTML, tolerated in XHTML Transitional. id is used in XHTML 1.0 Strict and XHTML 1.1, where name is actually forbidden. It's a tad complicated. The coding you choose depends on the DOCTYPE you have specified.

- If you're using XHTML Transitional, include both name and id so that old browsers that don't understand id but do understand name will handle your anchors properly. This applies only to elements that can take a name attribute in the first place, and they are `<a></a>`, `<applet></applet>`, `<form></form>`, `<frame></frame>`, `<iframe></iframe>`, img, and `<map></map>`. For every other element, you must use id alone in all forms of XHTML.

- If you're writing to XHTML 1.0 (any variant), you may *optionally* use name but you *must* use id. In XHTML 1.1, you must use id only. This syntax is new, so you can expect certain older browsers to ignore your anchors altogether. Yes, this does indeed mean that documents written in these variants of XHTML may not work properly in old browsers despite being perfectly valid. It's not as though we have not encountered this before.

- Within a single element, the name and id attributes have to be identical, and the same attribute cannot appear twice on a page.
- You can use character entities like é in name but not in id, which restricts itself to plain US-ASCII characters.

The examples in this book will generally assume XHTML Transitional coding and include both name and id. Sometimes I will use only id.

If you wish to use a heading as a destination (e.g., the section titles in a long document), you could name the destination breakdown and mark up the entire heading text:

```
<h3>
<a name="breakdown" id="breakdown">Cost breakdown, Europe/Mideast/Africa,
Q2 2000</a>
</h3>
```

(The <a></a> element sits inside a block-level element like a heading.)

An image can be an anchor.

```
<a id="map7" name="map7">
<img src="/map/7.jpg" alt="Map 7: Europe/Mideast/Africa" title="Territory Map 7,
covering Europe, the Middle East, and Africa" height="322" width="550"
border="0" />
</a>
```

Even a fragment of text, or nothing at all, can be a destination. You can use an empty <a></a> element that is plunked down in the middle of a document somewhere.

- With year-over-year revenues compounding by <a name="compound" id="compound">2%</a> in the E/M/A region
- <a name="EMA" id="EMA"></a>

In the latter case, you can deposit such an empty anchor after, say, a horizontal rule (either a graphic image or the HTML code, <hr />) or at the very top of a table cell.

But those were the easy examples. Theoretically, in XHTML it is possible to apply an id attribute to essentially any tag. It then becomes possible to treat such a tag as an anchor. The two previous examples could be rewritten thus:

- <h3 id="breakdown">Cost breakdown, Europe/Mideast/Africa, Q2 2000</h3>

- `<img id="map7" src="/map/7.jpg" alt="Map 7: Europe/Mideast/Africa" title="Territory Map 7, covering Europe, the Middle East, and Africa" height="322" width="550" border="0"/>`

The text-fragment approach can be modified: You may add an id to a paragraph tag, yielding, in this example, `<p id="compound">`With year-over-year revenues compounding by 2% in the E/M/A region> (and continuing on with the rest of the paragraph, ending in `</p>`).

As the saying goes, browser support for the technique of using ids on generic markup varies, but I have managed to get it to work in reasonably standards-compliant browsers — even Lynx — on opening element tags as diverse and improbable as blockquote, cite, code, dd, dfn, dl, dt, h1, li, ul, and var. If I can make it work there, you can make it work anywhere.

Coding the hyperlink

To actually send your visitor to the anchor, use the trusted `<a href=""></a>` link, but use a number sign (for pedants, an octothorpe — either way, it's #) followed by the exact, unaltered text of the id or name. You can add a title to `<a></a>`, if you wish; indeed, as per Chapter 7: "Text and links," if any links on your page have titles, they all must do.

- `<a href="#breakdown" title="Cost breakdown">costs are broken down</a>`
- `<a href="#map7" title="Map 7: Europe/Mideast/Africa (this page)">Map 7</a>`
- `<a href="#compound" title="Compound growth of 2%">year-over-year growth of only 2% (estimated)</a>`
- `<a href="#EMA" title="EMA">EMA</a>`

Some browsers — *Netscape 4, where are you?* — are case-sensitive in interpreting anchor names. (World Wide Web Consortium guidelines technically *require* case sensitivity.) For those browsers, #e3b and #e3B are different. We shouldn't have to worry about such minutiæ. Nonetheless, it is easier for human beings to keep things straight in their minds if they stick to all-lowercase anchor designations when writing pages, particularly since nearly everything else in XHTML is lowercase already.

Evergreen issues in internal navigation

Since the overlap of usability and navigation has been broached, I would be remiss if I did not point out that the more dour and orthodox of usabilitistas have tended to frown on internal navigation, using noble but passé reasoning.

Early browsers badly bungled the interplay of anchors and the Back and Forward buttons. If you hit an anchor link and decided you wanted to retrace your steps, selecting the Back button brought you to the previous *page*, not the previous position on the *current* page. This misbehaviour, long since cleared up (even Netscape 4 does it right), remains a source of stigma for some netters with long memories.

Critics offer the æsthetic complaint that anchors are ugly. Admittedly, a URL like http://store.newriders.com/products/clark/#bio has a face only a mother could love, but URLs are typically hidden from real-world users. (Using a title on your ‹a›‹/a› tags further distracts people from the status line where URLs are displayed in most graphical browsers, unless of course you use a JavaScript function like onload="window.defaultStatus='*text*'" to hide the URL completely.)

It has even been suggested that anchors are not "proper" or standards-compliant HTML, which is untrue.

None of those objections, then, holds water. Here are a couple that do:

- If the link and the destination are both visible onscreen in a graphical browser, and if the browser window is larger than all the content after the destination such that no scrolling is possible, selecting the link will do nothing whatsoever. (Why should the browser transport you to the anchor location when it's already right in front of you?) This confuses the heck out of people, including me, but it is self-evidently the correct approach.
- Even when scrolling happens, exactly where are you supposed to direct your attention? Browsers tend to place the anchor destination at the top of the screen, but which specific word, phrase, or image corresponds to the destination? Where are you supposed to look? Browsers do not highlight the destination text, something that is clearly possible technically: Google's cached search results highlight individual search words, and browser Find functions tend to do the same.

If you the author use a paragraph as anchor but really intend only a few words within the paragraph as the destination, don't people have to sit there and figure out which exact words they're supposed to be looking at? But if you go out of your way to be precise and use only the truly relevant segment of a paragraph as your destination, aren't you sending people to the middle of a paragraph? Don't they have to back up and read the whole paragraph just to understand what's going on? And if you use an image as a destination, how will that be entirely clear? While these are minor annoyances to sighted people (and this discussion is a tad abstract), they become a bigger deal for screen-reader users, who, you'll recall, cannot simply flit their eyes from location to location on a page. Sequential reading access, already confusing some of the time, becomes very confusing much of the time when anchor links are used.

It is unrealistic to expect Web authors to create separate files for each and every conceivable subdivision of a page merely to overcome the modest usability defects of anchors. Just think of a résumé: Do you really want the Education, Work Experience, and Career Goals sections to appear on different documents? Such an arrangement defies centuries of information design in the print medium, of which the Internet is merely an extension, not a refutation.

Besides, the problem of locating specific passages is in fact a holdover from print: Reference books (particularly in law, but think also of canonical works like religious texts) will list not only page number but also column and paragraph numbers to lead you to an exact target. HTML anchors are stepchildren of that practice.

And have you ever tried to locate a specific scene on a home videotape or find a few words on an audiocassette? How about locating a specific lyric in a song on a compact disc? The inconvenience of sequential access has antecedents in oldschool electronic media.

It remains unrealistic, moreover, to expect Web authors to cease using anchors because screen readers have a tough slog in grinding through unstructured text. There are some things we simply cannot do online, and providing random access to the contents of a Web page through speech or Braille is one of them.

Use anchors where necessary. It's that simple.

External navigation

Now that we've gotten the rather special case of within-page navigation over with, let's consider the kind of navigation that dominates the net: Between pages, wherever they may be hosted.

Terminology

There may be a few terminology issues here. Some phrases in current use:

- *Left-hand navigation*: Placement of navigation links at page left (for pages written in left-to-right languages, at least), usually in a table cell. Also achievable with all-stylesheet layouts. The typical appearance of this design in graphical browsers shows a column of links on the left-hand side of the page, hence the name. (We can also call it fixed navigation, since the navigation stays entirely or grossly the same from page to page and day to day.)
- *Top* or *bottom navigation*: Links at page top or bottom, respectively. Top navigation is often graphical; bottom navigation is usually text, very often provided as a rudimentary form of accessibility.
- *Navbars*: Navigation bars or banners of navigation links, usually graphical and usually horizontal. (Would they still be "bars" if they were vertical, or do they become "navcolumns"?)

It remains unrealistic, moreover, to expect Web authors to cease using anchors because screen readers have a tough slog in grinding through unstructured text. There are some things we simply cannot do online, and providing random access to the contents of a Web page through speech or Braille is one of them.

We're also dealing with the confusion caused by a single word with more than one meaning, and that word is *tabs*. I will often refer to the Tab key on a keyboard (note the capital letter). *Tabbing* refers to repeatedly depressing the Tab key. The term is used generically here, as "click" is used even if the visitor selects with a keyboard, not a mouse. Tabbing also encompasses the very inconvenient switch access, whereby a mobility-impaired person wades through sequences of possible actions and selects one at a time.

However, *tabs* as a navigational user-interface feature on a Website refer to Amazon-like graphical trapezoids, rectangles, or ovals that overlap or abut like shingles or simply sit there in a row and, when selected, take you to the section specified by their legends. Where necessary, I'll refer to these as "navigation tabs."

Another relevant concept is *focus*. An element on a Web page is said to have focus if it is selected or active or if the next action taken will apply to it. When you click a link, it has focus. When you tab *onto* a link but do nothing to it, the link has focus. If you select text in the browser window, that text has focus. If you merely click inside the browser window, it gains focus.

If you then move up to the address bar and type in a new URL, the address bar has focus. All very clear-cut examples. But sometimes it isn't so obvious. For example, if you select a Website from your graphical browser's bookmarks, its address will appear in the URL field and the page contents will display in the browser window as selected text. OK. So what happens if you press the spacebar? Will you replace the selected URL with a space character or will you scroll the contents by one screenful? Where is the focus?

Some browsers, like iCab on Macintosh, assume you want to scroll and force you to re-select the URL field if you really want to manipulate it. Others, like Explorer, retain the "selected" state of the URL text but explicitly alter the focus to the content area; click in the URL field again and you'll see that the full text is still pre-selected.

The issue of focus, then, is actually quite familiar. It just doesn't come up too much in everyday Web-surfing. In accessible navigation, you can't get away from it.

By the way, software tends to keep track of focus by tracing the location of an internal cursor or caret, a word you may recall as the name of the circumflex character in ASCII, ^. There may be more than one caret at any given time: The browser may place its focus in one spot, a plug-in (like Acrobat Reader) in another, and a screen reader in a third. Or there may be multiple possible carets, only one of which is in effect at any given moment.

Inconvenience and usability

It is somewhat inconvenient for a screen-reader or Braille-display user to contend with extensive navigation, like top or left-hand navbars with dozens or hundreds of links. The inconvenience stems from having to listen to the links in sequence; they cannot be skipped over or scanned visually.

The same scenario is massively inconvenient for a mobility-impaired person, particularly one using switch access. It takes a great deal of physical effort (exactly what is at a premium for someone with such a disability) to skip unneeded links.

It is bad accessibility practice to assume that your site is perfectly accessible merely because all images are accessible (always the biggest issue) and your site seems to meet every requirement. If there are a great many links or other intervening items to skip over between the top of the page and where the visitor actually wants to go, accessibility here overlaps significantly with usability. A hard-to-use site becomes an inaccessible site even if every other issue has been taken care of.

Years from now (see Chapter 15, "Future dreams"), Websites may be automatically self-reconfigurable to do things like shunting all the navigation to the *end* of a page. (All you the visitor would need to do is set a preference, which could be saved in a cookie.) The Composite Capabilities/Preferences Profiles Working Group at the World Wide Web Consortium (CCPP.org) is trying to make all this happen.

But we do not live in that idealized future. At present, we are forced to retrofit existing Website *concepts* like top and left-hand navigation.

> A hard-to-use site becomes an inaccessible site even if every other issue has been taken care of.

How and why to skip navigation

It is time, then, to bring up one of the rare cases in which you may be forced to add a visible element to your page to make it accessible. It isn't all that onerous, and you may be able to use an HTML accessibility code in addition to this mechanism or instead of it, though there are many provisos.

Let's start out by discussing the worst-case scenario – using plain-Jane HTML and visible added elements for accessibility. Later, I'll show you how to do the same thing with access-specific HTML, and finish with advice on which of those approaches to select.

Note that if your graphical browser lets you tab from item to item on a page (Netscape and Explorer on Windows let you do so, as do Explorer on Macintosh and Opera on all platforms, though Opera uses different keystrokes), then you can test the plain-Jane-HTML techniques yourself without any adaptive technology whatsoever.

LEFT-HAND NAVIGATION: TOO MANY LINKS

Left-hand navigation has become the norm among commercial sites online. While some designers use frames, piling dozens or a hundred links in a ‹td›‹/td› appearing early in a table row is an accepted practice. There's nothing wrong with it, no matter what some design purists would have you believe.

Here is the problem, though. With certain browsers and with certain older screen readers, you are stuck reading table cells in a linear order, rather like tiling a floor: Odds are you'll start at the upper-left cell, move across the first row a cell at a time, and then restart at the extreme left of the next row down. That's how tables are *linearized*.

For an all-stylesheet layout, dumber devices will read out page contents in the exact top-to-bottom order in which divs appear in the source HTML.

If you're using left-hand navigation, someone reading tables in a linear fashion will be presented with the entire contents of the cell, which in this case means dozens of links. And I really mean dozens of links: The homepage at ChicagoTribune.com presents me with 99 navigation links on what would be the left side of the screen in a graphical browser.

Visitors who cannot readily skip all those links must either page through them (as with Lynx, a text-only browser), or move the cursor to select each link in turn (as with some mobility-impaired people using any kind of browser), or attempt to skip the links using software commands, if that is even possible. But in doing so, visitors may skip links they actually want along with those they do not.

As a veteran Lynx user, let me tell you how it works. When presented with dozens of navigation links, I press the spacebar over and over again to bypass them a screenful at a time. If the first link of any resulting screenful happens to be a text field (e.g., a search box), I have to move the cursor off the field with the Downarrow or Tab keys, then keep on paging through the links. Or I can guess how many screenfuls of links are present and skip beyond that screenful: Typing 5p (p for *page*) brings me to the fifth screenful.

But I have it easy. While some mobility-impaired people do in fact repeatedly press the Tab key to move around a page, some people with more severe disabilities use adaptive technology that runs through a sequence of possible actions ("switch access"). You have to wait until the keyboard action comes up, then home in on the Tab key (which itself could take many steps), then actuate it. How would you like to go through that 99 times just to skip nagavation?

Then what if the link you really want is actually near the bottom of the page?

How long would you put up with that, if you don't already?

The table hack

If you use tables to lay out your page – and there will be *no* reason to stop doing so outright until most people online use browsers that can reliably render all-stylesheet layouts – you can take advantage of absolutely the cleverest trick in the brief history of Web design, the *table hack*.

Newspaper sites are notorious for piling dozens and dozens of links in left-hand navbars, causing extreme inconvenience for anyone with a mobility impairment: Imagine tabbing your way through link after link just to get to the actual editorial copy in the middle of the page. Screen-reader users also have to jump over these extraneous links, which, moreover, aren't even that usable for nondisabled people, either.

I credit Mark Pilgrim (a technical editor of this book; DiveIntoMark.org) for the idea, but he traces it back to Lauri Harpf of the Website APromotionGuide.com.

Our problem, you will recall, is that the top left cell in a layout table contains dozens of navigation links. Actual "content" appears in the cell immediately to the right (in a typical layout). Schematically, it looks like:

```
<tr>
<td colspan="height-of-full-table">Navigation links</td>
<td>Content</td>
</tr>
```

In the table hack, the top-left cell is replaced by a spacer GIF. But the next cell in the same row is unchanged: It's the "content" cell. The following row's first cell contains the navigation. You make it all work visually with colspan and valign attributes.

When read serially, it goes like this:
- Spacer GIF (rendered invisible with alt=""; a screen reader might beep to indicate a graphic, but that's about it)
- Main content (of any length)
- Navigation

And the HTML looks like:

```
<tr>
<td valign="top"><img src="spacer.GIF" alt="" width="1" height="1" border="0" title=""></td>
<td colspan="2" valign="top">Content</td> </tr>
<tr>
<td valign="top">Navigation</td> </tr>
```

The colspan="2" attribute merely makes the content cell twice as high as the other cells under discussion, one of which already measures a mere one pixel in height and width – unnoticeable in typical layouts. (You can futz with cell backgrounds if necessary to make it unobtrusive.) The navigation cell seems to sit at the far upper left to a sighted visitor; nothing looks different because the one-pixel spacer GIF is unnoticeable. But when experienced serially, you get the content first, navigation second (with, in some cases, a small screen-reader indication of the existence of a graphic, as through a beep or notification sound; it's up to the screen-reader user to deal with those details, not you).

Astonishingly, even *shockingly* simple, isn't it? It's a "Why didn't I think of that?" idea. Devilishly clever. And something I hadn't though of myself or had ever heard about until very late in the day.

This entire chapter is designed to accommodate people who lack neurosurgeon-calibre hand–eye coördination

Now, in subsequent sections here, I'll teach you the labyrinthine and painful procedures for skipping not merely left-hand navigation but anything else "extraneous" on the page, but nothing is going to approach the simplicity of the table hack. If you are forced to present enormous numbers of navigation links and if the only page element you wish to make easy to skip is that collection of links, then stick with tables and hack away!

Bypassing navigation

Now that we've learned the easy method, the fun is over. How do you code a Website to skip navigation if you're not using the table hack?

The gratuitous use of Flash on Websites – "Flashturbation" – has single-handedly spawned a new Internet buzzword: skip intro. Now I'm teaching you something else we sometimes need to skip – extensive navigation links. In certain cases, you will need to add an entirely visible hyperlink, a navigation-skipper, to your pages.

LINK FORMAT

We'll consider the link first and the anchor locations later. The link should look like this:

```
<a href="#body" title="Skip navigation">Skip navigation</a>
```

You can use whatever terminology you like for the title and link text. Feel free to add a little zing.

- `<a href="#body" title="Skip to article">Skip to article</a>`
- Site contents (`<a href="#body" title="Go directly to site contents">skip</a>`)
- `<a href="#body" title="[Read article]">Read article</a>`
- Don't need navigation? `<a href="#body" title="Skip navigation">Skip it!</a>`

Keep them visible!

Well-intentioned developers who already use page anchors to skip navigation will go to the trouble to set the anchor text in the tiniest possible font in the same colour as the background, rendering it invisible to graphical browsers (unless you happen to pass the mouse over it and notice the cursor shape change).

Or they'll use an invisible graphic (like a single-pixel GIF) with an alt text reading "Skip navigation" or equivalent. Here's an edited, but genuine, example from CNN.com:

```
<a name="top_of_page">
</a> <a href="#ContentArea">
<img src="1.gif" width="10" height="1" border="0" alt="Skip to main content"
align="right"></a>
```

An image ten pixels wide by one pixel high is essentially invisible. It's entirely invisible if its colour matches the background and it lacks a border, or, of course, if it's a transparent GIF.

This example, from the *Sydney Morning Herald* newspaper site at SMH.com.au, is super-minimalist:

```
<a href="#skip"><img src="/media/core/1x1clear.gif" alt="[skip navigation links]"
border="0" width="1" height="1"></a>
```

Individual pixels (in this case, a 1-by-1-pixel GIF) *can* be distinguished: Liquid-crystal displays often saddle you with a noticeable dead pixel or two. But in that case you're staring at the screen all day, and the dead pixel doesn't move. On a Website, a single pixel is fleeting. And besides, GIFs can be transparent. Even if the page background were black and the 1-by-1 GIF were white, nearly everyone would miss it nearly all the time. Nobody would think to click it. And only seasoned neurosurgeons would have enough hand–eye coordination to actually hit a single pixel with a mouse. This entire chapter is designed to accommodate people who lack neurosurgeon-calibre hand–eye coordination.

> The range of concepts that can be reliably evoked in little pictures is about as wide as a fly's wingspan. Words come first, then pictures, not the other way around.

Moreover, in late 2000 a nefarious use of 1-by-1 GIFs was discovered: Web bugs. Advertisers embed them in HTML-formatted E-mails and in Websites; once loaded, they register that your net connection is active, and permit the advertiser to place a cookie on your machine, read your E-mail address, or do something else without your knowledge. Reliance on single-pixel GIFs for navigation-skipping may be benign, but this subsequent use has cast suspicion on the entire practice.

TRADING OFF DISABLED GROUPS

In any event, the theory here is that, since Lynx users require a navigation-skipper, and since there is no such thing as small or invisible text with Lynx, and since alt texts are always displayed in Lynx, a hidden link serves Lynx adherents without inconveniencing anyone else. Similar reasoning applies to screen-reader users: The screen reader will enunciate the link, which the visitor can then select, skipping over the audible reading of up to 99 link titles.

Like a lot of kludges, this actually works quite well. But blind visitors are not the only ones inconvenienced by too many links in a navigation area. Recall that a mobility-impaired person with poor adaptive technology might be stuck tabbing through that morass. But, unless that person is also using Lynx or a screen reader (not impossible, but exceedingly rare), the skip-navigation link will remain invisible.

Why? A graphical browser with image-loading turned on (as is the norm) will load the essentially-invisible image, and the visitor won't notice it. With image-loading deactivated, the image is too small to display the alt text in its bounding box. Although some browsers expand the image space to display the alt, there are limits to the size of such expansion. You can't rely on it. Sometimes the visitor has to run the mouse over the image to see the expanded alternative text. But you won't run your cursor over something you don't know is there, and this mobility-impaired group isn't using a mouse in the first place.

Even if you place the navigation-skipper high up on the page and assume the visitor will tab onto it quickly, there is no reason to think the visitor will notice the link (it's too small), let alone understand its function. (Try it yourself. Even if your browser highlights successive links with a coloured border, can you spot a coloured border slightly bigger than ten pixels wide and a single pixel high? How about a coloured border surrounding a single dot? The purpose of the link is unclear, isn't it?)

We're not done yet: If you helpfully add a title to the link so that a tooltip will pop up in a graphical browser explaining the link's purpose, keep in mind that tooltips are tied to mouse movement. Navigating links by keyboard does not trigger a tooltip in any browser currently available. (Arguably, that needs to be fixed. Keyboard and mouse operation should be equivalent.)

You're not going to like this, but to make a lengthy list of links accessible, your "Skip navigation" link must be visible. It doesn't have to be intrusive, but it has to be apparent and self-explanatory in all browsers.

In evaluating your sites for accessible navigation, you will need to make intelligent decisions about landmarks on your pages.

Most of the time, it's enough to build the word "skip" or equivalent into the header of your navigation. Yes, I know, I promised I would make accessibility less of a pain in the arse. I'll have to make it up to you somewhere else.

Anyway, I would suggest a few model approaches:

```
<p><small>SITE CONTENTS (<a href="#body" title="Skip
navigation">skip</a>)</small>
```
is perfectly legal

Or, to reduce the conspicuity of capital letters, you could use a stylesheet to format small capitals. If your default font size is 12 pixels, you could use:

```
.caps { font-size: 10px; font-weight: normal; letter-spacing: 1px }
```

The last declaration above adds a wee bit of space between letters to pay respect to typography. Or use font-size: smaller instead of a specific size. Then code your header thus: <span class="caps">SITE CONTENTS</span> (<a href="#body" title="Skip navigation">skip</a>).

You could use a tiny graphic, a picture of text, in which is embedded a graphic image of the word "skip" (with required alt and title, of course).

Cries of woe at polluting your magnificent Web design with the single visible word "skip" ring somewhat hollow here. We're talking about a huge column of links, something that isn't exactly as beautiful as Liz Taylor in

Cleopatra. Even if you use a beautiful imagemap, it can't be *that* beautiful and will not be rendered *that* ugly by shoehorning in four wee characters.

Text, not icons

More philosophy:

Visualists embrace the utopian ideal that concepts can be boiled down to pictographs, transcending specific languages, which, the theory holds, inevitably someone will come along and fail to understand. The impression is that pictographs, through their "universality," are pure and noble, while specific languages, with their intimations of the Biblical tale of Babel, are sullied and improper.

Well, here's a newsflash for all the philosopher-kings and -queens out there: The range of concepts that can be reliably evoked in little pictures is about as wide as a fly's wingspan. Words come first, then pictures, not the other way around.

It is unwise to attempt to shoehorn complex ideas into stick-figure pictographs. There aren't a lot of pictographs that actually are universally understood on the Web. You might think that a little graphic of a house deployed to mean "homepage" might be one of them. To my chagrin, sites written in languages other than English have adopted it, which staggers the imagination given the gulf in meaning between "house" and "home" *in the original English.* It shouldn't even work there, let alone in other languages, where the English concept of "home" is often untranslatable and where the word "homepage" has a specific translation already in that language. Does your Website actually have a "housepage" if you use that navigation icon?

It will come as no shock to you that I strongly urge you not to attempt to dream up some kind of half-arsed pictograph for the concept "skip navigation." What are you going to use – a (leap)frog? a kid on a pogo stick? an arrow encircling a blob?

The solution is to use a word like "skip." Don't try to draw us a picture. But nothing says you cannot render the word in legible but discreet graphic form (a picture of text), with appropriate alt and title.

A final no-no: Don't try to double this function up with unrelated graphics. Do not, for example, turn the company logo into a navigation-skipper – unless you're also willing to add the words "Skip navigation" to the logo.

Where should the link end up?

Now that we have scrutinized the entrails of *coding* a navigation-skipper, just where should you end up when you select it?

The easy answer is: At the first point on the page that follows whatever you're skipping and represents actual content.

That point could be anything: A headline; a block of text; an image; a "slug" (listing of the current date and time, or an article byline); or – get this! – even more navigation.

In evaluating your sites for accessible navigation, you will need to make intelligent decisions about *landmarks* on your pages. Like a frog leaping across a pond from lily pad to lily pad, you are obliged to imagine which parts of your page can be skipped and which can be destinations.

BASIC CODING

Let's consider the simple case in which there is a clear distinction between navigation and "content" on a page. Here you'd need a simple anchor at the top of the content section.

```
<td><!– Start of real content (DO NOT DELETE) –>
<a name="body" id="body"></a>
```

If you're using Web-design software or, worse, a content-management system, vigilance may be required. You don't want your software doing your thinking for you and nuking your anchor tag. That may be especially true if you take the modern approach and simply add an id attribute to any arbitrary tag; your authoring program may nuke it behind your back.

That may be the simplest case, but the technique is transferable. You can set up as many anchors for navigation landmarks as you need. As you know already, your "skip" link would point to this anchor. In fact, the examples listed in the "Link format" section would immediately work here.

MORE THAN ONE NAVBAR

What if you've got more than one navigation area on your page? It's a pretty typical design, thanks to E-commerce sites like Amazon: A graphical navbar up top (maybe with tabs you can click) bolstered by left-hand navigation, quite likely in the form of simple text links.

Top and left navigation represent separate modules in appearance and function. It would be presumptuous to assume that a disabled visitor would want to skip both in their entirety. If you want to provide access through navigation-skipper links, don't force people to overshoot the mark by zipping from top navbar directly to page content, bypassing left-hand navigation.

There is no single solution to the problem, and you are hereby empowered to make intelligent judgement calls on which approach to take.

If your top navbar has only a few links (fewer than ten Tab keystrokes' worth, say – put yourself in the position of someone using only the keyboard) but your left-hand navigation has many more, you could probably get away without a "Skip navigation" link up top. Yes, you're expecting your visitors to page through those fewer-than-ten links, but that's tolerable if and only if you let people skip the mass of left-hand links. In this case, your table structure might look like this:

```
<table>
<tr><td>Company logo, or blank</td>
<td>Top navbar</td></tr>
<tr><td><a href="#top" title="Skip to content">(Skip)</a><br />Left-hand
navigation</td>
<td><a name="top">Regular page content</a></td></tr> </table>
```

For a top navbar with a plethora of links (like a set of navigation tabs), provide a navigation-skipper link on that top navbar. The destination of that link should be the top of the *next* navigation group (e.g., left-hand navigation). Don't use the first *content* cell as target.

Why?

A visitor can use any of the top navbar's links. Or the visitor can skip that navigation and end up at the beginning of the left-hand navigation region, making use of any of those links – or none of them, by skipping that group entirely. Remember, the whole purpose of this exercise is to spare people the necessity of tabbing through dozens of links they do not want without isolating them from links they do want.

Your HTML might look like this:

```
<table>
<tr><td>Company logo, or blank</td>
<td>
<a href="#left" title="Skip to next navigation block">(Skip)</a> Top navbar
</td> </tr>
<tr>
<td><a name="left"></a><a href="#top" title="Skip to content">(Skip)</a>Left-
hand navigation
</td>
<td>
<a name="top">Regular page content</a>
</td> </tr> </table>
```

It is legal to place empty <a></a> tags alongside one another. Targets must precede links. (You don't want an overlap.) You may, if you wish, use a non-breaking space character, , as a kind of placeholder within <a></a>, but

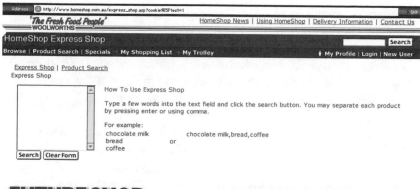

A search field located at the upper left of a page has become, in the post-Amazon era, a kind of standard, though just how it is applied may vary. (The first example has two search fields, one of them the size of a Hotmail text-entry field.)

my testing shows it to be unnecessary. Empty `<a></a>` tags work fine. So does adding an id to any arbitrary tag.

If your top navbar doesn't sit in a table (if it's one big image, or two side-by-side), the approach is unchanged. If you're using stylesheets for positioning rather than tables, the approach is also unchanged, keeping in mind that dumb devices will interpret and present to the visitor the contents of divs in the strict top-to-bottom order in which they are found in your source code. While that seems to solve the problem, here in the real world about the only device that does not understand stylesheets is Lynx; remember that screen readers sit on top of browsers, and nearly all those browsers interpret stylesheets.

TARGETING SEARCH

Search functions merit a certain wary or begrudging respect and are important enough to demand special treatment.

Amazon's search-box placement, at top left, has become a standard — a standard, but not the only one. I've seen search boxes at screen top, screen bottom, both (which I often use), and on the right. Since there are only four sides to a computer monitor, that pretty much covers all the options. (How often do you find a search field smack dab in the *middle* of a page? Occasionally, I suppose — on pages that do nothing but provide a search facility.)

If your search box is located at left or up top in a table-based layout, it will appear high up in a linearization of that table. While this is desirable, we mustn't forget all the other links that stand between the very top of the page and the search box. Will you need to provide a navigation-skipper?

Possibly. You can figure that out yourself at this point. But what you must not do is *skip the search*. If you're stuck tabbing through links on a page, search is a target of interest, not filler or an impediment. Make sure any search function that might otherwise be skipped is actually the target of the immediately-preceding navigation-skipper. If your left-hand navigation sits on top of your search box, your code could look like this:

```
< table >
< tr >< td colspan="2" >< a href="#left" title="Skip to next navigation
block" >(Skip)< /a >Top navbar< /td >< /tr >
< tr >< td >< a name="left" >< /a >< a href="#searcher" title="Skip to
search" >(Skip)< /a >Left-hand navigation
< a name="searcher" >Search fields< /a >
< a href="#top" title="Skip to page contents" >(Skip)< /a >< /td > < td >< a
name="top" >Regular page content< /a >< /td >< /tr >
< /table >
```

In this example, navigation-skippers move the cursor from top navbar to left-hand navigation to the search mechanism to the page content, by selecting your nav-skipper links in that order.

If your search box sits on top of your left-hand navigation (the converse of the previous example), you could write HTML like so:

```
< table >
< tr >< td colspan="2" >< /td >< td >Top navbar< a href="#searcher" title="Skip to
next navigation block" >(Skip)< /a >< /td >< /tr >
< tr >< td >< a name="searcher" >< /a >Search facility
< a href="#top" title="Skip to content" >(Skip)< /a >Left-hand
navigation< /td >< td >
< a name="top" >Regular page content< /a >< /td >< /tr > < /table >
```

What if your search facility lives on its own separate page? In other words, what if a visitor has to select a link to call up a separate page where he or she can run a search? This is unusual and certainly unwise (don't make people search for search!), but if you insist on this practice, make the link to the search page a destination in the skip order.

(This approach is unrelated to a search box that provides a basic text field right then and there and a link to a separate page for advanced searching. There are no specific access issues in that case. Normal cautions about adding text equivalents for graphics apply.)

Other landmarks

What other navigation landmarks are so important that you shouldn't skip them? What objects should become landmarks?

- A login section, with userID and password fields.
- Links to printable pages, "E-mail this article" functions, or similar alternate versions.
- Links to sidebars in an article (that is, supplementary articles).
- Next, Back, and Top of Page buttons.
- On a personal homepage, possibly a contact or mailto: link.
- Maybe bottom-of-page navigation, if you use it, but even then that may be a redundant destination if left-hand or top navigation is the same as bottom navigation. If they're different – well, "*Why* are they different?" is what I'd ask first, after which I would recommend adding it to the sequence of destinations.

> What if you could set up a Website so that whenever we hit a key something happened?

Page extremities

At the very end of your page content, you may use a "Back to top of page" link. For mobility-impaired people with no mouse access, there may be no immediately-evident reason to make that link a destination for navigation-skipping. Why? Some people with a mobility impairment relevant to Web accessibility are already using the keyboard. How many keyboards don't have a Home key, or at least PgUp? It would not be flagrantly presumptuous to code your page for the majority with standard keyboards.

(To be fair, a few keyboards lack those keys, particularly on Macs, given Steve Jobs' twenty-year hatred of typing and his unending stream of keyboard designs intended to impair expert touch-typists – like me, I must add. Or hardcore Unix sysadmin types may use the Happy Hacker Keyboard, with roughly the surface area of a FedEx waybill and severely limited function keys. Or, as on a laptop keyboard, you may have to hold down a so-called Fn key to produce those keystrokes, which isn't the sort of thing you want to have to hassle with if you can barely move your hands in the first place.)

Moreover, scrolling to the top of a document does not *deposit the cursor* there, requiring another keystroke or action. And remember users of the laborious adaptive technology known as switch access: Moving through a Website is an exercise in frustration for them. It is incumbent on you to alleviate that frustration.

Accordingly, then, not only is it always wise to make a Back to Top link a landmark on your page, perhaps all your pages ought to carry them, though the latter is just a suggestion.

Now let's consider the other extremity. At the very top of a page, the first item that actually does anything – like a link or a search field or a button as opposed to text or an image – should not be a search box (a text-input or textarea field). Why? Lynx users will find their cursors stuck in that search box because Lynx always selects the very first link or actionable region on a page.

The Lynx cursor is never invisible unless the page has no actionable items whatsoever; the cursor always sits on something. By contrast, graphical browsers hide the fact that they have a cursor at all, unless your browser responds to pressing the Tab key to move from item to item, at which point this cursor (or caret, or focus) pops out from behind the curtain and becomes apparent after all.

One way to fix the problem, if you happen to use a graphic image at the very top of a page, is to make that image a link back to the homepage of the site, a technique that I suppose will not work for the *actual* homepage. It is an imperfect solution for what is admittedly a minority concern.

Right-hand navigation

What if you're a free-thinker who locates side navigation on the right rather than the left? (Or just a part of the navigation, like a search box?)

This is where the training wheels come off. You will need to consider the layout of your page and come up with a logical tabbing order that includes navigation-skippers where necessary. But remember how such layouts would be linearized: Page content would likely appear before your right-hand navigation. Is that really the order in which people should interact with your site? Remember, nondisabled people can ignore the left-side content and skip immediately to the right-hand navigation links, but at this juncture we are not designing for nondisabled people.

It may make sense, then, to devise a skip sequence that puts the right-hand navigation segments before any page content even if that is not how they are coded in the base HTML.

I can envision a few scenarios:

If you have a top navbar and right-side navigation, let people skip from the top navbar to the right-hand navigation to the content. Make a pit stop along the way for search if necessary.

If you have a top navbar, left-hand navigation, and right-hand search, you may wish to skip from the top navbar to the search function, then to the left-hand navigation and finally to the content.

With no top or left navigation and nothing but a header, content, and right-hand navigation, things become conceptually complicated, because tabbing to the next element on the page may take you to a heading or a link *within the actual content*. But a mobility-impaired visitor may wish to skip the screenfuls of content and use the right-hand navigation. Ordinarily, you would embed a skip link in one block of navigation which, when selected, will send you to the next block. But here the first navigation block in the right-hand navbar is actually your destination, isn't it?

The solution may be to place a skip-navigation link before or after your header, making it the first link on the page. With any luck, that will be the first item selected when tabbing. It will surely be the case if you're using an ordinary browser that moves from link to link to link, bypassing everything else, but a visitor's adaptive technology may select the header (if it's in an img element). Still, it only takes one command to move off that header, which is not an unreasonable additional step by any stretch of the imagination.

Your job worsens if you are working in a language written from right to left, at which point what we are calling right-hand navigation here has the same role as left-hand navigation save for the fact that HTML is written in left-to-right English. You the visitor may *read* a Hebrew Website from right to left, but its underlying code has a left-to-right order, particularly where table cells are concerned. Such a dilemma, however, is a tad recherché; I would surmise that designers working in right-to-left languages, now armed with the concepts explained in this chapter, can make intelligent choices.

accesskey is something of a secret for nearly every Web-surfer.

Do I have to do all this?

Do you actually have to go to all this trouble? Just to recap, the answer is "Only if your navigation includes so many links they would be tedious to tab through." If not, the use of navigation-skippers is quite optional.

Alternatives with accessible HTML

Having endured the hazing ritual of HTML gymnastics to skip over extensive navigation, you may now matriculate to the full-fledged use of two HTML accessibility tags, accesskey and tabindex. They are widely applicable to online navigation, but are somewhat poorly supported and bring along their own problems. On the other hand, they're simpler.

Taking over your keyboard

What if you could set up a Website so that whenever we hit a key something happened? It can now be done — at the level of HTML rather than the browser, which already gives you certain keyboard control over Website content, as when you press Control- or Command-leftarrow to go Back one level.

Two tags let you take such control:
- accesskey assigns a character (virtually any imaginable character, not just plain ASCII) to any of several HTML elements, including links,

buttons, and text fields. You can give visitors one-keystroke access to such items.

- tabindex specifies the order in which a visitor will select items with each press of the Tab key or equivalent. Without using any kind of added link like a navigation-skipper, you can cause browsers to skip over whatever items you wish (as long as some other item exists for the cursor to land on).

At this point, you're muttering "Why didn't you say so in the first place?" The answer: Because the tedious and overt navigation-skipper approach works in any browser, while support for accesskey and tabindex is variable.

KEYBOARD NAVIGATION

You might consider accesskey and tabindex as akin to the ball and peen on the end of a handle. Together they make up the tool we know generically as a hammer, but you wouldn't want to mix up the two functions.

accesskey moves you directly *to* somewhere and does something right then and there. tabindex moves you *past* something and requires another step before doing anything.

In a moment of unexpected of clarity, the World Wide Web Consortium documentation of the accesskey attribute is understandable and self-explanatory:

> This attribute assigns an access key to an element. An access key is a single character from the document character set.... Pressing an accesskey assigned to an element gives focus to the element. The action that occurs when an element receives focus depends on the element. For example, when a user activates a link defined by the ‹a›‹/a› element, the [browser or device] generally follows the link. When a user activates a radio button, the user agent changes the value of the radio button. When the user activates a text field, it allows input, etc.
>
> The following elements support the accesskey attribute: ‹a›‹/a›, area, ‹button›‹/button›, input, ‹label›‹/label›, ‹legend›‹/legend›, and ‹textarea›‹/textarea›.

(Well, there is a *wee* ambiguity in the definition, but I'll cover that in due course.)

You simply add accesskey="" as an attribute on your element, inserting the character of your choice between the quotation marks. In page navigation, some examples might be:

- ‹a href="contact.shtml" title="Contact us" accesskey="C"›Contact us‹/a› (pressing C zips you directly to that page)

- [<a href="#top" title="Back to top of page" accesskey="t">Top</a>] (pressing t brings you back to the top of the page)

Or your left-hand navigation, if it is not too extensive, might use a letter or number on every link:

<a href="/home.jsp" title="Company homepage" accesskey="1">Home
</a>
<a href="/about.jsp" title="Company background/Job opportunities"
accesskey="2">About</a>
<a href="/prod.jsp" title="Products" accesskey="3">Products</a>
<a href="/ret.jsp" title="Where to buy" accesskey="4">Retailers</a>
<a href="/phone.jsp" title="Buy by phone" accesskey="5">Shop by
Phone</a>
<a href="/shop.jsp" title="Buy online" accesskey="6">Shop Online</a>
<a href="/contact.jsp" title="Phone numbers and e-mail and postal addresses"
accesskey="7">Contact Us</a>
<a href="/priv.jsp" title="What we do with your personal information"
accesskey="8">Privacy Policy</a>

In this case, all a hypothetical visitor need do is press a number on the keyboard to actuate the link. The effect is exactly the same as clicking the link with a mouse or tabbing onto it and pressing **Return**: The link is *activated* and you immediately go to the destination page.

When to use it

accesskey is the delinquent teenager of accessible HTML. It is difficult to make accesskey work.

The delinquency is mitigated somewhat if you limit your use of accesskey in the first place. Your mental model should be *keyboard shortcuts in software*. Typically, it is *frequently-used* functions to which we assign keyboard shortcuts in software — save, print, quit, cut, copy, paste. For *rarely-used* functions, menus and dialogue boxes are satisfactory.

accesskey is for all practical purposes a keyboard equivalent, though with all too many provisos. Apply accesskey only to very important areas of your page navigation — links that seldom change, if ever. Hit the high points only: It is rarely necessary even to *attempt* to assign an accesskey to every single link. (If you have very simple navigation, you certainly may do so. But adding accesskeys to links inside the "content" of your pages yields rather limited real-world results.)

Among the litany of user-hostile features of Microsoft Windows is the punishing difficulty it poses in typing accented characters.

What's wrong with this picture?

accesskey is something of a secret for nearly every Web-surfer.

True, Internet Explorer on Windows supported accesskey in version 4.0. You can hold down Alt and press the accesskey and it will work. Support was downgraded in IE 5 and later. According to a Microsoft source, "IE will support the accesskey attribute only on elements that you can get to via normal keyboard navigation (by tabbing). To do otherwise would be inconsistent." It's another case of Microsoft's reinterpreting World Wide Web Consortium standards, which specify *exactly* which elements can take accesskey with no "inconsistency" whatsoever.

What's the catch? (You've learned to expect a catch, haven't you?) The visitor does not know what the specific accesskey is. Explorer provides no visible indication that an accesskey even exists. In effect, Explorer plays Rumpelstiltskin, demanding that you say the magic word without knowing what it is.

Oh, but we're not done yet. We've hardly begun to list the incompatibilities. To continue with this example, some accesskeys may conflict with existing Explorer or Windows key commands, like Alt plus the first letter of a menu name, very much including F for File, E for Edit, and H for Help. In that case, by convention but not by any requirement, the accesskey wins out. (The same conflicts come up with Mac OS X 10.1 if you turn keyboard navigation on.)

This is a wee problem. Lots of people use keyboard commands to actuate menus. Keyboard fetishists like me do it all the time, and we're not disabled. And so do a lot of blind people, who are keyboard fetishists by necessity. Use accesskey to help out mobility-impaired people and you get in the way of blind people.

Such a conundrum could have been avoided if browser makers had ever interpreted the accesskey spec correctly. (I don't know of any who do it right.) The problem with accesskey is its name: It's really an access*character*, and you may use absolutely any Unicode character for that function. It all sounds very grand and internationalist.

Yet you still have to *type* the character. And the only time typing a character is an easy process is when you have to press only one key to do it. While it is obvious to everyone that 7 and *e* and # are all distinct characters, keep in mind that *a* and *A* and *å* and *à* are all different, too. In other words, case and accents make letters different. Accordingly, all of the following should be distinct and none of them interchangeable:

Contents

Web AccessiBlog

You're reading<Y> a Weblog of articles and sites dealing with the topic of **Web accessibility** (and not<N> other forms of media access – you can read about those **at my general Media Access page**).

Know of any items to add? **Mail me**. The date an item was added is provided in parentheses.

By press time, iCab remained the only visual browser to display an indication of accesskey assignments by default. The specification permits any character as an accesskey, including punctuation, numerals, exotic punctuation (¶, §, £, ¥, or whatever else), accented characters, and indeed any character that can be expressed in a Web-readable character encoding (like Japanese kanji). Even iCab's valiant efforts to indicate unusual accesskeys fail: Here the program displays everything incorrectly save for accesskey="&". Few of the assigned accesskeys actually work in iCab even if you do manage to type them. And remember, you're looking at the best implementation yet of a World Wide Web Consortium HTML specification that's been on the books since 1999.

- accesskey="7"
- accesskey="e"
- accesskey="#"
- accesskey="a"
- accesskey="A"
- accesskey="å" (that is, å)
- accesskey="à" (à)

In my testing, English-language browsers interpret upper- and lower-case accesskey letters as exactly the same and ignore most accented characters, even if the operating system makes them easy to type. Of the last four items in the list above, the first pair are treated identically (a and A) and the last pair are widely ignored (å and à). Of the seven items above, only three work properly.

accesskey="e" and accesskey="E" are in fact separate but are treated as interchangeable. Yes, on a Latin-alphabet keyboard you must actually press Shift to produce a capital letter, meaning that real-world accesskeys might end up being three-key combinations in Windows Explorer (Shift-Alt-*letter*). But if case were distinguished in interpreting accesskey, then at least accesskeys could be distinguishable from system-level commands (in this case, Shift-Alt-*letter* vs. Alt-*letter*).

This means, of course, that you can introduce your own conflict on a page by using two accesskeys differing only by case.

Nice.

So when do things get better?

You can use numbers – plus, I suppose, punctuation. If you're writing a foreign-language site and expect everyone to have a foreign-language keyboard, you can use an accented character, if it has a dedicated key and if the localized browser doesn't simply replicate English-language behaviour.

However, even keyboards specifically designed to type languages that use accented characters do not always give an accented character a key of its own. French keyboards, for example, may give *é* its own key, because that is the only letter that takes an acute accent in French. You might also find a dedicated *ç* key; no other characters take cedillas in French. But even in French, grave accents, circumflex accents, and diereses (umlauts or *trémas*) require you to press two keys – an accent key (called a "dead key" in oldschool typesetting) and then the character you want it to appear on.

On such a keyboard, you could make accesskey work with *é* or *ç, maybe,* but how do you make it work with *Ï* or *ù*?

If you wanted to enter such characters on an English-language keyboard, how would you do it? Among the litany of user-hostile features of Microsoft Windows is the punishing difficulty it poses in typing accented characters. How do you hold down **Alt** and also produce an *é* to trigger the accesskey when typing the accented letter *itself* requires you to hold down **Alt** and type **0233** on the numeric keypad?

Let us consider the Macintosh case, because typing non-English characters on Macs is quite simple. Here, you can just type **Option-e e** to produce an *é.* Nice and tidy. But will it work? Currently the answer is "probably not." A browser that understands accesskey, iCab on Macintosh, really understands only US-ASCII accesskeys. (You don't need to hold down a modifier key. As long as focus is placed in the browser window by clicking in it or tabbing to it, all you need to do is type the accesskey by itself.) iCab is also the only browser that actually displays the accesskey for you (in a superscribed sequence of ‹*accesskey*›; more details on display issues are coming up shortly).

If you use an extended character of any kind (non-ASCII punctuation or accented letter), iCab may or may not react properly when you type it and almost certainly will not display it properly. (The superscribed sequence is misdisplayed.) In iCab, some accented characters work as accesskey and some do not. Internet Explorer and Mozilla (hence also Netscape 6) on Macintosh ignore accented accesskeys (impossible to type anyway due to the requirement to hold down **Control** to trigger the accesskey).

On all platforms, browsers are not entirely to blame. Various Web Accessibility Initiative documents warn us to take care to provide input meth-

YAHOO! News   News Home - Photos - Help - Close Window

Photo Highlight

Multi. Photos<M> - Hide Summary<H> - Large Photo<L>
Slideshows: Top Stories | Entertainment | Lifestyle/Features | World | Sports | Science | Politics
Tue Jul 9, 4:19 PM ET   Prev.<P> | Start<T> | Next<n>   11 of 83

A Taiwanese rescue helicopter approaches a burning Chinese fishing boat, Tuesday, July 9, 2002, off Kaohsiung, Taiwan. Rescuers saved more than 110 Chinese fishermen from the burning boat as a tropical storm whipped up high seas and gales. (AP Photo/Yang Ja-yu)

It's not widely known, but Yahoo's photo slideshows use accesskey for navigation controls. In a compliant browser (and there are several, including Internet Explorer and iCab), as long as you somehow figure out what the accesskey assignments actually are, you can speed through the photographs by keyboard alone. Note that this example is an unwitting test of browser compatibility, since it uses accesskey letter assignments in both upper case and lower case (accesskey="H" but also accesskey="n"). Technically, what you type must match the case of the accesskey assignment; in practice, case is ignored by browsers.

ods relevant to various modalities (keyboard, mouse, voice, whatever), but accesskey is nothing more than keyboard control of Websites in drag. You could imagine entering an accesskey by voice. But how, exactly?

The entire accesskey system is set up as a keyboard substitute. It only works in some browsers, and is limited to 26 unaccented all-American letters, ten digits, and a few noncontroversial punctuation marks.

If accesskey were really a character you could "enter," then browsers would have to pop up a little windowette in which you could enter the character (using any input method you like, correcting any errors you make), and then press Return or click an OK button to actuate the accesskey. In other words, it would act something like the way Lynx handles numbered hyperlinks and form fields: Just type the number and hit Return and it happens. This, however, remains hypothetical, and massively inconvenient. Why bother? Shortcuts should not be more involved than the action they replace.

The show must go on

The poorly-thought-out accesskey attribute is severely compromised in practical application. I want you to use it anyway. You've got at least 36 characters you can stuff into the accesskey attribute, and that will surely be enough for you.

You need to consider accesskey an *adjunct* to your existing navigation system. Adding an accesskey to a link takes nothing away from that link. It will still work the way links have always worked.

Also, to reiterate, while accesskey can theoretically be added to every link on a page (or about three dozen of them, at least), that could be a case of too

much of a good thing. Use accesskey for major page navigation landmarks —
for only the highest-level or most important navigation links.

For instance, if your left-hand navigation included a list like
the following —

- Products
  - · For the car
  - · For the home
  - · For the office
  - · For the cottage and recreation
- Dealer locator
- Contact us

— it would be apparent that the major categories are "Products," "Dealer
locator," and "Contact us." If any links were crying out for accesskey, those are
the ones doing it.

In this limited example, with only four entries in the Producers subcategory, you certainly could use accesskey. It wouldn't hurt. But limiting the
addition of accesskey to major landmarks only is easier and provides good
added accessibility, all the many incompatibilities notwithstanding.

Overt listing of accesskey values

There's another option, and I've seen it a few times. Either the page that uses
accesskey, or a site help or FAQ page, or an accessibility statement, if there is
such a thing (see Chapter 14, "Certification and testing"), can simply list all
the accesskey assignments in plain readable text. It's a rather brute-force method
that would not be necessary were accesskey better-thought-out in the first place
and better-supported by browsers and devices.

Skipping navigation

Let us cast our gaze back to the entire tortuous concept of letting mobility-
impaired visitors skip huge masses of navigation links. While you can and
should use the oldschool-HTML method, you can add accesskey to your bag
of tricks.

Recall that accesskey can be added to the ‹a›‹/a› element, which we
usually use for hyperlinks in the form of ‹a href=""›‹/a›. That is, as the *source*
or *trigger* of a hyperlink. But remember ‹a id="" name=""›, the named anchor
or destination of a hyperlink? It's still an ‹a›‹/a› element, right?

Shouldn't it be possible to give a name and/or id to navigation blocks and
assign them accesskeys? Visitors could then select those regions via the
keyboard, subject to all the usual accesskey constraints. Couldn't they?
No, as it turns out, they could not. An accesskey merely actuates the element
in which it is included. ‹a href=""› actually brings you somewhere upon
actuation. But there is no particular meaning to the concept of actuation as

applied to ‹a name=""›. How do you actuate an anchor? (Testing shows it does not work.)

However, you can cheat a little bit in HTML. A link to an anchor can be placed anywhere in relation to that anchor. That includes the position of immediately preceding the anchor. This construct is legal HTML:

```
<a href="#zip_to_search" title="Zip to search"></a>
<a name="zip_to_search"></a>
```

The first ‹a›‹/a› links to the second. They just happen to be butting up alongside one another. Since there is no link text, the first ‹a›‹/a› is invisible; the second ‹a›‹/a› would be invisible anyway. Selecting this link via keyboard or mouse would have no particular effect – indeed, it might be impossible. But what happens if we add an accesskey?

```
<a href="#zip_to_search" title="Zip to search" accesskey="S"></a><a
name="zip_to_search"></a>
```

We have thus created a combo of link and anchor that will give itself focus when you press the **S** key, skipping absolutely everything else on the page. Miraculous, isn't it? We'll come back to this technique later.

ANOTHER TECHNIQUE

If the objective here is to let people skip over extensive navigation by moving from module to module without tabbing through the intervening steps, we can combine accesskey with the jiggery-pokery of oldschool HTML.

Let's add another trick. Just as two adjoining ‹a›‹/a› tags are a bit odd and somewhat mind-bending but perfectly legal, it is also legal, if odd and mind-bending, to place some text or a graphic inside the first ‹a›‹/a›:

- ‹a href="#navigation" title="Home | About | Login | Shop | Contact" accesskey="N"›**Top navbar**‹/a›‹a name="navigation"›‹/a›
- ‹a href="#pagetop" title="Company homepage" accesskey="H"›‹img src="/img/top.GIF" width="35" height="20" title="[Back to top]" alt="Back to top" border="0" /›‹/a›‹a name="pagetop"›‹/a›

Now we're able to do more than skip over what we don't want. We can directly select what we *do* want. We can refer to this technique as a link-accesskey-anchor combination.

In both the cases above, the sequence of events goes like this:

- Type the accesskey (by whatever means).
- The accesskey actuates the first ‹a›‹/a› element, which links to the second ‹a›‹/a›.
- The effect is equivalent to selecting everything contained in the first ‹a›‹/a›.

We can now do some entirely new things. Take this example:

```
<table>
<tr><td colspan="2"><a href="#topnav" title="Home, About, Products, Contact"
accesskey="T">Top navbar</a>
<a name="topnav"></a></td></tr> <tr><td><a href="#leftnav"
accesskey="L">First item in left-hand navigation</a><a href="#leftnav"></a>
Other items in left-hand navigation
<a href="#searcher" accesskey="S">Search function</a><a
name="searcher"></a></td>
<td><a href="#top" accesskey="C"></a><a name="top">Regular page
content</a></tr> </table>
```

Now we're able to do more than skip over what we don't want. We can directly select what we *do* want. How? By selecting accesskeys in the above example:

- Type T for top navigation (and then Tab from link to link).
- Or type L for any of the left-hand navigational links (and tab through them).
- Or hit S for Search.
- Or head straight for page content by pressing C.

If you add accesskey, then, you are really coding for a future utopia...

You no longer have to leapfrog over multiple modules to arrive at the module you want. You can bring it into focus immediately.

Display issues

At time of writing, only iCab on Macintosh automatically displays accesskey. It would be an understatement to describe the users of this browser as a minority.

Quite apart from every other roadblock stopping us from using accesskey, this is truly the killer: For users of nearly every browser, every accesskey on your page will be invisible even if their browsers support accesskey. Of course, this is not in any way maddening.

You can kludge together a couple of solutions that make the accesskey visible. One works better than the other.

If your accesskey is a letter (or, I suppose, a number) that actually appears in the text of the link, you can underline the corresponding letter. The el-cheapo way is to use the "deprecated" <u></u> element:

```
<a href="/index.htm" title="Homepage" accesskey="H"><u>H</u>ome</a>
```

Problems? Lots. Text links are underlined by default. Yes, you can and might turn off underlining in your browser or via a stylesheet, but by default the underline is there. People will think it is a link. Worse, interposing a <u></u> element interrupts the word. "Home" is a pronounceable word; "H ome" isn't. Once again, an access provision meant to make life easier for the mobility-impaired gets in the way of the visually-impaired.

Even if you use stylesheets, you still interrupt the word. A style declaration like this —

```
a:link { text-decoration: none }
span.u { text-decoration: underline }
```

— lets you underline arbitrarily-long sequences of characters, but you have to turn the underlining on and off with a ‹span›‹/span› element. While not "deprecated" and thus kosher, you're still breaking up a word:

```
‹a href="/index.htm" title="Homepage" accesskey="H"›‹span
class="u"›H‹/span›ome‹/a›
```

Evolt.org uses this approach. Here, an accesskey="a" is mirrored in an underlined letter A, ‹u›A‹/u›rticles, all within table cells and using accessible form markup of the sort discussed in Chapter 12, "Forms and interaction":

```
‹tr›‹td colspan="2" class="side"›‹strong›‹label
for="article_search"›‹u›A‹/u›rticles‹/label›‹/strong›‹/td›‹/tr›
‹tr› ‹td class="side"›‹input type="text" tabindex="10" accesskey="a"
name="keywords" id="article_search" value="" size="10" maxlength="50"›‹/td›
‹td class="side"›‹input type="submit" tabindex="14" value="Go"›‹/td› ‹/tr›
```

There may be a vaguely tidier solution: The p.initial:first-letter pseudoclass, to which you can apply whatever formatting you like:

```
a:link { text-decoration: none }
p.initial:first-letter { text-decoration: underline }
```

Then you can write your link text with confidence:

```
‹p class="initial"›‹a href="/index.htm" title="Homepage"
accesskey="H"›Home‹/a›‹/p›
```

Your confidence will, however, be shaken once you realize:

- This trick works only on stylesheet-aware browsers, and even they are not required to support the p.initial:first-letter pseudoclass. A fully CSS1-compliant browser can skip that pseudoclass entirely and still honestly claim full compliance.
- You need to wrap every such link in its own paragraph. This is no big deal, as you can style the paragraph's leading and other features at will, but is an additional task.
- Your accesskey choice is limited to the first character of the link. What happens if more than one link shares an initial letter, as in "Contact us" and "Career opportunities"? Or "Support," "Shop," and "Sitemap"?

You'd want to use different accesskeys, which this method of underlined display prevents.

Further, it is not helpful to list the accesskey value inside an image alt text. accesskey helps mobility-impaired people more than blind people, and most mobility-impaired visitors will not have access to the alt text. The issue of making accesskey values actually understandable and usable to visitors is not easy in the first place, but this is the wrong way to do it.

Possible solution

If we accept the principle that you have to make your accesskeys visible, you might as well just add the accesskey after the link. We'll call this an accesskey legend.

```
<a href="/home.htm" title="Homepage" accesskey="H">Homepage</a>
<small>[H]</small> |
<a href="/cust.htm" title="Already a customer? Log in here"
accesskey="L">Login</a> <small>[L]</small> |
<a href="/reg.htm" title="Register to shop" accesskey="R">Register</a>
<small>[R]</small> |
<a href="/search.htm" title="Search" accesskey="S">Search</a>
<small>[S]</small> |
<a href="/loc.htm" title="Store locations (and phone numbers) and opening
hours" accesskey="H">Locations &amp; Hours</a> <small>[H]</small> |
<a href="/cc.htm" title="Apply for a credit card" accesskey="C">Credit
card</a> <small>[C]</small> |
<a href="/about.htm" title="About us" accesskey="I">Company info/a>
<small>[I]</small> |
<a href="/faq.htm" title="FAQs" accesskey="F">FAQs</a> <small>[F]</small>
```

You can use whatever typography you like: <letter>, letter by itself, letter* with the asterisk as a link to a little explanation of accesskey.

You can add a title to the accesskey legend to explain the system you're using to a nondisabled visitor, or a mobility-impaired person who can handle a mouse for limited periods, or a screen-reader user.

```
<span style="font-size: smaller" title="Press this key (on Windows, use Alt plus
the key)">[S]</span>
<span title="Press to activate: S, Alt-S, or Ctrl-S"><small>[S]</small></span>
```

Now, since we have a multiplicity of keystrokes available to select an accesskey on our many browsers and platforms, we do not enjoy the luxury of a single keystroke to cite in the instructions above. So we end up stuffing the equivalent of a flowchart into our title. And it still might not work.

Are we done yet with the problems? No. For browsers that display accesskey (at present, only iCab), your explicit addition of accesskey legends will result in a double display of the selected accesskey. I suppose this is a lighter cross to bear than keeping the accesskey a secret.

Future plans

If you add accesskey, then, you are really coding for a future utopia where:

- browsers actually implement the XHTML standard, including accesskey, rather than picking and choosing which subcomponents to support
- the standard is clarified to make accesskey either a true accesskey (likely limited to US-ASCII letters, numerals, and some punctuation, irrespective of the damage this does to users of other keyboards) or an accesscharacter (which would require a recommended interface for entering characters that require more than one keystroke)
- visitors can use some capacity other than telepathy to figure out which accesskeys have been defined, and such visual display can be controlled and styled
- conflicts with browser and operating-system keypresses (on all operating systems, not just Windows) have been worked out
- enough other page authors are using accesskeys that your choice to use them will not make you stick out like a sore thumb or attract unwanted questions from your boss or client

I feel honour-bound to provide two pearls of advice that almost nullify one another save for the fact that adding an accesskey is technically simple:

- Include accesskey for very important, seldom-changing navigation landmarks on your pages.
- Expect almost no one to use it.

TABBING, TABBING, AND MORE TABBING

The tabindex attribute is next up to test our patience. When added to certain tags, tabindex determines the order in which those tags are selected with each press of the Tab key.

You can apply tabindex to the following:

- `<a></a>`
- area
- `<button></button>`
- `<input></input>`
- `<object></object>`
- `<select></select>`
- `<textarea></textarea>`

When retrofitting a Website, where do you place the landmarks on a page? Where would you place Skip Navigation links and tabindex attributes so a mobility-impaired visitor could skip tedious or unwanted links? Keep in mind that, in an ideal future, Websites will automatically reorder their contents to suit user requirements, but at present the issue is one of making existing sites less inaccessible. As we'll see in these and other examples, bad usability and overcomplex Web design significantly impair accessibility.

In this very difficult example (note the stack of competing navbars), you'd want the visitor to skip to the search box, then to the separate search tab, then to what appears to be the main topic-related navbar, then to the page's main content, and finally to the login section. Even that many landmarks might be a bit ridiculous.

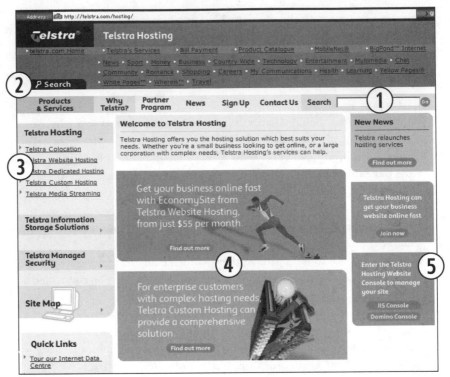

The use of tabindex on <a></a> (that is, hyperlinks) will be of greatest interest here.

The attribute takes the form of tabindex="". You insert a number inside the quotation marks. You can use any number you want, really, between 0 and 32767. Do not use negative numbers.

There is no requirement to use a consecutive sequence; all that matters is that one number must be lower than the next number in the tabbing sequence.

tabindex="0" is the same as having no tabindex at all.

In a hypothetical example consisting of seven links on a page, all of the following would produce exactly the same result – tabbing through the links in the order in which the numbers below are respectively listed.

- 1, 2, 3, 4, 5, 6, 7
- 1, 2, 4, 5, 6, 7, 8 (you can skip numbers at will)
- 1, 32761, 32763, 32764, 32765, 32766, 32767 (the jump from 1 to 32761 is no different from the jump from 32761 to 32763; the first number is less than the second in both cases)
- 100, 200, 201, 202, 203, 204, 300
- 10, 20, 30, 31, 40, 50, 60 (you can insert a number in sequence)

Even personal Weblogs can be complicated enough to warrant navigation-skipping links and tabindex attributes. You the visitor could zip to the search box, then to main content, then to the small navbar listing the last three posts, then to the main left-hand navigation, then to an archive-calendar table (itself tricky to navigate serially), and finally to the contact-the-author link.

In this unusual case, designers provide a link to a separate so-called accessible page (low graphics, and with much less content than the real page used by real visitors). While this is an unwise idea as implemented here, the navigation sequence would involve hitting that accessible-page link first, then the search box, then main content (with a carefully-crafted tabbing order through its two columns), then to the topic-specific and general navbars. Beyond that, skip-navigation links become a tad ridiculous.

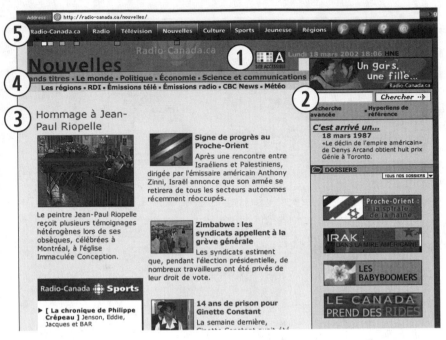

- 07000, 08000, 09000, 10000, 11000, 12000, 13000 (leading zeros are ignored)

To rework a previous example:

```
< a href="/home.htm" title="Homepage" accesskey="L"
tabindex="100">HomePAGE</a> <small>[L]</small> |
< a href="/cust.htm" title="Already a customer? Log in here" accesskey="C"
tabindex="200">Login</a> <small>[C]</small> |
< a href="/reg.htm" title="Register to shop" accesskey="R"
tabindex="300">Register</a> <small>[R]</small> |
< a href="/search.htm" title="Search" accesskey="S"
tabindex="400">Search</a> <small>[S]</small> |
< a href="/loc.htm" title="Store locations (and phone numbers) and opening
hours" accesskey="H" tabindex="500">Locations &amp; Hours</a>
<small>[H]</small> |
< a href="/cc.htm" title="Apply for a credit card" accesskey="C"
tabindex="600">Credit card</a> <small>[C]</small> |
< a href="/about.htm" title="About us" accesskey="I" tabindex="700">Company
info</a> <small>[I]</small> |
< a href="/faq.htm" title="FAQs" accesskey="F" tabindex="800">FAQs</a>
<small>[F]</small>
```

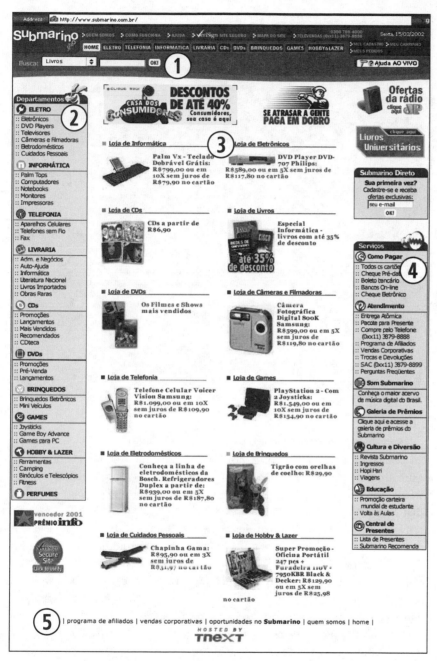

This E-commerce site (an E-commerce site that's not Amazon – believe it or not, they exist) reveals just how tedious it is to navigate link- and content-heavy sites with serial access. And remember, you come here to buy something. Start out at the search box, then the left-hand main navbar (a seeming expansion of the navbar that's immediately above the search field), then to main content (ideally with careful tabindex assignment), then to the customer-service navbar at screen right, and finally to the bottom navbar (important for its links to affiliate programs, jobs, and an about-us page). It's all a bit much, isn't it?

In this case, pressing the Tab key would move you directly to the Homepage link, and then, with each successive press of Tab, to Login, Register, Search, Locations & Hours, Credit card, Company info, and finally FAQs.

Even high-design artistique sites can require navigational retro-fitting. Curt Cloninger, author of *Fresh Styles for Web Designers* and a tech editor of this book, would place this site in the SuperTiny SimCity category. (It's one of many Websites created by Web designers for other Web designers.) Here, the iframe containing news items is clearly the highest-priority landmark. After that, zip to main content, the events listing, the navigation pull-down menu, and the main and right-hand navbars.

Remember, in all these examples, we are merely making navigation less bad rather than setting it up properly, which would require auto-reconfiguration to eliminate unneeded links and to reorder page contents for screen-reader and serial access.

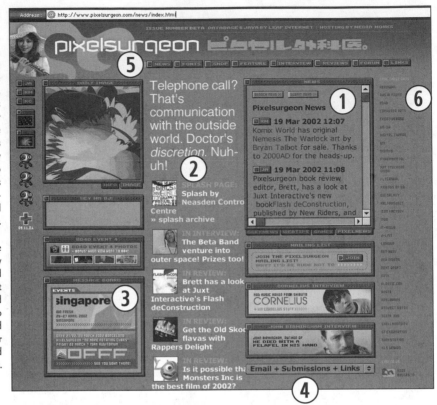

Awesome power, awesome responsibility

tabindex has no overt visible form, nor should it. An indexed tab is not a destination; it is a waypoint in a journey. You learn by doing: You find out where you're going by going there, by pressing Tab and watching what happens.

Now, it could be argued that this approach is not exactly optimal. You're used to tabbing ploddingly from one link (or item) to another, and now all of a sudden your cursor goes where the page author has told it to go.

Such cursor behaviour may come as a surprise, but it should be a welcome surprise. It signifies that you the designer have taken care to make the page accessible to someone using serial access via keyboard.

But with this awesome power comes responsibility. You need to add tabindex judiciously. As with accesskey, in the context of page navigation (as opposed, say, to navigation within forms; see Chapter 12, "Forms and interaction"), you should stick to high-profile navigation landmarks when it comes to tabindex use. Adding a tabindex to every little link on the page rather defeats the purpose; people can tab through every little link already.

What happens when you run out of tags with tabindexes? If you keep pressing the Tab key, where do you end up? This brings up the issue of browser compliance.

- In Internet Explorer 5 for Macintosh, tabindex is correctly supported. Once you're out of discrete tabindex items, you start tabbing through everything from the top of the page, as if there were no tabindexes.
- In Opera 4 and 5, and Internet Explorer 5.5 on Windows, Lynx, Netscape 4 on everything, and Opera and iCab on Macintosh: tabindex is simply ignored. (The magic commands to move through the links on a page in Opera, by the way, are Q to go backward and A to go forward. They're equivalent to pressing the Tab key in other browsers. tabindex remains unsupported.)
- In Netscape 6 and Mozilla: Only links with tabindex are selected, each in order. Then selection restarts from the beginning of the tabindex links. Other items are ignored. This means you can never tab off tabindexed links.

If you click in the document at some specific location, certain browsers (Explorer 4 and 5.01 on Windows, for example) will start tabbing *after* the point you clicked, not from page top. This only makes sense, but is not universal.

What about screen readers? With such adaptive technology, we're suddenly dealing with three levels of abstraction:

- The underlying HTML
- The browser
- The screen reader sitting on top of the browser

Screen-reader makers canvassed on this topic all stated that their devices defer to the browser. They don't particularly bother or attempt to interpret HTML in this case. So if your browser flubs tabindex – if you can never move the focus off tabindexed links and onto all the rest of the links – you have a wee problem. Except that screen readers have built-in controls to move from link to link anyway, and tabindex is of greatest use to mobility-impaired people, not the blind.

Skipping navigation

Can we use tabindex to skip navbars, that bugbear of accessible navigation?

Yes, in fact. Just add tabindex to the first link in each navigation island: First link in top navbar, first link in left-hand navigation.

What about search?

You can add tabindex to form fields, including search fields. You can easily place the form field for your search function in the tab sequence. Be sure to give the submit button the *subsequent* tabindex value. Then you can tab right into the search field, type whatever you want, and then tab directly onto the button that will execute the search.

Here's what I use:

```
<a name="search"></a>
<form method="get" action="http://search.atomz.com/search/">
<input size="20" name="sp-q" value="" accesskey="!" tabindex="20000"
title="Search" />
<input type="submit" value="" accesskey="\" tabindex="20001" title="Start the
search" />
<input type="hidden" name="sp-a" value="000500b5-sp00000004" /></form>
```

Note that I retain <a name="search"></a> as an anchor for any of several other purposes, including the tortuous oldschool-HTML navigation-skipping technique exhaustively documented in these pages.

So do you really need that tortuous oldschool-HTML technique after all? Unfortunately, yes, because it works in absolutely every browser.

You could, in theory, make a reasonable judgement call here. If your server logs show that almost no one is using a browser that does not support tabindex, you could migrate all your navigation-skipping to that method. But as of this writing it is laughably unlikely that any Website on earth would show such a pattern of browser identifiers. This reasonable judgement call turns out to be unreasonable in practice.

Since tabindex support is better than support for accesskey, use of tabindex does not signify coding for a future utopia. It is merely a feature some people can use and some cannot. But then again, so are titles on everything, which Netscape 4 ignores resolutely. I've already suggested adding titles hither and yon and they are imperfectly supported. This is no different.

Numbering

Quickie advice on enumerating tabindexes: You've got 32,768 slots to play with. Don't bunch them all together. There is no reason in the world to use a sequence of 1-2-3-4-5-6-7. What happens if you add a link between 3 and 4?

Even a vast Website with 80 or more navigation links can get away with enumerating tabindex by the hundreds: 100-200-300-400-500-600-700. You can then add intermediate tabindexes as you like. And that sequence works as well as any other ascending sequence. Sequential numbering is not required, or even desirable.

I would stay away from the extreme values of 1 and 32767. It might provide a sort of Cartesian satisfaction to use the very lowest or very highest figure, but you never know when you'll need to add a link to the top or bottom of your page. Even starting at 5 and ending at 32765 gives you some leeway. But there is no reason even to start numbering that low. Use increments of 100 and you can still apply 320 different tabindex attributes, more than anyone would actually want to tab through in the first place. And don't forget that a tabindex of 0 is equivalent to no tabindex at all.

(Why, then, does the W3C bother to list 0 as an option? So that you can add tabindex to every single link on a page but reserve its actual function for only some of the links, providing authoring consistency.)

The database problem

Perennially in this book, we find that maintenance of accessible Web pages is a bother. *Assets* like accesskey and tabindex give us one more thing to keep track of. You can't reuse accesskey assignments or tabindex numbers on a page.

There are advantages to maintaining consistent accesskey assignments or tabindex numbers on pages with equivalent content: Your navbars, if they are the same on multiple pages, should contain the same accessibility features. So how do you do it?

There is no unified method as yet, but some solutions are no-brainers. If you use a server-side include to add common navigation elements to your pages, accesskey and tabindex can be tucked handily away in your <a></a> tags. Ditto with search boxes or anything else consistently served into pages generated from a database.

But what if only certain elements recur in your pages, joined by other custom page-specific elements that are served from a database? You are going to have to come up with a system to avoid accesskey or tabindex conflicts. There isn't an authoring program on the planet that will keep these assets straight for you, though of course there ought to be.

CONFLICT-RESOLUTION TABLES

For accesskey, it may be as simple as maintaining a file in a common server directory that lists which keys are attached to which links and other items. Given that this can change for certain pages, a table or perhaps a spreadsheet could be used to keep these facts straight.

Set up such a table *after* the content of the navigational elements to be served has been decided on but *before* it goes into the database. Assign your accesskeys in your spreadsheet, commit them to the code, and save to the database.

(Given that you are advised to use accesskey sparingly, it will not be a heavy burden to maintain that spreadsheet. On your site, you may use accesskey for only ten or twenty out of thousands of possible links. Not a lot, but what if two of them are both assigned to the letter C? *Conflict resolution*, to coin a phrase, should become part of your production schedule nonetheless.)

To that spreadsheet you could add a quickie explanation of how to arrive at accesskey assignments, e.g., "Use the first letter of the link. If that letter is already taken, try the consonant after the first vowel in the link. Careers = C, Company Profile = M, Contact = N." That sort of thing.

Naming schemes

Since I'm here to solve your problems, I might as well expand that example and give you a few naming schemes you could use for accesskeys.

- Letters for top navigation, numerals for left navigation.
- If two links share a common first letter but at least one link consists of more than a single word, you have the option of using the first letters of *subsequent* words in the accesskey. Skip conjunctions, articles, and other function words: Hyperlink text reading "Press releases and photos" could use accesskey="p" or "r" but not "a".
- Use the *last* letter of a link – either as a first candidate or to resolve conflicts.
- If you use numerals, decide if zero is lowest or highest. Or, better yet, ignore zero because of that ambiguity (and its visual resemblance to O).
- If you run out of numerals and don't want to use letters, one not-so-hot approach is to use the punctuation on the Shift position of those numerals as seen on a U.S. English keyboard, namely !@#$%^&*(. (Remember, we're skipping zero.) There are all sorts of reasons not to do this (what are the symbols called? don't you need to press at least two keys to produce them? don't they look like mistakes, or swear words in old comic books?), but we are talking about battle conditions here.
- Certain punctuation makes sense for certain functions. Exclamation point to deposit the cursor in a form field and slash or backslash to execute a search (i.e., trigger the form submit button) are not bad. (Slash has a bit of a history as a search key, since it is used in Lynx and in vi on Unix. You could also use question mark.) Disadvantages: ? and ! need a Shift key; Alt or Command plus either slash or question mark will often call up a help screen in Windows or Mac OS, respectively.
- Geek sites with a super-hardcore Unix audience may tolerate accesskey assignments reminiscent of vi, elm, emacs, or other keyboard-driven software. For that specific and rarefied audience, punctuation or letter equivalents will have a built-in meaning that may please or reassure the cognoscenti, while of course confusing everyone else.

tabindex TECHNIQUES

For tabindex, you can use a spreadsheet to keep track of which links have which numbers. This task will quickly become even more tedious than sorting out accesskeys because you have thirty-two thousand possibilities at hand. Lessening the burden is the knowledge that only a certain limited range of links deserve tabindex.

Now, what happens if the contents of the link – what's inside the href="" – change continuously, as in a database-driven Website? In your spreadsheet, how do you keep track of which accesskey and tabindex go where?

If a certain string of text within that link never changes, the problem solves itself: Identify the link by that string alone. Examples:

- search-e.php?*lookup* (where an alphanumeric search query is appended to the link): Use "search-e.php" as the identifying string
- .../db/lang/query.php?*lookup* (where the same database architecture is used in various directories differentiated by human language): Use "query.php" as the identifying string

If, on the other hand, the full URL is autogenerated on the fly, and finding a pair of identical URLs is about as easy as matching up snowflakes, your conflict-resolution database may need to refer to the links by the database fieldname.

Since the prime use for tabindex is to provide stable navigation links, such autogenerated URLs may not really come up because autogeneration would not be used in those cases at all. (Why does the link to the Careers page or the search box need database backing? Does it need so much database backing that there is never a consistent string of characters in all variations of the URL?) Occasional examples are, however, possible.

If your site offers a section of, say, Five Most Popular Downloads, you may want to make them a tabbing target with tabindex. But the exact links will change, possibly every few hours.

Here, the Number 1, Number 2, and so on through Number 5 Most Popular Downloads occupy their own conceptual categories. Naturally, people are most interested in Numbers 1 and 5 (top and bottom of the list), but if it appears on the list at all it will be of interest. Maybe people will track the rise or fall of an item. (That's particularly true with a bestseller list, which will surely hold more than five items.)

The exact *identity* of the Numbers 1, 2, 3, 4, and 5 Most Popular Downloads will vary from time to time, but the five *categories* are invariant. You may wish to assign an invariant accesskey to each item in the hit parade, and you may also wish to establish a fixed tabbing order through them.

Your coding could look like this:

```
<ol> <li><a href="<var>database-generated-URL</var>"
tabindex="100"><samp>Number 1 most popular download</samp></a></li>
<li><a href="<var>database-generated-URL</var>"
tabindex="200"><samp>Number 2</samp></a></li>
<li><a href="<var>database-generated-URL</var>"
tabindex="300"><samp>Number 3</samp></a></li>
<li><a href="<var>database-generated-URL</var>"
tabindex="400"><samp>Number 4</samp></a></li>
<li><a href="<var>database-generated-URL</var>"
tabindex="500"><samp>Number 5</samp></a></li>
</ol>
```

If the URL constantly changes, but you want accesskey and tabindex to remain respectively unchanging, what do you do?

In cases like this, let us heed the advice of Rudy Limeback, Toronto Web and SQL consultant (R937.com, Rudy.ca):

> My suggestion is to use a name (like *Favourite1*) *that is stored* in the database and which acts as the selector of the particular database record which is retrieved for this href.
>
> The database should probably also store the accesskey and tabindex for each entry, so that these remain unchanged (or updatable if desired) across all pages that carry that link:
>
> ```
> <a href="database-generated" title="database-generated"
> accesskey="database-generated" tabindex="database-generated"></a>
> ```

In other words, in database-backed sites, you need to add accessibility features to the roster of data you track via the database.

How you do it will depend on your specific system. You know I'm here to help, but I'm not an expert on everything, and one Web topic on which I am assuredly not an expert is database programming; working up executable code you can drag and drop into your back end is half a book in itself, and a coauthored book at that. (Assuming it were even possible. Commercial content-management systems use proprietary coding methods that, apart from being essentially secret, can vary from installation to installation.)

I did do my homework here, querying various vendors of commercial content-management systems, all of whom refused to help. I have, however, given you a set of algorithms you can implement yourself. Some work remains your own.

Navbars and imagemaps

Now that we've gotten that over with, shall we move on to something a bit sexier, like navbars?

The term is rather broadly defined. Any set or block of navigation links can be called a navbar. A few styles are well-known; the continuum is well-represented by the text-only links of Yahoo at the low end, the tabs of Amazon in the middle, and so-called DHTML (dynamic HTML) drop-down menus at the high end.

There aren't a whole lot of accessibility issues in text-only navbars that you don't already know about. They're just links. You may wish to skip some of them, or assign accesskeys or tabindexes. Things get interesting when we concern ourselves with graphical navbars. And that really means imagemaps.

THE BASICS

Note: If you're already familiar with basic HTML, you can skip this section.

An imagemap is a graphic image whose parts are selectable (which usually means clickable).

In a hierarchy of complexity, imagemaps sit one step higher than simple images. You can easily turn an image *as a single unit* into a single hyperlink: Just stick the ‹img› element inside the ‹a›‹/a› element.

```
<a href="home.htm" title="Back to homepage"><img src="/img/home.gif"
height="40" width="30" alt="Homepage" border="0" title="[Back to
homepage]" /></a>
```

In this example, the visitor must select the image to get back to the home-page. The link is a picture. If the picture is absent or you can't see it, the alt and title provide text-only analogues. No problem.

You can, however, subdivide an image so that certain parts are clickable (and, optionally, certain other parts are not). The selectable areas are hyperlinks that are kept logically separate.

To create an imagemap, you use the ‹img› element you have come to consider a close confidant, adding the map="#*name*" attribute. Somewhere else in your HTML document, you define a ‹map›‹/map› with that same *name*; in almost every case, it will contain area elements that map out a set of selectable or clickable image regions.

In the simplest case, inside your ‹map›‹/map› element you list the hyper-links you wish to assign to each region of the image. You can define a region of any arbitrary polygonal shape, but nine times out of ten you'll use a rec-tangular section, which you define using the *x* and *y* pixel coordinates of the top-left and lower-right corners. (Start measuring at the top-left corner.)

A basic example might look like this:

```
<img src="a.gif" width="92" height="89" border="0" alt="About us"
title="Company information" usemap="#ona" />
<map name="ona">
<area shape="rect" coords="0,10,92,27" alt="Contact information"
```

This imagemap is almost perfectly coded for accessibility (all it needs is a title on the map element). Seen in Lynx, the text-only browser, the names of more than two dozen countries with bases in the Antarctic (code .aq, believe it or not) are all individually selectable. The secret? Add titles to everything. This approach is fully usable by screen readers, which will dutifully read out or transcribe the imagemap area titles.

LYNXIMGMAP:

http://www.comnap.aq/comnap/ comnap.nsf/P/Country/ ?Open&Start=1 &Count=4000#map

MAP:

http://www.comnap.aq/comnap/ comnap.nsf/P/Country/ ?Open&Start=1 &Count=4000#map

1. Argentina
2. Australia
3. Belgium
4. Bulgaria
5. Brazil
6. Canada
7. Chile
8. China
9. Germany
10. Ecuador
11. Spain
12. Finland
13. France
14. India
15. Italy
16. Japan
17. Korea
18. Netherlands
19. Norway
20. New Zealand
21. Peru
22. Poland
23. Russia
24. Sweden
25. Ukraine
26. United Kingdom
27. United States
28. Uruguay
29. South Africa

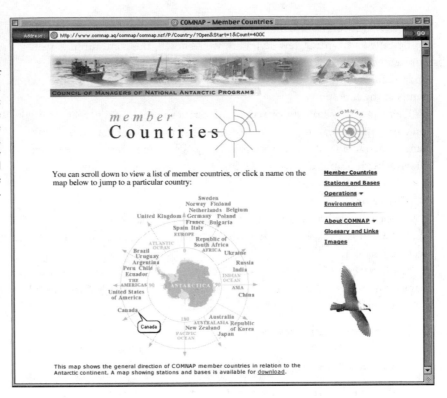

```
href="contact.asp" title="Postal and E-mail addresses, phone and fax numbers" />
<area shape="rect" coords="0,29,92,47" alt="Jobs" href="jobs.asp" title="Work
for us" />
<area shape="rect" coords="0,49,92,67" alt="Privacy policy" href="privacy.asp"
title="How we use your personal information" />
<area shape="rect" coords="0,69,92,87" alt="Copyright" href="copyright.asp"
title="Copyright notice" />
</map>
```

It should be noted that you can include more than a hyperlink in a <map></map>. Any block-level element, like a list or a <blockquote></blockquote> or even a paragraph, can be encompassed within the element. Here in the real world, however, the only use of <map></map> you will run across is the creation of image-based hyperlinks.

ACCESS TECHNIQUES

Surprisingly enough, imagemaps aren't hard to make accessible. HTML keeps the various components of an imagemap separate, and you can add access features to each of them. The results are usually quite pleasant.

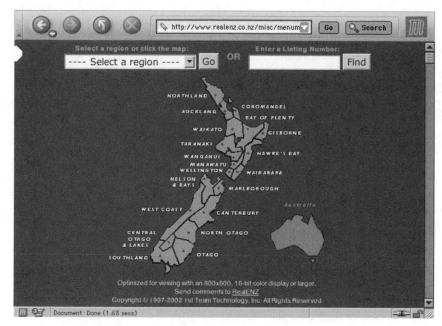

In another geographical example, this New Zealand real-estate locator also gets nearly everything right (but is missing a title on map). Easy to use in text-only or voice or Braille mode.

The alternative in both these cases? Without added titles, you're faced with the raw, savage URLs for each imagemap region. Hardly usable, let alone accessible.

LYNXIMGMAP:
http://www.realenz.co.nz/misc/menumap.cfm#districts

Click to select a Region...

MAP:
http://www.realenz.co.nz/misc/menumap.cfm#districts

1. northland
2. auckland
3. coromandel
4. waikato
5. bay of plenty
6. gisborne
7. hawke's bay
8. taranaki
9. wanganui
10. manawatu
11. wairarapa
12. wellington
13. nelson & bays
14. marlborough
15. canterbury
16. west coast
17. north otago
18. otago
19. central otago & lakes
20. southland
21. australia

Just as adding text equivalents to images is half the battle in Web accessibility in general, adding text equivalents to imagemaps is more than half the battle here. It's dead simple: Just use alt and title on any area that is graphical in nature. (If for some oddball reason you're using a text-only area, which I've never encountered in all my days on the Web, stick to title.)

You must use an alt on all graphics. It's not optional. Graphics inside area are not excepted. title is of course optional but helpful.

Among other things, if you use alt and title on area, Lynx users will have meaningful access to your imagemaps. Typically, Lynx displays a placeholder for an imagemap. Exactly what you see as a placeholder varies: [USEMAP] if you haven't specified an alt on your img link, or of course the actual alt if you have.

In either case, select that link and the otherwise-clickable URLs specified in area are presented as a tidy column of selectable links. That is, the URL is listed, in its full hideous spectacle, unless you have been thoughtful enough to give us a title on each of your areas. Which would you rather look at, a list of raw URLs or a nice tidy word?

(Note the asymmetry: For this specific purpose, you need an alt on the graphic that represents your imagemap and titles on all the selectable areas within it. So why bother with alt on those selectable areas? They're required, first of all, in order for your page to validate as XHTML; otherwise, they are used in the traditional way, as substitutes if the graphic isn't loaded and for assistive technology.)

MSNBC.com does it right on its homepage. Lynx makes it look like this:

TV News
MAP: http://www.msnbc.com/news/default.asp#ona
* Today show
* Nightly News
* Dateline NBC
* MSNBC Cable

Note that the four choices are listed in plain English.

Meanwhile, MSNBC does it quite wrong on the same page:

Navigation
MAP: http://www.msnbc.com/news/default.asp#nmMap
* http://www.msnbc.com/tools/nm/nmo.asp?c=N1
* http://www.msnbc.com/tools/nm/nmo.asp?c=N2
* http://www.msnbc.com/tools/nm/nmo.asp?c=N3
* http://www.msnbc.com/tools/nm/nmo.asp?c=N4
* http://www.msnbc.com/tools/nm/nmo.asp?c=N5
* http://www.msnbc.com/tools/nm/nmo.asp?c=N6
* http://www.msnbc.com/tools/nm/nmo.asp?c=N7
* http://www.msnbc.com/tools/nm/nmo.asp?c=N8
* http://www.msnbc.com/tools/nm/nmo.asp?c=N9
* http://www.msnbc.com/tools/nm/nmo.asp?c=N10
* http://www.msnbc.com/tools/nm/nmo.asp?c=N11
* http://go.msn.com/npl/msnt.asp

It is quite unreasonable to expect people to figure out what each of those entries means. The simple addition of title would have avoided this embarrassment.

In most graphical browsers, alt on area remains invisible unless the image is missing, while title on area pops up as a tooltip. It's very useful, actually, and it adds fun and richness. Your imagemap can be made up of inscrutable icons or short keywords; title fills people in on where they'll go if they select the link.

Writing imagemap text equivalents

Use the same principles applicable to creating alt and title for any other kind of graphic: The former sums up the function of the graphic, while the latter tells us more, in whatever manner you decide.

If your imagemap consists of pictures of text, your choice of alt is self-evident: Retype the words rendered in bitmaps.

Icons in imagemaps

If your imagemap is made up of graphic images, use alt to tidily summarize the function of the image ("Shop" for a shopping cart, for example). Hardly surprising advice at this point. You will be stupefied further by my advice to go nuts, if desired, with title.

And of course the dual approach must be considered: If your imagemap consists of little graphic icons *and also accompanying pictures of text*, then reproduce the text. Don't try to describe the little icons. Indeed, you cannot add a longdescription to an area. It rather staggers the imagination to contemplate an imagemap graphic so complex it would require one.

Tabbing

The tapeworm and hookworm of Web accessibility, accesskey and tabindex, can be applied to the ‹area›‹/area› element inside imagemaps.

All the usual principles apply: Use accesskey for significant and (in most cases) invariable navigational landmarks and tabindex for items you absolutely want visitors to tab through.

But there are added complications. Here in the real world, imagemaps are all graphical. How do you display the accesskey keystroke? At least with textual links, certain browsers would do it for you or you could kludge up a solution that might make you feel tawdry and cheap afterward but would actually work. Here, what are you supposed to do? Add a little letter C or numeral 7, as the case may be, to each tiny graphic?

Actually, in some cases that wouldn't be so awful. Nice big buttons could easily swallow up a tiny little character. You could position accesskey legends off in the corner or something. Rather conspicuous, but it could be done. For smaller images? Forget it.

And besides, what happens if the accesskey changes? (It could, you know.)

It may be practicable to make tabindex work with area in imagemaps, but accesskey remains impracticable.

You Are Here

As visitors move around your site by selecting destinations in its navbars, you'll want to let them know exactly where they are. The standard approach is to highlight the segment of the imagemap that corresponds to their current location. If the default appearance of an imagemap is white type on a grey ground for unexplored areas, you could use black type on cream to indicate You Are Here.

It works very nicely for sighted people. But what about the blind?

The use of colour as the sole differentiator of two items is prohibited by the Web Content Accessibility Guidelines. Now, there are a few tricky cases, fully explored in Chapter 9, "Type and colour," but in this particular example let's assume that the disabled visitor cannot see your navbars at all.

A You Are Here location can be inferred from the state of the region of the imagemap: The current location ceases to be selectable; it ceases to be a link. (If you have set up your imagemap so you can select a link corresponding to where you are already, *change* it, because that makes no sense whatsoever. Among other things, there shouldn't be a link called "Home" on the homepage or a link called "Contact us" on the Contact Us page. You can use plain text or a plain image to convey those words, but not a link. Seemingly obvious, but I do run across it from time to time.)

Screen readers, with uncommon exceptions, have no trouble differentiating a link from plain text. So this inference method can suffice if necessary.

But it won't kill you to do more than the minimum. Try using a different alt and/or title for the You Are Here location. In other words, tell people explicitly where they are through the alt and/or title. We can call this a "You Are Here legend." Some schemas to consider:

- Write text equivalents for selectable links in conventional upper- and lower-case, but write the You Are Here link in upper and lower case within parentheses or brackets: (HOME), [CAREERS], [FAQ]. The redundancy of capitals and punctuation may really only be needed if the underlying text uses acronyms: Compare FAQ (always capitalized; does that mean You Are Here?) and [FAQ] (the addition of brackets definitely means You Are Here). For this reason, do not pursue the technique I advocated in Chapter 6, "The image problem," of differentiating alt and title texts with brackets; such punctuation has a more important meaning in this application. (Yes, that makes your coding inconsistent, but images that are and are not *imagemaps* are different to begin with.)
- Spell it out for us by adding "You are here:" to the text equivalent, as YOU ARE HERE: Store locator.
- You could, if absolutely necessary, come up with a little catchphrase, like "Current" or "Position." But you're saving all of two words that way, and visitors will have to sit there and figure out what you mean. On the other hand, "You are here" means what it says.

Should you put these legends on the alt or the title or both? Both. It's important and you don't want anyone to miss it.

But wait: The You Are Here segment of the imagemap isn't a link, is it? I just finished telling you to make sure it is not. That means you can't put it inside an area element. How do you add an alt or title, then?

Well, you *can* add a nonlink to area. We have the nohref="nohref" attribute for just that purpose. An example might look like:

< area nohref="nohref" alt="You are here: Store locator" title="You are here: Store locator" COORDS="60,40,100,60" >

(In XHTML, attributes may not be "minimized." In oldschool HTML, we could simply use nohref by itself, but in XHTML an attribute must always equal something. Here we set the attribute to equal itself, as in nohref="nohref". Some older browsers choke on this notation, but they are older browsers, and we cannot help the aged forever.)

Using this technique, you or your content-management system can switch between an <area></area> that brings you to the store-locator page and another one that reminds you that you are already there once you arrive. The former has an active hyperlink, the latter does not. It's all fully legal HTML and is rather neat and tidy.

If you use *breadcrumb navigation* of the sort popularized by Yahoo, where the entire sequence of navigation steps from the homepage to your current location is listed, you may have nothing to worry about. I've never actually seen a graphical breadcrumb navigation system, which may indeed be conceptually impossible in the first place. It is generally obvious in breadcrumb-navigation schemes that the last entry in the list is the current location. In this example from Yahoo –

Home > Regional > Countries > New Zealand > Business and Economy > Business to Business > Health Care > Dentistry

– the only item that isn't a link in the actual Web page is the word "Dentistry," and it is evident even to screen-reader or Braille users that the last item represents the current location.

Now, it must be stated that breadcrumb navigation is meant to be scanned. Sequential access is inconvenient; it is a bother to have to listen to all the links read out or wade through them in Braille. But it is an unavoidable bother.

Hierarchies

What if your imagemap has two or more bands of navigation links, for example, city locations up top and services offered in those locations below? How do you communicate the visitor's location as an *intersection* of those imagemaps?

In all the discussions below, we're talking about marking up not entire navbars or imagemaps, but only the individual area elements that, when put together, tell visitors where they actually are. Imagine two rows of tabs on an E-commerce site: We're making one tab from the top row and another tab from the bottom row accessible. It is this combination of tabs that tells the visitor where he or she is in the hierarchy formed by two levels of imagemaps.

The strongest approach is to code each band of navigation links in a *separate* imagemap. That will be more work for you. It is quick and easy to load everything into a single imagemap; authoring programs will do that for you automagically. To do it my way, you will have to slice your graphic into two or more pieces (though authoring programs will do *that* for you automagically, too) and set up separate imagemap coding sequences for each.

Nonetheless, all this remains an imperfect solution. Sighted visitors can see at once that an upper-level navbar connotes a higher structural level, with each navbar below occupying a lower level. Sighted visitors have random access to the entire screen and can subconsciously understand relationships even without staring directly at one object, then another, and deducing the relationship between the two.

But when interpreted *serially*, as screen readers and Braille displays must do, the separation is less clear. Solutions to this dilemma are imperfect, to be frank. You can use a You Are Here legend schema on both levels, which will result in screen-reader users' being told where they are twice – once for the high-level or top or first imagemap, once again for the next.

While confusing at first blush, in the real world it is not particularly mindblowing to be in two places at once, at least if you expand your conception step by step through ever-larger degrees of detail. You can be in bed in your apartment; in Sydney in New South Wales; in the back seat in your car; in the waiting room of the doctor's office.

Online, you can be in the Consulting section of the Services department, or the Permits subcategory of the Licences & Permits division. Hearing "You are here: Consulting. You are here: Services" isn't all that confusing. It's not very clear, either, for that matter.

Or you can be very clever. You can use different writing styles for the respective navbars. You could use "You are here" for the highest level and a custom-written category label for lower level(s). To recast the foregoing examples:

- Upper navbar: alt="You are here: Consulting". Lower navbar: alt="The department is: Services"
- Upper navbar: alt="Licences & Permits". Lower navbar: alt="Permits desk"

In other words, use a descriptive approach. Imagine you're talking to a caller who was transferred from the main switchboard so many times that he or she is confused. "Who am I speaking with?" the caller asks. "It's the Permits desk in the Licences & Permits department."

There is another tack which, while radical and barely legal on paper, may be the most sensible. Add a You Are Here legend only to the lowest or most specific level in the hierarchy.

In the foregoing examples, the upper navbar would use alt="" title="". Lower navbars would provide alt and title along the lines of You are here: Services: Consulting or [Permits desk, Licences & Permits division].

In other words, tell people where they are at their final destination; don't nag at them at every step along the way.

If you have a *really* extensive hierarchy of navbars (three or more – almost unheard-of and generally inadvisable from a usability perspective), then this approach makes the most sense. And it is not illegal to use alt="" title="" by any means. We use alt="" on spacer GIFs and other meaningless graphics all the time. It is true that a screen-reader user may become aware of an absence in the topmost navbar, but really, won't it be only the superkeen screen-reader users who mentally compare one page's navbar to another on a site who will ever notice? And does it particularly matter, given that the lower navbar's legends are utterly clear and comprehensible?

By the way, this approach of splitting navbars into pieces may require the use of adjacent table cells with cellpadding="0" cellspacing="0" border="0", which adds manageable but unavoidable complexity. Suddenly the screen-reader user is manipulating not merely an imagemap but an imagemap in a table.

What if you use a cutesy navbar where the *lower* level is the main one (denoted, say, through larger type) and the upper level is the subcategory? (You might see this technique combined with a picture – big main navbar below the picture, smaller sub-navbar above.) Well, you may simply have to stop being cutesy. When these are interpreted sequentially, disabled visitors are going to hit the sub-navbar first.

What if some apparent hierarchy is actually an illusion? As an example, imagine a photograph bordered by graphical links at the top and bottom that are positioned for graphic effect and not because one set of links is more important. You may hope that people will see an order to the listing, but you don't want to give the impression that one set of links is higher up the food chain than another.

DHTML: Don't do it

What if you use one of those whiz-bang DHTML (dynamic HTML) drop-down navigation bars that mimic the menubars found in computer operating systems?

They're increasingly common, they're difficult to code (due largely to cross-browser incompatibilities), and in most cases they add needless complexity to Websites. They rely on the so-called Document Object Model, an amalgam of HTML, stylesheet, and JavaScript methods that is poorly standardized.

The knock against DHTML menus is their reliance on a mouse. Blind and mobility-impaired visitors cannot really use a mouse. There is currently no way to get DHTML menus to work purely via the keyboard. That makes DHTML menus nominally inaccessible.

There is one way to make DHTML menus work. Set up your pages so that the title of each menu – the word, image, or option that is visible even before the visitor attempts to explore or pull down the menu – is a plain hypertext link to a separate page that lists all the links inside the menu.

Imagine your DHTML menu displays the phrase About Us in its inactive state. When visitors click or simply mouseover that phrase, a list of menu options appears: Company Information, Jobs, Offices, Privacy Policy, Copyright. A nondisabled person could simply choose those options from the menu, and the hyperlink associated with the option chosen would be actuated.

In the accessible case, however, you must make the About Us region a plain hyperlink to another page that simply lists all the same options in ordinary hyperlinks.

Yes, this will require you to set up as many additional pages as there are headings or titles for your menus, but that is not exactly onerous. If the contents or URLs of menus change (as they might, especially on a newspaper site), then the contents or URLs must also change in the backup pages.

It is not good enough to fob off a disabled visitor to some kind of static navigation, like a fixed navbar or bottom-of-page links, when neither of those duplicates what the DHTML menu lets you do. In other words, you are not allowed to say: "If you can't handle the menus, you're stuck with whatever other navigation is on the page, even if it doesn't take you where the menus could." That does not constitute equivalence or accessibility.

DHTML menus are an advanced Web technique and I am raising the bar in response to that fact. If you have enough programming skill to create DHTML menus in the first place, it is child's play to set up ordinary backup pages. You may have to do some work to get your database or content-management system to propagate the same contents or URLs on those pages, but your fate was sealed in that respect the moment you decided to use drop-down menus and also make your site accessible.

There is no standard set of routines for keyboard handling in the World Wide Web Consortium's specifications for the Document Object Model. They say so right up front: "The DOM Level 2 Event specification does not provide a key event set. An event set designed for use with keyboard input devices will be included in a later version of the DOM specification." As of this writing, DOM Level 3 merely calls for keyboard handling as a future requirement: "The specification must define a set of key events to handle keyboard input. This key event set must be fully internationalizable."

At some later day, if the World Wide Web Consortium ever bothers to come up with standard keyboard routines for the Document Object Model on which DHTML menus are based, then we might be able to cook up an accessible technique that does not require something as inelegant as backup pages. I doubt this will happen at any time within the next five years. If you insist on using DHTML menus, you must also use the technique I have described.

Bottom-Line Accessibility Advice

Basic accessibility

- If you're using tables, try the table hack first.
- In any case, use skip-navigation links for large navigational regions.
- Use accesskey and tabindex attributes for important landmarks on the page, like search.

Intermediate accessibility

Use accesskey and tabindex attributes.

Advanced accessibility

Use skip-navigation links to allow easy focus movement from landmark to landmark on a complex page.

9| TYPE AND COLOUR

READING IS THE PRIMARY ACTIVITY OF THE WEB. For people with impaired vision who do not use screen readers, colour choices and, to a far lesser extent, type size become the accessibility issues.

The big surprise is how little work you must do to provide for big type on your Websites (in fact, no work at all for the group that truly is visually-impaired). Along the way, you will learn more than you ever thought possible about colourblindness. And that is where we'll start.

Goals

In this chapter:
- We'll learn about the anatomy of colourblindness.
- We'll explore the issue of meaningful objects in Web design and how to make them accessible to a colourblind person.
- We'll learn about a range of safe colours and colour increments.
- We'll understand how little typography has to do with accessibility.

Colourblindness

As we are all too aware, a perennial objection to making Websites accessible comes in the form of a reflexive bleating from Web designers per se: "What, I can't use graphics? You want I should make text-only sites? What is this, 1994?"

Accordingly, when I mention that you will have to take some care in selecting colours throughout your site, certain of my esteemed readers will immediately object: "What, are you saying I can't design now? Are you saying I can't use photographs?" and close this book in disgust.

Um, no. Go ahead and use photographs, assuming you include the appropriate text equivalents. The colour values of any particular photograph (or illustration, for that matter) are outside the purview of accessibility.

However, colours used elsewhere on your site must be selected with modest care. You don't have to go to extremes, and it won't take you more than a moment to decide what to do, particularly since this book and its included CD-ROM give you all the tools you'll need. You will, moreover, be an expert by that point.

The central problem

Our goal here is o make sure that everything expressed in a foreground colour that must be differentiated from a background or adjacent colour actually can be so differentiated. In practice, we're largely talking about typography, though icons, buttons, and large colour-filled expanses of a Web page are affected, as are combinations of typography and image (e.g., the word "Next" alongside a right-pointing arrow, or "Home" plus an outline of a house).

The assumption is that you as a designer will never have cause to use invisible text (foreground and background colours the same). That's barely worth mentioning, though you may recall the discussion of using invisible text for navigation-skipper links in Chapter 8, "Navigation." What we find far more often, though, is an *unwise* choice of foreground and background colours. Those of us who look at Websites have all seen it: Yellow type on white, or dark blue on slightly lighter blue. In rare cases, complementary colours, like red text on green, scintillate on the screen.

I will not pass judgement on these æsthetic lapses. The concern here is legibility. If, however, you do select colours for legibility, you stand a fair chance of being in good taste, if that even matters.

What is colourblindness?

The term is a misnomer: Few of us are *achromats* who are unable to see colours at all. (Oliver Sacks' book *The Island of the Colorblind* [Knopf, 1997] describes an unlikely community of many such people.) This book does not deal with that surpassingly rare group.

In practice, colourblind people confuse certain ranges of colours. The issue is nearly always colour discrimination or colour differentiation – that is, telling two colours apart (detecting that they are different). The issue is not identifying colours by name, though people with colour deficiency are often able to do so, even for colours they cannot actually see, because they have learned what objects are what colours throughout their lives.

But to reiterate, you must understand colourblindness as a problem of differentiating colours, not one of colour disappearing.

Colourblindness is not an equal-opportunity disability. Virtually everyone with colourblindness is male. The measured incidence of colourblindness varies by country and race, being most common among white males. The proportion of people in the Western world with any detectable colourblindness is usually quoted at 8%. Incidence in males hovers around 4%.

If your Website attracts a mixed male and female audience (most do, but realistically, a great many sites attract vastly more men than women or, rarely, vice-versa), you can estimate the proportion of your audience that is affected.

As usual, we are dealing with minorities here. You should not jump to the conclusion that, since the number of visitors with colourblindness may be 4% or less (assuming a fifty-fifty split between the sexes and a predominantly white readership), doing any kind of work to accommodate them is a waste of time or provides diminishing returns. If that were really the case, we wouldn't pay any attention to Web accessibility at all, because you would have to search high and low to find a site where a *majority* of visitors were disabled, which presumably would be the threshold at which accessibility would suddenly be worth it.

In fact, colourblindness is an easy disability to accommodate. It demands almost no special coding, usually requiring nothing more than intelligent and informed colour choices.

Anatomy

If you're old enough to be doing Web design, you're old enough to know that the retina is the light-sensitive lining of the eye, usually described as sitting at "the back" of the eye. In fact, the retina extends in three dimensions over most of the inside surface area of the eye. The retina really is a *lining* and is not at all like the screen of a drive-in movie theatre suspended at "the back" of the eyeball. If you dissected an eye in half from left to right, you would find a certain area lined retina cells even in the front half.

You will likely also be familiar with rods and cones, the two main categories of light-sensitive cells in the retina. The names come from the approximate shapes of the structures. Rods, which are far greater in number (typically over 100 million per eye) and are concentrated in certain areas, are almost completely insensitive to colours and react mostly at low light levels. It is not the case that cones detect colours and rods detect grey, black, and white; cones (fewer in number, at about 8 million per eye) need more light to actuate than rods do. Rods do well at low light levels, cones at high light levels. There is a considerable range of intermediate light levels where both rods and cones are active. At high light levels, rods are overwhelmed.

The reception of colour depends on pigmentation of the cones. It certainly surprised me to learn that cells in the retina could carry pigment, but cells in the skin and hair (and the iris, the coloured part of the eyeball) carry pigment, too, and *that* isn't particularly surprising.

In fact, colourblindness is an easy disability to accommodate. It demands almost no special coding, usually requiring nothing more than intelligent and informed colour choices.

(To keep rods and cones straight in your mind, remember the mnemonic of C for *cones* and *colour*.)

We see a rainbow of colours due to the activation of more than one kind of cone cell. Colour vision is additive: Different wavelengths of light combine to form the millions of hues detectable by a person with normal colour vision.

Colour deficiency

Through hereditary bad luck, and in rare cases through disease or exposure to toxins, some men and a very small number of women live with a colour-vision deficiency.

The technical terminology describing the various forms of colourblindness is tongue-twisting, confusable, and heavily Latinate. The lexicon takes a while to settle into understandability, but you absolutely must learn the various forms of colourblindness by name to make intelligent colour choices in Web design.

To make things easier, we should start with some general facts.

- Red and green are the colours most affected by colour-vision deficiency. Almost no one has a blue deficiency. Accordingly, nearly everyone can see blue, or, more accurately, almost everyone can distinguish blue as a colour different from others. (It was pure good luck that the default colour of hyperlinks is blue with underlining. Of course, plain blue hyperlinks smack of 1997, don't they?)

- Red and green are not uniformly replaced by grey. For some people with colour-vision deficiency, colours like beige and yellow replace red and green. With the exception of achromats, colourblind people *always see some kind of colour.*

- Errors of colour perception happen in some cases. Certain colours are shifted more toward the green or the red end of the spectrum, but this is rarely a make-or-break phenomenon in Web design.

- Colour is not the only issue. Brightness (or luminance, or intensity) of the colour comes into play in some cases. If your colours aren't bright enough *and* if nearby shades are poorly chosen, the dull colours may shift in apparent hue and be unreadable against their surroundings.

- Colourblind kids are like kids with dyslexia or learning disabilities: They often learn ways to adapt and function in a way essentially equivalent to nondisabled people. Over a lifetime, a great many kludges, rules of thumb, and forms of guesswork develop to make sense of a world whose colours they see differently. Since nearly all colourblind people can distinguish brightness and contrast, that's one way they identify that two colours are different. They may not know from direct experience what the colours look like to someone with "colour-normal" vision, but they know the hues are not the same. Colourblind people learn that certain objects are certain colours. If an unknown object comes along with an unknown true colour, they can make an educated guess based on the colour used to describe *other* objects with that same apparent colour and brightness. ("People tell me things that look this colour are dark red, so I'll hazard a guess that this thing is dark red, too.")

Types of colour deficiency

There are two main categories of colour-vision deficiency: One attributable to completely absent pigments in the cones ("anopia," or "anopic" deficiencies), another due to abnormal or "anomalous" pigments.

The three main varieties of colour-vision deficiency are protan, deutan, and tritan. You may notice from the roots of the words that they refer to the numbers one (*prot-*; think of "prototype"), two (*deut-*; equivalent to "deuce," which anyone who's ever played cards will know), and three (*trit-*; think "triple").

The conditions themselves (as opposed to the higher-level theoretical categories) are usually called protanopia, deuteranopia, and tritanopia. The terms refer to an insensitivity to light in the long, medium, and short wavelengths, respectively. To a person with normal colour vision, that translates to an insensitivity to red, green, and blue, respectively, in broad and somewhat inaccurate terms. (There is some overlap in colour wavelengths and perception, as you will likely know from arguing with friends over whether a colour is bluish green or greenish blue.)

Keeping protan, deutan, and tritan straight in your mind will not be that difficult if you think back to RGB colour. The acronym is always expressed in that order, not GRB or any other permutation. In fact, acronyms like RGB and CMYK roll right off the tongue.

If you can remember RGB and 1-2-3, you can remember protan, deutan, and tritan. Even before defining the terms fully, then, you have a range of mnemonics to keep them straight:

- Protan – one – red
- Deutan – two – green
- Tritan – three – blue

Red–green deficiencies

In both protanopia and deuteranopia and their related conditions, red and green are the colours that are confused. You get the two groups as a package deal: If you accommodate someone with red–green deficiency, you accommodate people with protanopia *and* deuteranopia, because their colour experiences are similar.

Why do these groups have problems differentiating red and green? It has to do with the cone cells. To distinguish red from green, the brain relies on the difference in stimulation of medium- and long-wavelength pigments in the cones (broadly analogous to stimulation of greens and reds, respectively). We're talking differences here, and to detect a difference, you need more than one item to compare. If your cones are insensitive to medium or long wavelengths (if you're missing one of those receptors), then you do not have a pair of input stimuli to compare. You cannot draw a distinction between the two *because you have only one to work with.*

Red–green deficiencies fall under the following categories.

PROTANOPIA

A person with protanopia is a *protanope* or a *protan.*

Protanopes cannot distinguish reds and greens; reds, moreover, appear dark.

If you're *missing* long-wavelength pigments in your cones but you *have* medium-wavelength pigments, you're a protanope. Those medium-wavelength pigments are not very sensitive to long wavelengths (the reds), so the hues that colour-normals would describe as red do not look red and seem dark compared to other colours that are actually equally bright.

This brightness deficiency will come up in practical use, so keep it in mind. (You can compensate for it by simply making the colour brighter.) Since most colourblind people are men, the following joke, a stock in the colour-vision trade, is not actually sexist: "The protanope wears a red tie to a funeral." Red and black can look the same if the red is dim enough.

DEUTERANOPIA

A person with deuteranopia is a *deuteranope* or a *deutan.* (Note that the terms are not parallel.)

Deutans, like protans, cannot distinguish reds and greens. Unlike protans, though, there is no brightness deficiency. Hues that colour-normals would describe as red do not appear red to a deutan, but they don't appear darker than other colours that are actually equally bright.

There are more deutans than protans in the world.

ANOMALOUS CONDITIONS

If protanopia and deuteranopia are a kind of pure or undiluted colour-vision deficiency, we also find colour deficiencies that are not necessarily as severe in practice but still related to the main deficiencies.

- *Protanomalous* colour-vision deficiency (*protanomaly*) is similar to protanopia. Protanomalous subjects have some ability to distinguish red and green (meaning they can identify certain colour pairs as different), but there is no reason to think they can see actual red or green. As with protans, red looks darker.

- *Deuteranomalous* colour-vision deficiency (*deuteranomaly*), not surprisingly, is similar to deuteranopia. Deuteranomalous vision is capable of better red–green discrimination; there is no reason to think deuteranomalous subjects can see red or green, but they can differentiate a certain range of shades. A small number of deuteranomalous people have such good colour discrimination that they can pass a standard colourblindness test.

PRACTICAL SIMILARITIES

As you can see, protanopes, deuteranopes, the protanomalous, and the deuteranomalous all vary in red–green deficiency *only in details*.

In building accessible Websites, you may consider all these groups roughly comparable (with the notable exception of darkened red sensitivity in protans). If you accommodate one of those groups, you accommodate all of them.

Tritanopia

A significantly rarer colour-vision deficiency is *tritanopia*.

Tritanopia is not exactly analogous to the red–green deficiencies; though it involves blue, it does not constitute a blue–yellow deficiency. Tritanopia *is* analogous to protanopia and deuteranopia in that *blues* and greens are confused.

- *Tritanopes* or *tritans* have no sensitivity to short wavelengths, broadly equivalent to blue. Tritanopia is quite rare in its hereditary form, but some diseases, including diabetes, induce tritanopia in people who formerly had normal colour vision; among elderly people, "acquired" tritanopia is more common than the hereditary kind.

There is no such thing as tritanomaly. There are no anomalous tritanopes.

THE YELLOW PROBLEM

Red and green are not the only hues affected. Some researchers believe that people with red–green colour-vision deficiency actually see shades of beige, yellow, or orange in place of red and/or green.

No one can be sure of what another person actually sees. Joel Pokorny of the University of Chicago, a leading scientist in colour vision interviewed for this book, was extremely reluctant to speak even in general terms about what hues colourblind people actually perceive, but the theory that red–green deficient people see beige/yellow/orange is not in wide dispute. The strongest evidence for this theory comes from the spectacularly rare group with one normal and one colourblind eye. With these subjects, it is possible to display colours to one eye and then the other, ask questions about colour differences, and draw inferences as to which colours are confused based on the subject's responses.

Here in the real world, however, beige, yellow, and orange are also used in and of themselves.

It follows, then, that hues a colour-normal person would describe as beige, yellow, or orange are the hues a colourblind person could actually confuse with red and green. Why? For the simple reason that red and green are perceived as those other shades. "True" beige/yellow/orange can be confused with "false" beige/yellow/orange.

The range of hues you have to be concerned about, then, is actually pretty wide: Red, orange, yellow, beige, and green.

What difference does it make?

You now have quite enough technical knowledge about colour-vision deficiency to stultify acquaintances at dinner parties.

How will it affect your work in building accessible Websites? Somewhat less than you might expect, actually, though you are not off the hook and you are not in a position to ignore the phenomenon altogether.

The range of hues you have to be concerned about, then, is actually pretty wide: Red, orange, yellow, beige, and green.

Recall that colour-vision deficiency concerns differentiating or discriminating between colours. That means making a comparison. Online, that further means making a comparison *in cases where actual meaning is involved.*

In accessibility terms, it is of no interest that a colourblind person might see a solitary block of colour on your page as something other than its intended red, green, or other confusable colour. Hues perceived in isolation, with no meaning attached to them, are neither here nor there.

Broadly speaking, then, it follows that photographs are exempt from accessibility considerations for colourblind visitors. The fact that a colour-deficient person doesn't see a photograph the way a colour-normal person does is largely irrelevant.

If, however, we are dealing with the rare case in which the whole purpose of the photograph is to differente one part from another, and those parts appear in confusable colours, then we have a problem. Actual examples of such photos are rare, even contrived. I suppose a photograph of a traffic light at an accident scene (with red and green illumination) is one such case, or a discussion of colours for exit signs inside buildings (red, blue, and green are all variously used worldwide), or maybe a shot of a row of otherwise-identical products differing only by colour, where red happens to be handy to green.

In any event, no accessibility guidelines anywhere suggest you doctor your photographs so that confusable colours are no longer confusable, and I'm not giving you that advice, either. Some accessibility provisions incur undue hardship or fundamentally alter the nature of the enterprise. The colour characteristics of photographs, in general, fall into that category.

(A clear exception: Type or navigation icons laid on top of or close by a photograph. Such items *definitely must take colour-vision deficiency into account* even if the rest of the image as a whole does not.)

So what *do* you have to worry about?

The crisis of meaning

On the Web, you have to worry about colour-vision deficiency when a meaningful object is on top of or near another object and the colours involved are confusable.

What is a meaningful object?

- Text.
- Links.
- Navigation, whether in HTML text or in graphics or both.
- Artwork, including logos, shopping-cart pictographs, warning messages, and any treatment of the two most infamous words online, "Skip intro."
- Interface elements like graphical search buttons.

There may be other such items. The salient test is: If I confuse this item with something else, will I make a mistake? Will I be unable to do what I want?

By contrast, graphic design used for its own sake or for beauty, effect, or appeal need not be adjusted for colour-vision deficiency. In these cases, you need not do anything special. If the text of your page occupies two-thirds of the screen, and the text is definitely unconfusable by a colour-deficient person (e.g., black text on white), but you did a nice design treatment at the left and top that uses red, green, or other confusable colours in an artistic way, you've got nothing to worry about, if that design treatment carries no meaning.

Graphic designers must separate their own responses from those of the rest of the world and acknowledge that emotional impact, sensations of pleasure, and artistic appreciation are not the same as meaning in this context. You may think it's important. It is not necessarily meaningful according to the definition we are using here.

The two phenomena may intersect. You may indeed have to change the colour of your text to make it unconfusable even though design elements on the very same page may stay untouched.

Only *meaningful objects* need be unambiguous.

You may alter other colour schemes out of the goodness of your heart, but nobody's expecting you to do so. Remember, we are not in the business of exactly duplicating the nondisabled experience for disabled visitors. Colourblind people can put up with seeing a site in a way the designer did not intend. What they can't put up with is not being able to *use* a site.

> Only meaningful
> objects need be
> unambiguous.

(And while we're on that topic, you know already that colour fidelity is an impossibility online. Ensuring that the specific shade of yellow you used in that swath of screen real estate remains that specific shade for all visitors cannot be done. Apart from the colour-gamut differences between Macintosh and Windows machines, colour bit depth can and will sabotage your colour choices; take a look at your page in 256- or 16-colour mode for a taste of this parallel universe. Colours aren't even consistent across a single monitor, a phenomenon quite apparent to anyone staring at a liquid-crystal display all day. Colour-deficient perception of objects that are not per se meaningful is yet another colour inconsistency we can add to the list.)

ADJACENCY AND OVERLAP

Applying these principles is easy. Keeping in mind that colour-vision deficiency deals with comparisons, you always have to think in groups.

When considering two items, is the first on top of the second? Or right alongside?

With three, five, or more items, what forms of adjacency and overlap are you dealing with?

When considering these comparisons, here's what you do not want to do. These prohibitions may seem excessively broad, but we will return to qualify them shortly.

- Don't set red on black or black on red. Red appears dark to protans, turning the combination into an effective dark beige/yellow/orange on black. (Dark grey itself, come to think of it, is probably just as bad as black when combined with red.)
- Don't set green on red or red on green. Apart from being tacky (is this a Website or a Christmas tree?), red and green are complementary colours and will sizzle onscreen even to the eyes of a colour-normal person; most colour-vision-deficient people confuse them.
- Don't place the two halves of a confusable pair next to each other.
- Don't mix beige/yellow/orange with red and green.

Is this unnecessarily restrictive? Am I taking the fun out of Web design?

Am I asking you to stop smoking *and* stop drinking? In the immortal words of Adam Ant, "You don't drink, don't smoke – what *do* you do?"

What you do is use your head. No, you may not use red/black or red/green combinations, nor may you mix them with beige/yellow/orange, *unless*:

- There is no actual chance of confusion.
  - If you've got a row of five graphical navigation buttons, all of which use white type with backgrounds of red, yellow, orange, green, and black, is there enough contrast to read the type in each button?

Red-on-green text tends to disappear for deutans and isn't very legible for protans. Even in monochrome rendering, it's hard to read. And by the way, red-on-green text is tacky. What is this, Christmas?

Yes, you can indeed place confusable colours (like red and green or green and blue) right next to each other if other cues make the items discernible. The multicoloured Amazon.com toolbar remains usable even with confusable colours. (It would be even more usable with alt texts, which the most sophisticated E-commerce site on earth still has not figured out how to incorporate into its site after all these many years.)

- If so, does it particularly matter that the backgrounds are *specifically* red, yellow, orange, green, and black? The space between the words, the (likely discernible) border between the buttons, the fact that *the words themselves* are not the same, and the difference in appearance of the five hues even to a colourblind person all combine to make the buttons understandable and differentiable. (Five shades of beige/yellow/orange that are nonetheless distinct to a colour-deficient person are exactly that: Distinct.)
- Red on black will likely always be confusable. Red near black may not be.
- The items are widely spaced. You can use red on the left side of the page and green on the right. As long as the "content" (logo, line art, type, whatever) is distinguishable against the specific background, it makes *no difference at all* that the two backgrounds might be confused since they are so far apart.
- The items have considerable difference in brightness. Light-yellow type on a dark-green button is OK, for example, because of the difference in brightness (or lightness). While it might be possible to develop formulæ to test for adequate lightness (Photoshop plug-in, anyone?), this is the sort of thing an experienced designer can just play by ear. If the lightness contrast is *indisputably* high, you've solved the problem.

As you can see, your true limitations are modest, but you do have to make intelligent analyses of the colours on a page.

Metadata

You cannot get away with using confusable colours while expecting that other features, like a title, longdescription, JavaScript rollover, or status-line message, will save the day and resolve the ambiguity.

First of all, if you're using JavaScript rollovers, all states must be unconfusable. Note that this means that all states may use confusable colours if, as in the previous examples, the type or foreground information is perfectly readable against any and all backgrounds.

(I'm saying "all states" here because it is possible to use an animated GIF as one of the states of a rollover. Animated GIFs contain a series of states unto themselves. Just as we can place tables inside tables or lists inside lists, graphics inside graphics must all maintain the same level of accessibility.)

It is bad usability and *certainly* bad accessibility to force people to scrub the mouse all over the screen until the cursor changes into a link indicator because they have no other way of finding the links on the page. It is no better to force people to wait for a rollover or a tooltip or a status-line display (very easy to miss) merely to understand what the hell an item is for.

(Fine-art and experimental sites do not have to be dumbed down. You may force the visitor to work to discover the page's links and other intricacies as long as a colourblind visitor is no worse off than one who isn't. If, on an artistic or experimental site, everyone is "disadvantaged" equally in broad terms, there is no inaccessibility in broad terms.)

Adding such metadata is always a good idea, but don't rely on it to absolve you of responsibility for colour choices.

Colour combinations

You now must carry a certain yoke as a Web designer. You now know that some colour combinations should be avoided under many conditions.

But since colourblindness follows well-known patterns, it follows that certain colour combinations are A-OK for everyone, right?

The answer is yes. Before delving into the matter, though, keep this important point in mind: Not all Websites use confusable colours, and even those that do so do not necessarily use them in confusable ways, what with the various other measures at our disposal. If, however, you wish to *maximally avoid* colour confusions, you have a range of colour choices at your disposal.

As it turns out, there's an impressive body of work available on colour choices for maps that is perfectly applicable to the Web. The lead author for most of this work is Cynthia Brewer of Pennsylvania State University.

Professional cartographers do not use colour merely as a differentiator; specific colour choices and intensity correlate with actual data. Online, though, colour is used mostly for differentiation. If researchers have pinpointed colour choices that work under the arduous demands of professional mapmaking, those colour choices are *certainly* going to work for Web design.

These findings (citations are found in the Bibliography) give us two sets of guidelines:

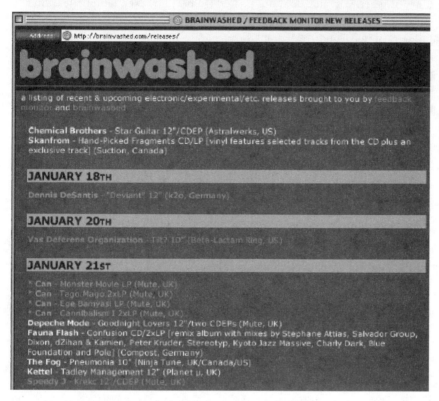

To paraphrase Steve Krug, don't make us think: Brainwashed .com tells us "Additions to this list in the last week or so appear in red. Release date changes in the last week or so appear in blue." Instead of cutely camouflaging these categories in a colour (hard to discern even with perfect vision), give us a separate section listing new releases, or add some text, or underline them or something (anything).

- Colour pairs that can be used together
- Colour steps (or gradations) that can be used to show a progression or to differentiate objects

If you have to differentiate two items clearly, you may use one of the colour pairs. If you need to differentiate a related range of items, you may use colour steps. (Online, with its reduced resolution and general difficulty of reading, you will want to provide redundant coding, relying on more than just colour. But you knew that already.)

It gets better. A problem related to colourblindness that affects everyone with any kind of colour vision is colour *naming*. People disagree on what to call certain shades. But experiments have shown that you can always find a range of shades that all subjects call by the same basic name (like red or blue or green as opposed to pink or turquoise or puce). The colour lists that follow are verbally unambiguous: What one person calls blue no other person will ever call brown.

For our purposes here (a fact confirmed with Brewer), the specific red, blue, or green you pick does not matter. Do not, however, tempt fate. Don't get fancy. Do not take this to extremes by selecting a hue that your better judgement tells you is really pink or turquoise or puce. Stick to shades that you have no doubt whatsoever can be described by the words in question. If you want red, pick a red; don't think too hard about it. Nearly everyone else who can perceive red will also consider it red. Interpret words like *dark*, *medium*, and *light* similarly.

Listed below, then, are colour pairs and colour steps that are safe for people with colour-vision deficiencies and whose names are also unambiguous.

- Red/blue
  - Steps: Dark red; medium red; light red; light blue; medium blue; dark blue
- Orange/blue
  - Steps: Dark orange; medium orange; light orange; light blue; medium blue; dark blue
- Orange/purple
  - Steps: Dark orange; medium orange; light orange; light purple; medium purple; dark purple
- Yellow/purple
  - Steps (note the restricted list): Yellow; light purple; medium purple; dark purple

Why is yellow special? Brewer explains: "Sequences of lightness steps are difficult to produce with yellow because basic yellow is a light colour and dark saturated yellows cannot be produced."

There's a B-list here. Brown/yellow and yellow/blue combinations are available. But under certain very severe conditions found in specific maps but not in real-world Websites, brown/yellow and yellow/blue pairs can be confusable. Of course, we are building accessible Websites, not accessible maps, so I have Cynthia Brewer's blessing to tell you to use the following colour pairs as much as you like.

- Brown/blue
  - Steps: Dark brown; medium brown; light brown; light blue; medium blue; dark blue
- Yellow/blue
  - Steps: Yellow (it's still special even here); light blue; medium blue; dark blue

We all know about the Web-safe palette of 216 colours that are more or less equivalent when rendered on different platforms. Should we go out on a limb and call Cynthia Brewer's list the colourblind-safe palette? How about the Brewer palette?

In any event, not every Website will require specific work to avoid confusable colour combinations. But if your site is one of those, now you've got six colour pairs and 32 colour increments to play with.

Creative uses

And playing with them is exactly what you should do.

The idea here is that, if you absolutely must use adjacent navbar buttons or something of that sort, you can ensure that they are differentiable by colour alone through the use of these well-tested pairs and increments. You will also enact other measures, like legible foreground coloration, borders, separation, and metadata. But these safe colours put you on a very firm footing.

Nobody's forcing you to use these colour steps exactly as listed, of course. They can be useful to you even if you don't have groups of exactly six or four items to differentiate. You can skip increments: Dark red, then light red, then medium blue could differentiate three items. Do you have six items? Enjoy the variation of using the dark-red/light-red/medium-blue step twice in a row. (Why not? That puts dark red and medium blue next to each other, and they aren't confusable.)

It is ill-advised to jump from pair to pair, however. The Brewer pairs are like DNA strands; do not let yourself play Dr. Frankenstein and recombine the DNA. Every one of these pairs contains blue. Remember learning that nearly everyone can see blue? Well, let's not try to ride that detail too far. If you mix and match, what are you going to be left with? Blue and blue? Red and orange? Red and purple? Red and brown?

Yellow isn't so great either if you try to extract it from one of the pairs above and use it inside another pair. Red and green are perceived as something akin to yellow by deutans and protans. If you use actual yellow as understood by colour-normals, you run the risk of having it confused with red or green.

White, black, and grey

Should these guidelines nonetheless cramp your literal and figurative style, keep a few things in mind:

White, black, and grey are perceived as such by pretty much anyone on the planet with functional vision (even those surpassingly-rare achromats). Those colours can provide a useful contrast against millions of other shades (and, in one combination or another, with all 216 Web-safe colours). You can mix white, black, and grey with confusable colours if the results, given foreground/background combinations, contrast, and other factors, are actually unconfusable.

You can even use black and red on the same page: Red type on white, white type on black, and white or red on top of each other in either combination.

And to reiterate a previous point, you can use confusable colours all you want if the confusion has no impact on the meaning or function of the site.

There is a small detail: For various physiological reasons, grey actually does become a confusable colour in some unusual combinations, as in the colour triplet magenta–grey–cyan. Now, when was the last time you used that combination? Grey confusability is unlikely to come up very often.

Plug-ins, guides, and utilities

If you have normal colour vision, these discussions of colour-vision deficiency are rather hypothetical. How do you apply your knowledge in the real world?

Well, colour-normals require simulators to approximate the appearance of Websites as perceived by the colourblind.

A word of warning: Looking at your pages in greyscale mode is not an adequate simulation of the experience of colourblindness. None of the groups discussed in depth here – protans, deutans, and tritans – sees the world without colour (as the very uncommon achromats do). Greyscale simulations are not bad as a tool for checking contrast levels, but you're checking contrast in the absence of colour, an unnatural condition for the groups you are trying to accommodate. I must have read a dozen instances of the advice "To ensure your site works for colourblind people, evaluate it with a black-and-white monitor" while researching this book. It doesn't work, and there is pretty much no such thing as a black-and-white monitor on First World computers anyway. It is usually impossible even to reset a colour monitor to greyscale. You should discount this advice altogether.

Web Accessibility Initiative advice

The Web Accessibility Initiative Web Content Accessibility Guidelines are blunt when it comes to colour: "Don't rely on colour alone."

That Guideline goes on to say:

> Ensure that text and graphics are understandable when viewed without colour. If colour alone is used to convey information, people who cannot differentiate between certain colours and users with devices that have non-colour or non-visual displays will not receive the information. When foreground and background colours are too close to the same hue, they may not provide sufficient contrast when viewed using monochrome displays or by people with different types of colour deficits.

On the face of it, if you have no particular knowledge of colour deficits, this sweeping prohibition does seem like a party-pooper. I suspect designers are misreading the guideline as "Don't use colour." That's not the intent.

There is certainly some debate as to what the intent actually is. It appears to mean "Don't use colour by itself to convey meaning."

At this point, we could pretend we were philosophers of art and launch into a discussion of the way the associative values of colour (red means blood, passion, also stop; green means grass, calm, also go) are a form of meaning, if you feel like stretching the term. Let's not.

I would suggest coming back to the test of colour confusability: If I confuse this item with something else, will I make a mistake? Will I be unable to do what I want?

In the case of colour-deficient vision, we considered colour combinations – pairs, triples, and beyond. The Guideline as written appears to force us to consider colour in terms of single objects. In reality, we are nonetheless meant to draw a comparison – between an item in a certain colour and another item with a different meaning.

The most common example of use of colour "alone" will clarify that there is really no such thing as using colour alone. I speak of financial tables, where negative numbers may be printed in red. ("Red ink," as they say.)

Red differentiates the number from a positive figure. A comparison is in fact being made with such positive figures, even if none exist on that page.

Take another example found online: If you make a mistake filling out a form, a Website may bounce you back into that form with the defective fields marked in red. You can disregard all the other fields, and to do so you draw a comparison with them.

Having spent a great deal of time wracking my brain on this topic, the only other case I could find involves dumb-arse Geocities-calibre Web "designers" who tell you "Click the green square to enter! Click the red square to exit!"

They're both squares, so a comparison based on shape won't help you. Apart from hovering over the images or otherwise inspecting the target filename, you have no particular means of telling the two apart other than colour.

In these specific cases, you must adjust your approach. You must make visible changes to your design in order to make it accessible. The groups involved here aren't merely the colourblind but also screen-reader users, anyone with a text-only browser, or a visitor using a monochrome display (not that there are many of those left in the world).

- If you want negative numbers to be differentiable from positive, you may use the colour red (but watch out for darkened red perception among protans) if and only if you also use a minus sign or surround the figure in parentheses. Or the number may be listed without a sign

You don't find examples like these very much anymore simply because designers have come to understand they represent bad usability, but if you instruct people to "Click the green [whatever] to do X!" and "Click the red [whatever] to do Y!" then a colourblind person might have to sit there and puzzle things out.

In the J-List example, the bitmap text is different enough that it can probably be read by a person with red–green colourblindness irrespective of its colour.

The "Click the green button to go to the open forum" example is somewhat harmless because the green button is right alongside the text. The same applies to the red and blue buttons. But why isn't the text a link? Why aren't the links simply "Open forum," "Send your e-mail," and "Enjoy last summer's ecotour," all in plain text?

Similarly, the "Hey, loser! You need Flash to view this site! Like, get lost and download it!" admonitions that are now familiar (and very tedious to those of us who do, in fact, have Flash installed, but undetected by the page author's inept scripting) certainly do not have to be expressed using colour-specific icons. "If you know you already have Flash 4, click the green button": Why not a plain-text link? And especially why not a plain-text link for the "text-only version" option denoted by a red button? (Is a text-only version really the only alternative to a Flash version?)

if it appears in a well-marked Loss or Deficit field, table cell, or column. (Use a real minus sign rather than a hyphen: − or −. Also, – or – will do in a pinch, though it's not the same.) Use the typographic formats appropriate for your language and region; a minus sign may trail the number, or parentheses may not be permitted, as the case may be for different languages.

• To indicate form fields with errors, add a warning icon with an alt text like Alert, Error, Correction needed, or Attention. You could even use an asterisk or exclamation point if you absolutely must, but some screen-reader users will miss those unless they've selected a setting to read every punctuation item. Or just add explicit, normal, everyday HTML text containing the warnings. You can also use stylesheets or HTML elements like <strong></strong> to emphasize the type, or you can draw a border around the field or a background behind it. (Watch for colour confusions.) Add however many levels of redundancy you wish.

- Do not ask people to select an item purely by colour. Nothing could be stupider. At the very first level, we aren't dealing with a newspaper here: "Read our editorial, p. A7." You should not force the visitor to hunt around for a link. The same words telling you to go hunting should be rewritten as *the links themselves*.

- If you're designing a children's site where a wild goose chase is the whole point and is all in good fun, then code redundantly: Set up a square, a rectangle, a circle, and a triangle, all with alt texts that define them as such. You may then add redundant coloration if desired, leading to alt texts like Red triangle, Green circle, and Black square.

Links and text

Whenever you specify colours on a Website, you need to specify at least five colours all at once: Body text, background, normal link, active link, and visited link. Why all five? If you specify fewer than that, your visitor's default colours may make the combinations unreadable even to someone with colour-normal vision. The visitor's preferred colours will be used for any setting you did not specify.

Now, obviously it is desirable for people to have the ability to override Web designers' colour choices, either for personal preference or to accommodate a visual impairment. But in a duel of colour assignments, both sides need to be equally armed: You need to specify every possible colour and so does the visitor, who trumps you with ultimate authority.

If the visitor has no special colour preferences, your colours come through in their entirety and not piecemeal. If the visitor does indeed have preferences, then those colours dominate in their entirety. In either case, someone is completely happy. Leave a colour unspecified, and you both end up unhappy.

How do you do it? In two places: The <body></body> element and in your stylesheet. Apart from the five main colours, you may optionally specify a few other link colours, like the colour a link adopts as it is being selected (usually clicked) or colours seen when you hover over a link.

HTML that is typical of a Website put together by a designer who cares (not all do, and that is not a criticism) might look like this:

Purely by accident, I happened upon what seems to be the worst of all possible worlds: "Mystery-meat navigation" united with confusable colours. In this TV-listings grid from TV3.co.nz, identical icon-lozenges differ only by colour (of course, by confusable colours like red, green, and blue). You are expected to remember what the respective colours mean. (Saving grace: The icon-lozenges do have alt texts, but no titles.) Visiting the site with an "unapproved" browser like Lynx traps you in an endless loop far, far away from the real site. And notice the enormous screen real estate occupied by what is in fact a modest amount of text? With better typographic choices and by using understandable letter symbols to indicate TV categories, this site's problems would disappear. I can't imagine the site is easy to maintain in this form, either.

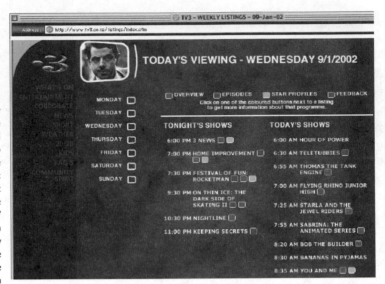

```
<body bgcolor="white" text="black" vlink="purple" alink="blue"
link="#990000">
```

- bgcolor is the background colour; text is the text colour. That much you figured out.
- A link that was never visited is assigned a colour by the link attribute.
- A link that was in fact visited is assigned a colour by vlink.
- alink sets the colour for a link as it's being clicked (an active link).

You need these assignments (which may appear in any order in the tag) to take care of those few graphical browsers that don't support the colour attributes of stylesheets, which nearly all graphical browsers in use today actually do.

XHTML 1.0 Transitional is the last document type in which specifying link and background colours on the <body></body> element is valid. XHTML 1.0 Strict and XHTML 1.1 prohibit it.

But since most browsers run on stylesheets, you need to duplicate your settings in the document's stylesheet, where you may add yet more settings.

To duplicate what's in the HTML <body></body> element, use a stylesheet that contains the following:

```
body { color: black; background-color: white }
a:link { color: #990000; background-color: white; text-decoration: underline }
a:visited { color: purple; background-color: white; text-decoration: none }
a:active { color: white; background-color: purple; text-decoration: underline }
```

(The actual colours are up to you. As for the text-decoration attribute, see the

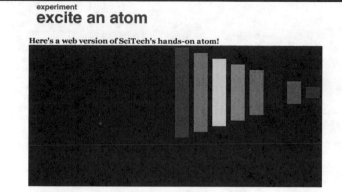

This model of a Hydrogen atom has three energy states.
It's usually in its **ground state**(lowest energy state). The electron is closer to the nucleus when the atom's energy state is lower. There are 3 energy states (n for short) for this atom: low (n=1), medium (n=2), and high energy (n=3). You can tell when the atom is in a higher energy state because the electron moves farther away from the nucleus.

What to Do:
Put more energy into the atom by shining light on it (clicking on a colored bar.)

Try these!
Excite the atom to its **medium energy state** by flashing a green photon at it (click the green bar)
Excite the atom to its **high energy state** by flashing a blue photon at it (click the blue bar)
When the atom is in its **medium energy state**, you can excite it to its **high energy state** with a red **photon** (click green bar, then quickly click red bar)

If you have designed a very clever interactive game or puzzle that, for some reason, relies on colour, you need to add usable clues that do not rely on colour. In this case (a particle-accelerator simulation), titles might be sufficient, or a different letter or number superimposed on each block, or giving the blocks different shapes, or a combination of those. Remember, accessibility is value-adding: You can keep your colour choices in this case; just give us some redundancy.

section on "Underlining links" later in this chapter.)

As in HTML, a stands for anchor or hyperlink, with the colon signifying "pseudoclasses," or approved minor variations, of the class known as a.

Though the background-color property is supposed to inherit from parent elements, it won't kill you to explicitly set the background colour for links. You may also use the specification background-color: inherit.

You've got one more commonly-used pseudoclass to play with:

a:hover { color: white; background-color: red; text-decoration: underline }

The a:hover pseudoclass governs what happens when you hover the cursor over a link without clicking it. It's kind of sexy. But it's optional.

A mobility-impaired person who uses switch access, tabbing, or some input device other than a mouse is unlikely ever to see the hover effect. For such visitors and for everyone else, you may set the a:focus pseudoclass, which governs the appearance of a link when it has focus, that is, when the next action you take will apply to it. In real-world use, focus can be distinguished from hovering or activation almost exclusively through keyboard input. If you tab through the links on a page, each successive link gains focus, not hovering or actuation.

A conventional way to signify focus is with a border. In fact, it's the default in many browsers.

For some reason, Web designers (and disreputable banner advertisers) make their sites look like operating-system controls, chiefly buttons (as in these Windows-like and Mac OS X–like examples). The Yahoo example deploys a Windows-like file-explorer icon. This usage is bad enough (what happens if one of those Windows-like banner ads is served to your Macintosh browser?); do we really want to extend this kind of operating-system infiltration of the Web to "system colours," the CSS colour definitions that make a Website look like an extension of your particular computer's operating system?

a:focus { color: #990000; background-color: white; border: solid 1px gray; }

You could use any other typographic technique, but you must keep a:hover and a:focus distinct.

Make sure your HTML and stylesheet colour declarations match exactly inasmuch as they overlap: There's no equivalent to a:hover or a:focus in HTML, so there's nothing to match there, but there *are* equivalents for background, text, and normal, visited, and active links.

Order of listing of a: stylesheet declarations is important because all a pseudoclasses have the same "specificity," meaning the last one listed wins if a link falls into more than ons category. The order suggested by Überexpert Eric A. Meyer is:

- a:link
- a:visited
- a:focus
- a:hover
- a:active

One detail remains: Extreme super-hotshot visitors may have set up a custom user stylesheet to override any of dozens of attributes on your pages. The difference between user stylesheets and simply selecting preferred colours in a browser's preferences is one of degree rather than kind. User stylesheets confer more power – particularly through the !important attribute, the doomsday weapon of user stylesheets that takes priority over any other definition. Even with this formidable quill in the quiver, the nature of the duel between the designer's colour preferences and the visitor's remains unchanged. What the visitor wants the visitor ultimately gets.

System colours

In Cascading Stylesheets Level 2 (CSS2) and later, we benefit from a range of new colour keywords of theoretical value in accessible design.

Instead of referring to colours per se as exact or approximate hues (as in rgb(255,51,51) or #f33 or red), these selectors refer to *system* colours, whatever they may be. Instead of using, say, red for a certain item, you may adopt whatever colour the visitor's computer operating system uses for text on buttons, or any of a great many system colour choices.

You the designer will not know in advance what the exact colours are. But that is the whole point: You are exercising your own design choices using a palette that respects the system limitations and personal preferences of the visitor. This may strike you as oxymoronic, but we'll get to that shortly.

Accessibility is listed as one of the official reasons to use these selectors: "They produce pages that may be more accessible, as the current user settings may be related to a disability." But browser support for these CSS2 selectors leaves much to be desired, at least at time of writing.

Yet even I, a hardcore accessibility advocate, have doubts about the worth of this feature. It is possible, even likely, that sighted Web-surfers enjoy the graphic design and variety of the Web. That is true for at least a portion of the visually-impaired audience, who may object to flashing animated GIFs or other excesses but, when pressed, might admit that Websites often look nice. There is no obvious movement to turn the look of Websites into the look of computer operating systems.

In other online contexts, we already deal with examples of grafting operating-system graphics onto the Web:

- Banner ads that look like Windows dialogue boxes. (I won't dignify them with a screenshot here.)
- Interface buttons at Apple's Website that look like Macintosh interface buttons.
- A button to view mail folders at Yahoo Mail that mimics the plus-sign-in-a-square of Windows.

We hear a lot about "Web applications" – application software that runs on the Web, usually via remote connection with a far-off server. Usabilitistas debate the merits of standardized vs. customized interfaces for such applications. I can imagine that the less-imaginative developers, or those working in fields where graphical originality is essentially nil (like engineering), will make their Web applications look exactly like Windows applications.

Do we wish to hasten this "standardization"?

More to the point, how are you better off specifying system-colour selectors?

- Browsers do not let people override those specific selectors. All a visitor can select are body copy, link types, and link underlining, if those.
- System colours are new and ill-known. The extreme super-hotshot visitors who specify user stylesheets are very unlikely indeed to select these system colours as a preference to override your settings.
- Specifying system colours negates the preferences of both designer and visitor, ceding control to whoever designed an operating system. You the designer do not even know in advance which operating system is in use. Is this not the worst of all worlds?

Underlining links

A case could be made that links should always be underlined. Virtually nothing else is underlined on Websites (though I have suggested a few such applications, as in markup for the ‹abbr›‹/abbr› and ‹acronym›‹/acronym› elements). Underlined text is almost always a link.

Many browsers allow the user to turn off link underlining. Some people do find it tacky. In stylesheets, the declaration text-decoration: underline turns underlining on, while text-decoration: none turns it off (for whatever item it refers to – in this case, a link expressed by the ‹a›‹/a› element).

The underscore itself adopts the colour of the link, meaning that colour-confusion issues may theoretically come up. In practice, text in a different colour that's also underlined is generally recognizable as a link even when minor colour confusions are possible. (If you have unwisely specified red links against a green background, the colour confusions involved are hardly minor. But you know better than to do that anyway.) The redundant coding of different colour plus underlining unambiguously identifies the link.

If you're looking at a greyscale monitor, the link text will appear in a different shade and also will be underlined. Also unambiguous.

On a monochrome display (single-bit, black or white and nothing in-between), all you've got to go on is the underscore (unless there's also something like ‹strong›‹/strong› involved).

Obviously, then, the case for underlining links is open-and-shut. Right?

No. Web-surfers have developed a range of heuristics for figuring out what a link is. A colour or font or size change can be sufficient. Left-hand navigation has trained people that stacks of words, images, or combinations of both tend to be links no matter what they look like. Top navigation is viewed similarly based on common experience. The subconscious thinking is: Anything in those broad regions is probably a link.

It is not uncommon for designers to use stylesheets to *remove* underlining from text links in navbars but *retain* them in body copy. Unlike navbars, it is not the case that anything in body copy is a link; in body copy we definitely need differentiation.

Sometimes links should be underlined and sometimes they shouldn't.

I'm not going to tell you which orthodoxy to adopt. You may even mix and match. You must nonetheless ensure that your typographic choices in totum are accessible to people with colour-vision deficiency. You have more than enough knowledge, and all the relevant software utilities, to carry out that task.

You may also use the more æsthetically pleasing dotted underline in all these cases. An example would be:

```
a { border-bottom: 1px dotted gray }
```

Type size

Now that we have colourblindness out of the way, let's consider visually-impaired people who have trouble reading "normal" type on Websites.

I am using the term "visually-impaired people" advisedly here. Even people with normal vision have to squint, peer, or work hard to read things from time to time – the instructions on a pill bottle being one example. Does that constitute visual impairment? For that specific task, yes, but not in general.

If people with normal vision find the type on a Website too small, are they visually-impaired? For that specific task, yes.

But that does not constitute a characteristic such people cannot change. Even if the type on a site is too small, if you look across your desk at a newspaper a moment later you are quite likely to be able to read that.

Transitory difficulty in reading a specific Website does not constitute visual impairment. Nor does a preference for 18-point type over whatever the designer specified because some sites were too small to read otherwise, prompting you to set your default at 18 point. (What about the sites whose type would have been quite large enough without your 18-point override?) These are not systemic and unchangeable conditions.

Experienced Web designers will be aware of the battles raging over which units of measurement to use if you want type on a page to be resizable. The ostensible purpose of such resizing is accessibility for the visually-impaired. In reality, you are merely accommodating normal-vision people who find the task of reading that specific page difficult.

While this is surely a form of accessibility, it is too low-level for this book to worry about.

It is generally accepted that pixel (px) sizing is the most compatible with text-zoom features on today's browsers, and that any type less than nine pixels in height is unreadable. It is further accepted that not every browser can zoom text, and that such a function is essential.

But I have a newsflash for everyone debating these issues: They are essentially irrelevant to actual visually-impaired people.

Screen magnification

Recall from the earliest pages of this book that visually-impaired people typically use screen-magnification software, which blows up *everything on the screen*.

If you use pixel-based sizing and are all proud of yourself for "accommodating the visually challenged," aren't you forgetting that the entire computer system has to be accessible, not just your very important Web page?

A Website with big, readable type is not very usable if your menubar insists on communicating with you via teeny 9-point type, if you can't read the names of the icons on your desktop, or indeed if you can't read anything except for the Website because it's all too small.

Screen magnifiers, then, magnify everything equally (or everything according to the settings the user selects). The menubar. The title bar of the window. The contents of the window (your Website). The Taskbar or Control Strip, if any. The trash or wastebasket or recycling bin. Toolbars. Everything.

To accommodate a visitor with a visual impairment severe enough to require big type but not so severe as to invalidate the use of a monitor altogether, there is nothing particularly special you should do. Indeed, there is nothing particularly special you can do.

I know this is a big shock to you, but look on the bright side: It's one less thing you have to worry about. Accessibility is handled exclusively by the visitor's adaptive technology.

One possible exception concerns type expressed in graphics or bitmaps, which scale rather poorly. (If you've ever used the resize command in Opera, which resizes text *and* graphics, you know this yourself.) On the other hand, screen-magnification software attempts to make an intelligent, high-quality magnification given that the intended user already has a vision loss. The bit-mapped type in your graphic should remain generally legible. An alt text is of course necessary, and can be relied on if the visually-impaired visitor has turned graphics off (which some do); an added title is always nice.

It may interest you to learn that some visually-impaired people use screen readers and screen magnifiers together. A screen reader can certainly read an alt and title if necessary.

There's another problem with screen magnification. To the extent that I could uncover (manufacturers were quite unhelpful, perhaps understandably based on what I'm about to mention), screen-magnification software blows up the bitmaps already on the screen. But most of the type on your screen has *already* been blown up from an outline font – a PostScript or (more likely) TrueType outline. The magnifier is not smart enough to re-poll the underlying outline font and provide a clean, smooth magnified character. Instead, it merely blows up the dots already on the screen; they may look nice and tidy at their existing size, but if you quadruple that size, the resulting characters will epitomize the term "jaggies."

From what I can tell, the only screen magnifier that *does the obvious* and blows up type from the underlying outline font (why is this not the expected behaviour in the first place?) is the limited ZoomView utility in Mac OS X 10.2, which I had not actually seen at press time. *Nothing else* blows up type correctly. (Magnifier manufacturers are invited to write in with corrections if I have overlooked something, but I rather doubt it.)

Now, given this fact, I have a hard time getting all high and mighty about pictures of text. Who says they'll be unreadable when blown up? All the type on the page may look unreadable! And pictures of text at least have alts to back them up, and preferably also titles.

What's the *real* problem?

HALATION

There is a small final detail. Due to a phenomenon known as halation or irradiation, light type on a dark background (*reverse* or *negative* type) looks bigger than the converse. When dealing with small type, as we usually do on the Web, the differences may be imperceptible (that is, less than a pixel's difference). If you have designed a site that uses somewhat larger type (14 point or above, let's say), you *may* wish to reduce the size of reverse type by maybe a pixel, or increase the size of regular or positive type by an equal amount.

Attention to this kind of detail, however, may be above and beyond the call of duty in general, and may make sense only when you are creating something like a navbar button with big reversed bitmapped text. The choice is yours.

Type selection

I suppose it is self-evident that a font that even nondisabled people with eagle-calibre eyesight find difficult to read will be even harder to read for a visually-impaired person. Old German blackletter fonts (mistakenly called Old English; they're about as English as Leni Riefenstahl) are an example of a hard-to-read font.

Beyond that, though, there are no immediate accessibility issues in type selection. Visually-impaired visitors and those with learning disabilities can override your choices. Totally blind visitors don't give a darn.

There is, however, one item of advice: In specifying fonts via stylesheets, specify a generic font family in each case (at the very end of the list, usually, meaning it will be the last resort). Why? If, in the exceedingly unlikely case that a visitor has none of the fonts you specify on his or her system, the browser can substitute its own default. The generic font families in Cascading Stylesheets Level 2 are:

- serif

- sans-serif (note the hyphen)
- cursive (that is, script)
- fantasy (no real correspondence to a typeface classification predating the Web, but think decorative or display or even "novelty fonts" here; the exact W3C specification says "[f]antasy fonts... are primarily decorative while still containing representations of characters... as opposed to pi or picture fonts, which do not represent characters")
- monospace

Pictures of text

The Web Content Accessibility Guidelines are unreasonably doctrinaire on the topic of using pictures of text to represent words. Checkpoint 3.2 declares:

> Content developers should use stylesheets to style text rather than representing text in images. Using text instead of images means that the information will be available to a greater number of users (with speech synthesizers, Braille displays, graphical displays, etc.). Using stylesheets will also allow users to override author styles and change colors or font sizes more easily.
>
> If it is necessary to use a bitmap to create a text effect (special font, transformation, shadows, etc.), the bitmap must be accessible....

Here we see another example of the real-world ignorance of the Web Accessibility Initiative and the antidesign bias of these visual unsophisticates.

I spent weeks assembling this chapter explaining just how to use colours in combination for *any* application, including pictures of text, while remaining accessible to the only group with a significant demand for colour control. The checkpoint assumes you the designer are too much of a rube to design your own Websites properly.

For screen-magnification users, blown-up pictures of text won't be all that much worse than blown-up text itself. Based on my research, screen magnifiers are not smart enough to use the operating system's own font-sizing and font-smoothing capabilities (that is, TrueType or PostScript outlines) when they blow up the screen image. If the unmagnified type size is 11 point and the desired magnified size is 200 point, the screen magnifier does not ask the operating system to draw a beautiful, smooth-edged 200-point character based on the underlying font outline. Rather, the magnifier acts as dumb as a sack of hammers and blows up the 11-point bitmap. How's that for stupid?

And how is your picture of text really going to fare worse than that?

In any event, the checkpoint invalidates its own initial advice by stating the obvious: A picture of text, like every single picture on every page of your Website, must have appropriate alternate text.

Bottom-Line Accessibility Advice

Basic, Intermediate, and Advanced accessibility

- Don't use confusable colours for meaningful objects unless you have to. In that case, make sure the meaning of objects can be understood from sources other than colour.
- Specify foreground and background text colours in every document that specified text colours at all.
- Specify a generic font family in each font declaration.
- If you use pictures of text, do so only for brief segments, as in navbars. Always use an alt text and, whenever possible, a title; both should reiterate the actual text.

10| tables and frames

Tables prompt eye-gouging hissyfits among accessibility advocates and Web designers of all stripes, whether oldschool or avant-garde. Both sides are saddled with myths and both argue in large part from ideology. Let's do a reality check, shall we?

Tables were introduced in HTML 3.2 back in 1997. (Not HTML 2.0. *Netscape* 2.0 supported tables, but they made their début in HTML 3.2. Very oldschool indeed.) Purists, take note: Even back then, tables were expressly permitted "to mark up tabular material or for layout purposes." Web designers who used tables for page layout were *not* violating the spec, working against the spirit of the true, glorious Internet, sullying the swimming pool, or committing any kind of sin.

Nested tables – tables within tables – have always been expressly permitted. Back to the HTML 3.2 spec: "A cell can contain a wide variety of other block- and text-level elements including form fields and other tables." The fact that nested tables take longer to display in a graphical browser is surely undesirable, but you cannot ascribe that behaviour to the inevitable effect of illegal coding. Nested tables have always been legal

The use of tables for layout has never been prohibited by the Web Accessibility Initiative. You are *not* creating an inaccessible page if it contains tables used for layout. You have committed no sin – *necessarily.* You will not be forced to turn in your trackball and badge while WAI Internal Affairs conducts an investigation. But you are not off the hook: You must code tables *properly*, which, for layout tables, is not difficult at all.

In fact, the strongest condemnation of tables in the WAI is as follows: "Do not use tables for layout unless the table makes sense when linearized." *Linearizing* refers to running the contents of cells together with no row or column structure. (How? In languages reading from left to right, start with the top row and read left to right. Then, in each successive row, concatenate cells in left-to-right order.) The *idée fixe* that layout tables are guilty until proven innocent – that they do *not* "make sense when linearized" by default, that you're doomed to labour over them forever to get them working – is an urban legend. Take my word for it: Having used the Web since the days of Mosaic, I can assure you that most layout tables do make sense, whether rendered as graphical tables or when linearized. You will nonetheless learn how to make even more sense with layout tables in this chapter.

Using tables for truly tabular data is actually quite rare online. In the immortal words of William Gibson, the street finds its own uses for things. The use the street found for tables is graphic design, not data structure. When you employ tables for layout, you can get away with minimal coding. Data tables require significant markup skills that take a long time to acquire. On the other hand, the information in data tables is intrinsically complex, and print designers struggle to this day with the difficulty of typesetting tables in existing desktop-publishing software. If no one's gotten data-table creation right in desktop publishing, a technology nearly 20 years old, why are we surprised that conditions are rough on the Web?

Here in the real world, you simply cannot produce Websites without tables. Don't think you're immune even if you have taken a vow of chastity and now do all your page layout with cascading stylesheets and sexy ‹div› elements (as described in Chapter 15, "Future dreams"). You'll have to get your hands dirty eventually by marking up true tabular data.

Goals

In this chapter:
- We'll understand the distinction between data and layout tables, and learn that the latter aren't so bad after all.
- We'll learn about table headers in all their forms.
- We'll explore access-specific table HTML.
- We'll put headers and access-specific table HTML together to arrive at a practicable coding approach that will improve table accessibility.
- We'll explain the small steps one may take to improve accessibility of frames.

The basics

Note: If you're already familiar with basic HTML, you can skip this section.
Tables have about as many components as a jet engine. You've got to go slow in learning to write tables or you'll become hopelessly lost. And you need absolute facility in basic tables in order to understand accessible table markup. This section will teach the bare bones of HTML tables, setting aside all issues of appearance.

Tables reside between ‹table›‹/table› elements. The building blocks of a basic table are rows. In case you were sick that day in grade school, understand something up front: Rows are horizontal. (Columns, which have a limited identity in Web tables, are vertical. Don't mix them up.) Rows sit inside ‹tr›‹/tr› elements. tr: *table row.* Easy to remember.

There is no such thing as a column per se in HTML. Various tags make reference to columns, but there is no ‹tc›‹/tc› tag for table columns. Instead, each table row is divided into cells. "Ah," you think. "Table cells. ‹tc›‹/tc› after all, right?" Nope: Try "table data," ‹td›‹/td›.

Each cell in a row is enclosed in ‹td›‹/td›. Each row has to have at least one cell; ‹tr›‹/tr› is technically illegal, while ‹tr›‹td›‹/td›‹/tr› is technically correct though very odd. A table can have only one cell or a theoretically unlimited number of cells.

It's possible to nest one table within another (almost always within ‹td›‹/td› elements). In fact, it's done all the time to achieve layout tricks. The practice is horrendously complex to develop and maintain (especially if you're coming back to a page for the first time in months) and causes slow rendering in graphical browsers.

Table rows have another variation, *table headers,* ‹th›‹/th›. They work exactly like ‹td›‹/td› but are usually found in the very first row or rows of a table. Technically, they can be placed anywhere, and indeed it's not unknown to encounter data tables with headers specified in the middle of the table – subdivisions, you might say. Headers provide structural or conceptual information about the rows below. (If a cell acts as a header and also provides data, a difficult-to-imagine, quasi-oxymoronic combination, you must use ‹td›‹/td›, not ‹th›‹/th›.)

Cells can expand in height and width. You can cause a cell to occupy more than one row in height with rowspan, while you can make a cell wider than one "column" with colspan. Examples:

- ‹td colspan="3"›‹/td›: A cell occupying three cell widths (three times the width of a standard ‹td›‹/td›)
- ‹td rowspan="4" colspan="2"›: A cell occupying two cell widths and four rows

You can mix and match cells with different rowspans and colspans, but rows and "columns" must add up. You can use four `<td></td>`s in consecutive order, or `<td></td><td colspan="3"></td>`, or `<td colspan="2"></td><td colspan="2"></td>`.

That merely scratches the surface of table tags, but it's enough to get you started.

Let's also define a couple of terms:

- *tabular material*: Information presented in rows and columns where the structure of rows and columns is essential to understanding the data.
- *rendering*: Displaying or presenting a table for human understanding.

Tables for layout

A table is merely a grid, like a sheet of graph paper, a spreadsheet, an unplayed game of tic-tac-toe, an octothorpe, a number sign. If you can imagine stretching cells in length and width, you can imagine using tables to lay out a Web page.

Actually, you probably don't have to imagine it: You work with layout tables every day. They're not per se inaccessible. There's a misconception that adaptive technology cannot read and understand tables. In fact, all major screen readers (on Windows, at least: OutSpoken on Macintosh is an exception) have specific commands for navigation inside tables. Since screen readers can also drive Braille displays, table-based layouts are accessible even to deaf-blind visitors. Layout tables pose surprisingly few access barriers.

What not to do

Absolutely none of the accessibility tags used in data tables may be used in layout tables. Technically, even summary="" is against the spec, but harmless. Do not use `<colgroup></colgroup>`, col, scope="", headers="", or any of the other tags fully explained in the balance of this chapter.

For layout tables, use only the most basic and unadorned `<table></table>`, `<tr></tr>`, and `<td></td>` elements. In fact, that is an exhaustive list of the elements you *may* use in coding layout tables.

Nested tables

The simple grids against which we may model HTML tables aren't good enough for designers. We crave complex structures, which are tricky to achieve online. Impatient with the slow deployment of layouts built purely by stylesheets, in the interim we have hacked our way to complexity through nested tables.

They look nice. But there is an underside. They're quite a bother to write, document, and maintain, especially when they're the output of an authoring program that hasn't been kept on a tight leash.

On the surface, nested tables do not pose an accessibility barrier. Screen readers and other adaptive technology can wade through the cells in a kind of brute-force way.

But if you're the human being at the controls of such a device, how do you figure out exactly where you are? A sighted visitor never has this problem: You can just glance around the screen. We use layout tables for their effects, not their structure, and to sighted people, the structure is quite invisible. (That is, unless for some strange reason you have set border to a value other than zero, in which case the skeletal grid structure comes to life.)

But not everyone using the Web can see.

UNDERSTANDING SCREEN READERS

The inaccessibility of nested tables is somewhat nuanced, and the best way to understand it, apart from testing your pages with a screen reader yourself, is to recall the way screen readers move around pages. Visitors using screen readers and Braille displays can chug through pages one word after another or navigate from one "item" to another, where "items" are defined by HTML markup. The commands to move through the items on a page vary from system to system, but we will model this process as akin to pressing the Tab key.

You can tab *to* a table and tab *within* a table. And here is where the problem starts. For simple layout tables not nested within other tables, it is no problem to move from cell to cell. With nested tables, though, a screen-reader user ends up working from within a maze formed by one table inside another.

Where a sighted visitor would appreciate the net appearance of all the nested tables put together, a screen-reader user navigates the underlying structure. As you know from attempting to code nested tables, the structure is damnably difficult to figure out. Now try reverse-engineering that structure via speech output.

In effect, by using nested tables, you conscript blind visitors into debugging the coding of your page by audio alone.

When you're using a screen reader, the feedback you receive is somewhat minimalist, but also confusing. Your screen reader can, for example, read out any text or links it encounters, speak the location of the cursor, and read any table headers that may be defined. You can skip from cell to cell or row to row, and you may request an audible signal as you pass each boundary. (Not every program has all those abilities, but we're working with a conceptual model here.)

Imagine, then, hearing dozens of audible signals as you step through the subcomponents of a Web page laid out with tables. It's OK when each cell contains something, or if a few cells are empty here and there, but it gets a bit redundant with table nesting.

If, for example, you embed a table, comprised of one row and one cell, inside a cell within a larger table (for example, to control cellpadding and cellspacing for a specific look), passing from that outer table to the nested cell involves traversing an entire ‹table›‹/table› element, plus individual tr and td tags.

Let's take an example of a Website listing statistical reports for sale. A cell within the outer table that contains the nested table might look like this:

```
‹td›Housing starts up 3.7% in April
‹table›
‹tr›
‹td›‹p›‹strong›In depth‹/strong›‹/p›
‹p›‹a href="/english/IPS/Data/01-004-RHS.htm" title="01-004-RHS Building
Permits"›Buy the full report‹/a› ($14.85)‹/p›‹/td›‹/tr›
‹/table›
‹/td›
```

To make your way to the link that lets you actually buy the report, you have to move the cursor into the outer cell, listen to the words "Housing starts up 3.7% in April," and then, in what appears to be the middle of a sentence, your screen reader tells you a whole new table has started.

Is the cursor now in the next column or something? Why have we skipped from one table to the next?

Now, this is not even a worst-case scenario. A single-cell embedded table, while not unheard-of, is child's play compared to what you can actually do — nest complex grids inside complex grids.

Also, in this limited example, the accessibility barrier is somewhat overstated, because not all screen readers are "verbose" in reporting the exact cell you are located in or the specific cells and rows you have moved through to get there. You can usually turn that verbosity on and off, but either way things are unclear: Even with verbosity off, a complex table nested inside another complex table will be read continuously as though there were no division between the two. With verbosity on, you hear every hiccup and burp along the route from outer table to inner table.

Not a pretty sight. Or sound.

So how do we fix it?

There has been some evolution in recent years in understanding the disadvantages of nested tables. Apart from the fact that they're convoluted to create and maintain, the complexity they add to a page may outweigh the improved appearance that is the intended result.

Also, due to bugs in the HTML rendering of Netscape 4 (yet again, perennially), it's often been necessary to code multiple *sets* of nested tables

Danny imagines his reinvention complete. "Do I look Jewish to you?!!" he explodes when interviewed by the tweedy *New York Times* reporter (well played by A.D. Miles) who has gleaned his story. (Actually, with his long cranium and death's-head 'do, Danny could double for Timothy McVeigh.) As Bean audaciously insists on Danny as a Jewish type—the tormented *apikoris*—the movie's more astute characters don't need the *Times* to give them the scoop. As Carla observes, only a Jew would be so obsessed with Jewishness. This cultural narcissism hardly makes anti-Semitism any less real— although the film does run the risk of suggesting that Jews are to blame for anti-Semitism, a formulation Bean attributes to Lina Moebius. Even before anyone suspects Danny might be Jewish, the fascists recognize him as an intellectual. (Why waste time with street brawls when he could be fundraising?) What they don't understand is that, closet Nietzschean that he is, Danny is casting himself as another Samson.

Developed by Bean over a period of decades with former *Voice* writer Mark Jacobson, *The Believer* has a script and a theme worthy of Sam Fuller. (The bravura opening in which Danny

The Believer
Written and directed by Henry Bean
Fireworks
Angelika
Opens May 17

Late Marriage
Written and directed by Dover Kosashvili
Magnolia
Opens May 17

You can use nested tables to intersperse arbitrary lengths of sidebar-like text within other text. A sighted visitor can just ignore the sidebar (due to a phenomenon similar to banner blindness, and due of course to a lifetime of scanning and reading printed pages). When experienced serially, as through a screen reader, the nested table will dutifully be read in its location in the main text.

to produce a roughly equivalent visual result in the Big Two browsers. And that says nothing of supporting small-fry browsers and platforms other than Windows.

Nested tables make your pages bigger (larger in byte count, or "heavier") and they take longer to render. Netscape 4 (*encore, toujours*) is the worst offender, since it won't display anything until it works through every single cell, row, and table. Or it might partially render a page, blank the screen, and start all over again after it recomputes certain widths.

Netscape will greet you with an empty screen if you fail to close any of several table tags. While validating your pages lets you spot such errors, it may be an understatement to say that not many coders validate their pages. Certainly not every single page. The more tables you use per page, the more likely you are to commit a typo.

Irrespective of the presence or absence of tables, some browsers display text before rendering images, others the reverse. Either way you're sitting there waiting for more information. Add that to the existing rendering complexity of tables, and you spend a lot of time waiting for pages to pop into view onscreen.

Need I mention that slow connection speeds and slow computers make matters even worse, even after all this?

I will not go so far as to recommend avoiding nested tables. Sometimes they're necessary or desirable. However, for the love of all that is holy, *please* don't design overly complex nested tables. Come up with some other way – like separate tables, or a stylesheets-only design.

Now that I've gotten that sermon out of the way, how do you decide if your tables are overly complex? For this purpose, we switch gears and momentarily turn our attention to Lynx.

The leading text-only browser (but not the only one), Lynx actually does interpret tables, though with the literalness and sophistication of a donkey. When people talk about linearization, they are singing the song of Lynx; nearly every screen reader can manipulate tables *qua* tables.

Lynx strings one cell after another in a single column. Cells arrayed horizontally in a row are unknown in Lynx. A table like this one:

```
<table>
<tr>
<td>Thyme</td>
<td>Rosemary</td>
<td>Oregano</td>
</tr>
<tr>
<td colspan="3">Marjoram</td>
</tr>
<tr>
<td colspan="2">Ginger</td>
<td>Cinnamon</td>
</tr>
</table>
```

would look exactly like this in Lynx:

Thyme Rosemary Oregano

Marjoram

Ginger Cinnamon

Lynx lays out tables serially. Remember serial access? Lynx is a program that lets you simulate serial access in the comfort and privacy of your own office. You can test the complexity of your table layouts with Lynx. (The program runs mainly on Unix, though it has been ported to other platforms; you can also, with some difficulty, find public Lynx sites. If you run any kind of Unix box, install Lynx yourself; it's free. Links and source code are available from lynx.browser.org.)

Fewer than 2% of Web-surfers of any description use Lynx. Do not take this statistic as licence to ignore Lynx users: Two percent of a million visitors is still 20,000 visitors. (Two percent of a hundred visitors, is two people. Are they too few people to worry about? You decide. I say no, particularly since Basic accessibility can serve them better with next to no added effort.)

Virtually no one uses a browser that cannot understand tables at all (that is, Netscape versions prior to 2.0 or any breed of Mosaic); you can ignore this group completely.

Preliminary HTML concerns

In the next section, you will learn an exhaustive array of accessibility tags you can use with data tables. But in nearly every conceivable case, you are not allowed to use them *at all* for layout tables. The Web Accessibility Intitative decrees it: "If a table is used for layout, do not use any structural markup for the purpose of visual formatting."

A couple issues:

- If you use the HTML Tidy authoring tool–cum–validator from the W3C, you'll be stuck with error messages for every layout table you write that lacks a summary attribute, whose majesty will be fully revealed in mere moments. If that happens to you, adding summary="" to your table element is legal and will shut the validator up.
- Don't use a title on a table element that lays out an entire page. If you do, the majority of nondisabled visitors will be stuck with a pop-up tooltip following the cursor everywhere on the page. You certainly may use a title on a table cell or row. If, for example, you have grouped all search functions into a cell, you can use a title, but do so only if you can add useful information. One of my sites, for example, provides a search field. I opted to add the detail that searching applies to the entire site, not just that specific page, to the title. You can live without that detail, and you can live with it, too, even as a tooltip.

The presence or absence of table borders has no bearing on accessibility for layout tables. The use of background and foreground colours, however, does have bearing. Colour choices are important enough to warrant an entire chapter, Chapter 9, "Type and colour."

Data tables

I have had to undergo personal hardship to understand access tags for HTML data tables. As in all good sob stories, the hardship can be traced back to childhood. In junior high school, every student in New Brunswick was saddled with provincial aptitude tests for two days straight. I aced all of them, except a little test that showed you a set of diagrams of wee odd-shaped geometric paper grids that, when folded up, produced a solid object resembling, in retrospect, those modernist houses featured in *Wallpaper*.

Our task was to decide which unfolded paper grid could be assembled, origami-like, to create the single solid object pictured. I needed every second of the allotted time to finish the test, I scored a lousy 60%, and I felt like I was about to burst into tears all the way through. It was that hard.

It seems I am no good at spatial reasoning. You should watch me try to screw a cap onto something I cannot actually see. My mind simply jams.

And here I am writing an entire chapter on the only feature of HTML that demands spatial mastery, if only in two dimensions. More than enough to confuse, I say.

The good news: Even I have figured it out. The bad news: Don't go thinking it's easy. HTML table accessibility tags are intrinsically complex, poorly supported (making them difficult to test), and time-consuming.

So let's start small.

METADATA

You've got two codes available to document the table itself: summary and caption. Kooky fun fact: Even if you use both, only one will be apparent in most browsers, though you may find the Easter egg–like richness of the other code rather amusing.

A caption sits at the top or bottom of a table and provides information about it. It's a wide-open specification: You can write whatever you want. The expected use, however, appears to follow the model of academic papers: "Figure 3b. Incidence of malaria among health-care professionals, 1965 to 1975." That sort of thing.

The HTML spec demands precise positioning of caption: It goes right after table and before anything else. You aren't limited to plain text: You can use so-called inline attributes like <strong></strong> and <em></em> and even img, but not block-level attributes like <p></p> or any of the hx series of headings.

Some examples:

```
<table>
<caption>Figure 3b<br />
<strong>Incidence of malaria among health-care professionals,
1965&ndash;75</strong></caption>
<tr>
<!— (and the rest of the table) —>
</table>
```

Here we snuck in a linebreak, shown by <br />. They're perfectly legit, no matter what you might have heard.

But if this really were a table of scientific data, wouldn't the figure label go at the bottom? Well, you can do that. caption defaults to a top placement (horizontally centred, at that), but you can select bottom.

```
<table>
<caption align="bottom">Figure 3b
<strong>Incidence of malaria among health-care professionals,
1965&ndash;75</strong></caption>
<tr>
```

```
< !— (and the rest of the table) —>
< /table>
```

"Deprecated" alignment values include left and right. You're expected to feel vaguely improper and abashed for using these and other deprecated features, and indeed they aren't very useful. You'd think a caption aligned to the left would place the caption to the left of *the whole table*, like car headlights side-by-side around a grille. Nope: left and right merely cause left- or right-alignment of the caption text.

caption is a rather brute-force instrument. It attaches text to a table with the subtlety of a nailgun. Yet in data tabulation, sometimes a table requires just the sort of explication caption provides. Using stylesheets, you can improve the appearance of the caption text. Apart from the usual typographic attributes, you can also assign alignment to left or right along with the top and bottom alignments built into the caption element. Even without style-sheets, you can use oldschool HTML like small and big.

* caption { font-size: smaller; text-align: center }
* < caption>< big>Table 3b</big>< br />

Remember the Web Content Accessibility Guidelines declaration not to use access markup in layout tables? A counterexample the braintrust at the W3C apparently failed to imagine is the use of a single-cell table to hold a photo-graph. In that case, the use of the caption element is warranted; the caption genuinely is a caption in that instance.

An example like this straddles the border between data and layout: We're using the table structure to position the image, but only so that we can use the caption element in the first place. And doesn't the image constitute the data of the table? In this case, the caption really is used to caption the photograph.

If you're reading this book while finishing off a double espresso, the caffeine may have energized your critical faculties beyond their ordinarily awe inducing levels. You may be tempted to slam down your cup and mutter "Why should I use this caption when I could just use another table row?" Well, you can. For any application where caption would work, so would adding a table row and typing in some text (even inside heading tags like h1 through h6).

So why use it? Structure. caption is a defined entity in HTML and adaptive technology like screen readers can seek it out and use it. A table row is merely a table row, with no defined relationship to the rest of the table.

The choice is yours, but caption is so easy and quick that, when applicable, you should use it.

But now the fun begins with summary. It's the only tag in all of HTML that is forbidden to manifest itself visually. The exact spec: "This attribute provides a summary of the table's purpose and structure for user agents rendering to non-visual media such as speech and Braille."

In other words, like sinking money into lottery tickets, you plug summary into a table and never see it again.

So why bother? (The perennial question in accessibility. I always imagine a tough-as-nails businessman [sic] in a black-and-white movie chomping a cigar, yelling at his comely secretary, and grunting "What's in it for me?") Because summary actually adds something useful, is dead simple, and is rather fun to deal with in certain cases.

summary is an attribute of the table element. Add it along with any other attributes, like border. For example:

< table align="center" border="0" cellpadding="5" cellspacing="3" summary=
"Unemployment figures in Queensland in 1994" >

You can, as ever, place the summary attribute anywhere in the tag, but typing it last may make it easier to edit. The mechanics of the attribute aren't the hard part. The hard part is writing the summary.

In the worst case (that is, in the most ill-advised case), the task may at first seem comparable to writing long descriptions, a task whose complexity you came to be all too acquainted with back in Chapter 6, "The image problem." It seems that this worst case is espoused by the Web Content Accessibility Guidelines. Deep within the morass of Web Accessibility Initiative technique documents is this case of a summary for a sample table (which you don't need to see to glean the complexity involved):

> Total required by pollution control standards as of January 1, 1971. Commercial category includes stores, insurance companies and banks. The table is divided into two columns. The left-hand column is "Total investment required in billions of dollars." The right-hand column is "Spending" and is divided into three subcolumns. The first subcolumn is titled "1970 actual in millions of dollars," the second is "1971 planned in millions of dollars," and the third is "Percent change, 1970 versus 1971." The rows are industries.

Now, if your screen reader spewed that out to you and then charged forward to read out the actual meat of the table, what would you do? Shake your head in confusion? Stop the process and re-read the summary?

And if this torrent of metadata is coming at you via a Braille display (an even slower serial interface than speech, which you can at least stop, start, and skip through), how do you handle it then?

The WCAG have not decided which form of accessible table markup ought to prevail — any of the one million header tags I'll get to shortly or this catch-all summary attribute. Looked at soberly, it's clear that summary should be short and sweet. Why? There's an emphasis throughout the Guidelines on using actual HTML structure for accessibility rather than using circumlocutions.

It's pretty clear: "When an appropriate markup language exists, use markup rather than images to convey information," say the WCAG. Elsewhere we are told: "Mark up documents with the proper structural elements.... [U]sing presentation markup rather than structural markup to convey structure (e.g., constructing what looks like a table of data with an HTML pre element) makes it difficult to render a page intelligibly to other devices."

So why do the WCAG advocate, in the lengthy example above, the use of unstructured, unpredictable summary text to "describe" the structure of a table?

It would appear that the summary attribute exists to provide a middling level of detail. If we think back to making images accessible, summary is possibly comparable to adding a title, not a longdesc. Imagine a page containing multiple tables. A screen-reader user might use the summary attribute to differentiate one table from another. (Admittedly, the comparison with image accessibility falls down here, because we used longdesc as a differentiator in that case.)

On the upside, summarys are quite easy to write. Just ask yourself "What is this table for?" and write that down in a concise sentence. It might require superhuman imagination to write a summary that doesn't begin with the words "This table..." or "A table that..." but we can live with it. Indeed, given all the other metadata that could be enunciated by a screen reader, a consistent writing structure might help keep summary separate from title or header information.

If summary is meant to be invisible in graphical browsers, how can it be "fun" nonetheless, as I promised before? Because some graphical browsers can actually speak. iCab on Macintosh is one of them, and it will dutifully read out a summary. You can impress your friends: Have them over to demonstrate a browser that talks without additional hardware or software and watch their eyebrows raise when the system utters words that simply are not present onscreen. Certainly, for the purposes of impressing your friends, I could not possibly suggest that you load up the summary attribute with song lyrics, Bible passages, or one of the raunchier personal ads in the alternative newsweekly of your choice. That would be irresponsible, and would simply require you to remove the fake text and use the summary properly, lest you inadvertently foist upon the world a table with summary text you'd prefer that strangers never hear.

Headers, headers, and more headers

All right. The party's over. Now we hit the head-scratchers.

HTML tables make provision for header information. In fact, they make bewildering, multilayered provision for headers. Over and over again, in so many confusing ways whose intentions and application are poorly explained in World Wide Web Consortium source documents.

To make matters worse, even some screen readers don't understand all the header substructures in HTML tables. Learning every nook and cranny of HTML table headings prepares you for the future more than it solves today's accessibility problems.

What is a header?

HTML specs are a tad vague on what a header actually is, how many of them there can be, what forms they can take, how one form can differentiated from another, and how they interact with related accessibility structures like groupings.

So it behooves us to come up with a functional definition. Headers use structured representations to elucidate or introduce tabular data. Headers usually precede data; a header that follows data can be called a footer.

Why "structured"? Because we're using HTML, which enforces several kinds of structure. Why "representations" and not words? Because nothing stops you from using images (like pictographs or product photography), with appropriate alternate texts and titles, as your headers; they're meant to be read by human beings, whose comprehension is not limited to written words. (Or you may also be stuck using a picture of, say, Japanese text rather than actual Japanese text because you lack fluency, the right fonts, or the expertise to type in Japanese.)

Why "elucidate or introduce" rather than just the latter? Because tables are two-dimensional: Your header information may sit in two places in the table, like the very top and the extreme left, and a reader must combine the two to understand the data. Or, in another case, you might look at the middle of a table, starting with a cell containing a number; then read up to find the Unemployment column header; read to the left to find the Queensland row header; and then, at last, understand that the number combines with the headers to mean unemployment in Queensland.

But that of course is the problem. A screen-reader or Braille user cannot simply glance at the row and column headers. Remember, those are serial-access devices, and in the worst case you'd have to traverse every intervening row or column until you hit the header, then step all the way back to where you started. Now, adaptive technology can automatically associate header information with cells, *if you provide it.* And you have a range of options. Let's start small.

First-level headers

Remember that table rows, marked up by ‹tr›‹/tr›, contain table cells or table "data," specified by ‹td›‹/td›? You also have the option of using ‹th›‹/th› instead of ‹td›‹/td› for cells in a row that are meant to act as headers for the "column" implied by the table structure.

It's permissible and encouraged to use ‹th› on cells in the middle of a table if those cells act as headers for the rows below them but not the rows above. You can also use a single ‹th› cell (like the first in a row) as a row header.

SECOND-LEVEL HEADERS

There is, however, another level of header abstraction in tables, known, surprisingly enough, as ‹thead›‹/thead› for table head.

Actually, in a strict interpretation, HTML tables contain a ‹thead›‹/thead›, a ‹tbody›‹/tbody› (the body or meat of the table, and there can be more than one), and a ‹tfoot›‹/tfoot› (a footer). You are not required to use any or all of those codes. Indeed, ‹tbody›‹/tbody› is implicit in every table (even an empty one: ‹table›‹tr›‹td›‹/td›‹/tr›‹/table› is legal, and the empty row is the body). By contrast, headers and footers must be explicitly specified.

To remain kosher, you will need to get in the habit of explicitly marking up ‹tbody›‹/tbody› if you also use ‹thead›‹/thead› or ‹tfoot›‹/tfoot›. If you're making a header or footer explicit, you must not leave the body implicit.

Again in strict interpretation, ‹thead›‹/thead› is intended for visual presentation. If your table extends beyond one printed page, every page can show the table header. The spec states: "This division enables user agents to support scrolling of table bodies independently of the table head and foot. When long tables are printed, the table head and foot information may be repeated on each page that contains table data."

Adaptive technology can nonetheless read and use the ‹thead›‹/thead› information. Or if it cannot, it needs to be upgraded by the manufacturer; you're doing your part and they need to do theirs.

What goes inside ‹thead›‹/thead›? Rows and cells. ("The table head and table foot should contain information about the table's columns. The table body should contain rows of table data," saith the W3C.) And of course those rows can also be headers, if you recall the ‹th›‹/th› or table-header element. Headers inside headers? Yup. And it gets better: You can use as many ‹tbody›‹/tbody› divisions as you want.

So we've got tables with headers inside headers and one or more bodies. Welcome, ladies and gentlemen, to HTML for tables.

Easy example:

```
‹table align="center" border="0" cellpadding="5" cellspacing="3"
summary="Unemployment figures in Queensland in 1994"›
‹thead›
```

```
<tr><th>City</th><th>Age</th><th colspan="3">Rate (%)</th></tr>
</thead>
<tbody>
<!— Rows and cells in any quantity —>
</tbody>
</table>
```

Footers

Footers are footers but also headers, in the way that a thumb is a thumb but also a finger or a leg is a leg but also a limb. Footers are merely headers that appear at the bottom rather than the top.

There is, in fact, an HTML construct for footers, which goes by the unsurprising name of <tfoot></tfoot>. Yet table footers, in the real Web as it is genuinely experienced as contrasted with the parallel-universe Web envisioned by the World Wide Web Consortium, are rarely necessary.

In the prehistoric medium called print, true table *footers* tended to limit themselves to tables in which headers and footers needed to be the same to make understanding the table easy. The canonical example is a printed transit timetable, with departure cities listed in a left-hand column and destination cities in header and footer. That way, even if your departure city were two-thirds of the way down a very long table, you could trace *down* to the destination city rather than traversing that two-thirds distance all the way back to the top. In cases, departure cities were listed not only in a column at left but the rightmost column for similar reasons. (All this applies, of course, to someone who can actually see, read, and manipulate a printed timetable.)

We could describe footers of this sort as structural. It is clear that the HTML table spec envisages this sort of structural footer, which is intended to appear at the bottom of successive pages were a lengthy table actually printed out. Structural footers, then, are more or less equivalent to the running footers of conventional print typography.

Now, you may be tempted to imagine that, say, the totals of a financial table, by virtue of appearing at the bottom of said table, are actually footers. That is rarely the case, if it ever is, because the totals represent one-time-only information that will not be repeated on later pages (or screenfuls, if online). One could imagine *running subtotals* appearing on each page or screenful, but there is no HTML mechanism for such a thing. (This isn't print, with its standardized dimensions. How do you determine the length of your visitor's screen? If you don't know even that much, how do you place running footers?) Running subtotals are hard to display even using a spreadsheet program.

In any event, footers are rarely encountered in Web tables. There's not a lot to know about them; the chief concern is placement of the <tfoot></tfoot> code. Let's quote the W3C: "tfoot must appear before tbody within a table definition so that user agents can render the foot before receiving all of the (potentially numerous) rows of data."

Yes, you have to list the end of a table before the middle of it, like so:

```
<table align="center" border="0" cellpadding="5" cellspacing="3"
summary="Unemployment figures in Queensland in 1994">
<thead>
<tr><th>City</th><th>Age</th><th colspan="3">Rate (%)</th></tr>
</thead>
<tfoot>
<tr><th>City</th><th>Age</th><th colspan="3">Rate (%)</th></tr>
</tfoot>
<tbody>
<!-- Rows and cells in any quantity -->
</tbody>
</table>
```

Note that the spec tells us to place <tfoot></tfoot> before <tbody></tbody>; it says nothing about where to place <thead></thead> in relation to <tfoot></tfoot>, so you might as well place it first for logic's sake.

In this example, we're duplicating the headers in the footer for easy scannability by a sighted person.

Does all of this have any relevance for screen-reader users?

Not a whole lot. In fact, as far as a screen reader is concerned, footers might as well not exist, except in the surpassingly rare cases where footers provide information that headers or body rows do not. (Remember, we're talking about *true* footers here, not unstructured, unrepeated text that coincidentally appears at the bottom.) It's like expecting a fly to be able to see, let alone care about, the soaring peak of a mountain. Footers are simply beyond the consideration of screen readers, which, as we know all too well, are sequential devices. Knowing about what appears at the bottom of a table isn't of much use to a machine that reads from the top down.

This argument does not excuse you from coding table footers correctly should you blaze a trail and actually write a table that requires them. They're just not something you particularly need to worry about in day-to-day Web design.

Structure

HTML provides a bewildering array of header tags and attributes below the level of <thead></thead> and <th></th>. The list includes:

- colgroup and col
- scope
- headers with id

We need to hack our way, as if with a machete, through this thicket of definitions by relying on structure at all times.

As we learned in Chapter 7, "Text and links," it is quite possible to specify a heading (not a header, a heading) as ordinary text typeset in a large bold font such that any typical sighted visitor would immediately recognize it as a heading. A screen reader, being as dumb as a sack of hammers, cannot read your mind and understand that a line of text marked up with ‹font face="Arial" size="+3"›‹bold›‹/bold›‹/font› (to use a particularly garish example that is common in more ways than one) is actually intended as an introduction to the next block of text.

If, however, you avail yourself of one of the six header tags of the ‹hx› series, screen readers will get what you mean. If you format that enclosed text with a stylesheet, you can produce more or less whatever look you want (and, in fact, an improved appearance compared to the brute-force ‹font›‹/font› element).

As HTML authors, we are at least passingly familiar with a mental model of text that includes six levels of headers. We are not, however, accustomed to a mental model of tables that includes groups of rows and of columns and a practically unlimited set of headers that must be explicitly associated with them.

Vertical groupings

Columns are neglected stepchildren in HTML tables. There is no specific tag for a table column (there's only ‹td›‹/td› for table data; compare this with ‹tr›‹/tr› for table row), yet you have a ton of options for clumping related columns together.

The first of these is ‹colgroup›‹/colgroup›, which does just what it says: It groups columns. In defining your table, you can allocate as many ‹colgroup›‹/colgroup›s as you want. It's a confusing tag that smacks of being thrown in at the last minute.

In the way that every table has a ‹tbody›‹/tbody›, whether listed explicitly or not, every table has an implicit ‹colgroup›‹/colgroup›. But if you add that tag yourself, you can specify how many columns are encompassed by that grouping and apply certain formatting options to them in one fell swoop.

Stick your ‹colgroup›‹/colgroup› element or elements right after the ‹table› opening tag itself (and after a ‹caption›‹/caption›, if you're using one). Use span="" to specify how many columns are part of that group. You can set up as many ‹colgroup›‹/colgroup›s as you need to structure the information the table conveys.

The following are all legal examples and all apply to a table with a total of eight columns.

```
‹table›
```

```
<colgroup span="8"></colgroup>

<table>
<colgroup></colgroup>
<colgroup span="3"></colgroup>
<colgroup span="3"></colgroup>
<colgroup></colgroup>

<table>
<colgroup span="2"></colgroup>
<colgroup span="2"></colgroup>
<colgroup span="2"></colgroup>
<colgroup span="2"></colgroup>

<table>
<colgroup span="7"></colgroup>
<colgroup></colgroup>

<table>
<colgroup span="1"></colgroup>
<colgroup span="1"></colgroup>
<colgroup></colgroup>
<colgroup span="1"></colgroup>
<colgroup span="1"></colgroup>
<colgroup></colgroup>
<colgroup span="1"></colgroup>
<colgroup span="1"></colgroup>
```

It is vaguely disturbing that the opening and closing tags can contain nothing at all yet be entirely valid.

Indeed, column groupings give you a kind of magisterial power to impose structure on a table. But we're not done yet.

COLUMNS WITHIN COLUMN GROUPS

Uniformity is *so* twentieth-century. What makes us think that every column within a group will be exactly the same?

There is, in fact, provision for diversity within unity through the use of the col element. The duckbill platypus of table tags, it's even stranger than `<colgroup></colgroup>`: Among other things, you are forbidden to use a closing tag. (Accordingly, in XHTML you must close col with a space and a slash.)

col elements sit inside ‹colgroup›‹/colgroup›s. It has essentially the same function as ‹colgroup›‹/colgroup›: It lets you identify columns (in any number, using the span="" attribute) and treat them specially.

Why, then, don't we simply nest ‹colgroup›‹/colgroup› elements the way we can nest lists? If we're trying to achieve recursion in structuring columns, why not set things up so that the higher-level element (‹colgroup›‹/colgroup›) recurs?

Beats me. The differences between ‹colgroup›‹/colgroup› and col are pedantic at best and merely add to the confusion. But we are stuck with this confusion.

To use the span="" attribute: span="1" is implicit unless otherwise specified, and ‹col /› is the same as ‹col span="1" /›. I have shied away from documenting the innumerable table formatting attributes through this chapter, but I will note that you can set the alignment of the contents of cells with cellhalign and cellvalign (note the oddball spellings).

Actually, in that case, now we see a way in which ‹colgroup›‹/colgroup› and col differ: You can set alignment for a column group and override it individually with ‹col›. We could fondly imagine doing this with nested ‹colgroup›‹/colgroup›s, but we do not live in that imaginary dreamworld.

To recast an example from above:

```
‹table›
‹colgroup›
‹col span="1" width="35" /›
‹!— Explicitly specifying a single column 35 pixels across (above) —›
‹/colgroup›
‹colgroup span="3" halign="left"›
‹col /›
‹col cellhalign="center" /›
‹col /›
‹!— Centre the middle column only —›
‹/colgroup›
‹colgroup span="3"›
‹col span="3" /›
‹!— Redundant, but legal —›
‹/colgroup›
```

These column groupings are quite the bother. And, at time of writing, the Big Two authoring programs, GoLive and Dreamweaver, cannot insert them automatically for you. So you're stuck typing them in yourself. An appetizing prospect, tisn't it?

scope **and** headers

For users of adaptive technology, "associating" headers with table cells is necessary to interpret the table. A great deal of effort has gone into defining HTML structures for this purpose.

It may be heretical to note that reading tables through speech or Braille is a pain in the arse in the first place. Correct header coding merely reduces the chance that reading a table will be a pain in the arse *and* you won't be able to understand the table even after all your efforts.

We can learn a few things from old media here. In the talking-book field, tables are read aloud by a human being. One approach, which I've actually used myself, is to provide a reader's note explaining what the top and left headers are (in one common example), then to read the rows one at a time.

It's a good system, really. I don't even need to show you how such a table would look. It is so self-documenting that you can figure out the structure just from this simulation of reading a table in talking-book format:

- Nova Scotia: males 18–35, 12.4%; males 36–51, 8.0%; females 18–35, 14.4%; females 36–51, 7.7%
- New Brunswick: males 18–35, 19.9%; males 36–51, 9.7%; females 18–35, 17.0%; females 36–51, 8.7%

You don't even have to bother envisioning how a table with this information would look because the information is right there in an understandable form.

But in talking books, a kind of *information-searching* purpose is uncommon, and even when it happens it's not very difficult compared to the Web. Most of the time, talking-book listeners do not particularly care about what any specific cell of a table actually says. They are not on the hunt for particular information. If, say, you're a scientist and you *do* actually care, then it is a simple matter of sitting there and waiting until the right information is read to you. Admittedly, this is a bother if the table consists of an alphabetical list of country names with related data and the country you're interested in is Zimbabwe, but one can always fast-forward and rewind talking books. It's a low-tech, slow-moving, genteel medium, optimized for light usage.

On the Web, however, it is much more likely that you're interested in one specific table cell with its specific data. You the reader must take active steps to find and read that cell. This of course requires that your adaptive technology support accessible table tags, which, at time of writing, is far from universal.

In any event, the relatively simple HTML scope element duplicates the genteel talking-book approach. When you add scope to a table cell, you designate that cell as having scope over a column or row – in other words, that it is a form of header.

So, to set up a *column* header, add scope="col" to any table-header cell (‹th›‹/th›) or even to a normal cell (‹td›‹/td›). Voilà: You have now told the world that the column of cells *below* that cell has the scoped cell as header. This tidy solution is muddied somewhat by the fact that HTML lacks a true conception of columns; they are defined by inference. (It's as though the World Wide Web Consortium realized its mistake and later gave us a *scope* attribute that explicitly designates a cell as a *column* header, but was unable to rewrite the old HTML spec to include columns per se. Understandable, but inelegant.)

Somewhat more usefully, you can designate a cell in a row as the header for that row. Yes, finally headers can extend horizontally. Just add scope="row" to that cell.

This remarkably easy and effective approach takes almost no time at all. How would we code the talking-book example above?

```
<table>
<tr>
<th scope="col">Province</th>
<th scope="col">Males 18-35</th>
<th scope="col">Males 36-51</th>
<th scope="col">Females 18-35</th>
<th scope="col">Females 36-51</th>
</tr>
<tr>
<td scope="row">Nova Scotia</td>
<td>12.4%</td>
<td>8.0%</td>
<td>14.4%</td>
<td>7.7%</td>
</tr>
<tr>
<td scope="row">New Brunswick</td>
<td>19.9%</td>
<td>9.7%</td>
<td>17.0%</td>
<td>8.7%</td>
</tr>
</table>
```

The column headers, then, are: *Province, Males 18–35, Males 36–51, Females 18–35, Females 36–51.* The row headers are *Nova Scotia* and *New Brunswick.*

Simple, huh?

You can vary the scope="" attribute a little. You can also use scope="rowgroup" or scope="colgroup". The latter is self-explanatory; scope applies to whatever colgroup immediately encloses it. But there is no such thing as a rowgroup per se in HTML. Instead, scope="rowgroup" applies to "the

remaining cells of the ‹thead›‹/thead›, ‹tfoot›‹/tfoot›, or ‹tbody›‹/tbody›,"
according to the HTML specification. (Here we are yet again with the asymmetry between rows and columns in HTML, except here it's the *rows* that are
not true defined structures.)

It is not clear how often structures like these will come up in actual use.
How often does a cell have *horizontal* scope on groups of *columns?* Horizontal
scope on groups of rows is somewhat easier to envision, I suppose.

However, we have a problem. We run across multiple rows of headers all
the time. I routinely see two-layer headers, and I have seen three-layer
headers in scientific papers. We're dealing with heavily qualified data sets of
this sort (setting aside every header tag for clarity):

```
‹tr›
‹td colspan="8"›Males‹/td›
‹td colspan="8"›Females‹/td›
‹/tr›
‹tr›
‹td colspan="4"›Nova Scotia‹/td›
‹td colspan="4"›New Brunswick‹/td›
‹td colspan="4"›Nova Scotia‹/td›
‹td colspan="4"›New Brunswick‹/td›‹/tr›
‹tr›
‹td›Grade school‹/td›
‹td›High school‹/td›
‹td›University‹/td›
‹td›Postgraduate‹/td›
‹td›Grade school‹/td›
‹td›High school‹/td›
‹td›University‹/td›
‹td›Postgraduate‹/td›
‹/tr›
```

The scope attribute handles one level at a time – a single column, a single row,
or a single rowgroup or colgroup. HTML does have a mechanism for setting up
networks of headers and cells, but it is a pox on all our houses.

- Add id="" and a unique name to each header cell.
- For each data cell, add headers="" and list every header id that applies to
  the cell, separated by spaces.

The headers of our current example could look like this (adding a few other
headers while we're at it – note the transformation of td to th):

```
<thead>
<tr>
<th colspan="8" id="males">Males</th>
<th colspan="8" id="females">Females</th>
</tr>
<tr>
<th colspan="4" id="males-ns">Nova Scotia</th>
<th colspan="4" id="males-nb">New Brunswick</th>
<th colspan="4" id="females-ns">Nova Scotia</th>
<th colspan="4" id="females-nb">New Brunswick</th></tr>
<tr>
<th id="males-ns-grade">Grade school</th>
<th id="males-ns-hs">High school</th>
<th id="males-ns-uni">University</th>
<th id="males-ns-post">Postgraduate</th>
<th id="females-ns-grade">Grade school</th>
<th id="females-ns-hs">High school</th>
<th id="females-ns-uni">University</th>
<th id="females-ns-post">Postgraduate</th>
</tr>
</thead>
```

Note that every header cell's id must be obsessively microdetailed. Oh, but it gets worse. Now we deal with the *data*.

```
<tbody>
<tr>
<td headers="males males-ns males-ns-grade">
18.7%</td>
<td headers="males males-ns males-ns-hs">
19.3%</td>
<td headers="males males-ns males-ns-uni">
11.1%</td>
<td headers="males males-ns males-ns-post">
7.4%</td>
<td headers="males males-nb males-nb-grade">
16.3%</td>
<td headers="males males-nb males-nb-hs">
19.0%</td>
<td headers="males males-nb males-nb-uni">
13.2%</td>
<td headers="males males-nb males-nb-post">
7.6%</td>
```

```
<td headers="females females-ns females-ns-grade">
14.1%</td>
<td headers="females females-ns females-ns-hs">
18.8%</td>
<td headers="females females-ns females-ns-uni">
9.0%</td>
<td headers="females females-ns females-ns-post">
7.6%</td>
<td headers="females females-nb females-nb-grade">
19.9%</td>
<td headers="females females-nb females-nb-hs">
15.8%</td>
<td headers="females females-nb females-nb-uni">
14.1%</td>
<td headers="females females-nb females-nb-post">
7.9%</td>
</tr>
</tbody>
```

And that's *just one row*.

For *n* layers of table headers, each data cell must carry *n* custom-added headers="" references. The example above is not atypical; there will be tremendous confusing redundancy at every level of exposition. True, the headers="" codes are not meant for human reading, but you are a human and you have to *create* them.

The case can be made, however, that the example above is the most complex way to code the headers. The most specific id of each row is the last one, so the other two could be left out:

```
<tbody>
<tr>
<td headers="males-ns-grade">
18.7%</td>
<td headers="males-ns-hs">
19.3%</td>
<td headers="males-ns-uni">
11.1%</td>
<td headers="males-ns-post">
7.4%</td>
<td headers="males-nb-grade">
16.3%</td>
<td headers="males-nb-hs">
19.0%</td>
```

```
< td headers="males-nb-uni" >
13.2%</td>
< td headers="males-nb-post" >
7.6%</td>
< td headers="females-ns-grade" >
14.1%</td>
< td headers="females-ns-hs" >
18.8%</td>
< td headers="females-ns-uni" >
9.0%</td>
< td headers="females-ns-post" >
7.6%</td>
< td headers="females-nb-grade" >
19.9%</td>
< td headers="females-nb-hs" >
15.8%</td>
< td headers="females-nb-uni" >
14.1%</td>
< td headers="females-nb-post" >
7.9%</td>
</tr>
</tbody>
```

Tedious nonetheless, don't you think?

And, moreover, adaptive-technology support for this coding is essentially nonexistent. Does this mean that complex tables with multi-layered headers are essentially inaccessible no matter what you do? Yes.

So why bother?

Indeed, *why bother?*

What we need is for authoring programs (spreadsheets among them, *very much* including Excel) to insert these headers="" codes automatically. It ain't happening yet. Then we need adaptive technology to *really* use them. That ain't happening yet, either.

I would recommend, then, adding these tedious id/headers="" codes when you are able. *Always* use the scope attributes; they are easy to add, even by hand.

As support for the tediously overdetailed id and header="" coding increases, so can your use of it.

Abbreviations

One quickie point. On the `<th></th>` element only, you may add an `abbr=""` attribute, which, not surprisingly, means "abbreviation."

It's strictly optional. The purpose is to abbreviate an especially long header so that, if you're stuck listening to it a dozen times during table readout, you will be less likely to yearn for a quick and merciful death. This provision does seem to imply that the adaptive technology will read out all the *other* headers (in their many shapes and forms) so you can fully understand the context. It also seems to imply that adaptive technology would be smart enough to read the *full* form the first time and the abbreviated form thereafter.

It is my experience, though, that verbose table headers are verbose for a reason — it takes that many words to express the concept and/or you need that many words to differentiate the header from other headers. It is not immediately obvious how one abbreviates these headers meaningfully. If it were actually possible, *we wouldn't write a long header in the first place.* And, in the print medium, people already use abbreviated headers anyway, often expanding the abbreviation in a footnote. (For that purpose, we would enclose the abbreviation in the `<abbr></abbr>` *element.* Note the difference, and see Chapter 7, "Text and links.")

In the case of short headers, I suppose trimming "Meeting date" to "Date" is harmless, but barely worth the trouble.

The `abbr=""` attribute on the `<th></th>` element seems to be a character in search of an author, really. Use it if you wish, but it is optional.

Frames

Frames do not elicit quite the eye-gouging hissyfits that tables do, at least among accessibility experts (self-proclaimed or otherwise). The big knock against frames is their usability — frame-based pages are hard to bookmark, slow to load, and difficult to program, and tend to insist on being displayed in windows of a certain minimum size.

Nonetheless, the leading screen readers (i.e., not OutSpoken for Macintosh) can all handle frames. They are not per se inaccessible, and the accessibility additions are rather modest.

Note, though, that as with tables, moving around inside frames with a screen reader adds levels of complexity. Generally you are informed whenever you traverse a frame boundary. If frames also enclose tables, you get to hear warnings about tables, too.

If the big knock against frames is usability, this knock gets even bigger when accessibility is considered. My recommendation is not to use frames unless you have no other way of achieving your layout.

The basics

Note: If you're already familiar with basic HTML, you can skip this section.

Frames *themselves* are merely HTML documents. You specify frames inside a larger container document that must, by the way, carry a so-called Frameset DOCTYPE, which, for XHTML, is as follows:

```
<!DOCTYPE html PUBLIC "-//W3C//DTD XHTML 1.0 Frameset//EN"
"http://www.w3.org/TR/2000/REC-xhtml1-20000126/DTD/xhtml1-frameset.dtd">
```

In the grand tradition of using the same words over and over in HTML (abbr! header!), after declaring a Frameset DOCTYPE you immediately use a different kind of ‹frameset›‹/frameset›. That is the element that surrounds however many frame elements you're using (as many as 16, in my experience). It also surrounds the critical ‹noframes›‹/noframes› content. You have a great many formatting attributes at your disposal (to set width and height of frames, for example), which you can look up yourself.

```
<frameset cols="200, *">
<frameset rows="75%, *">
<frame src="frame_left.html" name="Navbar" title="Navigation" />
<frame src="frame_botleft.html" name="Search" title="Search the site" />
<frameset>
<frame src="main.html" name="Main" title="Main body" />
<noframes>
<body>
<p>
You need a frames-capable browser to enjoy our site to the utmost. However,
our <a href="main.html" title="Main body">
main content</a>
is still available.</p>
</body>
</noframes>
</frameset>
</frameset>
</frameset>
```

The approach is rather similar to nested tables (and vaguely reminiscent of ‹colgroup›‹/colgroup› and col) in that framesets contain frames or other framesets.

A frame element simply links to an HTML document (through src="*filename*"). You must assign a name (and optionally an id — here's another case where id and name are not interchangeable); a title is useful for accessibility, as we'll see shortly.

Also inside ‹frameset›‹/frameset› you must — and I really mean must — include a ‹noframes›‹/noframes› element, which can contain ‹body›‹/body› elements or any block-level element below that level, like paragraphs and headings. As the name implies, your noframes content will be seen by browsers that cannot render frames (e.g., Lynx). In fact, here in the real world, the only device you'd ever run across that cannot handle frames is Lynx. Yes, we do get the wireless zealots who insist we not forget people browsing Websites on cellphones, but this theoretical activity does not actually happen in the real world; if people surf anything at all on a tiny mobile device, they surf special wireless-friendly Website variants.

Exactly what to put inside <noframes></noframes> is no longer very clear. In the days of simple Websites, you could duplicate nearly all the main content, where "main content" was defined as whatever wasn't a navbar or a search box or some other fixed entity that appeared across multiple pages. (Or you could define "main content" as the homepage, the default page served up when someone surfs to your domain.)

Back then, you could get away with that approach if you also duplicated any frame-based navbars in plain text (or accessible imagemaps, I suppose) inside the main content itself. You could add a search function, too. The fact that it was even possible to carry out such duplication added fuel to usabilitistas' fire: Why bother with frames if you can fit all your markup inside a normal HTML document?

Complex database-driven Websites very often have complex database-driven navbars (and other edge-of-screen frame content) along with generated main content. So what *do* you put inside <noframes></noframes>?

I do not have an answer, or not a very good one. At the very least, include a sitemap if you've got one, a search function, and an E-mail address or a reply form directed to your Webmaster. <noframes></noframes> content, while necessary, is a bit outdated and is certainly noncritical.

What you absolutely must *not* place inside the noframes tag is anything remotely resembling the following:

- This page requires frames.
- You need frames to use this site! Upgrade your browser, buddy! It's just good form.
- This site is optimized for Netscape Navigator and Internet Explorer version 4 at a resolution of 1024 x 768.
- You don't have frames. Your browser is even worse than mine. And mine's *really* old. Click here to see the menu and continue with your pitiful little life.
- Frames are like so totally your friend.
- This page uses frames, but for some reason you are using a browser that is so behind the times that it doesn't support them. I'd suggest you get yourself together, baby, and get with the program, cuz this is 2001, not 1994.

In other words, do not tell people to get lost until they upgrade to equipment you consider acceptable.

Accessible frames

The World Wide Web Consortium added only a couple of attributes to the <frame></frame> element, one of which is simple and makes sense, the other quite the opposite.

As with essentially everything else you can imagine in HTML, you can add a title to your frame element. You're already required to include a name, so the distinction between the two resembles the alt/title distinction in graphics. Use the name attribute for an indication of basic function (Main, LeftNav, Search, Footer, Contact) and add a title for a fuller explanation (Company homepage, Navigate our site, Search, Copyright and credits, Contact us):

```
<frame src="main.html" name="Main" title="Company homepage" />
<frame src="leftnav.html" name="LeftNav" title="Browse our site" />
<frame src="search.html" name="Search" title="Search" />
<frame src="copyright.html" name="Footer" title="Copyright & credits" />
<frame src="contact.html" name="Contact" title="Contact us" />
```

As in the case of *Search*, the two texts don't always have to differ.

What you *could* argue about is the use of a longdescription. Yes, for some unfathomable reason the esteemed Consortium has equated longdesc for images with longdesc for frames. The actual spec for longdesc tells us: "Describe the purpose of frames and how frames relate to each other if it is not obvious by frame titles alone." Why do you need to drone on and on and on about the function of a frame?

There is no set limit on the length of a frame title (or any title), though 1,024 characters (1 K) of title text is the recommendation I have made for alt and title on images. Yet if you cannot differentiate two frames in 1 K of text, accessibility is not your problem; confusion, overcomplexity, and lack of usability are. longdesc is not going to help you.

The Web Accessibility Initiative prompts a bitter little chuckle when it suggests using longdesc to describe the *appearance* of frames. I could not think of anything of less interest to a visitor who cannot see frames. This suggestion appears to be a failed analogue of a description of the appearance of an entire *page*, another hobbyhorse the WAI loves to ride (see Chapter 6, "The image problem"). Think about it: Does a screen-reader user or someone browsing with Lynx particularly care what your page or, worse, your frame happens to look like? I doubt it. By definition, overall appearance of this sort is irrelevant to such visitors. Ignore the WAI's advice to longdescribe frame appearance.

If you really must use a longdesc, remember that it is simply an HTML file. Every technical recommendation in the use of longdesc for images applies here – naming conventions (*framename*-LD.html), use of anchors, and the like. (Have a look back at Chapter 6, "The image problem.") But really, this does seem a bit *de trop*.

In summation

Tables are a bother. Until authoring programs *and* adaptive technology conveniently support the full HTML spec, it is sometimes not *worth* the bother. Nonetheless, there are enough accessible table tags that are well-supported and easy to use that you are now well equipped to noticeably improve the accessibility of your tables even without titanic effort.

To make frames accessible, use ‹noframes›‹/noframes› and title, and think carefully about usability; don't use frames unless you truly have to.

Bottom-Line Accessibility Advice

Basic accessibility
- Use tables for layout if they make sense when linearized.
- Use basic header information for data tables (the ‹th›‹/th› element). Use ‹caption›‹/caption› elements and summary attributes whenever possible; summary="" is desirable for layout tables.

Intermediate accessibility
- Use the scope attribute for complex data-table headers.
- Use titles on every frame.
- Provide ‹noframes›‹/noframes› content for every page laid out in frames.

Advanced accessibility
- Use id and the full range of data-table header attributes.
- Use column and row groupings.

11| Stylesheets

Cascading stylesheets (CSS) hold the grand promise of enabling Web authors to separate presentation from structure, form from function, decoration from essence. In *principle*, that is.

Also in principle, stylesheets provide for increased accessibility, though the actual accessibility provisions of CSS are so poorly supported that the entire project amounts to vapourware.

I should point out that this book, conceived as it was for developers and designers, limits itself to the stylesheets a developer or designer, not a Website visitor, would create. If you're already *au courant* with accessible CSS and feel I'm leaving too much out, keep that limitation in mind.

Goals

In this chapter:
- We'll learn how to link stylesheets to Web pages.
- We'll understand the limitations of accessibility-specific stylesheets, particularly so-called aural stylesheets.

Media stylesheets

With modest exceptions to be discussed later, the weight of CSS accessibility rests on the shoulders of so-called *media stylesheets*.

In general, and quite apart from the issue of accessibility, stylesheets attempt to separate the details of a document's presentation from its underlying HTML structure. If you would prefer your first-level headings to appear in bold Verdana capitals with a hint of added letterspacing, that's just what you can have. A device unable to interpret such a stylesheet will simply ignore it, or at least interpret whatever features it actually can. (Consistent with the philosophy of this book, we will not concentrate on disastrously standards-noncompliant interpretations of CSS.)

Underlying the whole system, of course, is well-written HTML that uses, for example, actual heading styles for headings rather than tarting up paragraph tags to make text look big and important to a sighted reader.

If we broaden our understanding of "presentation" to mean something more like "representation," thereby obviating even an implied *visual* form, it becomes possible to customize CSS for a range of output media. It becomes possible to write separate stylesheets for media whose modes of presentation vary enormously, from Braille to printers to computer screens.

CSS Level 2 media types were defined in 1998. Their details (as excerpted from the World Wide Web Consortium document focusing on accessibility-specific media) are as follows:

aural
Intended for speech synthesizers.

braille
Intended for Braille tactile feedback devices.

embossed
Intended for paged Braille printers.

print
Intended for paged, opaque material and for documents viewed on screen in print preview mode.

screen
Intended primarily for colour computer screens.

tty
Intended for media using a fixed-pitch character grid, such as teletypes, terminals, or portable devices with limited display capabilities.

Kray-zee, huh? Now you can write a stylesheet that works with Braille. In *principle*, at least.

Specifying a media stylesheet

It is quite possible to *embed* stylesheets in a document, by typing out the many attributes within <style></style> tags inside the <head></head> element. Then each document carries its own stylesheet, meaning you must manually alter each document should you change your mind or make a mistake.

It's also possible to specify style information *inline* inside nearly any element, as in this example:

```
<h2 style="font-weight: bold; font-family: Verdana; font-size: 18px; text-
transform: uppercase; margin-bottom: 0.5em; letter-spacing: 0.2em">
```

It's best to reserve this practice for emergencies or rarities — e.g., the one and only time you might ever need the cursive generic font family, where you could specify it as style="font-family: cursive" inside an element.

By far the preferred method of styling a document involves *external* stylesheets — separately-maintained documents that can be included by reference in an unlimited number of HTML files and updated in one fell swoop. It will probably not surprise you to learn that external stylesheets are called via a link element inside the <head></head> element. An oldschool example that does not set a media type might look like this:

```
<link rel="stylesheet" href="stylesheet.css" type="text/css" />
```

The rel="" segment signifies a relationship between the link and the current document. The external stylesheet's filename (actually, it is a URL or address) goes inside href=""; the MIME filetype declaration type="text/css" is not technically mandatory but is highly recommended; some browsers refuse to load the stylesheet if the declaration is missing. You also must close the tag with a space and a slash.

To use media stylesheets, simply add one more attribute to the link element: media="" (which can go anywhere in the element). Some possible examples (note the filenames):

- ```
  <link rel="stylesheet" href="stylesheet-tty.css" type="text/css"
  media="tty" />
  ```
- ```
  <link rel="stylesheet" href="stylesheet-aural.css" type="text/css"
  media="aural" />
  ```
- ```
  <link rel="stylesheet" href="stylesheet-braille.css" type="text/css"
  media="braille" />
  ```

I suggest a naming convention like the one above: Decide on a name for the default stylesheet and add a hyphen and the full name of the medium before the file extension for each media variant. Unlike, say, my recommended naming convention for long descriptions (*imagefilename*-LD.html), you can't rely on two-letter abbreviations due to the conflict between br for *braille* and br for *Brazil*, for which one could readily envision a localized stylesheet. (There is little likelihood of confusion with the language code br, as it refers to the Breton language, with half a million native speakers in France. Brazilian Portuguese is specified by pt-br.) If you find that level of detail academic and extraneous (*a first for this book, shurely?!*), feel free to devise your own naming scheme.
  ```

If you do not specify a medium for a stylesheet, graphical Web browsers default to an interpretation of media="all". That may not be true for cellphones, toaster-ovens, or other Internet-connected devices, not that any of them actually make use of media CSS.

In CSS Level 2, you do not have to use separate stylesheets for different media; you can use the @media rule to specify the media. That is not, however, a basic technique, so we will skip the details here.

Accessibility-specific media

From an access standpoint, the media stylesheets that matter are screen, aural, braille, and tty. (You may be wondering: "Is the term written Braille or braille?" In XHTML, attribute values do not need to be lowercase, as elements and attributes themselves must. For consistency with official documents, however, in stylesheets we will consider braille correct, even if it causes mild affront to the legacy of Louis Braille.)

The screen medium might seem unrelated to access because of our continuing interest in people who cannot actually see a screen. As you know, though, many low-vision people and essentially all mobility-impaired and deaf or hard-of-hearing people look at conventional computer monitors to surf the Web. As you learned in Chapter 9, "Type and colour," there is nothing special you can do to make type legible for a low-vision person that screen-magnification software cannot more properly do.

But you'll also recall that colour combinations are an accessibility issue for colourblind people. It is generally recommended to specify colours in a stylesheet. What kind of stylesheet? A default stylesheet, invariably interpreted as media="all" by graphical browsers. A stylesheet explicitly marked as media="screen" self-evidently falls into the same category.

Further, user stylesheets created to accommodate a visually-impaired visitor's colour, size, and presentation preferences are always of media="screen" by definition. However, the print media style can be an indirect form of accessibility given that typical print stylesheets produce black-on-white text, which some visually-impaired people find easier to use with screen magnifiers.

OTHER MEDIA

There is some evidence that CSS media types created for accessibility were not all that well-considered by the World Wide Web Consortium (W3C), a concern that is quite separate from implementation issues subsequent to their introduction.

tty is an example. We start with the terminology problem. Just as the name of the oddball accesskey attribute tricks you into thinking the issue is keystrokes on a keyboard (an accesskey is actually an accesscharacter), the tty nomenclature may conjure the following images among oldtimers in the computer and/or accessibility demimondes:

- Ancient teletype machines, of the sort used to compose and print out telegrams and Telexes.
- TTYs as understood by deaf and hard-of-hearing people – teletypewriters or telecommunications devices for the deaf (TDDs) or, in the international euphemism, text telephones (TTs). (In the U.K. and Ireland, the term Minicom is used, a former brand name turned into a generic term à la Kleenex or Xerox. It's still a TTY.)
- A dot-matrix or letter-quality printer of the early 1980s, when our fondest word-processing wish was for our documents to look as good as a typewriter's.

Indeed, recapping the tty CSS specification tells us it is "[i]ntended for media using a fixed-pitch character grid, such as teletypes, terminals, or portable devices with limited display capabilities." So much for divorcing presentation from structure: We are explicitly told not to use proportionally-spaced fonts, and that "[a]uthors should not use pixel units with the tty media type." But do the writers of the specification understand the true range of presentation modes of "media using a fixed-pitch character grid"?

- Ancient teletype machines were limited to uppercase alphabets and printed out sheets (remember continuous tractor-fed paper?) letter by letter and line by line.
- Ancient teletype machines, interfaced with acoustic couplers and voice telephones, were used as TTYs, with the same teletype output styles.
- Free-standing, compact TDDs almost invariably use a single-line visual display capable of rendering uppercase letters and a reduced punctuation set. (Really sexy models might use a two-line liquid-crystal display with full upper and lower case.) Characters on such a display *crawl* from right to left. (The very first characters may start at the leftmost position, but after the display is full up, characters at the *left* edge are pushed off the display into oblivion to make room for new characters appearing at the *rightmost* position.)
- People who make extended TTY calls (for example, the minority of deaf people in well-funded office jobs) use TTY software on their computers. It's still a telecommunications device for the deaf, but screen size varies, and you have access to upper and lower case and colours.
- "Terminals," back in the day, used a host of display dimensions, like 80 or 132 characters by 24 or 25 rows. Fonts were monospaced, with rare exceptions. Colours and double-high/double-wide fonts were available, as was "inverse video" (dark characters on a light background). You could draw boxes and lines using special characters. Accented characters were possible, with occasional difficulty. Quite significantly, *every position on the screen was individually addressable.* You could

A typical TTY (teletypewriter), also known as a TDD (telephone device for the deaf). The model shown has oldschool acoustic couplers to receive a telephone handset, but in practice all TTYs are connected directly to a phone line. Note the cramped keyboard and single-line display (here deactivated).

plunk a word or a character or a line or a box anywhere you wanted.

- And those were just the terminals themselves – like the old-style DEC and Wyse terminal hardware, "dumb" terminals that couldn't do any thinking of their own. Terminal-emulation software on personal computers superseded those old machines and is a tad more flexible: I regularly run terminal sessions at 80 columns by a very uncommon 42 rows, for example.
- MS-DOS displays came in a number of flavours, some of which even allowed italics. (Anyone remember playing around with WordPerfect display settings on VGA and XGA monitor cards?)
- "Portable devices" like personal digital assistants and cellphones come with bitmapped displays that can and do offer multiple fonts intermixed with graphics. (None of this "fixed-pitch character grid" nonsense. What decade is the W3C working in?) My ancient Apple Newton MessagePad 130 can itself do more on its little screen than any of the other devices in this list. (It is not clear how all this differs from the handheld media style: "Intended for handheld devices [typically small screen, monochrome, limited bandwidth].")

Are we to assume that the tty media stylesheet is meant to simultaneously accommodate devices that print out in capitals, display single lines of text (and cause preceding text outside that window to disappear), offer full-screen addressing in double-high, double-wide type, let you use coloured italic fonts, and give you full bitmapped graphics?

The under-researched tty style appears to have been created as a theoretical exercise. To the ill-informed, it must *sound* like a good idea. It certainly seems to have been devised in near-complete ignorance of the kind of tty implementation the W3C should have had in mind all along: Lynx, the text-only Web browser. It ignores CSS completely, but does nothing less than a spectacular job of rendering even ill-formed HTML in plain old characters and lines, just like MS-DOS. A typical Web designer could never write a tty stylesheet that makes Web pages look better than Lynx does without stylesheets at all.

All right. How about Braille?

It's fun to envision your Web pages automatically reformatting themselves into raised dots. But you'll recall that Braille intended for adults isn't a transliteration of a single printed to a single Braille character. Dozens of contractions are in use, some of them representing entire (short) words. Stylesheets do not handle that kind of character substitution, full stop. (The same sort of thing happens in Arabic and Farsi, where the shape of a letter varies with its position in a word; in Greek, with its regular and word-ending sigmas; and in Latin-alphabet languages with the many ligatures involving the letter f. Stylesheets do not handle those substitutions, either.)

The under-researched tty style appears to have been created as a theoretical exercise.

A Braille stylesheet could, for example, turn all ‹h1›‹/h1› elements into capitals (there are Braille codes for all-capitals text) preceded by a blank line, but it could not properly encode the characters between the opening and closing tags, except at a juvenile grade of Braille.

(This says nothing of the related embossed media style, "intended for paged Braille printers." Apart from accessible media types, CSS2 also introduced styles suited to the formatting of printed pages. The embossed media style is a cousin to those styles. But Braille transcriptionists undergo months of training and practice before they are competent to be unleashed on the reading public. Braille has its own set of conventions for page layout and division that a simple stylesheet, even making use of those *other* page-related CSS2 features, could not possibly accommodate. It's another concept that sounds good to the ill-informed.)

Who are we really serving here?

That isn't a rhetorical question. Which disabled groups are genuinely served by these media stylesheets? Not these:

- People who read Braille use refreshable Braille displays that employ their own logic to translate Web text into Braille.
- Deaf people do not attempt to surf the Web on their TTYs. After nearly a decade's effort, the old TTY protocol can barely be twisted and deformed into accommodating the text equivalent of interactive voice response systems ("To speak to an operator, press 0"), let alone the complexity of a Website. (While there has been an ongoing push to bring the Internet to voice telephones – the Japanese i-Mode system is

a clear-cut success; Wireless Access Protocol in Europe is a clear-cut failure – there is no push to bring the Internet to TTYs. Those net-enabled voice telephones, moreover, ignore the tty style, as everything else in the observable universe does.)

Aural stylesheets

When it comes to accessibility, however, the star of the media-stylesheet show is the aural variant. It's discussed often enough that the acronym ACSS (for *aural cascading stylesheets*) is used in online discussions of the bright and promising future of what is obviously a unique, valuable, and terribly clever invention.

The name itself is the first strike against it. *Aural*, a term favoured exclusively by pedants, sounds exactly like *oral*. When chatting with your friends about aural stylesheets at the local espresso joint, they may begin to wonder what CSS has to do with the human mouth. ("'Oral' stylesheets? Is that like oral hygiene?" is one of the few G-rated jokes you're likely to hear.) You simply cannot discuss "aural" stylesheets out loud without causing confusion and sounding like a twit.

Words like *audio*, *audible*, and even *auditory* are far less ambiguous, not to mention less pretentious, but it's *aural* we're stuck with. (The minor differences in meaning among those words are less of a cross to bear than the homonym *oral*.)

Where "visual" CSS permits you to set myriad details of graphical presentation (size, margins, borders, fonts, and beyond), aural CSS gives you control over audible characteristics, including:

- Selection of voice (male, female, or specific voice profiles available in your operating system or other software) and many vocal features.
- Volume.
- Whether or not a defined item, punctuation, or numbers are even spoken.
- Pauses.
- Cuing: You can play a sound before or after an item, for example.
- Mixing: You can play a sound while another item is articulated or voiced.
- Spatial locations: Assuming the right hardware, you can locate voices and sounds in three-dimensional space.

A whole new set of toys to play with, right?

> When it comes to accessibility, however, the star of the media-stylesheet show is the aural variant.

The knowledge gap

As everywhere in *media* access per se (think of captioning, audio description, subtitling, and dubbing), even if we enjoyed a flawlessly reliable technical infrastructure for aural stylesheets, how many working Web designers and developers would know how to write them?

You're pretty handy in Photoshop, and you can even write all-CSS layouts. You've written entire back ends in SQL. Audio? You can handle audio, kind of. You've certainly ripped MP3s to compact disc. Now, though, your boss (or the World Wide Web Consortium, whichever is worse) wants you to craft computer voices, position them in three-dimensional space, and specify background music and tones for special components.

You simply don't have that training. Nor should anyone expect you to have it. Nor is there anywhere you can *get* that training.

At the authorial level, aural stylesheets are a character in search of an author. Literally.

Aural application

"Who's gonna use this?" you ask. The answer is: Effectively no one.

Media stylesheets in general are poorly supported. Even a simple print stylesheet – for printed pages as opposed to screen display – will be ignored by certain browser versions (and some media-stylesheet combinations will crash our old friend, that carcinoma of the Web, Netscape 4).

We also face the issue of appropriateness of device. Remember the summary attribute of HTML tables? The W3C specification tells us unequivocally: "This attribute provides a summary of the table's purpose and structure for user agents rendering to non-visual media such as speech and Braille." It is not even a subject of debate whether or not a graphical browser should support summary. It must *not* do so, except inasmuch as such a browser has a speech or "non-visual" mode. (iCab on Macintosh can read Web pages aloud, and when it does so it reads the summary aloud, too.)

Why should graphical browsers support aural stylesheets?

Shouldn't that support be hived off onto screen readers?

But those programs already offer a vast range of controls for vocal characteristics. To make a visual analogy, a low-vision person may find the graphical defaults chosen by Web authors mildly annoying and may set up browser defaults or a user stylesheet to override them. But if Web designers set up aural stylesheets that override a screen-reader user's very-carefully-thought-out speech choices, honed over weeks and months of use, in favour something you slapped together because you liked the idea of using Elmer Fudd's voice to enunciate link text, the blind visitor may well end up far more than mildly annoyed.

It is a greater sin to mess with an individual blind visitor's speech settings via ACSS than any sin you could imagine that affects low-vision or colourblind people. Annoying sounds are far more annoying than annoying images. Rejigging a user's volume settings alone is more than enough to make you an enemy for life. Among other things, sound settings are harder to avoid: If you think a blackboard is ugly, you can look away, but you cannot look away from the sound of fingernails scratching a blackboard. If you dislike the appearance of a Website, you have a remarkable armamentarium at your disposal to reformulate that site's visual rendering to your liking via user CSS. But if you're stuck with somebody else's voice and sound choices, you truly are stuck.

It's all vaguely academic, though. Quite a bit of research and digging has uncovered exactly one existing assistive technology that supports aural stylesheets: Emacspeak, a rather advanced Linux software package that goes well beyond what conventional screen readers can do. (A screen-reader program whose name has the strangest capitalization ever encountered, pwWebSpeak, allegedly supported ACSS, but the program is no longer sold.)

Of course, Linux is a hacker playground. Very few real-world blind (or sighted) people use Linux, let alone Emacspeak. In fact, Emacspeak's greatest proponent happens to be the worldwide authority on audio interfaces for computers: T.V. Raman, formerly of Cornell University and Adobe Systems and, at time of writing, a researcher at the IBM Almaden Research Center in California working on the "multimodal" Web. Raman literally wrote the book on audio interfaces, entitled, surprisingly enough, *Auditory User Interfaces: Toward the Speaking Computer* (Kluwer Academic Publishers, 1997).

I interviewed Raman on current and future uses of aural stylesheets. He agrees that browser support for ACSS is nonexistent, but adds that support for stylesheets among assistive devices is also limited for technical reasons. Screen readers, for example, sit on top of browsers and do not have independent access to Web content of all kinds. "The problem is that mainstream browsers are not self-voicing browsers. It's not the browser that talks," Raman notes. "It's some third-party aid that comes along and talks. And when that happens, the third-party tool does not have access to the browser's internal CSS implementation." Someday that may change, of course.

Raman, a blind person, enjoys the luxury of ACSS support via Emacspeak, and he often uses it to make certain sections of long and tedious documents silent. Just as user stylesheets can be applied post-facto to alter an author's stylesheet (or act alone if the author didn't specify one), under Emacspeak it is possible to write user aural stylesheets that modify the rendering on the visitor's computer of prewritten, prestyled documents without the original author's knowledge.

Raman can thus skip over paragraphs coded as <p class="note"> or similar by altering his aural stylesheet to make such classes silent. That option may be an augury of the future: Raman's advice to Web authors is not to worry about

ACSS for the moment, but to provide as much meaningful stylesheet markup as possible.

Paragraphs of a certain type, for example (notes, navigation, meeting minutes) should be marked as such using `<p class="classname">` rather than just `<p></p>`. "If they use the class attribute in some meaningful manner, even if they don't write aural presentation rules... then either now or down the pipe someone would be able to potentially map aural representations to it," Raman says.

What this implies, of course, is limiting the use of inline styles – along the lines of `<p style="font: 18pt/22pt Impact">` – to very unusual cases, since you aren't identifying a class whose manifestation an aural stylesheet can manipulate. (In that example, it's better to define `.impact { 18pt/22pt Impact }` and invoke it with `<p class="impact">`.)

(Raman, by the way, does see a use for aural stylesheets in self-voicing electronic books, but those are not Websites.)

Don't worry about it

It appears, then, that your job as Web author need not include worrying about media stylesheets for accessibility. They're poorly thought out and are effectively unsupported in the real world.

Your greatest contribution to accessibility through stylesheets appears to rest on the proper, thorough, but indeed somewhat inconvenient use of class selectors for paragraphs and other elements. It requires you to consider the purpose of each section of your document and mark it up accordingly.

It appears, then, that your job as Web author need not include worrying about media stylesheets for accessibility. They're poorly thought out and are effectively unsupported in the real world.

Additional functions

At the authorial level, though, there are a couple of tricks you have at your disposal to use CSS for accessibility.

Remember the dilemma of specifying accesskeys and somehow "exposing" them to visitors so they could actually be noticed and used, assuming the browser supports them in the first place?

It turns out that, in Cascading Stylesheets Level 2, you can "generate content" to appear before or after an item through the :before and :after pseudo-elements.

It would then be possible to set up virtually anything to which an accesskey can be assigned – even a link that is an image (`<a><img></a>`) – so that the actual accesskey is listed after it. You simply add :after to the declaration of whatever item you wish to affect.

An example:

```
[accesskey]:after { content: "[" attr(accesskey) "]" }
```

The brackets in the sequence [accesskey]:after are used to specify that we're after that specific *attribute* of the element in question. (You could specify generated content for an element unconditionally: p:after { content "*" } would add an asterisk after every single paragraph, for example. Here we're just interested in the accesskey *attribute* of any applicable element.)

There are a couple of rules for marking up the content to be generated by the browser. Place literal characters (entities work fine) inside neutral quotation marks; that part you probably figured out. You can also use variables, as we do here: attr(accesskey) will substitute whatever value you have selected for the accesskey attribute. And as you can see, you can combine literal and variable content.

Using that previous snippet of stylesheet, an element like ‹a href="home.html" title="Homepage" accesskey="H"›Homepage‹/a› might be rendered as Homepage [H] in a browser rather than just Homepage.

This does not completely solve the problem of hidden accesskeys. For one thing, your visitors still have to know what the letters in brackets signify, and that invariably means writing it out somewhere on your site. Moreover, Cascading Stylesheets Level 1 support remains imperfect among browsers, and CSS2 support is even spottier. We're dealing with overlapping minorities here: The small subset of browsers that support accesskey *and* support the :before and :after pseudo-elements.

You may also be displeased with the visual impact on your page. You are, after all, littering it with brackets and (usually) letters. But as you know, on rare occasion appearance must be modified (let's not say "sacrificed") for accessibility.

You may, moreover, use :before and :after to spell out the expansions of abbreviations and acronyms, though that rather defeats the purpose. (Why would you want to read the acronym *and* the expansion, which succeeds merely in being longer, wordier, and harder to understand?) If you really must use this technique, the style looks like so (using parentheses to enclose the expansion):

- abbr[title]:after, acronym[title]:after { content: " (" attr(title) ")" }

The W3C actually suggests using :before and :after to make alt texts visible:

- img:after { content: attr(alt) }

The W3C helpfully notes that "the value of the attribute is displayed even though the image may not be (e.g., the user has turned off images through the user interface)." I thought alts were substitutions, not additions; for that we have title. The whole approach is a bad idea.

Fonts

As mentioned in Chapter 9, "Type and colour," authors are strongly encouraged to name a generic font family (generally serif or sans-serif) whenever any
font is specified by name. In that way, under battle conditions a graphical
browser or other visual device will at least have a fallback font it can use. (In
the rare case that a serif font does not exist on the system while a sans-serif font
does, the device can simply ignore a serif declaration.)

Bottom-Line Accessibility Advice

Basic, Intermediate, and Advanced accessibility

• Use stylesheets to control presentation of documents. Do not bother
  with accessibility-specific stylesheet media types.
• Specify a generic font family in each font declaration.

12| forms and interaction

Your visitors can do more than just sit there and admire your Websites. Through forms and a few other mechanisms, they can "interact" with your site, to use a heavily-debased buzzword – typing into type-in fields, pulling down pull-down menus, checking check boxes, and engaging in other intellectually taxing pursuits.

Without doing anything special at all, typical forms are not very inaccessible. The additions you can make to bring forms up to spec are not onerous.

Goals

In this chapter:

- We'll understand the difficulty of using forms with adaptive technology.
- We'll explain how to improve keyboard navigation *to* forms and *within* them.
- We'll learn why it's best to give visitors control over what happens next in filling out a form rather than allowing actions to happen automatically.
- We'll explore real-world issues in forms design that are not immediately obvious.

Who are we serving?

Forms contain information unto themselves (the names of buttons, the labels for fields, the values of check boxes and radio buttons). Forms also accept information, as in type-in boxes. We have to make forms' own information accessible, make it easy to manipulate form controls, and facilitate entering new information.

As is pretty much always the case in Web accessibility, we're mostly trying to make life easier for blind visitors (as such – visually-impaired people have very few barriers). But given that adaptive technology has had a long time to adapt to the use of forms, the improvements you can make are actually quite modest. Mobility-impaired people stand to gain quite a bit through keyboard access – namely our old friends accesskey and tabindex, which we flogged to the point of stupefaction back in Chapter 8, "Navigation." (We are stuck with the same old compatibility problems with those attributes, of course.) Also, we can make minor contributions to the accessibility of forms for learning-disabled people.

ISSUES WITH ADAPTIVE TECHNOLOGY

If you're using a screen reader, it is possible to get lost inside forms. Even if developers write a form that validates as proper HTML, some screen readers are incapable of telling you where the cursor is located or what any adjoining text might say.

These quirks bring back unpleasant memories of nonstandard browsers (not including Netscape 4, shurely?!) that are unable to interpret anything vaguely resembling proper HTML. There seems to be an expectation that you, the author or designer, are required to know all about these quirks and do every-thing necessary to accommodate them, rather after the manner of writing nonstandard HTML just so a browser (in an entirely hypothetical example, Netscape 4) will not actually crash.

I cannot support this approach. This book often suggests the use of HTML structures that, while fully legit, can be interpreted by few, if any, browsers or devices. Someday that will change, and you always have the option of writing more minimalist HTML that, while valid, does not make use of unsupported features. It is improper, however, to be expected to attempt nonstandard modifications because some makers of adaptive technology haven't figured out how to interpret standard HTML. I've suggested accessible approaches that exceed very conservative HTML, but I'm not about to suggest a practice that fails to meet even that basic and simplistic level of programming.

Besides, without vast testing of particular Websites and combinations of browsers, platforms, and devices, I could not diagnose the problems in sufficient detail to actually tell you how to fix them.

What you need to do is write valid HTML, including accessible form tags and attributes where possible. If certain screen readers or other devices cannot handle valid markup, it is not your problem. Yes, arguably it is blind visitors' problem, and they're the ones who suffer, but they need to seek redress from the adaptive-technology developer, not you or me.

One more issue is relevant. To make a form look tidy and resemble paper forms, we often resort to the use of tables for layout. That is not a prohibited practice and never was, but screen readers sometimes fail to make it clear

If you're using a screen reader, it is possible to get lost inside forms

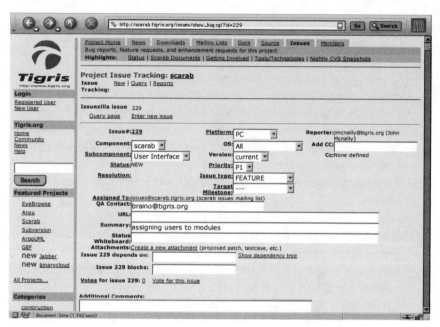

An unusually complex example of a form laid out using tables. It's easy to imagine getting lost inside here when using a screen reader or other serial-access device.

which cell containing text (that is, a field name) relates to which other cell containing the actual field. This phenomenon is not universal, but it is actually avoidable through better HTML coding, as we'll soon see.

The basics

Note: If you're already familiar with basic HTML, you can skip this section.

Forms are doggedly complex and intricate structures rivaling Stonehenge and the Mayan ruins. I really am going to give you just the basics here (and not a lot of examples), since it is quite possible to write a book half the size of this one purely on forms design. (Indeed, in the print medium, you can find a range of such books, not to mention books on PDF forms.) I did say at the outset that basic HTML knowledge is required to understand this book; forms, however, *are well beyond basic*.

I ask the reader's forgiveness for my inability to reinvent the wheel when it comes to teaching forms. I regret that I have but one life to give to writing an accessibility book, not one and a half.

Forms, unsurprisingly, sit inside <form></form> tags. A range of form *controls* are available, including input, <select></select>, <textarea></textarea>, and <button></button>. But since <form></form> is a so-called block-level element, you can use all sorts of regular HTML markup inside it (like paragraphs and headings), turning forms into documents inside documents.

What do these form controls do? Defining them becomes an exercise in tautology, actually (that is, input is for inputting, ‹select›‹/select› selects, the options for ‹select›‹/select› are called options), but here we go anyway. I'm leaving out the accessibility tags and options for now.

- ‹input› permits the visitor to interact with the form. The tag takes a vast range of parameters, of which the most important is input type="*typename*". Among many options, the Website visitor may enter text inside a small field (using type="text"), select from radio buttons (only one selection permitted; type="radio") or check boxes (multiple selections permitted; type="check"), or upload files (where supported; type="file").

- ‹select›‹/select› permits the selection of options. The user interface for this facility varies, but tends to express itself in a pull-down menu. Each available option sits inside an ‹option›‹/option› tag.

- textareas are vaguely reminiscent of input type="text" in that they constitute tidy fields into which to type text, but ‹textarea›‹/textarea› can take on a specific size (rows="*rowdimension*" and cols="*columndimension*") and allows multiple lines of text. If you've ever used a Web-based E-mail service, you have typed inside a ‹textarea›‹/textarea›.

- A ‹button›‹/button› is vaguely reminiscent of input type="button". Again with the tautologies: By using the type="button" attribute (yes, ‹button type="button"›), you can do anything you want with it in postprocessing, though you're more likely to use the type="submit" and type="reset" variants that are predefined in the specification for Submit and Reset buttons, respectively.

Setting up a form is one thing, but processing its contents is another — using the famous method="get" and method="post" attributes of the ‹form›‹/form› tag, among other methods. And boy, is that topic ever not basic. I would suggest entry into one of the leading Silicon Valley monasteries to learn the full manipulation of the runes of the ‹form›‹/form› tag.

Jukka K. Korpela wrote a bit of useful explanation for me on dynamic forms: "Form processing itself takes place behind the scenes, so there are no direct accessibility issues. But usually the processing ends with sending a result page to the browser, and the accessibility issues of that page are very important. In particular, it should present the most essential information first, details later, and if it contains a new form, the form should appear after the results proper. However, these accessibility issues might be beyond your control, or you might have just a few things you can do, by selecting among available forms-processing software and perhaps by setting its parameters."

Accessible additions

Fortunately for all of us, there isn't a whole lot to do in making forms accessible. Let's start with navigation.

KEYBOARD CONTROL

Improving keyboard access to forms isn't of huge benefit to blind people, but it certainly helps someone typing with one finger or using switch access. (You'll recall – from Chapter 3, "How do disabled people use computers?" – that switch access involves using a single control to cycle through all keyboard and mouse commands in descending order of generality until you encounter the command you wish to actuate. "Slow" doesn't begin to describe it.)

Moving to the form

All the standard barriers related to bypassing left-hand navigation or other links and content remain in force. If the purpose of the page is the completion of a form, or if a form is a small but high-profile component of a complex page (e.g., "Type in your E-mail address to subscribe to our newsletter"), you *definitely* want to be able to skip to the form and move conveniently through it.

Make sure any form on a page – and I do mean any form – becomes one of the landmarks accessible by tabbing. For this, we use the tabindex attribute, which cannot actually be added to the form tag. Among the tags that *can* take the tabindex attribute are input, <select></select>, <textarea></textarea>, and <button></button>. You've got two options:

- Add tabindex to the first input field or control in the form, as input tabindex="300".
- Apply tabindex to one of the access-specific tags about to make their grand début in this chapter.

Either method will make it possible to simply tab from landmark to landmark on the page and eventually hit the form. Now, if the entire *raison d'être* of your page *is* a form, even if it has a few paragraphs of introductory text, a case can be made that you should use a very low tabindex value (like tabindex="10" or tabindex="200"), possibly even the lowest (tabindex="1"), so that the visitor can tab to it early, if not first. In this case, getting right to the form may be more important than getting past a navbar or getting right to a search field.

(And a search field, you will note, is actually a form. Of course, if there's a search field on every page but the *content* of the page in question consists of a separate form not duplicated elsewhere, then that big form is what takes precedence.)

Moving inside the form

Getting around within the form is sometimes more complicated, but the complications are often beyond your control. Macintosh users are not very accustomed to manipulating forms entirely by keyboard – anywhere, in any application, not just Web browsers. Compared to Windows, it's virtually impossible. (Mac OS X 10.1 was the first system version to permit global keyboard usage, and even then there were bugs.)

On Windows, in fact, there are a whole host of keyboard shortcuts to move among and within form elements – Tab, downarrow, spacebar, the Return key (which Windows insists on calling Enter). You can select check boxes and radio dials, pull down menus, and type in your own entries, among other actions.

Most blind people relying on screen readers use Windows. They're all very conversant indeed with keyboard commands, particularly since screen readers themselves demand exceedingly obscure, finger-mangling keystrokes just for basic operation. (Actual examples from the screen reader Jaws: Hold down the Insert key on the numeric keypad and type the 5 key there twice quickly; Ctrl-Insert-F; Ctrl-Shift-[pressed twice quickly.) The standard keystrokes for moving around form elements are child's play compared to the necessary overhead of the screen reader's keystrokes.

We have the accesskey attribute at our disposal in marking up forms. It is perhaps superfluous for blind visitors for the reasons just described, along with the perennial issue of making the accesskey actually visible to or detectable by any visitor with any disability or lack thereof. accesskey is, however, useful for mobility-impaired people, though exactly how we make them aware of its presence is a source of frustration.

For this application, you can intelligently add accesskeys to form fields and controls to which people would want to skip directly – the high-profile controls, you could say. Nothing's stopping you from adding accesskey to most or all form controls (though you might run out of letters and numbers soon enough, and they must not conflict with accesskeys defined elsewhere on the page), but it's a lot of work with minimal benefit.

Why? If you have two type-in fields (city and state/province/territory, for example) close enough that you could move from one directly to the next via the Tab key, it is actually more trouble for the mobility-impaired visitor to press the accesskey, assuming he or she knows what it is. Tab is Tab is Tab; it's a primitive, an irreducible key on a keyboard. To actuate an accesskey, you typically have to hold down a modifier key and type the accesscharacter (which you'll recall is what they actually are, not keys per se). That's two or three or more keypresses depending on circumstances. If your switch gives you a chance to make an actuation of any kind only every few seconds, every keystroke counts.

Some criteria for selecting high-profile controls:

- In a simple but important form like a search box, add accesskey and tabindex to the text field. Adding accesskey to the Submit button is desirable but optional. A well-programmed Website lets you simply press Return to trigger the search. (If you're using a graphical Submit button, you can add accesskey to an ‹a›‹/a› tag, ‹button›‹/button›, or ‹input›.)
- In a long form where you expect (or know, through user testing) that visitors will usually fill out most or all fields, add accesskey and tabindex to the first item where an action is possible (a text field, a radio button, a check box). Visitors can thereby zip directly to the first live field of a form. If a Submit button, or any similar control applying to the entire form, is far away (at the bottom, say), then add an accesskey and tabindex to that.
- If you've created a lengthy form in which you expect people to skip entire areas – for example, in a form where a marital-status field might cause you to skip to one later field or another based on your response – assign an accesskey to at least the first field of any such grouping. (We'll return to groupings later.)
- If, for some inexplicable reason, you use a button to perform exactly the same task as a link (e.g, a Go Back link in the form of a button), such a button merits an accesskey.

Have you ever had to specify the country you reside in via a pull-down menu listing a couple of hundred of them?

This entire approach represents another instance of the practice of placing landmarks throughout a page in an order that can be selected by keyboard access.

Reset buttons

In general, Reset buttons are a miserable idea. Real-world visitors are quite likely to hit the button by accident and wipe out everything they have entered in the form. Web developers seem to include Reset buttons because HTML makes it easy. I've been online since before there even *was* a Web and I can tell you categorically that I have never once found a Reset button that truly needed to be there.

If you absolutely must be contrary and include such a button, do not give it any kind of keyboard control. Make it impossible to actuate accidentally by keypresses. Do not under any circumstances give the Reset button an accesskey. It is too easy to press the accesskey accidentally, *especially* because today's browsers and adaptive technology do a very good job of keeping the accesskey secret in the first place. Not knowing which key to avoid pressing, you might end up pressing it anyway.

Don't give a Reset button a tabindex, either. You don't want to make it *easy* to select the button. Leaving the button bereft of access features merely makes it no better or worse than a plain, standards-compliant HTML button. It might make sense to give tabindex values to whatever item *precedes* the button and whatever item *follows* it so that the button will be skipped.

If you must assign a Reset button a tabindex, give it the very last numeric value of the page. I'm sure a number like 32767 will do (one less than the very maximum). In fact, let me advance that as a convention: If you absolutely must, inexplicably, include a Reset button in the first place and if you stubbornly demand to give it a tabindex, let's all use 32767.

Grouping options

Think back to the difference between reading a Website with the naked, nondisabled eye and with adaptive technology like a screen reader. The difference pertains to random vs. sequential access.

Forms give the deceptive impression of being perfectly suited to sequential access. You're dealing with one form component at a time, right? So your attention is focused on one item at a time, isn't it?

Yes, true enough, as far as it goes. But real-world Websites pack a lot of information into a single form field. Have you ever had to specify the country you reside in via a pull-down menu listing a couple of hundred of them? Or had to select certain occupation categories from a job site? (If you want more than one category, you must use particular keyboard commands.) Have you filled out a poll or survey online, whose dozens of questions all have exactly the same seven response options formatted as radio buttons?

Usability specialists ("usabilitistas") would argue that two of these examples constitute bad form design. You should be able to type in the name of your country (or its two- or three-letter code) and type in a number from 1 to 7 corresponding to your poll response. Arguably, you should be permitted to type in keywords in a text-entry field to specify job categories.

Web developers favour overly complex and regimented form interfaces like these because they preclude errors. There is no chance of mistyping *Liechtenstein*, or entering a response value of 0 or 3.7, or of requesting a job category of *despoiler of worlds*, *smithy*, or *yo mama*. If it's hard for the user to make a mistake, programmers don't have to worry about fixing up errors after the fact, which, frankly, is a programming hassle.

Further on the topic of form design, one entry on a form may be listed right after the previous entry. (It's quite possible to include intervening text or graphics, but that is not common. Fields tend to follow one after another.) On a credit-card application, for example, address may be related to city and name may not be unrelated to both, but credit and employment history, income and expenses, and other required information really are islands unto their own. Yet, when read sequentially, one topic bleeds into the next.

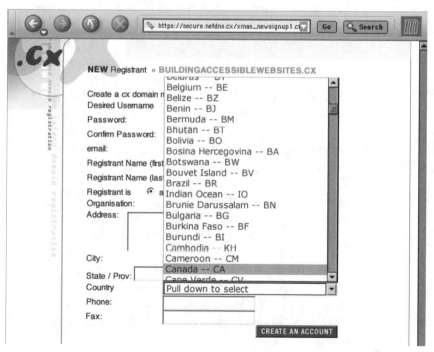

A typical, confusing, low-usability example of a pull-down menu of country names. First, "Pull down to select" is not the name of any country on earth. Second, most-frequently-selected countries should be at the top of the list. Third, the list is too long, and, in this case, its text is unwieldy: Why not sort countries by country code?

Imagine listening to hundreds of country names, one after another, in a screen reader, all because you are unlucky enough to live in the United Kingdom (U is pretty far down in the alphabet).

It's theoretically possible to use optgroup to divvy up countries into groups (by continent?), but even that does not really solve the problem. Menus like these are convenient for programmers; they prevent unintentional errors (like typing "Untied Kingdom"). But they're a pain in the arse for everyone else. Why not just let people type in a country name and error-check it in postprocessing? That requires actual programming skill rather than a drag-and-drop country menu widget.

Oh, and quickie questions: Where is "Bosina" Hercegovina, where is "Brunie" Darussalam, and just who exactly will be using this form in Burkina Faso? The entire trope of country-name pull-down menus needs to be scrapped.

This approach creates a few barriers:

- It is tedious beyond belief to be forced to listen to an interminable list of country names through a screen reader — a list that is somewhat predictable (Andorra comes before Australia which comes before Austria) yet inescapable (you cannot skip all the As through Fs to select Germany faster). During such interminable periods, you have ample time to wonder what irreplaceable portion of your lifespan this needless tedium takes up, and what you could have done with the time saved by simply typing the word "Germany" were you given the option.

- Because of screen-reader incompatibilities mentioned earlier, it is possible to lose track of exactly where you are in a complex form. Then there's the importuning of what we now call the Real World. If the form gives you pull-down menus for province or state and country, and you're sitting there listening to the various options *and the phone happens to ring*, by the time you can return your attention to the computer you may have forgotten where you were. Without accessible coding, you may be stuck starting from scratch and listening to the whole damned list all over again. (How long would you put up with that, if you don't already?)

- Long lists and mixes of topics are confusing to some people and are often very confusing indeed to learning-disabled people.

- It may be particularly tedious for a mobility-impaired person to step through extended form items.

SOLVING THE PROBLEM

In HTML, you can group related fields and options.

Fieldsets

You can use the `<fieldset></fieldset>` tag to chunk up form fields into "sets." There is no preordained arrangement you must adhere to. Instead, think about the conceptual groupings on your form. In the example of a credit-card application, all the following are viable fieldsets:

- First name, middle initial, surname
- Street address, city, state/province, postal code, country
- Telephone numbers (all of them as a group, not individual entries)
- E-mail and Web addresses
- Work history
- Housing history
- Income and expenses
- Other credit lines
- Date, signature, and declarations

You can SEARCH all my sites at once:

<!>

Search all Joe Clark sites <\>

A typical fieldset with its typical ugly bounding box, removable via stylesheets. (Note the accesskey indicators iCab uniquely displays.)

The HTML technique involved is ludicrously simple, so I won't dress it up: Just slap a ‹fieldset› tag at the beginning of a set and a ‹/fieldset› tag at the end. It's analogous to using ‹div›‹/div› tags to break up chunks of content anywhere else in a Website.

Optionally, you can add a ‹legend›‹/legend› tag directly after ‹/fieldset›. Between the opening ‹legend› and closing ‹/legend› tags, you can enter a name for that fieldset:

- ‹legend›Personal information‹/legend›
- ‹legend›Address‹/legend›
- ‹legend›Telephone‹/legend›

Such a legend acts exactly like ‹caption›‹/caption› in ‹table›‹/table›, with the same alignment values: align="top" or bottom or left or right. You may add an accesskey to a legend; what support there is for this usage appears to give focus to the first item in the fieldset. (I got it to work in Netscape 6, but not iCab.)

At time of writing, browsers that support ‹fieldset›‹/fieldset› surround each of them in an ugly bounding box. I suppose it can be argued that these fieldsets should be visible, in part because they benefit a learning-disabled person who can see the groupings. But perhaps it should be possible to turn this visibility off and on. To turn a border off, add this line to your stylesheet:

    fieldset { border: none }

You may have to add padding to produce an adequate visual appearance, and in my experience fieldset margins require tedious fiddling with width or percentage parameters. If you can produce a reliable and tolerable visual appearance for your target audience's browsers, then you must use fieldsets. They're simple and effective.

If, however, you are saddled with a stylesheet or browser incompatibility that refuses to make the intrusive bounding box go away, this may be one case where the overt visible form of an accessibility provision is too intrusive to be justified in any site that attempts to control its general appearance. (Not all sites do.) The Web Accessibility Initiative tells us: "Content developers should group information where natural and appropriate." fieldsets may be natural, but they may not be appropriate in the (possibly rare) case where their default visual display cannot be modified and clashes intrusively.

Use this exemption sparingly, if at all. I have not found a reasonably standards-compliant browser yet that is unable to deactivate the default border. You may be stuck with one of them, in which rare case you may refrain from using fieldsets.

On the other hand, you may kind of like the overt visual clustering. You could experiment with other border settings (like dotted 1px gray) to make the border more visible and yet also more palatable.

Option groups

Meanwhile, options in a <select></select> tag (a pull-down menu, effectively) can be grouped together using <optgroup></optgroup>.

The use of the tag is simple, and quite akin to <fieldset></fieldset>. Surround any related option tags with an <optgroup> and an </optgroup>. Always add a label attribute to the tag (which must be unique per page). A generic example looks like this:

```
<select name="country" id="country">
<optgroup label="A1">
<option></option>
<option></option>
<option></option>
</optgroup>
<optgroup label="A2">
<option></option>
</optgroup>
<optgroup label="B1">
Any number of option tags
</optgroup>
</select>
```

You cannot nest <optgroup></optgroup> tags; they may contain nothing but <option></option> tags.

Browser handling of option groups varies, but is not entirely bad.

- Internet Explorer 5 on Macintosh turns the option groups into submenus.
- iCab, Netscape 6, and Mozilla show you an unselectable heading corresponding to the label value of the option group.

In practice, the exact content of your menu will likely not be compatible with this approach. Not every option list can be subcategorized. Maybe only a minority ever could be. In the worst-case scenario of a vast list of every country name on the planet, you could divide everything up by continent. More-current browsers will group the list of options in a way that most people will find helpful. Reading the lengthy menu may be made less onerous by the submenus or visible headings in browsers that provide them. But this case is perhaps exceptional.

Since you have only one level of grouping to play with, this facility is somewhat limited, but it is substantially better than nothing, it actually improves the appearance of menu items, and it is terribly slick and clever. Use option groups whenever possible.

As Jukka K. Korpela points out, in form designs where optgroup might help, it may be better better to ask the visitor to make choices in different steps (using server-side intermediate processing when needed) than to create nested menus.

Do not, however, succumb to the temptation to use the ‹optgroup›‹/optgroup› syntax to provide instructions, add advertising, or be cute. (Do you still use ‹dl›‹/dl› to indent text?) Don't enter option-group text that does not actually categorize the option group. Do not flout the laws of Nature.

Field labels

There's a rather oddball tag called ‹label›‹/label› that lets you "associate" textual or graphical labels with specific form controls.

Some older screen readers have a hard time linking a form control to nearby text, particularly across the boundary of a table cell. The ‹label›‹/label› tag solves the problem two ways:

- You can specify a label for a form control located virtually anywhere on the same page; adaptive technology will link the label and the control – theoretically.
- You can enclose a control inside a ‹label›‹/label› tag.

QUESTIONS OF DISPLAY

‹label›‹/label› takes a form rather similar to ‹span›‹/span›. It can contain any "inline" element, like text or even an image (with appropriate alternate text, of course). That means the inline text, image, or other material will be overt and visible, as labels generally are in the real world.

Accordingly, even though you can place a label for a form control anywhere on a page at any distance from the actual control, wherever you place the label is where it will show up.

USAGE

If you do want to separate a label and a form control in your HTML, you must use an identical assignment of id (not name) for the form control and the label. The "oddball" part comes into play here. The syntax to specify the id looks like this:

```
‹label for="idvalue"›Label text‹/label›
```

It seems a bit bald-faced and contrived to use "label for *x*" in HTML, but since the label tag was added to HTML only very late in the day (in version 4.0), these syntactic oddities must be tolerated.

In any event, having set up your label tag in that manner, all you need to do is add id="*idvalue*" to the form control, wherever it is. (Note that you must use id, not name.) Any kind of form control will work – buttons, check boxes, radio buttons, menus, text inputs, file selectors, and anything else that's valid HTML.

It makes a bit more sense to enclose a form control in a <label></label> tag. In this case, you may use for="*idvalue*", despite the redundancy. Preferably, just surround the form control, and any necessary plain text, with <label></label>. Some examples using a simple control like input:

- <label><img src="location.gif" alt="Location" width="42" height="20" border="0" title="Where are you located?" /><input type="text" id="location" /></label> (you may use an image or any other inline element)
- <label accesskey="s"><span class="bigger">Home</span><input type="text" id="home_phone" /></label> (inline stylesheet markup is fine)
- <label accesskey="G" title="Don't forget the area code"><abbr title="Phone number">Ph#</abbr><input type="text" id="phone-number" /></label>

TITLES

As in that last example above, you can add titles to essentially everything in HTML, including the entire range of form tags. Even if you're also using the accessible HTML catalogued in exacting detail here, there is no harm and possibly quite a bit of benefit in using titles in forms.

There is some indication (which I was not really able to verify) that certain screen readers have trouble wading through forms whose elements lack a title. That really means every single element – every check box, every radio button, every text-entry field, the lot. I am something of a title fetishist and do tend to use them religiously, but I am not quite willing to advise you to add a title to absolutely everything. Why? Screen readers, like all other HTML-aware devices, must be upgraded to understand standard HTML. Requiring an *optional* attribute like title just to use a form suggests that the screen reader in question needs to be fixed.

I would say it is most useful to assign titles to input and textarea fields – anywhere you must enter your own information. Since titles provide "advisory information," use this facility to *advise* what you want us to include in that field. Examples:

- Enter your phone number (area code first)
- Type your surname (last name, family name), then any other names
- Explain the problem you are having (in under 100 words, if possible)
- If you don't know your postal code, leave the field blank
- If you usually take a half size, order a full size UP

Imagine you're a disembodied voice piping out of the speakers of your visitor's computer. What advice would you give on how to fill out that field? Take that advice, write it succinctly, and include it in a title.

Radio buttons are another application. To use a previous example, a poll in which you are expected to select one of seven response buttons, duplicated in the dozens all the way down a page, can become confusing. Which button refers to Strongly Disagree? Strongly Agree? Agree Somewhat? Adding a title to each button makes that information clear to most visitors (through tooltips, status-line display, and screen-reader output).

A perennial goal of accessibility is to provide redundancy of information. Using all the HTML accessibility tags customized for forms along with ever-present titles gives us about as much redundancy as anyone has a right to expect.

Keyboard access

A label may also take an accesskey; the HTML specification tells us simply: "When a label element receives focus, it passes the focus on to its associated control." Selecting the label via accesskey, then, is the same as selecting the associated control. Kookily enough, this also means that a label and a form control associated via id="*idvalue*" can theoretically be actuated by the accesskey irrespective of the distance between the label and the control. I suspect this was one of the many unintended consequences of undertested Web Accessibility Initiative modifications.

Graphical buttons

As elsewhere in accessible Website design, you must use text equivalents for graphics, including alt, title, and longdesc. alt is the standard method for the img and embed tags, as you well know, and you are free to use either of those tags for, say, a graphical button.

However, input type="image" itself can carry an alt, which is a good thing, since there is no actual img tag that could carry it within that usage. But we're dealing with a new addition as of HTML 4.0 here; older documents won't have alt inside input. (Or if they do, it wasn't legal at the time the code was written — people did improvise in the old days, sometimes with good intentions.)

Text-only browsers and graphical browsers with image-loading turned off could always avail themselves of two other attributes of the input tag, namely value and name. Back in the day, oldschool browsers used one of those entries as a text equivalent, substituting for the alt text that was not legal at the time.

Nowadays, though, you have *all* those at your disposal, plus id and title. That's five possible text equivalents or text-equivalents manqué: alt, name, value, id, and title. Based on my own research (I'll spare you the details), I would suggest the following:

- Use alt, name, value, and id, all with the same text and all at once on every input type="image" tag. (If your validator chokes on the id attribute because you have specified a DOCTYPE predating HTML 4.0, take it out. If the validator chokes on name because you are using an XHTML 1.1 DOCTYPE, take that out.)
- Consistent with distinguishing alt and title when using the img tag, if you're going to use exactly the same text as the four previous attributes for title, enclose it in brackets []. Otherwise, feel free to explain the purpose of the button or what will happen next inside the title.

Syntax like the following is legal:

```
<input type="image" src="button-6.gif" alt="Continue" name="Continue"
id="Continue" value="Continue" title="Proceed to checkout" />
```

It's redundant, redolent of outdated coding kludges, and vaguely laughable, but legal nonetheless.

(With all five text equivalents present, Lynx displays value; using only one at a time, or simply deleting value, my testing shows that Lynx displays alt by preference but no alternative text at all if you use only title, id, or name. The details are somewhat academic, I know.)

Prefilled form fields

The Web Content Accessibility Guidelines list the following as a Priority 3 (advanced) measure: "Until user agents handle empty controls correctly, include default placeholding characters in edit boxes and text areas."

Evidently some very early screen readers could not detect the presence of an empty text-entry field at all. It simply ceased to exist. This is yet another case of adaptive technology's inability to interpret standard HTML, and in this example the cure may be worse than the disease.

One of these outmoded screen readers may be able to detect your form field due to the default placeholder text it contains, but the visitor must then listen to the text. Fine so far — but where did the text come from? Is it text adjoining the field that attempts to provide instructions on how to fill it out, or is it indeed text inside the field? (You may have to hunt around with keyboard commands that force readings of nearby objects to find out.) Further, if a field carries prewritten text, you must delete the text to use the field.

As a nondisabled person who has been online forever, is a quick typist, and knows all keyboard shortcuts in wide use, even I very often have to struggle to delete every last character inside a field. I know all about key sequences like Select All and Delete, but half the time I'll mistype the Select All command (selecting everything in the browser window), or I'll try to select the text with the mouse and click the adjacent button instead, or delete everything but one character. It's nothing but trouble. And I'm not blind and I

have no trouble manipulating a keyboard and mouse. Imagine how much of a
bother it is for those groups.

Besides, we can't keep working around the quirks of nonstandard devices,
be they an Ebola-like browser (could it be Netscape 4?) or creaky old screen
readers. It is probably a bad idea to prefill your text fields if this is the only
reason you're doing it.

One does occasionally happen across a Website whose text fields (a search
box, for example) are prefilled, though the text disappears instantly when
you deposit the cursor in the field. Based on queries submitted to screen-
reader makers, screen readers are not confused by this technique and indeed
do not bother to read the prefilled text once the cursor is deposited in the
field. This practice seems to be gilding the lily anyway; thousands of Websites
get by just fine with entirely blank text-entry fields.

Rethinking layout

You now have a lot of knowledge about forms, but how do you apply it?

Apart from adding these accessibility tags, you may wish to rethink the
layout of your forms. The access additions, particularly label for="*idvalue*",
allegedly solve the problem of associating form controls with their labels.

We wouldn't have had to go to all this trouble if designers had not resorted to hacks like the use of table cells to align form fields and text. There
seems to be an effort to emulate the design tropes of printed forms – in
particular, a desire to place the label of a field to the left of the field itself.
Side-by-side positioning is difficult in a linear language of expression like
HTML. So the table hack and its ilk were not unforgivable, though they
brought up unforeseen problems with noncompliant screen readers, which
made it difficult or impossible even to detect certain form elements when
dispersed through tables. Moreover, the task of navigating table cells is always
slower using serial access; depending on your settings, your software may
let you know every single time you pass from one cell to another. It is all
unduly complicated.

Maybe the online medium needs to make a virtue of necessity. If it's
difficult to align components horizontally, then let them appear stacked on
top of one another. That might not be such a dire fate. The Web is not print,
as they say.

If you use structural groupings like <optgroup></optgroup> and even
<p></p> (abetted with stylesheets for acceptable appearance), there is very
little chance that a visitor relying on adaptive technology won't be able to
figure out what goes with what. It's merely a suggestion.

Error-checking

It is helpful to provide error-checking that does not merely *alert* us to a
mistake we've made but attempts to *correct* it.

If you want side-by-side positioning of the sort found in print typography, you are pretty much stuck with using tables in HTML. A very pretty and yet hopelessly complicated example here. In serial access, you have to contend with navigation with the table and within the form – all because we want HTML tables to look as space-saving as tables on the printed page.

What if I told you that you should just give in to the inherent nature of HTML and lay out your tables in a linear rather than a side-by-side manner? It's perhaps unæsthetic, but it's easier to use and more accessible.

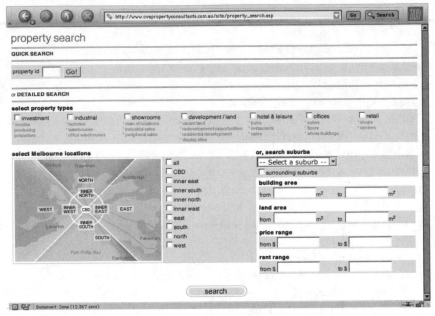

If you take my advice about providing type-in fields rather than menus for, say, country names in forms, and if I type "Gremany" in that form field, it is better practice for your system to map that misspelling to "Germany" or *at least* present a list of likely options. (I suppose that is not a very good example given that few country names are confusable. Mistyping "Austlia" could mean Austria or Australia. Or a state name like Dakota or Australia could be ambiguous – is it North or South Dakota? Western Australia or South Australia?)

Error correction of this sort provides improved accessibility for dyslexics. And for bad typists. It's a very good idea. A bother to program, but useful nonetheless. Retrofitting functions like these might be too much to ask, but I would be pleased if all readers who create complex forms promised themselves that they would add error-checking to any new forms they create and over whose back-end programming they have influence – even something as simple as a search interface that would check mistypings against likely correct entries.

If you need to alert us to an error, you must use redundant methods. You may not simply present the form to us again with the erroneous fields marked in red. An entire chapter of this book (Chapter 9, "Type and colour") explains why that method will be inaccessible to pretty much anyone who is colourblind or reliant on a screen reader.

Dynamic forms

Forms that don't just sit there and let you use them as plain-Jane HTML — as though this were still 1994 and our expectations were pretty low — are increasingly common. You've probably run across *dynamic* forms: As soon as you make an entry in one field, the rest of the form changes altogether.

This approach can be intelligent and well-conceived. Localization is one reason to design a dynamic form. To return, yet again, to our example of a vast list of country names, you could set up your form so that only the most relevant fields for postal address or phone number appear once the visitor specifies a country name. The form may default to U.S.-style addressing (street address, city, state, ZIP) but change to province and postal code for a Canadian address or provide something more free-form for a Swedish visitor, given that Swedish addresses aren't as structured as those in the U.S. or Canada. Or a phone-number field could assume a country code and provide just the right number of possible digits for area code and number (an issue Americentric forms, with their demands for three-three-four number formations, flub notoriously).

Another example is found at the PlanetOut.com personals. When setting up an advanced search, the system asks you to select first a continent, then a country, then a city. But only one of those options appears at a time, building up from top to bottom in reaction to your inputs. (What am I doing searching the PlanetOut personals, you ask? The accessibility specialist–author, lonely and dispossessed in his northerly garret, is sometimes forced to cast his drift net wide.) It's a very intelligent and respectful method of handling a worldwide (though still English-speaking) visitorship.

But by far the most common dynamic form device is a pull-down menu that actuates as soon as you make a selection. Usabilitistas have a fair bone to pick with this approach:

- It requires JavaScript. (In fairness, at time of writing the overwhelming majority of browsers have JavaScript turned on, and I have found no evidence of severe incompatibility with screen readers for typical JavaScript uses.)
- It provides no escape route if you make mistakes. If you select the wrong option, off you go in that direction anyway. I personally make that mistake at least six times a year.

The solution is easy, actually. Always provide a valid HTML button or control to advance to the next step. A *Go* button next to a pull-down menu is perfectly standard. A *Continue* or *Proceed* button in a sophisticated form will do fine. If you use a graphical button, all necessary text equivalents must be supplied. (You may also wish to enclose a *Go* or *Proceed* button in a < noscript >< /noscript > element so that only JavaScript-unaware browsers even render it.)

A surprisingly sensitive and clever implementation of dynamic forms. At PlanetOut.com, you can select Canada from the pull-down menu, which immediately switches from "Zip Code" to "Postal Code." (Good internationalization there.)

If, on the other hand, .you are not in the U.S. or Canada, you can build your own location step by step by selecting a region, a country (whose field pops up out of nowhere), a city (ditto). You may then fine-tune the distance from that city, if necessary – all done via self-generating forms.

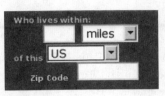

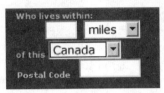

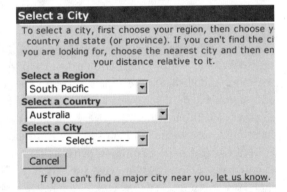

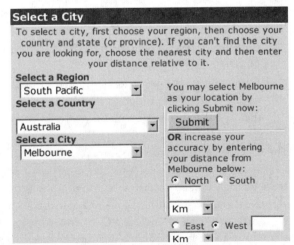

Another questionable technique: Instead of assigning the menu any kind of label (even plain text outside the <select></select> coding), the first entry in the menu options acts as the title or explanation of the menu. Funnily enough, though, there is no nation called "Choose your country," nor does anyone speak "Choose your language" — but you'd never know that from the way developers rig up their menus. You now have a range of accessible methods (even the use of plain text outside various form elements) to solve such problems.

Real-world issues

Our goal here is accessibility and not a narrow form of compliance with pubished standards. It is not enough to code a form accessibly; you must also accommodate accessibility in the real world.

Telephone numbers

If a form you design has an entry field for a telephone number, aren't you assuming that every visitor can use a voice phone? Newsflash: Deaf people typically cannot talk on the phone; they use TTYs, which consist of a keyboard and a display (usually single-line) with a modem that only other TTYs can connect to. Deaf and hard-of-hearing callers, and those with speech impediments, can type back and forth in real time. TTY software and modems for personal computers are also available and are employed by power users who spend a lot of time on the phone.

If your Website form assumes that a visitor's home or office phone number is voice only, your staff are in for a rude surprise when they actually dial the number and hear the distinctive TTY tones (which actually do not sound like a fax machine or a modem).

There would seem to be two telephone-number issues at work here:
- *Location:* Home, office, mobile or cellular
- *Modality:* Voice, TTY, fax

Depending on context, your form may not need to take location into account, but I am telling you that your forms *must* take modality into account, even if you don't care about fax numbers.

You will not have much of a problem making this accommodation. Everywhere in the U.S. and Canada (and some U.S. territories, like the Virgin Islands), Australia, and the U.K., relay services are available. (The U.S. federal government has its own relay service.) You call a hearing operator who acts as an intermediary between a TTY and a "voice" caller, typing what a hearing person says and reading what a deaf person types. (There are other variations: If you can speak but not hear, *voice carryover* is often available, for example. The range of relay services is quite extensive. There are, however, no really comprehensive Websites on the topic.)

In any event, a hearing person can always call a TTY user (any TTY user anywhere) wherever there is a relay service in the hearing person's location. There is no extra cost for the call, and very often there is a discount due to the longer times required to communicate this way. Similarly, TTY users can call any voice number (at all – anywhere in the world).

Yes, it's a bother, and you do have to train your staff to handle TTY calls through relay services, but it is still a notable improvement over having your staff dial a TTY number without knowing it actually is one. If you're looking for training on relay-service use, call the relay service itself. In most parts of the United States, dialing 711 (just those three digits) connects you to local relay service. In Canada, 711, when it works at all, connects you to the TTY-to-voice end of the relay system; there is no uniform national phone number for voice-to-TTY service. Other numbers are available; since there are literally dozens of relay services operated by different vendors in North America alone, you need to check your local phone book or do a Google search on the keyword relay service plus whatever state or province you live in.

In Australia, call the Customer Relations department of the Australian Communications Exchange relay service at 1800 555 630 (TTY) or 1800 555 660 (voice). In the U.K., call Typetalk Customer Support at 0800 500 888 (TTY) or 0800 7 311 888 (voice). Elsewhere in the world, consult your local listings.

Now, ideally your business would own an actual TTY device or TTY software, and probably have a dedicated TTY number. But unless you're a large retail concern with a lot of TTY callers or have a known demand from TTY callers, it is unnecessary to own your own equipment. That's why we have relay services in the first place.

For each phone-number field on your forms, then, I want you to specific-ally add another field that allows visitors to specify voice or TTY (or fax). I would not worry about the somewhat common case of a household or busi-ness that can handle either TTY or voice; in practice, individual Website visitors always have a preference and will select one or the other.

Markup like this will suffice:

```
<input type="radio" name="voice" value="voice" title="Voice number" id="voice"
accesskey="v" checked="checked" />Voice
<input type="radio" name="tty" value="TTY" title="TTY number" id="tty"
accesskey="t" />TTY
```

Or you could create a small pull-down menu, or a type-in text field, or any of several possible interfaces. The exact approach is up to you; I just want you to do it.

Alternate formats

If one of the forms on your Website invites visitors to fill in their postal address to receive printed information by snail mail (*poste escargot*), do keep in mind that not everyone can read print, very much including the blind.

Now, it is clearly unreasonable to expect an online bookstore to stock all its products in Braille, large print, and/or audiotape; the central activity of the business is selling (inaccessible) printed books. On the other hand, a company that sells products or services other than books to the public should take into account the need to provide its information in accessible formats.

I am not advising you to have your company brochures Brailled, retypeset in large print, and/or audiotaped in advance of any known demand for those. I will, however, advise you to allow Website visitors to *request* such formats.

All you need is a plainly apparent indication on the form used to request the literature that says something like "Alternate accessible formats available on request." You could add a little text area in which the visitor could type a request (if there isn't one already – good design of feedback forms generally requires a Comments field), or simply let the visitor check a box saying something like "Contact me to discuss accessible alternate formats for this information."

If someone actually takes you up on your offer, you will then be faced with having the literature in question converted to Braille or audiotape. Leave that job to the professionals. I would suggest another Google search using keywords like **blind braille conversion** or **blind audiotape conversion** plus the state or province you live in (if you are in Canada or the U.S.), or a similar approach for residents of the U.K., Australia, or elsewhere.

Large-print production you might be able to handle yourself. Provide the customer with the original, unaltered source brochure with regular or small print and a separate document with all the brochure's text set in large type (at least 18 point, with lots of leading). Don't use Arial as typeface, and do not use any kind of fancy or novelty font. The American Printing House for the Blind, APH.org, is a good resource, and indeed for U.S. readers, APH can convert literature into Braille, audiotape, or large print.

It may seem archaic to have to worry about print in the first place; we are, after all, building accessible Websites. I am, however, responding to the real world here. We *do* use the Web to order printed literature; I've done it myself. You must take disability into account in providing such a service.

Similarly, if your organization offers a promotional or informative video or audio product via Web ordering, it may be incumbent on you to provide captioned and/or audio-described video and, at the very least, a transcription of an audio product. Chapter 13, "Multimedia," describes this process.

How far do we take this? Do *all* products a disabled person could even theoretically order via the Web need to be accessible? The blanket answer is yes. The reality is that they are not. Only a minority of products are accessible; so-called universal design is a rarity, and indeed universally-designed products are usually the most custom-designed products there are. In any event, you should consider the issue and take necessary steps.

Bottom-Line Accessibility Advice

Basic accessibility

- Group related form options using < fieldset ></ fieldset > and < optgroup ></ optgroup >.
- Always account for telephone modality (voice vs. TTY), and make allowance for the provision of alternate formats on request.
- Do not code forms so that an action takes place as soon as the visitor makes a selection. Include a Go button (or similar function) so the visitor has control over what happens when using the form.
- Use as many of the five possible form-element text equivalents – alt, name, value, id, and title – as is legal for the HTML version declared in that page's DOCTYPE.

Intermediate and Advanced accessibility

- Use accesskey and tabindex to improve keyboard navigation.
- Add titles to as many form elements as possible, giving preference to type-in fields.

13| multimedia

AUDIO ON THE WEB WORKS VERY NICELY. Video is still a bit of a boondoggle. And making video accessible is so difficult you had best leave the job to the experts. And at present, there is no way for you the Web developer to become an expert.

Goals

In this chapter:
- We'll understand the Big Four access techniques of captioning, audio description, subtitling, and dubbing.
- We'll explore the state of the art outside the Web and how the Web compares.
- We'll come up with a list of options for low- and medium-budget accessibility.

What's the problem?

Well, that depends on how we define "problem."

The *accessibility* problem is simple: Deaf people can't hear audio and blind people can't see video. The *infrastructure* problem is trickier: There are too many player and file formats for the various operating systems. While essentially every player can handle "universal" formats like MP3, each player's specific file format is proprietary to that player. It's much worse than the VHS/Beta discrepancy canonically cited as a parallel: Back in the day, it was always possible to find an A-list movie in both home-video formats. But, as if to spite real-world users, media files online are routinely offered in only one format, absolutely forcing you to run multiple players. Considering accessibility specifically, different players and versions have different capacities and are incompatible, to varying degrees, with assistive technology like screen readers.

The *appropriateness* problem is intractable. Despite a few promising experiments here and there, there isn't enough bandwidth in the world to duplicate even the quality of broadcast television online. Nor is there any reason even to make that attempt, a fact lost on executives at media juggernauts, whose quest for some kind of ill-defined "convergence" threatens to ruin the Web as we know it in an ill-conceived effort to make it just like television.

We have the Web. We have television. Like matter and antimatter, the two should remain separate.

I am not wild about the use of video on the Web. (Audio is fine by me.) Yet I am not so religiously opposed to its use that I refuse to recognize that accessibility must be taken into account. But the utility and practicality of online video access actually mirror those of online video itself. Just as online multimedia aren't even remotely as good as TV, online multimedia *accessibility* isn't remotely as good as TV's. In fact, it's not as good as TV's was in 1989.

Defining our terms

As you read back in Chapter 4 ("What is media access?"), the broad categories of accessible media predating the Web are *captioning* for deaf and hard-of-hearing viewers and *audio description* for blind and visually-impaired audiences. These are two of what I call the Big Four access techniques; the other two are subtitling and dubbing, which this book does not really cover.

Closed accessibility features are hidden until they are activated. *Open* access features are always present and cannot be turned off.

The basics

Note: If you're already familiar with basic HTML, you can skip this section.
HTML coding for multimedia leaves a lot to be desired. The oldschool technique is widely compatible but officially "deprecated," while the standards-compliant technique is poorly supported and has been known to crash browsers.

The oldschool technique is the embed element, which takes attributes similar to those of img. (In fact, technically you can use embed rather than img to specify a graphical image if you want.) An easy example:

```
< embed src="announce2.mov" width="320" height="256" />
```

It will not surprise you to learn that the width and height specifications govern the size of the window in which the file identified by src will play.

Closed accessibility features are hidden until they are activated. Open access features are always present and cannot be turned off.

Netscape devised the embed element. It was never actually approved in a World Wide Web Consortium "recommendation." It is of course widely used nonetheless.

The other oldschool technique, reserved for Java applets, is the ‹applet›‹/applet› element, with a vast panoply of parameters. Life is too short to list them all in a section entitled "The basics," but here's one example:

```
‹applet codebase="http://img.socks-online.co.uk/applets/classes"
code="sizes.class" width="350" height="200" alt="SockSizer&trade;"
align="left"›
‹/applet›
```

‹applet›‹/applet› has a few advantages, like the ability to include marked-up text or even graphics between the opening and closing tags (in theory, a browser unable to display the Java applet could display such content instead). You can and should also add an alt text inside the tag itself.

However, both those oldschool elements are now "deprecated" in favour of the allegedly superior ‹object›‹/object› element, which is so generic it can encompass essentially anything — any "object," including images, imagemaps, video, audio, lists, plain text, entire HTML documents. You can, for example, set up multiple ‹object›‹/object› elements that enclose:

- a QuickTime video
- an ordinary still image that can be displayed if the video cannot
- a still image in a different file format if the previous file were undisplayable
- plain text that can be displayed if the image cannot

Such an example could be written as follows (and is not entirely farfetched given today's limited browser support for the PNG format used here):

```
‹object data="conf.mov" type="video/quicktime" title="Press conference (May
7/01)" width="300" height="300"›
‹param name="pluginspage" value="http://quicktime.apple.com/" /›
‹param name="autoplay" value="true" /›
‹object data="desrosiers2.png" type="img/png" title="Yves-&Eacute;tienne
Desrosiers, CEO"›
Yves-&Eacute;tienne Desrosiers, CEO
‹object data="desrosiers2.jpg" type="img/jpg" title="Yves-&Eacute;tienne
Desrosiers, CEO"›
Yves-&Eacute;tienne Desrosiers, CEO
‹/object›
‹/object›
‹/object›
```

Note the nested objects. You can place one object inside another in (usually) descending order of desirability or technical sophistication: A movie file, then maybe a sound file, then an image in a high-quality format like PNG (with enclosed alternative text), then maybe a JPEG image (ditto). The oft-cited principle of graceful degradation is at work here, or ought to be, if the element actually functions properly.

(The param elements, by the way, specify "initialization data"; compliant devices could, for example, automatically refer you to the download page for the QuickTime plug-in if you didn't already have it.)

You don't add an alt text or a longdescription to `<object></object>` per se. Any text that an `<object></object>` element might enclose will become the alternative text.

The bad news is that, for all its marvels, `<object></object>` is so poorly supported by real-world browsers – actually crashing Internet Explorer 4.01 for Windows in some unusual cases – that it is quite unusable. For video and audio files, you're stuck with embed. Your choice then becomes writing a standards-compliant page that breaks browsers and doesn't actually do what you want or writing a noncompliant page that works just fine. For the foreseeable future, noncompliance is the way to go. Yes, I know, I promised never to authorize or promote nonstandard HTML use, but if I stuck to that faithfully here, online video would essentially disappear.

Technical infrastructure

Online video can hardly be considered "new media" in any strict sense. Video is not exactly a new addition to homes and businesses. Video on computer screens reaches all the way back to 1993, actually predating the Web. (Remember the Macintosh TV, with its cable-TV tuner and remote control?)

Unlike the entirely new task of making text-and-graphics Websites accessible, we have decades of experience in accessible video *outside* the Web. This history has rather raised expectations of what should be possible online. We should *at least* be able to exceed the capacities of "old media."

So let's consider television and home video.

- In North America, the so-called Line 21 captioning system, in use since 1979, gives us two usable streams of captioning. (Technically there are four channels, but only two are practicable. The first pair of channels – CC1 and CC2 – is sent down one pipe, while the other pair – CC3 and CC4 – has a separate pipe. To use CC1 and CC2 together, each gets half the total bandwidth. But if you use CC1 and CC3, each can have all the bandwidth of their respective pipes.)
- We also get two usable channels (out of four, with the same distribution as above) of text information that occupies all or half the screen depending on the device you're watching.

DVD subtitles (from Tom Tykwer's Run Lola Run). True to the subtitling idiom (as opposed to captioning), the titles are an edited translation; they don't move to show who's speaking (in fact, who is speaking in this scene?); and no "non-speech information," like sound effects ("phone rings," "footsteps receding") or manner of speech ("sarcastically," "whispering") is shown. Subtitles are insufficient as an accessibility technique for deaf viewers.

DVD closed captions (also from Run Lola Run). Here we see the vaunted non-speech information crucial to making a film understandable to a deaf audience. One could dispute the caption positioning here. Note the white-on-black typography, and the lousy caption font my television set sticks me with.

- In Europe, the U.K., Australia, and other countries using World System Teletext (WST), several streams are available, with hundreds of available channels of full-screen text.
- Also in certain WST countries, a separate captioning system — Line 22, a variation of the one used in North America — has been available since 1992, with one caption stream.

- Home videotape devices in North America have always been able to record and play back captions. Videotape devices in WST countries cannot record World System Teletext captions (with rare exceptions); the transplanted North American Line 22 captioning system works with any VCR. In North America, then, home video has offered closed captions for nearly a full human generation, and for almost a decade in certain WST countries.

- Stereo television is widely used, in analogue and digital formats, around the world. In North America, it is uncommon but quite possible to use the second audio track (its actual name is Second Audio Program, or SAP) to deliver audio descriptions mixed in with main audio.

- Digital television systems – even those that are little more than tarted-up present-day analogue TV – offer at least two and usually many more audio channels. It then becomes possible to run a program with original audio, descriptions for the blind, dubbed dialogue, and descriptions in the language of the dubbing.

Flash:
Nothing whatsoever.

- DVDs offer up to 32 subtitle tracks (not exactly the same as captions, but the tracks can be put to equivalent use) and up to eight audio tracks. (The number of bits available on a DVD is finite; given that video is the whole point of DVDs and that video eats up a lot of space, you usually run out of available bits well before you run out of possible audio tracks. Subtitle tracks occupy far less space, but even I find it hard to imagine 32 titling variations.) NTSC DVDs can also carry closed captions – chiefly DVDs in Region 1 and in Japan (Region 2).

That's what we get to play with in the real world. What does the virtual world give us?

- QuickTime: No predefined limit to the number of text and audio tracks.
- RealVideo: Captions (one stream) and audio description (one stream), though the exact numbers are muddied given that you get one of each stream per language.
- Windows Media: "Multiple" captions, but no audio descriptions.
- Flash: Nothing whatsoever built into the data structure, but you can add text in a way that functions as captions.

Even if you wanted to duplicate the degree of accessibility available in North America (let alone in a medium like DVD), you couldn't do it in all the multimedia formats currently in use online. Pick one that seems to work well (like QuickTime) and you leave out everyone who doesn't have that player. (Admittedly, this would be more pressing if you chose Windows Media, which is new even for Windows users and essentially unused on Macintosh.)

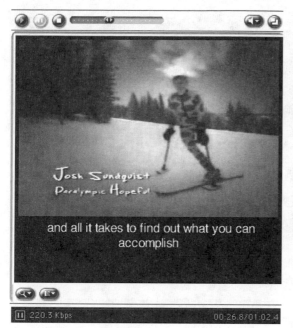

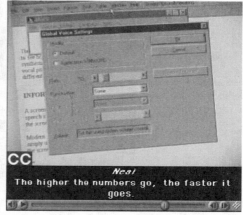

Captioning as seen in RealPlayer (left) and QuickTime. Fonts and positioning are terrible (in some ways worse even than on TV); QuickTime makes it difficult to turn captions on and off (the "CC" button was added to make that possible), though doing so is much easier in RealPlayer. On the plus side, unlike on television, you can position captions outside the frame. It is not easy to "author" the separate text files necessary to create the captions and synchronize those files with the online video.

SMIL

There does exist a platform-neutral, industry-standard markup language with which to create files for accessible media, including captioning and audio description. The so-called Synchronized Media Integration Language or SMIL is a World Wide Web Consortium "recommendation," which is about as forceful and standardized as the W3C gets.

SMIL lets you cue text, audio, and video together in any combination. It is, in effect, a metalanguage (indeed, it's based on XML) that describes *what* should appear *when* in a "time-based medium." We're not just talking about cinema, TV, radio, and music here: A slideshow or a PowerPoint presentation falls under the same category even if it contains nothing but words. (So would an animated GIF, theoretically.) SMIL handles anything that doesn't just load once at a random moment unforeseen by the designer or author and sit there.

SMIL has been around since 1998. Player support is pretty good: QuickTime 4.1 and later and RealPlayer 8 and later support at least SMIL 1.0, while SMIL 2.0 support is present but incomplete in Internet Explorer 5.5 and later for Windows.

When it comes to creating a SMIL file, though, we harken back to the early days of the Web's commercial boom. Is it better to code by hand (preferred by oldschool Web programmers; allows precision and full standards compliance, but is as slow as it is error-prone) or use a graphical

This all-QuickTime captioning experiment by WGBH gives you English or Spanish captions (true captions even in Spanish, not just foreign-language subtitles) and/or English or Spanish "enhancements"—paragraphs of description of the musical style, instruments used, and the like. Very slick, and a massive programming task.

editing program (preferred by neophytes; tends to produce nonstandard, hard-to-maintain markup but is noticeably faster)?

A great many professional Web developers mix and match, and indeed the seeming duality of text vs. graphical HTML editing barely scratches the surface of all the software involved. You might design your comps in Photoshop, touch them up in ImageReady or Fireworks, create HTML layouts in Dreamweaver, write CGI and database programs in a text editor, and test in a range of browsers.

Now you need to ask yourself: On top of all that, do I want to learn a new markup language known as SMIL, or do I want to learn new *software* that will produce SMIL files for me?

You actually have quite a few options for authoring programs; a good listing is found at the W3C site itself, at w3.org/AudioVideo. Your source video track, any descriptions, and any captions or transcripts you create (which you will learn about shortly) are all files that SMIL can manipulate.

Naturally, Microsoft marches to the beat of a different drummer. Support for SMIL in Windows Media Player is somewhat nonstandard. (Of course, to be "somewhat" nonstandard equates with "nonstandard, period," but when it comes to accessibility, standards have a tendency to be imperfectly supported.) Windows Media supports a subset of SMIL 2.0, which Microsoft has given the charming name of HTML+Time. A standards-compliant SMIL document will not necessarily work in Windows Media, but captioning and description files are simple enough that they will usually work. (Or so I gather. Quite a bit of research, including questions posed directly to Microsoft, failed to provide a definitive answer.)

Further, Microsoft has its own SMIL-like markup language for time-based media, the Synchronized Accessible Media Interchange or SAMI. Like SMIL,

SAMI resembles HTML and is not particularly difficult to learn. Yet there are no authoring programs for the format; it's nonstandard; and it works only in Windows Media Player, and even then only imperfectly. (A Microsoft Web page tell us simply: "Windows Media Player 5 supports a subset of the full SAMI specification." It's Microsoft's own file format and a Microsoft player supports only "a subset" of it?)

SAMI has been rendered obsolete by SMIL and its stepchild, HTML+Time. Unless you are creating accessible media for an intranet or some other installation that you absolutely know uses Windows Media Player and you are entirely sure you will never, ever need to migrate accessibility files anywhere else online, you should do no authoring at all in SAMI. Use SMIL instead.

Interface issues

There's also a wee problem with user interfaces. While this is not technically your problem as a developer or designer, it is a necessary detail in understanding the practical obstacles standing in the way of accessible multimedia.

A deaf or hard-of-hearing person has no particular difficulty using the visual controls of media players. A blind or visually-impaired or a mobility-impaired person definitely does have difficulty given that it is normal for players to emulate VCR-style control buttons that you have to click with a mouse. There are two classes of player: Stand-alone (running as its own application) and embedded in a browser. It is quite often impossible to use the Tab key to move from a surrounding Web page to the player application and within the regions of the player. Keyboard equivalents are incomplete and insufficient in all players except Windows Media on the Windows platform per se, though all players, even Windows Media, suffer from the separation of stand-alone use vs. embedding in HTML pages. (How do you traverse the boundary?)

Screen-reader users are particularly ill-served. They're already dealing with layer upon layer of abstraction:

- The computer hardware. (With screen readers, extensive and unusual keystrokes are the norm.)
- The computer operating system.
- The screen reader (and/or Braille display, for that matter).
- The application software, like a browser or player, with possibly numerous open windows.
- The content within the software.
- The accessibility features of that content.

Yes, the tendrils of accessibility really do extend that deep. How else do you gain access to the audio descriptions of the video file running in your RealPlayer window inside Microsoft Internet Explorer for Windows under the

Multimedia players can pop up as free-standing miniapplications (even if still under the control of the browser), as in the example at top, the trailer for the Australian film Let's Get Skase.

Or the multimedia player (actually, the multimedia itself – the player is merely spawned by the browser) can be embedded inside an HTML document, typically within <frame></frame>, <iframe></iframe>, <embed></embed>, or <object></object> or in a table cell. The Bourne Identity example at bottom shows the embedded approach, which is admittedly nicer to look at.

At time of writing, by the way, I had never seen a single online movie trailer with captions or descriptions (both of which are readily achievable given movie-studio budgets and levels of expertise).

ægis of a screen reader you operate using the split keyboard you find pleasant to type on?

At time of writing, leading screen readers provided incomplete access to all the controls and features of multimedia player applications. There's nothing you the author can do about it. In fact, it is in no one's interest for authors to view this layer cake of incompatibilities as a technical challenge to be solved for their own particular Websites. It is not all that helpful for you to beaver away at programming a kludge that blind visitors can use to gain access to audio descriptions on your site, for example, to overcome some technical limitation of the sort just described. That same kludge probably relies on nonstandard methods (as a lot of JavaScript programming could be described) and definitely won't work anywhere else.

Even the seemingly simple case of an incompatibility of interface for captioning shows us how deep the technical obstacles run. The free Quick-Time Player and the QuickTime Pro variant you must pay for will handle text tracks differently. If you encode hidden text tracks in a QuickTime movie, only the Pro version can turn them on. The free version has no access to the text at all through the player's native controls; it might as well not be there. (If you save a version with text tracks visible, they stay visible forevermore. Then the titles are open, not closed.)

As you can see, even simple tasks face multilayered technical barriers.

You can work up a little onscreen button that turns captions on and off through calls to the QuickTime scripting language known as ActionScript. In fact, this is so convincing a solution to the problem that contacts at Apple and the WGBH Educational Foundation all enthusiastically support it (rather than the more obvious permanent solution of fixing the players).

You'd think this approach would be just fine given that deaf people can see the nice onscreen button you havee programmed. Here's a question for you: How does someone who can't use the mouse click the button? The question is somewhat unfair, actually, since you can assign a keyboard equivalent to an ActionScript, though you then have to include a very clear visible statement explaining which key to press (reminiscent of the accesskey problem discussed in Chapter 7, "Text and links").

As you can see, even simple tasks involve multilayered technical barriers. The players themselves have technical limitations; interfaces to actuate access features are inconsistent; and even if you solve those problems for one disabled group you might not have solved them for another.

Closed or open?

Why are captions and descriptions *closed* on television and home video? Why, in other words, do you have to explicitly turn them on? Why isn't accessibility *open* or available as an intrinsic feature that cannot be deactivated?

The philosophy, backed up by essentially no research, holds that nondis-abled people cannot stand captioning (especially) or audio description and hate having either form of accessibility rammed down their throats. Accordingly, we have invented heavily-compromised and expensive technical systems to hide captions and descriptions from the vulnerable, delicate eyes and ears of nondisabled people.

On TV and in video, there's exactly one signal to play with. (Yes, if you have a satellite dish, you may indeed be able to watch multiple feeds of MTV or CBC or the BBC, but that is the rare exception, not the rule.) When you watch a TV station, you watch exactly the same feed every other viewer sees. That single feed must accommodate sensitive nondisabled people and also the deaf and the blind. Bandwidth is a scarce resource in TV and video, you might say. Main picture and sound and all access features must be bundled together.

But that is not the case online. We can run as many separate feeds as we like, each of them as different or as similar as we like. Outside the access field, we find a couple of examples. If you want to download, say, a video player, you may be asked which server is closest to you (North America, Europe, Australia, Africa); those are multiple feeds as we understand them here. Or you may use Akamai or a similar technology to distribute the load of serving multiple copies of the same file across many different servers in different locations.

In accessibility, we can use the capacity for multiple feeds to get around the shortcomings of closed accessibility. Instead of replicating the television model by providing, say, a single QuickTime file with every access feature hidden inside, why not give us a number of different but related QuickTime files?

- Plain – no access features at all.
- With open captions.
- With open descriptions.
- With both.

> Until players are all at least as capable as existing TV and video, fully support certain standards, and are completely and effortlessly compatible and manipulable with screen readers and other adaptive technology, open accessibility is the way to go.

Sure, you're encoding and saving four files rather than one, but disc space is cheap. Sure, you're transmitting four files rather than one, but we have a range of ways to distribute server load at our disposal. In any event, individual visitors will tend to choose only one of the available file options; you're rarely serving more than one file per visitor. You're going to the trouble of creating captioning and descriptions anyway, so there is no real added effort there. And it is often technically simpler to add open captions and descriptions than closed ones.

We are faced with a thicket of incompatibilities in making "closed accessibility" work online. Recall that various players have various abilities. But it's actually worse than you think: Some players can't even do basic things right, like aligning text. The choice of fonts alone is a severe stumbling block: Untrained people generally have poor taste in typography; they do not understand the special demands of reading onscreen text, particularly onscreen text overlaid onto video; their available fonts are limited; and finally, untrained people have an annoying habit of considering the font known as Arial appropriate for any purpose. (It is not appropriate for any purpose.) Worse, with rare exceptions the ultimate viewer *must own the actual font* in order to see it.

Until players are all at least as capable as existing TV and video, fully support certain standards, and are completely and effortlessly compatible and manipulable with screen readers and other adaptive technology, *open accessibility is the way to go.*

There's a notable disadvantage to open accessibility: Caption text is rendered as bitmaps or pictures and cannot be scanned, searched for, captured, downloaded, or printed the way a separate text track can be. It's a problem, but not such a pressing problem that it invalidates the whole approach. (Incidentally, a separate transcript, easily derived from the task of creating the open captions, is helpful to provide.) You needn't worry about a similar problem with audio description; as I explain later (see "Text descriptions"), the only kind of descriptions you ever want to deal with involve recordings of actual human speech, which itself cannot be scanned, searched for, captured, downloaded, or printed as text can be, and that is just the way things are.

The knowledge gap

Why am I not teaching you how to do captioning and description right here?

That was originally the plan, I must confess. I then had quite a lot of time to consider what would be involved. And that turns out to be an entirely separate training course that is longer, more involved, and more taxing than this entire book. It is difficult to *explain* captioning and audio description without sitting down in person with tapes rolling. It is impossible to *teach* either discipline without extensive actual video to use as practice material. As with typography, it takes a very long time to develop an eye for it.

A written manual that attempts to teach media access, without actual media at hand to work with, could never do much good.

In effect, in producing accessible media your room for creativity is severely hindered by the source material. You *cannot* do whatever you want. Cinema is a blank canvas; accessibility is a paint-by-number set.

This isn't merely my opinion. Captioning has been widespread since the 1980s (and dates back to the 1940s); audio description of film and television is nearly fifteen years old. While there is room for improvement in the existing practices, the fact remains that *there are existing practices.* You simply cannot make it up as you go along.

You need to ask yourself a few questions, then:

- Do I have these kinds of skills?
- Are these skills even remotely relevant to the rest of my work in development for the Web?
- Is this even the sort of thing I want to learn well enough to do a good job?
- Where would I go to learn these skills in the first place?

The answers to the first three questions rest with you. The answer to the last question is "Nowhere," and it pretty much queers the whole enterprise.

LEARN BY WATCHING

I would suggest that everyone hoping to perform, oversee, manage, delegate, or simply understand any form of captioning or audio description spend a couple of weeks doing nothing but watching captioning and audio description.

Readers in the U.S. and Canada have the most options. First, turn on captioning on your television set. Virtually all televisions built since mid-1993 (and ancillary TV-receiving devices like computer video cards) have included caption-decoder chips as standard equipment under U.S. law. (Canada receives the same TV sets and equipment, by and large, but there's no legal requirement.)

It is still possible to buy an external decoder for an old TV set, but you get better results (including colour captions) by using a new TV. It could be time to upgrade. (If you buy a television for the office for the purpose of learning captioning, it could be a deductible business expense.) Some sources for external decoders are United TTY Service (UnitedTTY.com), Harris Communications (HarrisComm.com), and Hear-More (HearMore.com).

You can watch audio descriptions on a few U.S. television networks. At time of writing, the complete list appears to be ABC, CBS, Fox, Lifetime, NBC, Nickelodeon, PBS, TBS, TNT, USA Network, and Turner Classic Movies. Schedules are extremely hard to come by; the searchable listings at TV.Yahoo.com appear to be the only listing of U.S. described programs (look for the malapropist acronym "DVS"). Global and CTV regularly air described programming in Canada, as do a few other networks and broadcasters on occasion.

You can and should buy, rent, or borrow home videos with audio description. I can provide a firm recommendation for DVS Home Video, found at DVS.WGBH.org. At press time, nine DVDs in Region 1 (U.S., Canada, U.S. territories) and about three dozen in Region 2 (Japan, Europe, South Africa, Middle East) offer descriptions. (Eight of the Region 2 discs are in German.) That's not really a lot. I maintain a list online: joeclark.org/dvd/.

For readers in the U.K. and Ireland, Western Europe, Australia, and other areas served by the World System Teletext technology, captioned TV broadcasts are widely available. You generally need a teletext television set (typical midrange and high-end models offer that feature), though you can find a very few external decoders and VCRs able to decode teletext captions. There are a few sources of open-captioned home videos, but not many – the Australian Caption Centre is one (auscap.com.au). It's also possible to watch closed-captioned home videos that use the Line 22 system, for which you need a separate decoder (the so-called Videocaption Reader) or a VCR or TV with that separate decoder chip. (Line 22 is not the same as World System Teletext. Yes, you need two decoders to watch all forms of closed-captioned programming.) Sarabec.com sells Videocaption Readers.

Audio description is present but rare on analogue and digital television in the U.K. and Germany. The Royal National Institute for the Blind in the U.K. sells a line of described home videos (RNIB.org.uk).

Japan uses the same television system as the U.S. and Canada, and Line 21 captions are in reasonably wide use there, though you generally need a separate decoder.

Readers pretty much everywhere in the world can watch subtitled DVDs, though the conventions used in subtitling aren't even remotely comparable to those used in captioning. That is true even for the technique euphemistically known as "subtitles for the deaf and hard-of-hearing," about which I will refrain from launching into a diatribe.

It takes two solid weeks of watching captioning and audio description before it becomes comfortable.

This is not a short-term commitment. You can't just watch one or two shows and then *turn the damn things off*. It takes two solid weeks of watching captioning and audio description before it becomes comfortable. Rather like breaking in a new pair of shoes, the task of assimilating main audio and video and captions and/or descriptions all at once is foreign and unsettling at first. (For people over 40, anyway. Kids today are much more adept at handling multiple simultaneous streams of information.)

You will undoubtedly notice a wide divergence of captioning styles (if not in audio description). Who's doing it right? To answer that question would require another book, plus a full-on training course, and I have to take things one step at a time. Consider your task one of learning the range of acceptable practices. Take note of who captioned whichever programs you like, and keep watching for that firm's work; if you're going to emulate anybody, emulate only one style, not a mishmash of styles from this captioner and that.

Low-budget access

After gaining all this knowledge, you may wish to try your hand. You can do captioning and audio description yourself, but do not underestimate the difficulties involved.

There's more than one way to publish on the Web, and sites of every description, with budgets of zero on up, can be made accessible to varying degrees. Think of the Priority 1 through 3 guidelines from the Web Accessibility Initiative, or this book's Basic, Intermediate, and Advanced accessibility advice.

Out in meatspace, for example, there's a whole underground movement of home subtitling of Japanese *anime* videos. Fans go so far as to write their own software to do it. No one particularly cares how good or bad the subtitles are. They're better than a Japanese soundtrack you cannot understand.

If your Website has just a few videoclips, which themselves aren't exactly of Stanley Kubrick quality, does it particularly matter that amateurs are doing the captioning and description?

I would certainly endorse this kind of homegrown captioning and description, with reservations. The reservations have little to do with the probably low quality of the captioning (for small-time applications, that is not altogether important) and more to do with the enormous effort required. And audio description is another matter entirely.

CAPTIONING AND TRANSCRIPTION

Captioning starts with text. Transcribing the video accurately is the first problem. You are unlikely to have experience in transcription. Neither is anyone else nearby, for that matter. Among neophytes, there is a tendency to be at once too literal in transcription ("Um, yes. Um, I think, um –") and too free ("No!!! [*laughs hysterically!!*] I DIDN'T SAY THAT!!!").

The best way to learn how to transcribe is to watch captioned television. Failing that, reading existing transcripts and comparing them to the original audio is a good way to learn. (And where *are* you going to find those?) The problem with this advice is the fact that a great many rules of written English are literally invisible to most of us: At least at the level of grammar and punctuation, well-written English doesn't call attention to itself, and the mechanisms it uses are hidden. It actually takes a lot of work to make a transcript, or anything else, read effortlessly.

There are a couple of shortcuts available in transcription. If your videoclip is based on a script, start with that, taking care to note any deviations from the script.

If you're transcribing from scratch, there are a few good practices to follow.

Every transcription file should state what is being transcribed, ideally with links back to the source page, the homepage of the entire Website in question, and the original audiovisual file. Give an E-mail address for questions about the transcript; you may wish to set up an alias for this purpose (transcripts@*yourcompany*.com), and you may also wish to credit transcribers by name. If you hired an outside transcribing firm, definitely credit them. Provide a copyright declaration.

Indicate a change of speaker. Cascading stylesheets come in handy here (consistent with the advice of T.V. Raman, as found in Chapter 11, "Stylesheets"). Give each speaker his or her own paragraph style:

- ‹p class="george"›
- ‹p class="announcer"›
- ‹p class="man1"› (for an unnamed first male speaker)
- ‹p class="man2"› (for a second male speaker)

In this way, you assign styles to each paragraph based on who's speaking. Inside a paragraph, however, you should mark up the name of the speaker by using a single ‹span›‹/span› class. All actual character or speaker names inside a document share the same class; there is no need to differentiate them.

‹span class="s"›‹/span› (s for speaker; keeping things short is helpful but not required)

A transcribed paragraph might begin like this:

‹p class="george"›‹span class="s"›George‹/span›: *Transcribed words*‹/p›

This method marks the paragraph as being the words of George and the word *George* as being the name of a speaker. Later on, it becomes possible to search for and extract only George's speech, or to eliminate the names of all speakers, or to assemble a list of all the people who spoke. Isn't that a bit more useful than a plain-text transcript where none of these transformations are possible? (The added effort is not great, as we'll see shortly.)

You can define typographic attributes for the class known as s to give it, say, a bold sans serif font. You could also cause these speaker names to appear in capital letters:

span.s { font-family: Verdana, Geneva, sans-serif; font-weight: bold; text-transform: uppercase }

For browsers and devices that do not understand stylesheets, it is not wrong to nest a ‹strong›‹/strong› element inside ‹span›‹/span›, taking care to redefine the s class to avoid redundancy. A transcribed paragraph could begin like so:

‹p class="george"›‹span class="s"›‹strong›George‹/strong›‹/span›: *Transcribed words*‹/p›

using a class like this:

span.s { font-family: Verdana, Geneva, sans-serif; text-transform: uppercase }

What about the paragraph classes for speaker identification? They don't have to look any different from other paragraphs per se. There is no requirement to actually define these classes in your stylesheet. Heretical, isn't it? "Why else do we declare styles?" you ask. Well, in this case the goal is future manipulability rather than present-day appearance. A screen-reader user could remap the interpretation of such paragraph styles to speak in a different voice or volume. Or, later on, you could do a search of the file to extract everything that George said.

If it seems like a lot of work to type something like `<p class="george">` `<span class="s">George</span>`: in front of every paragraph, you can take the easy way out. Just type the speaker's name and a colon at the opening of each paragraph in a simple text editor or word processor (yes, even Microsoft Word). As long as there's a consistent structure to your paragraphs – for example, two blank lines, then the character name, then a colon and a space – you can do a search-and-replace later on. You can even close the preceding paragraph (using `</p>`). Example:

- Search for: [Return][Return]George:[space]
- Replace with: `</p>`[Return][Return]`<p class="george"><span class="s"><strong>George</strong></span>`:[space]

Here is a final detail that is strictly optional. It helps to start each sentence on a new line. Web browsers will ignore such a linebreak (unless it's inside an unwise tag like `<pre></pre>`, which I rather doubt you will use), but if you encode sentences separately, even through the innocuous method of separating them with a carriage return, it will be easier to transform the transcript into chunked-up or scrolling captions later. If you were truly keen on this, you could use a linebreak element, `<br class="sentence" />`, which you could later search for and replace. This is not *quite* the best way to do it, since you are only marking a sentence boundary and not the beginning and end of each sentence, but it could be useful. If you'll permit me to pursue this detail even more exhaustively, a usually-invisible HTML character entity like the zero-width non-joiner – `&zwnj;` or the more reliable `&#8204;` – can act as a sentence boundary.

Non-speech information

It is necessary to transcribe all relevant non-speech information. What does "relevant" mean? It's similar to evaluating which parts of a page must be modified for colourblind people: If you missed a notation of the sound effect, would you be confused, fail to understand a later event or statement, or make a mistake?

For example, if the video shows a person walking up to a podium and the floorboards creak en route, there is no particular reason to note that sound in writing. If, however, a floorboard *breaks* and the person stumbles, the sound is suddenly more important. If the speaker bumps the microphone out of frame (invisibly, in other words) and says "Oops! Sorry!" then it is necessary to explain why the speaker is apologizing. (A notation like [Bumps the microphone] will do.)

Some sound effects are obviously always important (or nearly so): A ringing phone, a knock on a door, a crying baby.

Because sound effects can occur as events unto themselves or right in the middle of dialogue, you need to use markup for both cases. A paragraph- and a class-level style declaration will do. Some examples:

- <p class="nsi">[Phone rings]</p>
- <p class="george"><span class="s"><strong>George</strong></span>: Good morning and welcome to the first day of our – <span class="nsi">[Bumps the microphone]</span> Oops! Sorry! Good way to get the ball rolling. Welcome to the first day of our AGM. *Transcription continues*</p>

Here, nsi means "non-speech information."

You don't necessarily have to assign typographic attributes to these styles. Why? Because you absolutely must use some kind of delimiter – parentheses ( ) or brackets [ ], but never angle brackets <> or braces { }, which are not used in English writing – to surround the text that conveys the non-speech information. This redundancy obviates the absolute necessity to define styles. (Screen readers, Braille displays, and other adaptive technology can recognize such punctuation.)

If you want to define a style, though, it's perfectly fine. Italics are nice.

    .nsi { font-style: italic }

You don't have to transcribe words in a language you do not understand. Annotate a foreign-language segment inside a larger file:

- [Speaking Japanese]
- [Asks question in Japanese]
  [Responds in Japanese]

If an interpreter is used, state that the resulting text is translated:

- George (translated):
- George (through interpreter):
- Interpreter:

(Despite common usage by American newscasters, who seem to think "translator" sounds grander or more objective than "interpreter," keep in mind that translators work with the written word while interpreters work with spoken and/or signed language.)

If the entire segment contains nothing but foreign-language dialogue, you can either send it out to a translation house for a proper transcript or

The way to make a video accessible is to work on it, not to produce a separate analogue. Separate hasn't been equal for rather a long time, has it?

provide an excuse on your actual Website along the lines of "This audio file consists exclusively of dialogue in Japanese which we cannot transcribe." Don't pretend there isn't any dialogue; tell us what's happening. Being up-front and honest about your limitations is the way to go.

Why bother with transcription?

The goal here is to provide a captioned videoclip. But there are other forms of accessibility when captioning is impossible.

Under battle conditions and as an absolute last resort, it is permissible to provide a separate, free-standing text transcript of a videoclip. The practice is to be discouraged except where utterly unavoidable. The way to make a video accessible is to work on it, not to produce a separate analogue. Separate hasn't been equal for rather a long time, has it?

If, however, you just don't have the time, money, or expertise to produce even homegrown captions, you are not off the hook. You do have to provide a transcript, which ideally should be available as soon as the original clip is available but can be delayed a reasonable period while you put it together.

Since online video is usually of short duration, I doubt it would take your company more than a day or two to produce even a rudimentary text-only transcript. If you're providing hours of video online, your budgets are already pretty high, and presumably you could at least send an audiotape of the video feed out of house for transcription. Or you could transcribe it in-house in chunks – two hours per day, for example.

Your obligation is to come up with some method of making your video accessible to deaf visitors. A number of options are at your disposal, not all of them technically onerous or expensive.

Even if you *do* provide a captioned clip, by the way, it is a good idea to give people a separate transcript, too. It can be scanned, searched for, captured, downloaded, or printed. Your captioners or your captioning software can provide a dump of plain text with a minimum of fuss; it's preferable to convert that plain text into proper HTML, but you could get by without it.

Linking

Place a link to the transcript near the link to the source video file. It may be helpful to use a standard filename convention for transcripts, like using the video filename prefixed or followed by trn:

- announce2-trn.html
- trn-announce2.html

Audio description

There's an asymmetry involved in making video accessible to the blind or the deaf. Blind people can follow a videoclip with no picture much more easily than deaf people can follow it without sound. Nondisabled people can run their own experiment: Watch TV for a day with the volume all the way down (and no captions). Then watch TV the next day with your back turned (and no descriptions).

The most pressing need, then, is captioning, not audio description. If you have to choose one over the other (as will often be the case in small business), choose captioning. However, if you have more time than money, I expect you to do captioning first and pick away at the task of audio description gradually. You may be able to produce a captioned clip (or at least a separate transcript) for publication at the same time the uncaptioned clip goes up on your site, with a described version published two weeks later. What you may not do is ignore description completely.

That kind of staggered accessibility schedule is not completely kosher. We are violating the principle of equal access. Blind people aren't less important than deaf people, nor are they more important, nor is either group more or less important than others. But the intrinsic difference in understanding an audio-visual medium when you have access to only the audio or the video means we have to set priorities.

What about posting just an *audio* track, complete with descriptions, in lieu of a videoclip whose audio contains the descriptions? That would not be equivalent access; it's not as though you are presenting deaf people with visuals only and no sound.

What you *can* do, though, is provide both of the following:
- Your actual videoclip with descriptions.
- A separate file (in, for example, MP3 format) of main audio plus descriptions.

Some visitors may have so little vision that they don't need the images at all. They can download the much smaller MP3 file. But the option of video plus descriptions is always available.

How to do it

Frankly, I always hate it when authors take the easy way out, explaining away their refusal to document a specific topic by calling it "beyond the scope of this book."

For better or worse, that is genuinely true in this case. Teaching you the mechanics of crafting a comprehensible text transcript is one thing. Training you to provide full-on audio description is quite another – something else indisputably beyond the scope of this book.

I acknowledge I am committing a sin, however venial, by telling you to add audio descriptions but not telling you how to go about it. I am also at risk of accusations of hypocrisy here given that I have spent a couple of decades arguing that lousy accessibility is worse than no accessibility at all. Through this book's advice or lack thereof, it is virtually certain that the captioning and description you create will not be up to professional standards. But for small-budget productions and for online video that is of low quality to begin with, professional standards are beside the point and some kind of accessibility is better than none at all.

Text descriptions

Another option, which I discourage altogether, involves writing text descriptions of videoclips. Since we're creating descriptions for blind people, and blind people online have adaptive technology like Braille displays, screen magnifiers, and screen readers, if we provide understandable text then we've solved the access problem, right? No need to bother with voice recordings, right?

Not really. It's theoretically possible to synchronize such text with video: It's called captioning, or maybe subtitling, depending on the application. But try to imagine how this would work. You have a videoclip running in your player (with main audio and video), and somehow your speech synthesizer is supposed to keep tabs on a hidden text track and read it out loud at just the right moment. The speech must finish at just the right moment, too.

Screen-reader users already have to sit there listening to computer speech all day. (It's not uncommon for blind computer users to prefer to do things on the phone or face-to-face as much as possible just to relieve the tedium of that droning voice yammering at them all day.) Now we want to add dreary computer speech, through a technical apparatus that isn't as reliable as a simple human recording, to a videoclip that already contains human voices and other high-quality sound.

Why muddy the waters? The correct way to provide descriptions of a videoclip is to use human narrators.

In any event, the technical infrastructure I have just described does not exist. Screen readers have no way to read bits of text aloud at just the right moment – not when they're somehow embedded (likely through nonstandard means) inside a videoclip. We've got enough incompatibilities to deal with already. And if your player offers exactly one text track, who gets to use it – blind people or deaf people? If there are two or more tracks, how does a person using adaptive technology find out they are available and select them?

"Well, can't we just write up a text file full of descriptions?" you now ask. (The Web Accessibility Initiative actually recommends doing so.) How will that work, exactly? How do you explain which descriptions relate to which sections of the video? The entire concept is oxymoronic and ridiculous on its face. While separate transcripts suffice as a form of accessibility for deaf viewers if there is no other choice, they are a last resort in that setting. There is never a case where a separate text description file suffices as a form of access for blind viewers. Don't even think of it.

The only way to describe video is with an actual human voice. Accept no substitutes.

Software

Transcription is complicated enough that it's possible to earn a community-college degree in the discipline, and thus transcription actually *is* beyond our scope. But in this section, we're concentrating on a sort of amateur or home-grown transcription that doesn't have to be Pulitzer-quality. You may have to get the hang of transcription on your own, or simply choose not to worry about quality if you're only transcribing a handful of clips.

OK. Once your transcript is completed, what do you do with it?

One option is MAGpie, the so-called Media Access Generator, a Windows and Mac OS X software application by the National Center for Accessible Media at the WGBH Educational Foundation in Boston. (This book's CD-ROM has a link to the current version of the software.) MAGpie lets you add captions (and, with difficulty, audio descriptions) to RealVideo, QuickTime, and Windows Media files. (Not Flash. Not yet, anyway.)

You can use the transcript you previously created as a source file in MAGpie. You'll love this part: After I just finished telling you that you should prepare your transcript in HTML, not only will you need a plain-text version for MAGpie, you'll have to chunk up the transcript into sentences. For this and all other MAGpie tasks, you'll need to follow the directions in the MAGpie documentation. MAGpie can add audio descriptions to a videoclip. The version available at time of writing could add descriptions that you have *already recorded*; a later version, which had not been released at press time, lets you actually record your own descriptions as well as add them to a file.

(What's the easiest way to create a plain-text variant of an HTML file? Do a Save As Text from your browser, or Select All, copy, and paste into another program, like a text editor. Or use a program like BBEdit to remove HTML markup. Or – and here's a little-known feature – upload the file to a server and mail it to yourself using the Print command in Lynx, resulting in a superb and pristine text-only rendering.)

Moreover, this book's CD-ROM contains a demo version of CCaption, an application for Macs and Windows machines that can caption QuickTime and other video files. You can use your plain-text transcript as a source file with CCaption.

Given that two of the Big Three multimedia players and later Internet Explorer versions support SMIL files, and given that SMIL is a W3C recommendation, and given that the inventor of the SAMI file format doesn't even support it properly, it behooves you to use SMIL whenever possible, which pretty much means always.

Big-budget access

What if you are required, as under the U.S. Section 508 regulations (described in Appendix A, "Accessibility and the law"), to provide accessible video? Or if you decide to do it anyway, for reasons that should be familiar by now?

The following advice applies to any prosperous organization, firm, charity, or enterprise. If you have a budget large enough to carry the costs of serving a large quantity of discrete video files, or any number of files to a very large audience (possibly using Akamai or a similar technology to distribute the load), then you have more than enough money to make your video accessible *properly*. And to do it properly, you hire outside professionals.

I am not providing a hard-and-fast income or earnings or asset or wealth cut-off point below which you are excused from doing things the right way (i.e., the expensive way). That is not how the assessment of undue hardship or other forms of financial appropriateness is ever undertaken. It is always a relative or comparative analysis.

In the present case, though, this is a time for you to be honest with yourself: Deep down, do you know perfectly well that your wealthy organization – perhaps with hundreds of thousands or millions in annual revenues – can afford to do accessibility right? I'm going to leave it up to you to decide if you fit the description.

If you do, then you are well-advised to send out your video for captioning and audio description by recognized professionals in the field. Depending on the length, difficulty, and turnaround time, such captioning and description could cost hundreds or thousands of dollars per item. Yes, that much. It's still cheap in production-budget terms.

Whom should you hire? I have my favourites, but I'm not going to plug them. Some guidelines to follow:

- Never under any circumstances use a postproduction house, dubbing operation, ad agency, or any other business that considers captioning or description Just Another Add-On Service We Provide for the Convenience of Our Clients. Hire only firms that do nothing but captioning or description.
- Don't hire any captioning company with less than five years in the business. (Description is too new for that time restriction.)
- Treat Canadian vendors with great skepticism, since I know firsthand just how poor Canadian captioning and description actually are. (Exception: Real-time English-language captioning of live events, where Canadian captioners are generally good to excellent.)

- Be prepared to send the work out of town, out of state or province, or out of the country. In particular, Canadians may be forced to bite the bullet and hire American vendors, who will bill in painfully expensive American dollars.

Some advanced vendors can make a good-faith but insufficient attempt at producing a file with closed accessibility features. You're much better off asking for open captions and descriptions (in separate files, with both of them added to yet a third file).

WORKING WITH VENDORS

Here is how things will probably transpire when dealing with outside vendors. In this section, the phrase *online files* refers to a videoclip in an electronic format, or possibly on a CD or a DVD, but in any event, no videotape is involved.

For captioning, you should be able to provide your uncaptioned master in essentially any tape format, or even as an online file. You can ask for a closed-captioned "submaster" tape in return, if you are using a physical tape format, but you will probably simply ask for decoded closed captions, which can be added to any source of video footage. Decoded closed captions don't look very nice, but they are perfectly functional. They are burned into the tape, thus making them open.

Some captioning houses can use a character generator or titling software instead of a caption decoder to produce the captions, which will *sometimes* result in a nicer appearance and better legibility. That is not by any means guaranteed, though; see the discussion of "Screenfonts" below. An advantage of this technique, certainly, is how easy it is to use colours. Yellow captions are often very nice. Sometimes a background colour or "mask" is desirable, at least part of the time (over a white image on the screen, for example). You can talk this over with your captioner and come up with a few ideas.

It is actually quite possible that your vendor of choice can handle *only* videotape and not online formats. You may be faced with digitizing from videotape yourself after you have received the captioned and/or described submasters. If your vendor can accommodate online file formats, they should be able to give you exactly the file format and degree of compression you require. Insist, in fact – this is a case where the captioner or describer can't be a little bit pregnant. Either they offer cradle-to-grave service with online files or they don't.

For audio description, you will receive a new file or tape with audible descriptions. Or you could ask for an audio file by itself without video, which you may use as an adjunct to a video file with descriptions but not as a replacement.

Theoretically, your vendor could provide either descriptions mixed in with main audio (that's what is used most of the time in the field of described TV and video) or a file consisting only of descriptions, which are of course timed to start and stop at just the right moment and silence at other times. It is hard to imagine an actual use for the latter on the Web, and indeed the typical real-world use of such a format is for description in first-run movie theatres – you listen to the main soundtrack of the movie via the cinema's normal speakers and follow the descriptions through a headphone.

If you have opted to offer a video file with open captions and open descriptions, you need to plan for that up front and tell your captioning and description providers what you want to do. It is not particularly difficult to mate the description track to the open-captioned master, but you may want your vendors to take care of that for you rather than messing around in a video-editing program.

(I am not really discussing closed accessibility here. Consistent with my general advice, closed access doesn't work very well online. If you want to give it a whirl, though, at time of writing only the Caption Center and the Descriptive Video Service at WGBH could attempt closed online accessibility, and even then pretty much only in English; see access.WGBH.org.)

Copyright is an issue. The holder of the copyright must authorize the creation of the derivative works known as captions or descriptions. Most of the time the copyright owner will be you, and you simply sign a standard work order authorizing the process. If your videoclip includes songs or music, you will, I assume, have the right to reproduce such songs or music online; you may not have the right to transcribe the lyrics, which is what captioning does. Licenced works contained within your videoclip may require an explicit sublicence permitting them to be captioned or described.

Screenfonts

Typography is important in captioning, though it is possible to provide only general advice in a general-interest book. The cheapest method uses closed-caption fonts decoded and burned into the picture. Such fonts are ugly everywhere on earth. They are, however, tolerable. (I've done tests with real-world video using decoded Line 21 closed captions. They're unsightly but perfectly readable.) Your vendor may be able to use subtitling software that offers better fonts.

We don't have a range of well-tested fonts at our disposal. The Royal National Institute for the Blind in the U.K. commissioned the design of a face named Tiresias engineered to be readable for visually-impaired people. It's fine, except, insanely enough, there is no such thing as Tiresias Italic. A typeface without italics is like a knife without a fork – unusable by itself here in the real world.

AG Schoolbook™ Regular A 1966-1988: Günther Gerhard Lange	**LILLIPUTIAN COGS** 11 Illicitly coerce gypsy ABCDEFGHIJKLMNOPQRSTUVWXYZ abcdefghijklmnopqrstuvwxyz1234567890
Bell Centennial™ Sub Caption 1978: Matthew Carter	**LILLIPUTIAN COGS** 11 Illicitly coerce gypsy ABCDEFGHIJKLMNOPQRSTUVWXYZ abcdefghijklmnopqrstuvwxyz1234567890
Bell Gothic™ Bold 1938: Chauncey H. Griffith	**LILLIPUTIAN COGS** 11 Illicitly coerce gypsy ABCDEFGHIJKLMNOPQRSTUVWXYZ abcdefghijklmnopqrstuvwxyz1234567890
FF DIN™ Regular 1995: Albert-Jan Pool	**LILLIPUTIAN COGS** 11 Illicitly coerce gypsy ABCDEFGHIJKLMNOPQRSTUVWXYZ abcdefghijklmnopqrstuvwxyz1234567890
FF Info Text™ Book 1996: Erik Spiekermann & Ole Schäfer	**LILLIPUTIAN COGS** 11 Illicitly coerce gypsy ABCDEFGHIJKLMNOPQRSTUVWXYZ abcdefghijklmnopqrstuvwxyz1234567890
FF Letter Gothic Text™ 1997: Albert Pinggera	**LILLIPUTIAN COGS** 11 Illicitly coerce gypsy ABCDEFGHIJKLMNOPQRSTUVWXYZ abcdefghijklmnopqrstuvwxyz1234567890
Lucida Sans™ Roman 1985: Charles Bigelow & Kris Holmes	**LILLIPUTIAN COGS** 11 Illicitly coerce gypsy ABCDEFGHIJKLMNOPQRSTUVWXYZ abcdefghijklmnopqrstuvwxyz1234567890
FF OCR F™ Regular 1995: Albert-Jan Pool	**LILLIPUTIAN COGS** 11 Illicitly coerce gypsy ABCDEFGHIJKLMNOPQRSTUVWXYZ abcdefghijklmnopqrstuvwxyz1234567890
FF Schulbuch Nord™ Normal 1991: Just van Rossum	**LILLIPUTIAN COGS** 11 Illicitly coerce gypsy ΛBCDEFGHIJKLMNOPQRSTUVWXYZ abcdefghijklmnopqrstuvwxyz1234567890
Tiresias PCfont™ Regular 2000: Royal National Institute for the Blind	**LILLIPUTIAN COGS** 11 Illicitly coerce gypsy ABCDEFGHIJKLMNOPQRSTUVWXYZ abcdefghijklmnopqrstuvwxyz1234567890
Tiresias Infofont™ Regular 2000: Royal National Institute for the Blind	**LILLIPUTIAN COGS** 11 Illicitly coerce gypsy ABCDEFGHIJKLMNOPQRSTUVWXYZ abcdefghijklmnopqrstuvwxyz1234567890

The choice of fonts for captioning is not an obvious one. Any typeface that looks classy and elegant in the pages of a book will end up spindly and mushed on low-resolution monitors. Nor are conventional (overused) sans serif faces like Helvetica suitable because too many characters are confusable. (Do not use Arial for any purpose.)

The faces illustrated here are at least marginally well-suited for captioning, if only for short video segments. Yes, you have to go out and buy them; fonts are not all free. On the plus side, Tiresias is included at no charge on this book's CD-ROM. Though it lacks an italic, it's certainly a bargain.

The good news is that italics and other variations are under development. In the meantime, the RNIB has licenced the inclusion of two Tiresias variants, Screenfont and PCfont (the latter for computer displays), on the CD-ROM accompanying this book. Yes, you get two fonts for free.

In any event, custom-engineered screenfonts not specifically intended for titling are also rare. Georgia and Verdana were designed for Microsoft by the undisputed greatest living practitioner of typeface design, Matthew Carter. They're free to download at microsoft.com/typography/; if you've installed anything by Microsoft in the last five years, you own one or the other, and new computers ship with either or both. They'll do fine for open captioning. (Bold, italic, and bold-italic variants are available, and, at least on Windows, the character set is gigantic.) Tahoma is a slightly narrower variant of Verdana that may be better for titling. Trebuchet, another Microsoft screenfont (designed by Vincent Connare), also works nicely.

Don't use Helvetica. Typographic neophytes think Helvetica is "legible." Try running a few tests with confusable characters like Il1i!¡|, 00Q, aeso, S568, or quotation marks. Related *grotesk* typefaces like Univers suffer similarly. (One more time: Don't use Arial. It's a bastardized variant of Helvetica, it's ugly, it bespeaks unsophistication, and it sticks you with all the same confusable characters as other grotesks.) Sans serif faces like Franklin Gothic, News Gothic, Officina Sans, Info Text, Thesis, Syntax, and Cæcilia do a better job of solving the problem of confusable characters.

Serif fonts work, but require care. So-called *slab serifs* or *egyptians* (with serifs cut square and perpendicular), like Stymie, Rockwell, Lubalin Graph, Boton, and Serifa, are surprisingly effective. So are a couple of novelty fonts entirely dismissed by graphic designers, like Souvenir and Benguiat. Don't even think of using traditional book typefaces like Times, Bookman, or Century. In fact, any typeface that would look classy and elegant in small sizes in a very serious and expensive book must be avoided like the plague in titling. Resolution is poor; you're looking at the type from a greater distance; the words move; foreground and background colours mix and move; and displays are luminous while print is reflective.

Colour choices? White characters with a slight black edging; white characters on a black background, as is the norm in Line 21 captioning; and yellow characters with or without edging all work well. It is possible to colour-code captions for different speakers; leave that up to the pros, and only if they have years of experience doing it. In all cases, open up the *tracking* (or *letterspacing*), the space between letters generally, as distinct from *kerning*, the space between *pairs* of letters. Glowing letters tend to bleed into each other; letters that are nicely spaced for print are too close together in video.

DVD subtitling houses, software, and techniques are generally usable in producing open captioning.

LANGUAGE VARIANTS

Canadians may have to live with American spellings in their captioning; since Canadian captioning of prerecorded programming is substandard, the use of American captioners may be wise. Putting up with American accents in audio description is less onerous; American newsreader accents are similar to Canadian ones, and those are the sort of voices heard in audio description. I assume that the use of British audio-description narrators for American English materials is somewhat annoying, as the converse would be. (The British already describe U.S. programming and vice-versa; perhaps I am overstating the case.)

If you're American, could you tolerate Canadian, British, or Australian spellings? I know the answer already: You didn't know there was such a thing as Canadian spelling, and now that you *do* know, nothing but American orthography will do. Fortunately for you, the U.S. offers a vast selection of professional and qualified captioners, so your linguistic gene pool need never be tainted, at least in accessible video.

Can you handle British or Australian spellings or accents if you aren't British or Australian? Decide for yourself.

Flash accessibility

Something quasi-miraculous came to pass while I was writing this book: Macromedia Flash went from completely inaccessible to quite accessible overnight.

I can and will take partial credit for this event, since I had written an article in December 2000 explaining all that was wrong with Flash from an accessibility perspective. I also chatted on the phone with Macromedia and yentaed its developers to various (other) luminaries in the accessibility biz.

A year and a half later, Flash MX (the development platform) and Flash 6 (the player program) were released, and lo and behold the single biggest deficiency had been remedied: Suddenly Flash "content" was accessible to screen readers. At press time, there remained quite a lot of work to do, but what Macromedia managed to accomplish is nonetheless impressive.

The screen-reader problem

The Flash MX "authoring environment" and the Flash 6 player solve a few accessibility problems.

Screen-reader compatibility is the first Macromedia access milestone. In ordinary HTML Web sites, screen readers can read text on the page, plus text equivalents like alt, title, and longdesc.

Nearly every blind or visually-impaired person online who uses a screen reader does so on the Windows platform. Apart from the large general installed base of Windows machines, the reason for Windows' dominace traces back to a Microsoft software infrastructure known as Active Accessibility. MSAA acts as an intermediary between the structure and appearance of Windows software programs (including Windows itself and various browsers) and adaptive technology like screen readers.

Adaptive technology can poll MSAA to find out where the cursor is located, where text, toolbars, and icons are located and what they say and mean, and more.

In order to make a computer accessible, a screen-reader manufacturer merely has to write software compatible with MSAA calls, plus the usual caveats about compensating for individual programs' incompatibilities (including Microsoft's own software). This is not a small task, but it is a much easier task with MSAA than it would be if adaptive-technology makers were forced to reinvent the wheel, which is actually the case on, say, Mac OS, which offers nothing in the way of an accessibility infrastructure. The Gnome Accessibility Project is an ongoing but incomplete effort to write an access infrastructure for Linux.

MX/6: The first hurdle

Macromedia's "authoring environment," Flash MX, and the new Flash 6 player offer substantial, real, and only slighly incomplete screen-reader support. Among other things, you can assign text equivalents (similar to alt and longdesc in HTML) to buttons, input fields, movies, and a few other items, all of which screen readers can find and read out.

Text per se is automatically "exposed" to screen readers, meaning that many parts of many existing Flash sites are instantly made accessible if you're using Flash 6 and the right adaptive technology. Authors don't have to lift a finger.

HTML equivalence

HTML is itself not completely up to the task of making Web pages accessible. But the capabilities or HTML are a useful baseline of comparison.

Among the things you can do in HTML that you can't do in Flash:

- Set and change text languages (though you can *detect* a language setting in Flash using ActionScript)
- Add titles to nearly everything
- Add long descriptions to certain data types (like frames and iframes); Flash does not use equivalent data types, but you can nonetheless make frame- or iframe-like components in Flash
- Mark up acronyms and abbreviations (dubiously useful in HTML, but the capability is there)
- Include multiple levels of alternative content (like nested < object >< object ></ object ></ object >, or the many alternatives in iframe)

- Group and annotate form elements (using input, legend, fieldset, and the like)

(Some commentators accuse Macromedia of pulling a Microsoft by developing self-contained proprietary programming realms that undermine the universality of HTML and standardized Web technologies. Macromedia denies it, but if that happens, Flash has to be at least as accessible as HTML. At present, it isn't.)

Unfair testing

The list of what's possible in HTML are in many ways an unfair comparison. Flash isn't HTML, and even some of the HTML-specific access capabilities are not very useful (like acronym and abbr). Colourblindness is poorly understood, and the existing requirements, which call for essentially random or arbitrary colour replacement, not only are absurd in the real world but don't necessarily solve the inaccessibility for people with colour deficiencies.

HTML has been around long enough that its capacities have influenced accessibility requirements. Accessibility experts are, moreover, generally hostile to good visual design. There's a considerable bias within Web accessibility toward "universal" HTML and away from "proprietary" software like Flash and PDF. People are just gonna have to get over that. DVDs, home videotapes, television, and the movies are all accessible in slightly different but functionally comparable ways. HTML, Flash, PDF, and whatever new technology comes along can all be accessible in their own ways.

This issue may clarify the general objections of some Flash critics. Instead of complaining about Flash-only Web sites, shouldn't we be concerned about appropriate alternatives? An HTML site should be available in parallel with a Flash site; the HTML site should be as HTML-like as possible, with the Flash site as Flash-like as possible. You can have similar but not identical content and functions in both sites.

Similarly, Flash-only sites should be as accessible as possible in Flash-specific ways, while HTML-only sites should have HTML-like accessibility

Multimedia

The most significant deficiency in accessible Flash is the absence of primitives – built-in procedures and capabilities – for captioning (for deaf viewers) and audio description (for blind viewers).

Flash animations – even very discreet, tasteful, highly usable animations, including those that do nothing but move text around onscreen – are a form of cinema. Cinematic works are already made accessible in a variety of media and settings (TV; tape and disc; movie houses; online). There is no such thing as a perfect system in any of those media; some access provisions are only barely adequate.

Nonetheless, data structures are already in place for captioning and audio description in non-Flash media. There are, in effect, slots into which you can stick caption text or a recording of an audio description. In "traditional" online video of the QuickTime/Real/Windows Media ilk, we suffer from a profusion of data structures, including RealText, QTtext, SMIL, and SAMI.

It is not particularly easy to add captions and descriptions to traditional online video, which in many ways is significantly worse than very old media like TV. But it is at least possible, using, for example, the WGBH Educational Foundation's MAGpie software, a link to which is included on this book's CD-ROM. You *can* hack your way through the existing text primitives in Flash to create a captioned animation; it is merely difficult and clumsy. It is also theoretically possible to add a second audio track using the existing Flash sound structures that will function as descriptive narration.

But the reality is that it remains impossible to caption or describe a Flash animation *within a Flash authoring program itself.* You the viewer cannot simply select a standardized, universal command in the Flash player itself to turn on captions or descriptions.

Macromedia knows all this, in part because I have talked to them at great length to make sure they don't overlook captions and descriptions and don't blow it when they try to implement those features. The issue is that the development team for accessibility at Macromedia is small (never more than four people full-time, usually more like 2½ people). The company wisely chose to get screen-reader access working first and worry about everything else later.

I am told that rudimentary captioning support will appear in a dot-level Flash upgrade this year or next. It is a fair supposition that MAGpie will play a large role. Freebie suggestion: Add support for SMIL, which is a full-fledged W3C recommendation.

There remains the general problem, applicable to all audiovisual media, of the lack of training in accessibility, which Macromedia developers will not be able to solve but must eventually be solved anyway by someone, somewhere, somehow. Even if we had a perfect technical infrastructure for audiovisual accessibility, there's no training on how to do it properly.

A good start

Macromedia has taken serious steps to fix its accessibility deficiencies. There's still a lot that's missing, but Macromedia is aware of nearly everything that needs to be done and will presumably fix it all. Still, the Macromedia case is a concrete example of a high-profile company with a *kewl* product embracing accessibility in an unbegrudging way.

Audio

Online audio is much easier to make accessible than video.

First, only audio files that are entirely or largely comprised of words, narration, or dialogue need to be made accessible – not, in other words, your entire MP3 music collection. That includes music with lyrics. However, a documentary *about* a musical group must be made accessible. You may not have the rights to reproduce actual song lyrics; in cases like those, use annotations like [Playing "Don't Fear the Reaper"] or, if you absolutely must, something as vague as [Music plays].

Second, synchronization is not necessary. Some will tell you otherwise. Synchronization is *nice*. It is quite possible to accomplish using SMIL. Go ahead, knock yourself out.

But all you *need* to do is provide an accurate transcript. The link to the transcript must be near the link to the source audio file. The techniques used are the same as with transcribing video. Do not unreasonably delay producing such a transcript.

Live feeds

All the foregoing advice applies to prerecorded audio and video files. But what if you're Webcasting a live event?

For nearly 20 years, we have enjoyed *live* or *real-time* captioning or *stenocaptioning* of events as they happen. The technique does not involve someone gamely typing away at a standard computer keyboard; there isn't a typist on earth who can keep up with human conversation that way. Instead, trained court reporters, using stenotype keyboards, listen to the audio and enter what they hear in phonetic shorthand. Software translates the keystrokes into visible words by looking up the phonetic shorthand in a dictionary.

Stenocaptioning can be and is being done in English, French, Spanish, German, and Italian. It's a tremendously demanding profession, which nearly anyone can learn but few can master. Start with the hardware: Stenotype machines have very few keys (24, in fact), which you must press in combination just to produce one phrase, word, syllable, or phoneme. Then you have to press another combination of keys for the next phrase, word, syllable, or phoneme. (Repetitive-strain injuries were commonplace among court reporters before anyone who used a personal computer ever heard of them.)

According to interviews with experienced pros in the field, it is easy to learn *stenotypy* (an actual term in use) well enough to keep up with, say, a 120-words-per-minute conversation. But, in the real world, conversations run at 180 to 220 words a minute ("wam" – again, an actual term in use). Your ability to keep up with such speeds is preordained: You top out at some maximum speed, and only if you have a hereditary predisposition can you reach 180 to 220 wam. In other words, you have to go through extensive training just to find out if you can actually do the job.

Furthermore, said training requires you to learn the keystrokes for thousands of syllables and words, and in fact you must devise separate keystrokes for homonyms (like there/their/they're) so that those words will be translated into correct spellings by the software. Also, proper names and unusual or foreign-language words require their own keystrokes, which, save for rare cases, you cannot look up; you simply have to know them.

It is quite possible to use real-time captioning online. People have tried to send out captions to browsers using JavaScript, and I suppose it is theoretically possible to transmit real-time captions in a closed format in SMIL or some player-specific format, but why bother? The technical incompatibilities here are even worse than with prerecorded video.

I strongly advise you to hire qualified, experienced real-time captioners to caption your live event. They will interface their software with a standard television captioning decoder to produce open-captioned video, which you can then stream online. You may need to set up two video streams (captioned and uncaptioned) if you wish to spare sensitive hearing people the agony of watching captions.

Every real-time captioner can deliver a plain-text file after the fact – instantly so, in fact. You can post that file as a separate transcript (though I recommend adding proper HTML markup, as described previously).

In North America, very advanced captioners can stenocaption in mixed case, though most of the time you'll see captions in capital letters only. Text editors can do a reasonably intelligent conversion from all-caps to mixed case, or you can just leave the file as-is if you have to.

I should note that a product called eScription from Speche Communications (pronounced "Speech"; www.speche.com) can intercept real-time captions emanating from the captioning software and insert them into the closed text-track or caption fields in RealPlayer, Windows Media, or QuickTime formats. Does it work? I don't know; I've never tried it, having merely spoken with staff from Speche. It is an available option.

There is no way to make live audio Webcasts accessible to deaf and hard-of-hearing visitors – not without turning them into live video Webcasts whose video segment consists of a blank screen with visible captions. That is not necessarily a bad way to do things. A workable alternative is to run the live audio feed inaccessibly, but transcribe it later, or, better yet, hire real-time captioners to transcribe the audio as it happens and post the transcript immediately after the event is over.

An extended audio feed, like that of an all-day conference, should be chunked into segments if you choose the latter approach. Post the chunks as you get them (e.g., after each speaker; after morning and afternoon sessions;

or once a day). Don't save up the entire huge set of transcripts until absolutely everything is finished.

You can post text files first and marked-up HTML versions later if necessary. Posting a *raw* text file (with, say, a **.txt** filename extension) is not the best idea because browsers handle plain-text files unpredictably. The chief problem is linebreaks; browsers do not always wrap lines of text to fit inside the browser window. Add at least minimal HTML coding, like paragraph tags <p></p> around paragraphs. (A quickie search-and-replace will usually suffice to add those.) Don't use the <pre></pre> (preformatted) element, since it will cause lines to scroll offscreen in many browsers.

Bottom-Line Accessibility Advice

Basic accessibility
- Set up a schedule to provide at least a transcript of the dialogue and meaningful sound effects of any posted online video or audio.
- Use all available accessibility features in Flash.

Intermediate and Advanced accessibility
- Provide captioning and audio description for online video.

14| **certification and testing**

RATHER LIKE BEING FORCED TO APPLY FOR A PERMIT to hold a demonstration, it seems contradictory to be expected to certify one's Website. The Web is supposed to be "anarchic," right? Anything goes.

That, at least, is the dream. The reality? Compliance, whether legally enforced or not, is an increasingly pressing criterion in Web development. You may be required to certify that your Website is accessible, or may voluntarily choose to do so. Then there's the issue of testing your site to prove that it *is* accessible.

Ideally, both certification and testing would be automated processes akin to spellchecking in a word processor. I will continue my tradition of heresy and iconoclasm by explaining just how difficult automated certification and testing actually are. Along the way, you will learn how to develop and post accessibility policies.

Goals

In this chapter:

- We'll explore levels of accessibility certification.
- We'll consider retrofitting issues.
- We'll learn how to write and post an accessibility policy.
- We'll understand the difficulties involved in including disabled people in user testing.

Certifying accessibility

In industrial applications (like manufacturing an engine component), we are faced with the issues of *spec* and *tolerance* – what the standard or specification requires and how close you come to meeting it.

In Web accessibility, the specification from which all others derive is the Web Accessibility Initiative's Web Content Accessibility Guidelines (WCAG). You've got three levels of compliance, as I described in Chapter 5, "The structure of accessible pages":

- Level A: You meet all Priority 1 requirements.
- Level AA: You meet Priority 1 and Priority 2 requirements.
- Level AAA: You meet Priority 1, Priority 2, and Priority 3 requirements.

In practical terms, Level A compliance is easiest to attain and does the greatest good in accessibility terms because Priority 2 and 3 requirements are harder to meet, serve smaller and smaller audiences, and apply to less and less common Web techniques.

Certification and policies

A terminology issue here. A certification level forms only one part of an accessibility policy. *Certification levels* relate to WCAG requirements; a *policy* stipulates the promises and requirements you and your team will abide by.

In practice, there may not be all that much of a difference. Your policy may simply say "Our pages conform to Level AA compliance as articulated by the Web Content Accessibility Guidelines," short and sweet. Or your lawyers may demand something more lengthy and qualified.

Choosing a certification level

Unless you are working for a government department or the rare "private" organization with actual requirements, you will not be obligated to certify the accessibility of your sites. If you actually are required or simply elect to do so, you need to decide which level of certification you wish to claim.

Do not mistake this for an easy decision. The salient issue is the future vs. the past.

RETROFITTING

Through concerted effort and after a lot of internal training (based largely on this book), it may be possible for your Web team to attain, for example, Level AA compliance on all new Web pages and templates. OK. What do you do with the two thousand database-generated pages already available? It is not *impossible* to retrofit even many thousands of old pages, no matter what anyone tells you; it is merely *expensive* to do so. If you've got the money, do it.

I would be very surprised if even a single reader of this book were willing and able to retrofit more than a dozen old Web pages. I myself am an expert on the topic and should have tremendous motivation to get my own house in order, but of the 200 or more old documents on my various Websites, I have rewritten, upgraded, and retrofitted only about 60. That does not imply that the remaining pages are inaccessible; they are merely unap-praised or less than ideal (due largely to the sloppy HTML 2.0–era coding practices, a phase all Web old-timers went through).

It is much more likely that you will adopt an approach similar to the U.S. government's Section 508 regulations (described in Appendix A, "Access-ibility and the law"): Old pages may remain unappraised and potentially inaccessible as long as they are untouched. But if an old page is updated or altered in any way, no matter how minor, full-on accessibility must be provided. Also, a page must be upgraded on reasonable request from a visitor.

Such a policy in no way represents shirking your responsibilities or copping out. In human-rights legislation throughout the Western world, accommodation must be provided for people with disabilities up to but not beyond the point of undue hardship or burden. There are limits to what can be done, and those limits are not always the same as refusing to do the work because it is very difficult and expensive. Even very difficult or expensive accessibility provisions may nonetheless be required; undue hardship is defined differently in every case. But there is no blanket requirement to do absolutely everything conceivable to improve access. (It may surprise you to hear that I fully support this limitation. It is a necessity in the real world.)

Accordingly, I can't give you a specific rule to live by here. I cannot offer a magic threshold combining staff complement, budget, and back catalogue of existing Web pages above or below which you must or must not retrofit those pages. I will, however, offer some guidelines that are consistent with other advice given in this book:

- If you believe it is necessary – and not merely expedient or cheap – to avoid retrofitting old pages, say so in an accessibility policy. (More on those later.)
- You may also check your Web logs and draw up a list of the most-frequently-requested pages on your site. (How many of them will you work on? Fifty percent? Eighty? Twenty-five? Arrive at your own proportion by your own calculations. Just don't be skimpy.) It is perfectly OK to establish a policy that the most popular old pages – maybe the ten most popular, a nice round number – will be upgraded within a reasonably quick period (like six weeks), with, say, half the remaining list upgraded within a year. I know it is strange to think a year ahead given that we are working in so-called "Internet time," but a certain professionalism must take hold. The Web isn't going away, and neither is your Website. It is quite acceptable to phase accessibility in over time for old pages. Even if you have a hundred pages to modify, that's only two a week over the span of a year.
- I strongly encourage every organization to post a policy stating that you will make reasonable efforts to repair any actual inaccessibility on an old page or anywhere on the site if reported by a visitor. (Set up a

dedicated form and/or E-mail address for that purpose. access@*yourcompany.com* will do it, aliased to webmaster@*yourcompany.com* if desired.) You don't have to specify a turnaround time, but you do have to promise to fix such problems quickly. I suppose you could treat such reports the way you would treat any other report of a broken or misbehaving page; the discipline of quality assurance has developed entire triage criteria for deciding what gets fixed first. It might be better to alter your procedures to make every reported accessibility problem a top-priority issue. (Remember, it could be something as simple as a missing alternative text, which could be fixed in five minutes flat.) You are free to specify that the complaint must concern *actual* and not *hypothetical* inaccessibility: The respondent has to demonstrate a problem.

- If, upon honest and thorough examination, you conclude that you cannot fix anything but the most severe accessibility deficiencies (at the level of "Visitors can't use this page at all") on older pages, or, worst of all, you cannot fix *anything* on older pages, then say so explicitly, but provide a dedicated form or address for feedback. (Do not say, in effect, "Take it or leave it." Let people respond.)
- It may be permissible, on the grounds of undue hardship or burden, to make every part of a page accessible except for multimedia if the costs for captioning and audio description would be insupportable. (There may be other unusual extreme cases, like heavily-nested tables you cannot figure out how to rewrite.) Yet you may still be able to add the task of *transcribing* the multimedia to the many tasks you will accommodate over your year-long phase-in period. In a case like that, do everything but the hard stuff first, set up and adhere to a schedule for the hard stuff, and explain all the above in your policy.

What to look at?

When retrofitting old pages, you have to decide what issues to consider, a decision intricately related to certification level (Level A vs. AA vs. AAA). It would be nice to be able to automate the process.

Some utilities and services almost make that possible. The CD-ROM included with this book contains a copy of the A-Prompt program from the Adaptive Technology Resource Centre at the University of Toronto, which walks you through topic after topic in Web accessibility for selected pages. (The program is small enough and self-explanatory enough that I'm not documenting it here. Later versions may support Mac OS under Java, but for now A-Prompt is Windows-only.)

You can find a few other accessibility testing services, many of them available for a fee, on the Web. There's a whole list over at the Web Accessibility Initiative site: w3.org/WAI/ER/existingtools.html.

These programs will attempt to *identify* problems and let you fix them. I'm going to rain on your parade a bit here and tell you that there is no substitute for human oversight of each retrofitted page. Even if you have an automated tool that alerts you to a missing alt text, you still have to write it. That will probably require looking at the graphic itself (or at least the filename – you can probably tell at a glance that spacer.gif will take alt=""). Then you may further wish to add a title, and, in rare cases, a longdescription. Can software do that for you? Hardly.

I will strengthen my reputation (*notoriety, shurely?!*) for heresy and iconoclasm by advising that you might as well forget about Bobby (cast.org/bobby), the alleged Website accessibility testing tool that is always immediately mentioned by everyone who doesn't know the first thing about accessibility.

Bobby is just too primitive and outdated, and, far from solving the problem of human intervention, Bobby makes matters worse, flooding your monitor with error messages along the lines of "This may be a problem. You should look at it." Um, yeah. I *should* look at it, and I don't need computer software nagging me about it.

At any rate, to explore a real-world example, if you find that the same shared graphics are unannotated on page after page, you'll yearn for some kind of automated *modification* system, not just an automated *identification* system. Perhaps a site-wide search-and-replace will do, unless you were using sloppy HTML 2.0–era coding practices at the time and were not consistent in the order of attributes inside a tag. (Did you write the tag as ‹img height width› sometimes and ‹img width height› some other times?) As with automating accesskey and tabindex (Chapter 8, "Navigation"), this is the sort of thing a database should do for you, not that any such program actually exists.

For every retrofitted page, then, you the designer or developer must survey the page's condition and make informed, specific, conscious decisions on how to fix problems. Such a procedure *cannot be automated*.

Accessibility advocates are hesitant to admit all this; we all seem to want to pretend that accessibility is easy. Conversely, when confronted with the prospect of retrofitting large numbers of pages, developers tend to immediately reject the notion out of hand. Both camps are overreacting. Accessibility generally *is* easy, as access advocates claim – for *new* pages, at least. And it *is* a lot of work to fix up old pages, as developers claim. The degree to which it is actually practicable varies case by case, and that determination must remain yours.

But there is a parallelism at work here. Just as repairing access defects in old pages requires human judgement and equivocation, so does evaluating *the entire issue*. You must decide how much work you are willing and able to do, and, while doing it, you must decide how that work will express itself.

New pages

Life is *so* much simpler when it comes to producing new pages. Here you have no choice. You absolutely must include accessibility features. Priority 1 or Level A access will do just fine to start, unless your content demands a higher level (as with online video). I'm not talking about legal or regulatory requirements, though you may have those to deal with, too; this entire book is based on the premise that you cannot build a Website in the 21st century and beyond without including accessibility features, no matter how modest.

Making a final decision

You are under no obligation to decide on the same certification level for old and new pages. The following combinations are all defensible depending on the resources at your disposal:

- Old pages, when retrofitted, and new pages upon creation are written to Level A compliance.
- Old pages are retrofitted to Level A compliance while new pages are written to Level AAA.
- Old pages without multimedia are retrofitted to Level AA compliance; old pages with multimedia are initially retrofitted to Level A compliance, with Level AA phased in according to a published schedule (e.g., rollout over a year – exact filenames and due dates do not have to be given). Meanwhile, all new pages are written to Level AA compliance.
- Old pages are not certified at all. Upon request, accessibility deficiencies will be rectified so the repaired page meets Level A compliance. New pages are written to Level A compliance.
- No certification will be claimed for old pages until all of them have been assessed and repaired. The goal is Level AA accessibility for older pages; the evaluation and repair project is expected to be completed by [*a certain date*]. Meanwhile, new pages are all written to Level AA compliance.
- Some old pages were originally written to the equivalent of Level A compliance. Other old pages will be upgraded on request to Level A compliance. New pages are written to Level AAA compliance.

Any policy that was reasonably considered after a full and thorough understanding of accessibility issues, and after an honest assessment of what your team can *actually do* as opposed to what it *feels like doing*, will suffice.

Line-item exceptions

Remember the issue of spec and tolerance?

What happens if you can meet every WCAG provision except one or two? What if, in other words, you cannot accommodate certain line items in Priority 1, 2, or 3 requirements?

The most likely case is, I suppose, an inability to make multimedia accessible on a page where everything else meets the spec. In any case such as this, you had better have a very good explanation for such noncompliance. If you do, then a posted policy must explain which line items you do not comply with. Stating that you meet all guidelines but one is arguably better than nothing and has the virtue of honesty. Moreover, the policy can list specific pages or sections that do not meet a given guideline, or you could add such a notification to the pages or sections themselves.

By implication, then, you should not refuse to post a policy merely because you think you must meet every component of a WCAG requirement before doing so. Yes, technically you cannot pick and choose which items to comply with, but here in the real world it is occasionally unavoidable. And remember, there's always a way to meet every part of the guidelines, particularly for Priority 1; in the tough case of accessible multimedia, over time you will be able to provide a transcript at the very least. At that point, you may have fulfilled the entirety of that level of WCAG compliance, at which point you should update your policy.

Writing and posting the policy

The first rule of writing an accessibility policy is "Cut the crap." Don't waste our time with bromides of this sort:

> [Company name] strives to provide market-leading user experience to its customers. To that end, we are proud to embrace cooperative standards for performance and user satisfaction. One of many [Company name] initiatives in this regard is accessibility to the handicapped. [Company name] undertakes to make best efforts to work toward ensuring that all parts of Companyname.com are accessible to handicapped people. Specifically, this page and many others at Companyname.com are optimized for World Wide Web Consortium (W3C) Web Accessibility Initiative (WAI) Web Content Accessibility Guidelines (WCAG) Level A (single-A)/Priority 1 conformance.

Don't waste our time, OK? Life's too short.

Tell us, in a sentence or two, to what standard your pages are written. (See the previous section to learn how simple it can be.) You may optionally wish to specify other standards you adhere to, like XHTML or Dublin Core metadata.

You have a few options in making your accessibility policy known. Absolutely place a link to it on your homepage (or all of them, if you have multiple entry points, as a multilingual site might). It's a must. A link saying "Accessibility policy" is all you need. I suppose you could give the link a certain accesskey and a relatively low tabindex. Any "About us" or corporate-information page must carry a link. So must a copyright or privacy-policy page, if there is one.

Optionally, you may include a link to the policy in page footers throughout your site. This may be gilding the lily a bit. It is theoretically possible to add such a notation even to old pages if they are constructed from a database where footers are specified by include files (or moral equivalent). Alternatively, for pages where your best current efforts aren't very good (e.g., a page with multimedia you have not made accessible yet), you may wish to include a link to the access policy. You could even write slightly different wordings for different applications – one for general usage, another for troublesome pages, a third for new pages. (I would set up separate documents rather than using HTML anchors within the same document. You want people to know unequivocally what policy applies.)

You may also list accesskey assignments in your accessibility policy (as mentioned in Chapter 8, "Navigation"). That may be too specific a level of detail for a site-wide or company-wide policy.

Now, this book is not a thoroughgoing, general-interest manual on accessibility. I am not attempting to counsel you on how to reno your bathrooms so a person in a wheelchair can use them. Nonetheless, this is a golden opportunity for you to consider "enterprise-wide" accessibility, which could cover everything from workplace accommodations to TTY telephone access to provision of materials in alternate formats like audiotape.

If you don't have such a sweeping policy ready, don't wait for one before posting a *Web* accessibility policy. The latter could, however, be a nice talking point for and instigator of the former.

Legal compliance

I am not providing an opinion one way or another on the issue of complying with legal requirements apart from stating the obvious: Follow the requirements to the best of your ability. In practice, most of my readers affected by legal compliance work under the ægis of U.S. Section 508 regulations, which are not exactly the easiest things to understand, making full compliance a matter open to debate. If you are forced to comply with a regulation, you may also be forced to provide a statement of compliance; for all I know, eventually a form of outside auditing may be instituted to prove your claims.

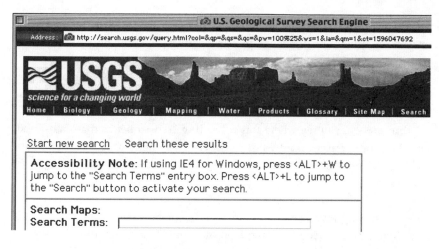

Meeting WCAG specifications may be quite different from these legal requirements, though in practice achieving at least Priority 1 accessibility gets you most of the way to meeting every other Web-accessibility rule on the planet.

If you are not actually required to meet certain standards, even those of the WCAG, but do so anyway and post an accessibility policy, it may be easier or harder for a visitor to file a complaint or a lawsuit alleging inaccessibility, that is, discrimination or unequal treatment. There is no jurisprudence in this area at time of writing, and even if there were, it wouldn't necessarily apply where you happen to live. It *seems* self-evident that stating your level of accessibility compliance indicates forethought and responsibility, but that is mere supposition on my part.

Testing

How do you test Websites for accessibility? The same way you test Websites in general – with real people.

Usability testing has become an accepted component of the more expensive and sophisticated Websites. If nothing else, prototypes are tested on a couple of people in the office, or the developers themselves attempt to perform certain functions as if they were neophytes, or the company's existing quality-assurance department, if there is one, is pressed into service to test the prototype. You can hire consultants and labs to perform user testing for you, if you can afford it.

However, while experts may be able to pretend to be neophytes, nondisabled people are not very good at pretending to be disabled. To a certain extent, it is possible: You can unplug the mouse and attempt to operate your site purely via keyboard, including the use of all navigation elements. (Suddenly accesskey and especially tabindex don't seem so obscure after all.)

So how do you simulate being blind? You can't just unplug the monitor or turn the brightness down completely, because then how do you interact with the system? You need a screen reader, don't you?

What about simulating visual impairment? You can't just bump up the font size on your Website; that is not how low-vision people use computers: The *entire screen* is magnified using software.

I'm sure you can see where this is heading. To do a better-than-half-arsed job of testing for accessibility, at the very least you need your own adaptive technology and, preferably, you need to include actual disabled users in your user testing.

Buying your own

I can highly recommend investing a bit of money in a screen reader. Several are in wide use, all on Windows: Jaws (by Freedom Scientific), Window-Eyes (GW Micro), and IBM Home Page Reader. You might as well forget about Macintosh screen readers until Alva Access Group upgrades OutSpoken for OS X.

In rough terms, screen readers cost a thousand bucks American, which isn't a lot of money for a mid-sized firm. That's about five hours of a project manager's time at typical rates. If you're a Web consultancy, you can bill the cost to a client, or swing a deal with several clients to split the cost – and keep the program for your own use.

Adding to the overhead is the absolute requirement to run the screen reader on a separate computer. These programs are finicky and unstable; you do *not* want their tendrils infiltrating an important production machine. On the plus side, they run just fine on old iron.

So for a couple of thousand dollars American, you can test all your designs (for the life of the software license term) for screen-reader compatibility. Yes, you will probably test against one screen reader only, and I can certainly tell you that the three leading products interpret HTML – and generally behave – quite differently. You'll also receive different levels of support when asking for help and reporting bugs (lots of it and immediately from GW Micro, next to none of it and begrudgingly from the other two).

Someone in the office will have to learn the labyrinthine keystroke commands to run the program. You may have to draw straws for that task, but I suspect you'll find a keener on staff who is just geeky enough to find the idea *kewl*. Definitely use headphones for speech output, though having a good speaker (one is enough) on hand for meetings and presentations can be nice.

Do *not* unplug the monitor or attempt to simulate blindness while running the screen reader. You must be able to compare the full visual information against the auditory version. (Similarly, to evaluate captioning, you must leave the sound on, and to evaluate audio description, you must watch the visuals.) It may be somewhat overwhelming at first to correlate vision and

speech in this way. You will get the hang of it after a few hours of acclima-
tion, and remember that you can always rerun a test any as many times as
necessary until you catch everything. You can also slow down the speech rate.

If all this seems too expensive, note that each of the screen readers mentioned here can be downloaded in a demo version. Additionally, you can buy
a time-limited version of Jaws (for 60 days' use) for next to nothing. It would
still be advisable to install it on a nonessential machine.

As for visual impairment: Since there's not a whole lot you can do to craft
your pages for magnification of the complete screen (see Chapter 9, "Type
and colour"), it is strictly optional to buy a screen magnifier and run your
own tests.

Disabled testers

Including actual disabled people is the gold standard of accessibility testing.
It is, however, essentially impossible in practice.

- Does your testing facility have its own adaptive technology?
- But then, don't disabled users thoroughly customize their own
  computers and their own adaptive technology?
- How do you find these disabled people in the first place?
- How accessible is everything surrounding the test session – the
  building, the washrooms, the existing Website, the information
  describing the session? How are you handling transportation? (Blind
  people can't drive.)
- How much experience does your testing staff have in dealing with
  disabled people, let alone understanding access issues?
- If you're running a group test (as is admittedly unusual), how can you
  include a disabled user in the group? Invariably, that person will take
  longer to do everything.
- How do you interpret success and failure? Your testing facility may
  have experience comparing test scores against previous tests, but do
  you have a corpus of data on disabled users' performance? And if so,
  doesn't that vary by disability?

It may make more sense to bring the test suite to the disabled user. OK – but
where do you find them? And aren't you running special surveillance software
on your test systems to monitor keystrokes and mouse movements and to
time responses?

Also, remember that in all cases you need to test for multiple relevant
disabilities – blindness, mobility impairment, maybe deafness if you run
multimedia. That will require more than one disabled testing population.

Consider the experience of the most famous usability consultancy on the
planet, the Nielsen Norman Group, home of Jakob Nielsen. (Yes, *I know, OK?*
Jakob Nielsen. *I know.*) The firm conducted a set of usability tests with

disabled subjects while I was writing this book. Kara Pernice Coyne of the Group refused to disclose even how many subjects were involved, but confirmed that the Group was forced to search high and wide for blind and visually-impaired subjects, going so far as to get in touch with other accessibility experts and more or less beg them for contacts. Do you think you can do better? I could not.

DISABLED EMPLOYEES

It is also possible that you yourself are a disabled person who does usability testing, either for your employer or as a consultant. Or you could be a disabled employee doing other work who is pressed into testing service as other employees might be.

This is, admittedly, rather unlikely. The public image presented by the Internet industry is one of ecumenism and equal opportunity, where no configuration of sexual orientation, hairstyle, embedded hardware like nose rings, fashion sense, or ethnicity could possibly be an impediment to getting hired if *you have the right skills*. In reality, Web firms hire within a specific range of employee types; while the range is larger than, say, the accounting business, there are actual limits to who is acceptable and who isn't. (As an example, I am entirely unacceptable to Web firms for reasons of personality. On the upside, I can't stand *them*, either.)

As described at the outset of this book, disability is upsetting and foreign to nondisabled people. Employers in every sector save for public service are unwilling to hire a disabled employee if it would require any accommodations whatsoever. While illegal, this bias is in wide effect. A blind Web programmer, for example, may be disqualified from consideration because of a claim that it is necessary to view and evaluate the appearance of client Websites, or at least because the blind employee is assumed to work more slowly than someone who can see. (It's usually true. But accuracy may be higher. Still, discrimination is often irrational, so I won't bother trying to argue against the bias.)

I would be very pleased to hear of even a single Web consultancy, or Web-related department of an old-economy consultancy, with a blind or mobility-impaired or deaf employee working on Web design. I expect not to enjoy such a pleasure. In the hypothetical case that such a person does exist, I would urge the employer and employee to work out a way in which the disabled person's experience and skills could help the testing process.

Having someone on staff can be a quick and easy way to find obvious problems. Do keep in mind, though, that a blind person cannot simulate the accessibility barriers faced by someone using switch access. On-staff disabled testers do not eliminate the need for more thorough testing, either in-house or out-of-house.

A problem in search of a solution

There is no immediately obvious or attainable solution for the problem of testing Websites with actual disabled users. Ideally, the industry will adopt the following changes:

- Outside consultancies will expand to offer accessibility testing. Nondisabled staff can simulate a great many testing conditions; simply running a range of screen readers may be useful for clients uninterested in doing such testing themselves.
- Consultancies will band together to develop a database of disabled subjects in various cities who can be called upon to do user testing. The population may be small, and after participating in one or more tests, standard protocols require those subjects be disqualified from further tests for a number of years. (Otherwise they become "professional testers.") I argue that this nicety must be sacrificed if we're ever going to get anywhere in testing by actual disabled users. It can further be argued that you *want* the most experienced users working for you because they have the greatest fluency in adaptive technology and Web use. It might be oxymoronic to imagine a novice disabled Web-surfer in the first place; you need such advanced software skills just to duplicate the basic functions of a nondisabled person that there may be no such thing as actual newbies.

Doing pretty much anything that puts actual disabled people to work testing Web accessibility is all to the good. If you can figure out a way to make it work, however imperfectly, I say *go for it*.

Bottom-Line Accessibility Advice

Basic accessibility

- Write and post an accessibility policy. State the pages to which it applies — for example, new pages only or pages retrofitted after a certain date.

Intermediate accessibility

- Certify the accessibility of your pages against a known standard, such as the Web Content Accessibility Guidelines priority levels. Note any known or deliberate deviations from those standards.

Advanced accessibility

- When conducting user testing, include users with disabilities if it is at all possible.
- Buy your own adaptive technology for user testing.

15| future Dreams

YOU NOW HAVE WORLD-CLASS ACCESSIBILITY KNOWLEDGE. You border on guru status. You're just *super*.

The rest of the world, however, is not.

In so very many cases, the Web accessibility techniques I have presented in this book are retrofits, workarounds, kludges. Accessibility can be made practicable, yes. You know how to do that in spades right now. Yet it is difficult to make accessibility elegant. We will need to invent entire new technologies to reach that goal. And an entire new discipline of accessibility training will need to be brought into the world.

Serial vs. random

Over and over in this book, tediously, inescapably, we have faced the Sisyphean burden of rejiggering Websites designed for random access by the naked eye into some kind of half-arsed compatibility with devices that read sequentially. Quite simply, much of the content on Websites is made to be ignored most of the time, but it is impossible to ignore part of something when that something is presented to you in its entirety as a stream of computerized yammering from a screen reader.

We have been more or less successful in our efforts. With techniques like skipping navigation and moving from one well-labeled table cell to another, it is quite possible to read, understand, and enjoy a Web page with minimum fuss, even via screen reader or Braille.

But let's be frank here. We may have achieved practical or passable accessibility, but what we have not achieved is elegance. What we have done, in effect, is to focus a camera at a stageplay and pretend the result is cinema.

How can we create Websites that look appropriate for nondisabled users of graphical browsers (containing within themselves basic accessibility features) and parallel Websites offering the same or analogous information that are optimized for screen-reader or Braille access?

Our challenge is simple to express but onerous to achieve: Shoving all navigation to the bottom of the document, leaving "content" and possibly search facilities up top. Which would *you* rather hear first?

AUDIO INTERFACES

Setting Braille aside, in effect we are faced with the dilemma of asking visual Web designers and Web programmers to create *audio interfaces* – a means of interacting with a computer system through sound. In practice, this really means sound *output* and not input, but that isn't different in principle from the graphical Web: The Web may communicate with you through visual output, but you don't communicate with the Web through visual input.

Some work has already been done on audio or auditory interfaces, chiefly by T.V. Raman, author of the book with the surprising title *Auditory User Interfaces* (Kluwer Academic Publishers, 1997). Raman formerly worked at Adobe, developing the PDF2txt and PDF2HTML utilities that convert PDFs into plain-text and HTML documents. (Look for them at access.adobe.com.) At time of writing, Raman is a researcher with IBM, working on the so-called multimodal Web. (We met Raman in Chapter 11, "Stylesheets.")

Bill Buxton, formerly of the University of Toronto and now the chief scientist at Alias Wavefront, has promoted a range of common-sense ideas in human–computer interaction, such as the use of two hands and the sense of hearing, including stereo sound. Other researchers have been exploring auditory interfaces since the mid-1980s. Development has been pronounced in the field of *earcons* – "non-verbal audio messages that are used in the computer/user interface to provide information to the user about some computer object, operation or interaction," according to Meera M. Blattner's definition. Earcons are not sounds we would recognize from the real world (dog barking, typewriter bell, rustling of leaves), but arbitrary sound sequences, usually musical in nature. The typical proposed application is to alert the computer user to an ongoing process (like downloading a file), though some experiments have been conducted on the use of earcons in user interfaces. Imagine your computer playing a musical note as you pull down a menu. That sort of thing. (Citations and abstracts are provided in the Bibliography.)

Web-specific audio interfaces have also been studied, with promising results. On the vexing problem of navigation of data tables, researchers at the University of Glasgow added tones whose pitch increased as you moved down and/or across a table. The addition made the task of finding the answer to a question from deep within the numbers in a table significantly faster, easier, and more pleasant. Meanwhile, the University of Hertfordshire developed a prototype system using earcons and other non-speech sounds to navigate through "hypermedia information" (don't you love the academic terminology?); in effect, the researchers wrote their own screen reader. Most subjects found it easy to navigate through a purpose-built, self-contained "hypermedia" virtual world using voice and sound cues. (The virtual world included descriptions of paintings and artworks. "Participants were very pleased with the tactile pictures and accompanying descriptions; for example, they were excited to find out what a Beefeater, the Houses of Parliament, and famous paintings looked like," researchers reported. Don't underestimate the blind population's thirst for information about the visual world.)

Meanwhile, one screen-reader manufacturer, Alva Access Group, is cooking up a putatively new approach to reading the screen, one that simplifies commands and uses "multispatial" sound and voice.

All very futuristic.

Characters in search of an author

Unfortunately, none of this research and development is going to matter in the real world without standardization and its kissing cousin, ubiquity.

Let us cast our thoughts back to the dark prehistory of HTML 4, or "oldschool HTML" as I have so charmingly dubbed it. It was impossible to find a browser, any browser anywhere, that supported every single accessibility feature. (Possible exception: The World Wide Web Consortium's testbed application Amaya, a stillborn Edsel of a browser/editor beloved by an Übergeek cadre of W3C policy wonks.) Even as I write this there is no browser at all that supports every nook and cranny of accessible HTML, not even Mozilla.

And accessible HTML has been documented for years. It's also simple to put in place – certainly simpler than the coloured scrollbars or "extended" JavaScript "standards" that Microsoft saw fit to include in Internet Explorer for Windows.

Now, though, we are contemplating opening the experience of Web browsing to an almost-entirely-new dimension, sound. It's as big a jump as leaping from oldschool HTML to Java applets. Bigger, even. It's almost as significant as jumping from Usenet and E-mail to the Web itself. For once in our blessed lives, the debased catchphrase "paradigm shift" is genuinely applicable.

Auditory interfaces would have to manifest themselves at the level of the screen reader or, better yet, the browser. The kinds of auditory metadata and cues that researchers have laid out for us would have to become as commonplace as visual-interface metadata and cues, like tooltips for titles or a shift in cursor shape when you run the mouse over a link. And their specific meaning would have to be as widely understood as left-hand navigation, tabs, and underlined links.

> Don't underestimate the blind population's thirst for information about the visual world.

What's more, developers today do not make use of the access tags that are already supported. Still, to this day, we find images without so much as an alt text, a laughably simple, widely-supported and actually obligatory access attribute. Now we're imagining the creation of a parallel auditory interface to accompany a Website's visual interface.

At present, it is difficult even to specify the fonts you prefer in certain HTML tags. Something as conceptually simple as relative font sizing in cascading stylesheets (from xx-small to xx-large) is improperly implemented in visual browsers. And now we want people – developers or "end users" or both – to be able to select little sounds and tones that relate to Website constructs, like links, text, input fields, and navigation? I don't think so.

There's another parallel: Skins. The rampaging popularity of WinAmp, with its selectable appearances and interfaces ("skins"), suddenly made us wonder why we were putting up with software designers' deciding for us how their programs would look all these years. Apple implemented and then crippled Themes and Appearances in the Mac OS, for a plausible reason: It is sobering to imagine tech-support staff having to explain how to perform action X when you've turned your entire interface into Teletubbyland. Windows XP and Mozilla support skins. Is it time for auditory skins, with sounds you yourself select to indicate Website landmarks?

A feeling of déjà vu will surely sweep over you, esteemed reader, as you think back to the vexing dilemma of making Flash animations and online video accessible. Even if we had perfect tools for that purpose, we are nonetheless faced with the prospect of training creators in the artistic development of access formats like audio description. In the present case, we somehow expect visual Web designers, whose all-too-frequent crimes against usability are merely the most prominent of their many venial sins, to master a new means of expression that they themselves will never use by choice.

Somehow, the use of auditory cues will have to become instantly widespread for it to reach a "tipping point" (*pace* Malcolm Gladwell) and become standardized.

Static Web design at least follows in the footsteps of print design; multimedia stands on the shoulders of cinema and static Web design. But what are the antecedents of auditory interfaces? They were all born of research projects. There are no real-world examples to rely on. This vicious cycle in and of itself will smother the deployment of audio interfaces.

Section tags

In the catechism of Web authoring, HTML corresponds to structure and stylesheets to presentation. The distinction is not always clear-cut, and I am about to propose a muddying of the waters.

We should be able to mark up sections of our documents with standardized tags describing the structure and purpose of those sections.

Note that section-level structure is largely unconsidered in HTML. You could argue that any content below a heading tag (up to but not including another heading tag) is a conceptual section, as is any kind of list. Certainly a frame is a section, as is a free-standing table inside a page.

All right, fine. So we do have sections after all. Fine. But do we have sections called, for example, TopNav, LeftNav, BottomNav, AnchorNav (for navigation purely within the page), Searchbox, Body, or Sidebar (as in newspaper sites)? How about sections with names suited to auction sites? help-wanted sites? search engines?

Now, if we had a standardized vocabulary of section elements (including foreign-language translations where applicable – the French should be able to use navgauche instead of LeftNav), wouldn't we be able to set up our pages for re-manipulation out in the field?

If you wrap your navbars in coding like –

- ‹div class="TopNav"›‹/div›
- ‹div class="SearchBox"›‹/div›
- ‹div class="LeftNav"›‹/div›
- ‹div class="Body"›‹/div›
- ‹div class="BottomNav"›‹/div›

– then couldn't a really intelligent browser or device happen along and reorder those segments for screen-reader display as follows?

- ‹div class="SearchBox"›‹/div›
- ‹div class="Body"›‹/div›
- ‹div class="TopNav"›‹/div›
- ‹div class="LeftNav"›‹/div›
- ‹div class="BottomNav"›‹/div›

You would never have to bother maintaining alternate page structures. With your document properly marked up, anyone who requires an alternate can rejigger the page at their end, unbeknownst to you and without affecting anyone else's experience of the site. (It's the closed-access philosophy, à la captioning and audio description: Build accessibility into the original source and let people turn the features on and off as desired. Do so even if the result is so very different from the inaccessible original that many who don't need accessibility would never tolerate being stuck with it permanently.)

Standardized grammars are not without precedent. Dublin Core metadata (dublincore.org) are a standardized means of adding information about a page within its ‹head›‹/head› element. In theory, compliant devices can sort and reorder such documents based on the metadata contents. If, for example, 20 of the 300 pages at your site deal with a specific topic (e.g., a topic for which a Library of Congress subject heading exists, like "Closed captioning" or "Video recordings for the visually handicapped"), a device could skim through all 300 pages and present a hitlist of only the documents matching that subject heading. By strictly limiting the range of permissible classifications, it becomes possible to engage in pinpoint manipulations – a triage much more precise than you'd get from a search engine chugging through the words in all your pages, to continue with the preceding example. (Among other things, there are fewer items to look at if you concern yourself only with Dublin Core metadata. It's easier to examine 300 `<head></head>` elements than 300 full texts.)

Now, of course, as with anything smart and promising *and of true practical utility* in the wide world of the Web, Dublin Core metadata are essentially unused. (But Flash? Flash everybody is using!) There is little incentive to invent devices that can manipulate such metadata if no one is using it. The same fate may befall section tags.

Or perhaps the use of section tags will eventually become widespread. There's already a World Wide Web Consortium group working on what are called Composite Capabilities/Preferences Profiles (CCPP; see CCPP.org), which will definitely encompass the kind of accessibility reconfigurations discussed here. But like all voluntary standards, CCPP faces an uphill battle. Frankly, it is much more expedient to hack a few alt texts into a Web page and call it accessible (an approach this book does not merely authorize but actively teaches you to do) than to reprogram a site so that it becomes *elegantly* accessible.

The database problem

A very big, very necessary new invention can be summed up in a very few words: An authoring tool that maintains accessibility assets in a database for manipulation. Assets in this category include:

- alt, title, and longdesc associated with images, so that when an image is used or reused in a site or is shared with other sites, its prewritten text analogues automatically appear. (You need write such analogues only once per language.) Multilingual sites must keep track of multiple-language variants. Sliced images must be maintained as a unit, with the full panoply of text equivalents.
- accesskey and tabindex, either fixed or variable, according to page and site requirements.
- acronyms and abbreviations maintained sitewide (tricky, since the same character strings used on different pages might or might not actually be acronyms or abbreviations).
- Caption, audio-description, subtitle, and dubbing tracks that never get separated from the inaccessible source file. Multiple related caption or description tracks (e.g., easy-reader captions and verbatim captions;

continuous descriptions and descriptions of a certain item in a scene that are heard only upon special command) must all be accommodated. When entirely separate files are required to provide access, maintain them and keep them available. We don't want a recurrence of the television experience, where a program once captioned goes uncaptioned in rebroadcast.

- Section tags.

"Once accessible, always available" should be the philosophy here.

Now, all this is readily achieved in a costly content-management system, and I can envisage Broadvision or Vignette marketing a $50,000 module that takes care of these tasks. I can also imagine shareware applications using MySQL or other free tools. I am having a hard time imagining Macromedia or Adobe ever getting around to adding these functions to Dreamweaver or GoLive. Call me a pessimist.

On the other hand, the blossoming of homegrown content-management tools – Blogger, Greymatter, and Movable Type are the Big Three among so-called independent Websites – gives me cause for optimism. If anyone's going to implement intelligent database structures and reconfigurable site structures along the lines of CCPP, these dedicated hobbyists are; the diamond-studded content-management systems won't get around to it until there's cash on the barrelhead paying for such development. Open-source content managers like Zope are another glimmer of hope.

The repair problem

As discussed in Chapter 14, "Certification and testing," the degree of accessibility of a Website is not cut-and-dried; it's all relative. Fixing access problems at a Website is, at present, rather inconvenient. It is quite possible to quickly check for the absence of text analogues on images through search and replace, but subtler issues, like the use of acronym and abbr or navigation, require careful thought and subjective evaluation. Then again, even a "quick" check of images ceases to be quick if you're stuck doing it for dozens or hundreds of pages or templates.

Our authoring tools should take a good run at automating this process for us. We could imagine a system that, working in tandem with the asset database, presented a custom-made screen of allegedly inaccessible components. Imagine a list of all the images on your site that do not come equipped with alt texts laid out before you, with type-in fields alongside. Enter an alt once and it propagates automatically not merely through that page, but everywhere on your site (and on any other sites whose files reside on a server you specify). If a graphic with a single function has two appearances in two different languages, the authoring tool is smart enough to show them to you together so you can make the text equivalent; you can also enter language-specific text (e.g., for an invariant shopping-cart icon whose alt must differ on English- and French-language E-commerce sites).

Such a tool could display a thumbnail of your page, onto which you could drag and drop (or add via keyboard commands) a set of accesskey and tabindex values. (We can't rely solely on drag and drop. The authoring tool itself must be accessible to a disabled person. In this case, one could tab from element to element and take action through keyboard commands where necessary.)

A very intelligent repair tool would spot typographic attributes used to make text look like a heading (e.g., 20px and red) and suggest a stylesheet attached to an actual ‹hx› heading tag to take its place.

Unlike the nag known as Bobby, repair tools of this calibre would let you select the complexity for which you wish to test. Don't feel like adding titles to all your images? Deselect that option. Don't particularly care about acronyms? No one says you have to, necessarily. Yet the tool would be smart enough to actually require what is required: You could not opt to skip an alt text, for example.

We do have something along these lines: A-Prompt from the University of Toronto (APrompt.ca), a Windows application that walks you through the entire range of accessibility issues on a site. It lacks the database function, random access, and pseudointelligence of what I have in mind, but it gets us more than halfway to our goal. (It's included on this book's CD-ROM.)

Ultimately, every midsized Web developer, whether in-house or in a consultancy, will require automated accessibility repair, because their clients will require repair services. Eventually, though, building access into original designs will become so commonplace that the need to retrofit accessibility will diminish. That fact in itself may discourage developers from inventing the repair tool envisioned here.

Art for access' sake

Online accessibility requires subjective interpretation. It's hard enough summing up still images in words. The Big Four access techniques for multimedia — captioning, audio description, subtitling, and dubbing — are exacting and ill-understood, and demand a range of skills that Web designers and programmers do not immediately have.

- In captioning: Can you accurately transcribe extended dialogue and sound effects? (I really mean *accurately*, with perfect spelling and punctuation.) Can you break that transcript into self-contained chunks, editing the original if necessary to maintain a comfortable reading speed without altering the meaning of the original words, or their feel? Then, can you wrangle what passes for captioning software online? (Is this what you thought you'd end up doing back when you took a Photoshop course in community college?)

- In audio description: Can you watch and listen and distill what isn't understandable purely from audio alone into tight, evocative prose? If you're dealing with a wordless or soundless animation (as most Flash pieces still are), are you prepared to sum up the entire visual experience in coherent words that, when spoken, occupy the same span of time as the original visual work? Can you pack enough meaning into that little time?

Do you, in all honesty, have anything resembling the skills necessary to carry out this kind of work?

Probably not. But can you learn it? Probably so. Even the tough stuff.

But *where* are you going to learn it? There's barely any training at all for conventional Web design these days. Bookshelves groaning under the weight of how-to books like this one do not constitute training, and spotty college and night courses here and there don't cut the mustard, either. Yes, Web design is a new field, meaning that everyone who's any good at it is *doing* it rather than teaching it. But that just proves the point: We're working in a medium of mass communication populated largely by autodidacts.

So it may be idealistic to imagine training for the subjective aspects of accessibility. Or maybe it isn't: Maybe the same companies that caused the problem of inaccessible imagery and multimedia in the first place should join forces to fund the development of training courses and materials that will teach any halfway intelligent person to do halfway intelligent access work. One could imagine a multilingual off-the-shelf product, containing DVDs, CDs, and print materials, training Web designers and programmers in the Big Four access techniques, with conventional Web access, as documented in this book, also explained.

Such a training program would be a worldwide first. Are you aware that there is no standardized training at all for the *existing* industries of captioning, audio description, subtitling, and dubbing? (This explains why quality and technique vary so appallingly in those fields.) Adding the responsibility of adapting those techniques to multimedia is a lot to ask. But we need it anyway, no matter how difficult the task may appear.

This is a particular concern of mine, and by the time this book hits those groaning bookshelves there may already be news on that front. But at present, the only training that's widely available forms part of this book, which is quite insufficient even by my own admission.

The solution

This chapter is entitled "Future dreams," so let's do some dreaming. What we need are:

- A standardized grammar of section tags, which could grow over time and be automatically updated by compliant devices.

We're working in a medium of mass communication populated largely by autodidacts.

- Browsers that fully support every crumb of accessible HTML (indeed, fully support *all* of HTML), *and* media stylesheets, *and* permit the user to select a preferred default stylesheet medium after the manner of selecting a default natural language.
- Content-management systems that can apply section tags, and also do the dirty work of section tags while we're waiting for them to catch on — automatically reformatting pages on demand.
- Content-management systems that, furthermore, read a browser's preferred media setting and automatically send pages formatted for that medium.
- Within browsers (by preference — let's not relegate this function to the gulag of screen readers), a network of sonic cues, selectable by the user in a system analogous to skins, that can be activated to denote structures and landmarks inside a Web document.
- Authoring tools that give easy, automated access to the full range of HTML access features *at the time of creation*.
- Related tools that repair inaccessible Websites.
- Widespread, thorough training programs for the subjective manifestations of online accessibility, including the development of text analogues of still images, captioning, audio description, subtitling, and dubbing.

There. I have thrown down the gauntlet.

How will we turn these future dreams into everyday reality?

APPENDICES

a| accessibility and the law

IN THE MANY INDUSTRIALIZED COUNTRIES WITH HUMAN-RIGHTS or disability-discrimination laws, you are legally *required* to provide accessible Websites. The requirement may not be explicitly stated in the relevant legislation (which invariably predates the Web), but there is ample evidence that human-rights and antidiscrimination laws apply to the Internet.

I brought up the issue of legal requirements in Chapter 2, "Why bother?"; this appendix will provide American readers with a greater understanding of the requirements of the Americans with Disabilities Act and the U.S. Section 508 requirements. I'll also provide an analysis, in lay terms, of the only known legal case involving Website accessibility, which, while occurring in Australia, has worldwide implications.

The ADA and the Web

The Americans with Disabilities Act calls for the removal of barriers to participation faced by people with disabilities in employment and entertainment, to name but two spheres of everyday life it covers.

The ADA was signed into law in 1990, meaning it predates the commercial explosion of the Internet. The applicability of this wide-ranging civil-rights legislation to the Web has been unclear, or at least little-discussed. However, the issues were quite authoritatively explained in the article "The ADA and the Internet: Must Websites be accessible to the disabled?" by Dana Whitehead McKee and Deborah T. Fleischaker. The periodical is a bit obscure, but the advice and information contained in the article are exemplary. Dana McKee, of Brown Goldstein Levy, LLP (BrownGold.com), has licensed the adaptation of her article for this book.

The version that follows has been edited to remove legal citations solely for the purposes of easy reading, but they are all present in the electronic version found on the CD-ROM included with this book.

I'd like to extend my gratitude to Ms McKee for the opportunity to bring this valuable information to a broader public.

THE ADA AND THE INTERNET: MUST WEBSITES BE ACCESSIBLE TO THE DISABLED?

By Dana Whitehead McKee and Deborah T. Fleischaker. Published in the Maryland Bar Journal, Nov.–Dec. 2000, v33 i6 p34–36. Reprinted with permission.

Many companies today either choose to disregard the issue of accessibility or simply forget to consider the disabled when designing and updating their Websites. This article examines how Title III of the Americans with Disabilities Act of 1990 (ADA) [42 U.S.C. §§12181–12189 (1994)] can and will have a dramatic impact in making the Internet accessible to the disabled.

Title III of the ADA

The ADA is a remedial statute designed to eliminate discrimination against individuals with disabilities and "to assure equality of opportunity, full participation, independent living, and economic self-sufficiency for such individuals." The scope of the statute is broad and prohibits discrimination in:

- employment (Title I);
- public (i.e., government) services, activities, and transportation (Title II);
- public accommodations and services operated by private entities (Title III); and
- telecommunications services (Title IV)

Of these sections, only Title III is applicable to private entities whose operations on the Internet affect commerce outside of the employment context.

Title III provides that:

> No individual shall be discriminated against on the basis of disability in the full and equal enjoyment of the goods, services, facilities, privileges, advantages, or accommodations of any place of public accommodation by any person who owns, leases (or leases to), or operates a place of public accommodation.

To have a cause of action under Title III of the ADA, usually the plaintiff must prove that:

- he or she is disabled;
- the defendant is a "private entity," which owns, leases, or operates a "place of public accommodation";
- he or she has been denied the opportunity to participate in or benefit from the goods, services, facilities, privileges, or advantages, or has been given the opportunity to participate, but in a manner not equal

to that afforded to others, or the benefit is separate and different from that afforded to others; and

- the defendant has failed to make reasonable or necessary modifications which would not fundamentally alter the nature of the public accommodation.

If the challenged discrimination is caused by a communications barrier, the plaintiff must also prove the existence of such barrier and suggest or prove a readily achievable method of removing the barrier. Cases such as *Pascuiti vs. New York Yankees* and *Gilbert vs. Eckerd Drugs* reiterate those principles.

THE ADA's APPLICATION TO THE INTERNET

The application of the ADA to owners of Internet service providers and Website owners is likely to be fraught with litigation over the issue of whether they own, lease or operate a "place of public accommodation." Many people, including some courts (for example, *Parker vs. Metropolitan Life Ins. Co.*), equate a place of public accommodation as a physical structure, such as a school, restaurant, or hotel. However, a careful reading of the statute and the regulations promulgated under the ADA clearly suggests that the definition is not so limited.

Title III does not define "place of public accommodation." Instead, it provides a laundry list of the type of private entities that would be considered public accommodations if their operations affect commerce. This list includes places of lodging, establishments serving food or drink, places of public gathering, sales or rental establishments, service establishments, stations used for specified public transportation, places of public display or collection (i.e., museum or library), places of recreation, places of education, social service establishments, and places of exercise or recreation.

The regulations, however, define a "place of public accommodation" as a "facility, owned by a private entity, whose operations affect commerce and fall within [the statutory] categories." The term "facility," as used in this regulation, is not limited to buildings or structures, but includes "sites, complexes, equipment, rolling stock or other conveyances, roads, walks, passageways, parking lots, or other real or personal property."

Most Websites seem to fall squarely within the definition of a "place of public accommodation." Many are owned by non-government entities for commercial gain and often fall within the broad categories of sales, rental, or service establishments or places of recreation or education.

Websites are also "facilities" as defined by the regulations. They are personal property to their owners and, as the name implies, they are "sites." Indeed, according to the federal district court in Massachusetts (*Digital Equip. Corp. vs. Altavista Tech., Inc.*), a Website is a group of related documents that share the same address on the Web. These related documents that comprise the Website are stored in a space that is either leased or owned on a server, as the court in *Shea vs. Reno* found.

Although no court has yet decided whether a Website is a place of public accommodation, at least one court has found it to be so, though not as part of a specific case on that topic. In *Doe vs. Mutual of Omaha Ins. Co.*, the Seventh Circuit, in describing the scope of Title III, noted:

> The core meaning of this provision... is that the owner or operator of a store, hotel, restaurant, dentist's office, travel agency, theater, *Website*, or other facility (whether in physical space or in electronic space...) that is open to the public cannot exclude disabled persons from entering the facility and, once in, from using the facility in the same way that the nondisabled do.

(Emphasis added.) Like the Seventh Circuit, the United States Departments of both Justice and Education have indicated that Websites are places of public accommodation.

DEFENSES TO INTERNET ADA CLAIMS

Nevertheless, businesses that are unwilling to make their Websites accessible may argue that Title III should not be applicable to Internet commerce. In support of this argument, they will most likely claim that the services or benefits that are inaccessible to the disabled through Websites or Website portals (i.e., the gateway page to the World Wide Web) do not fall within the scope of the ADA because these sites are not places utilized by physical access.

This argument may meet with some limited success. The courts are divided on whether a "public accommodation" under Title III is applicable in nonphysical access cases. The issue has arisen most often in two contexts: the application of Title III to membership organizations and to insurance benefits. Several courts have required that there be a close nexus with a physical structure for Title III to apply. In *Ford vs. Schering Plough Corp.*, the court held that disability benefits provided by an employer were not covered by Title III because no nexus existed with the insurer's office. Similar nexus requirements were found essential by the following courts: *Parker vs. Metropolitan Life Ins. Co.*; *Schaff vs. Association of Educ. Therapists*; *Pappas vs. Bethesda Hosp. Ass'n.*; and *Welsh vs. Boy Scouts of Am.*

Other courts, however, have not interpreted the term "public accommodations" to require a physical structure or a nexus between the physical structure and the discrimination for Title III to be applicable. For example, in *Pallozzi vs. Allstate Life Ins. Co.*, the court stated: "Title III's mandate that the disabled be accorded 'full and equal enjoyment of the goods [and] services... of any place of public accommodation' suggests to us that the statute was meant to guarantee them more than mere physical access."

The court, in *Walker vs. Carnival Cruise Lines*, concluded that when the private entity falls squarely within the ADA definition of public accommodation, no issue with physical access is necessary. Other courts have also concluded that the ADA's access requirements apply to more than physical structures. The court, in *Lewis vs. Aetna Life Ins. Co.*, may have said it best: "It is difficult to believe that Congress intended to withhold the protections of the ADA from the millions of disabled persons who buy their goods by telephone, mail order, or home delivery without ever entering the physical premises of a business establishment."

Arguably, Websites and Website portals are facilities under the ADA regulations, and therefore fall within the scope of a "place of public accommodation." The fact that the disabled only access the site electronically, as opposed to physically entering an office, should not result in the ADA's being inapplicable. To hold otherwise would mean that stores like the Gap could legally discriminate against the disabled on the Internet by having inaccessible Websites, but would be prohibited from having inaccessible stores in local shopping centers. Certainly Congress did not design the ADA for such disparate outcomes.

Private-entity defendants may also try to avoid liability under Title III under the theory that the necessary modifications are "unreasonable," would "fundamentally alter" the nature of the public accommodation, would result in an "undue burden," or are not "readily achievable," i.e., "easily accomplishable and able to be carried out without much difficulty or expense." In most cases, none of these defenses should be persuasive because the necessary modifications are quite simple to achieve, are not cost prohibitive, and should not result in fundamentally altering the nature of the Website.

Website designers and owners do not even have to incur any costs in determining how to make Websites accessible to the disabled or whether an already existing site has accessibility problems; they may consult World Wide Web Consortium Web Accessibility Initiative documents or use the Bobby validation service. While these are only two of the cost-effective options available, they serve to demonstrate that public Websites can be made accessible without undue burden.

Although no court has yet decided that the Internet and Websites are public accommodations covered by Title III of the ADA, there is little doubt that such a decision will ultimately be made. To require businesses on the street to comply with the ADA while permitting those in cyberspace to freely discriminate against the disabled would defeat the purpose of the ADA. Therefore, to avoid potential costly litigation, owners of Websites and Website portals should make sure that their sites are constructed so that they are accessible to the disabled.

> Arguably, Websites and Website portals are facilities under the ADA regulations, and therefore fall within the scope of a "place of public accommodation."

> To require businesses on the street to comply with the ADA while permitting those in cyberspace to freely discriminate against the disabled would defeat the purpose of the ADA.

I hope the foregoing article is useful to readers concerned with complying with U.S. laws.

Note that, as ever, the fear of getting sued should not be the impetus to provide accessibility. Besides, there is but a single known case of anyone's having actually been sued, as we shall now see.

Mighty Olympics vanquished!

At time of writing, only one legal case concerning Web accessibility is known: *Maguire vs. SOCOG*. A single individual was triumphant in pursuing a complaint of Web inaccessibility. His adversary: Nothing less than the Olympic movement itself, as manifested in the Sydney Organizing Committee for the Olympic Games.

This case teaches us that the legal need for accessibility is so clear-cut, and the means of achieving basic accessibility so straightforward, that even an unspeakably wealthy and powerful international organization can lose in a judicial proceeding.

BACKGROUND

In Australia in June 1999, Bruce Maguire lodged a complaint with the Human Rights & Equal Opportunity Commission (HREOC) under a law called the Disability Discrimination Act. His complaint concerned the Website of the Sydney Organizing Committee for the Olympic Games (SOCOG), which Maguire alleged was inaccessible to him as a blind person.

According to the complaint, Maguire, unlike most blind people online, does not use a screen reader to read aloud the elements of a Web page. Instead, he uses a refreshable Braille display. But neither technology can render into voice an image that lacks a text equivalent. Nearly all Web pages online have some kind of graphics, including high-profile sites like those associated with major sporting events.

Maguire contended that significant parts of the SOCOG Website, Olympics.com, were inaccessible to him.

On 24 August 2000, the HREOC released its decision and supported Maguire's complaint, ordering certain access provisions to be in place on the Olympics.com site by 15 September 2000. SOCOG ignored the ruling and was subsequently fined A$20,000.

To respond to the objection that this case, having taken place "far away" in Australia, is unrelated to Web design in other nations, I would suggest examining the similarities among the Disability Discrimination Act, the Americans with Disabilities Act, and the Canadian Human Rights Act, not to mention provincial, state, and territorial human-rights codes. The legal principles of unequal treatment ("discrimination"; "unfavourable" treatment) and unjustifiable hardship ("undue" hardship or "burden") are effectively identical in Australia, the U.S., and Canada, if not elsewhere, and the case of *Maguire vs. SOCOG* will inevitably come into play as precedents for legal cases worldwide.

Some history of the complaint

Maguire had tangled with SOCOG before on matters unrelated to the Web, and those complaints are referred to extensively in the decision. However, the crux

of his complaint involved a demand that the Olympics.com site provide the
following accessibility features:

- That SOCOG include alt text on all images and imagemap links
  on the Website
- That SOCOG ensure access from the Schedule page to the Index
  of Sports
- That SOCOG ensure access to the Results Tables on the Website during
  the Olympic Games

Withholding information

SOCOG attempted to derail the proceedings through several means. One
involved withholding information Maguire claimed he needed to understand
the size and scope of the task of improving accessibility at Olympics.com.

The information Maguire asked for included:

- A sample page in electronic format from the proposed Results Table
  on the SOCOG Website relating to the Olympic Games
- The current content plan for the Olympic Website
- The number of templates to be used
- The details of the tools used to generate the pages of the
  Olympic Website
- Calculations of certain ballpark figures

HREOC commissioner William Carter stated flatly:

> I pause to mention that the relevant information has never
> been provided nor had it been provided by the time of the
> hearing on 8 and 11 August 2000. By letter dated 4 August
> 2000, the solicitor for [SOCOG] sought relief from the need
> to provide the requested information on the basis that it was
> "highly commercially sensitive information within the
> knowledge of SOCOG and its contractor." Its contractor
> was IBM.

Commerce takes place in a competitive system of sellers and buyers. IBM and
SOCOG had outright monopolies on Sydney Olympic Websites. There were no
competitors – even licensed television networks' Web ventures weren't in the
same league. There was no competition per se in the way there is competition
between Ford and Toyota. While it could be argued that IBM's competitors
might have stolen its ideas, Maguire did not seek public release of the information, merely release to him and his lawyer. The claim of "commercially-sensi-
tive information" was clearly false.

Later, SOCOG claimed that "'the provision of the HTML source code of the
Results Pages' would not be made available because it was 'highly commercially
sensitive information.'" It is unclear if SOCOG or HREOC didn't understand the

lingo or if this was meant literally. Anyone could view the source code for the results pages once the site went live; it would become the worst-kept secret in the world. What we wouldn't see is the underlying database programming, which in itself is not necessarily accessible or inaccessible. SOCOG's claim could have been dismissed immediately if it was meant literally. If not, perhaps there was some kind of intention to confuse.

Further, although SOCOG advanced this "commercially sensitive" defense, HREOC stated it could have accommodated SOCOG by coming up with some means of "protect[ing] the commercial sensitivity of the information, assuming of course the information qualified for that description."

Partial progress

Maguire filed his complaint on 7 June 1999 (15 months and eight days before the start of the Sydney 2000 Olympics). The decision notes that "on a visit to the SOCOG Website on 17 April 2000, some changes had been made to the site since his original complaint but that in certain other respects the site remained inaccessible."

At the hearing for this complaint, SOCOG claimed the alt-text problem had been solved "and that access to the Index of Sports from the Schedule was available and had always been available by a different route; namely, by entering the URL for each sport directly into the Web browser." In other words, SOCOG attempted to suggest that typing in a lengthy URL could provide equal access. SOCOG did not, however, describe any circumstances in which sighted people would have to type in full URLs.

What constitutes discrimination?

In Australia, under the Disability Discrimination Act, "It is unlawful for a person who... provides goods or services, or makes facilities available, to discriminate against another person on the ground of the other person's disability... in the terms or conditions on which the... person provides the other person with those goods or services...; or in the manner in which the... person provides the other person with those goods or services or makes those facilities available to the other person."

Just on the face of it, the requirement to type in URLs if you're blind but merely click a link if you're sighted constitutes discrimination.

"The provision of the Website was a service relating to the provision by the respondent of information relating to the largest and most significant entertainment or recreation event in the history of this country," the decision holds.

SOCOG attempted to claim that the site was "promotional." As we all know, "promotional" Websites don't cost tens of millions of dollars and attract six billion hits over their lifespans, as SOCOG would claim in the proceeding. HREOC didn't buy it, fortunately: "The provision of information by the respondent via its Website is, in the Commission's view, a service relating to the entertainment which the respondent will provide to the world in the course of the Sydney Olympic Games."

What is unjustifiable hardship?

In antidiscrimination laws throughout the Western world, anyone alleged to have discriminated is not required to remedy the discrimination if doing so would dramatically alter the nature of business or put the party in financial jeopardy. In other words, there is a test of reasonableness, extent, and expense when assessing disability discrimination. It is possible, therefore, for a body like the HREOC to conclude that there *was* disability discrimination but that the way to fix it is too complicated or expensive.

SOCOG argued that retrofitting its site for accessibility would cause unjustifiable hardship, estimating the cost at A$2.2 million.

Accessibility guidelines

World Wide Web Consortium accessibility guidelines, SOCOG maintained, were too new to graft onto Olympics.com, which had already undergone "substantial implementation." HREOC countered that Olympics.com "is and has been in the process of continual development. Indeed it is alleged, particularly in relation to the provision of alt text, that this has been ongoing. A letter from IBM... asserts that alt text was being added to images on the SOCOG Website and 'expected' that this task 'would be completed by 8 August 2000.' "

Obviously, if the guidelines were truly so new and the site so substantially complete, it would not have been possible to add so many alt texts, which, the decision fails to note, have been a feature of HTML for years (since at least HTML 2.0, dating from December 1996, "based upon current practice in 1994")and are a *requirement* of HTML 4.0, issued in December 1997.

Yet Maguire and an expert witness explained that not all images had been adapted with alts, and there is no discussion of the adequacy and understandability of the alt texts.

Type-in URLs

HREOC agreed with Maguire that typing in sport-specific URLs did not constitute favourable ("equal") treatment. As Maguire plainly put it, "that is not the way that people use Web pages." The Commission agreed: "[T]he proposed alternative is both unorthodox and cumbersome and need not be resorted to by a sighted person."

It must also be pointed out that the URLs in question are tongue-twisters. As examples, five sports have very long URLs differing by exactly one character. Can you guess what sport relates to each URL below?

www.olympics.com/eng/sports/CS/home.html
www.olympics.com/eng/sports/CF/home.html
www.olympics.com/eng/sports/CM/home.html
www.olympics.com/eng/sports/CR/home.html
www.olympics.com/eng/sports/CT/home.html

In order, the URLs relate to canoe/kayak slalom, canoe/kayak sprint, mountain biking, road cycling, and track cycling. You can't assume some kind of acronym system at work: "Canoe/kayak slalom" and "canoe/kayak sprint" both share the acronym CKS, but the URLs use CS and CF.

SOCOG, in all seriousness, advanced the manual typing-in of mile-long, hard-to-remember, confusable URLs as an accessibility measure.

Inaccessibility of the Results Table

Tables are a recurring bugbear for blind Web-surfers. Not only are tables used for page layout, but when put to use in their putative intended sense, to structure tabular data, Web authors need to add coding to make navigating the table understandable to a screen-reader or Braille user.

However, that task is quite manageable. It's difficult to do using authoring programs like Dreamweaver, unless your site is so sprawling and enormous that you're writing your own HTML-generating tools in the first place, as SOCOG apparently did. In that case, it's a question of adapting the software to produce accessible code. There is no evidence that SOCOG did so.

HREOC states flatly that "the Results Table remains and will remain inaccessible to the complainant." It gets worse for SOCOG:

> In the Commission's view, the respondent has discriminated against the complainant... in that the Website does not include alt text on all images and imagemap links, the Index to Sports cannot be accessed from the Schedule page, and the Results Tables provided during the Games on the Website will remain inaccessible.

And furthermore:

> Because of the manner in which that information was made available, it could be accessed by a sighted person. Because of the manner in which that information was made available it could not be accessed by a blind person because of his or her disability. This meant that, in respect of the same information, the respondent, in the manner in which it used its computer technology to service the needs of the public to have access to that information, made it available to sighted persons, but it made it unavailable or only partly available to a blind person because of the latter's disability. It follows that, because of his or her disability, the blind person was treated less favourably by the respondent than the sighted person.

Degree of difficulty in providing access

SOCOG attempted to present the line of reasoning we usually encounter with corporations: Our site is too big to make accessible. Perhaps interestingly, such sites are never too big for all the other infrastructure the corporations decide is worth the money: Database back ends, professional graphic design, custom JavaScript and Java applets, expensive content-management systems.

SOCOG's claims include:

- The site currently consists of 6,000 pages and approximately 55,000 pages will be generated in the course of the Games.
- There are 37 sports Web page templates, each with approximately 35 results templates – in total 1,295 templates for results alone.
- The tables of results will contain "wrapped text within cells."
- There will be approximately six billion hits on the site and the site needs to be fast and highly responsive.
- To reformat the site and its contents in a way which will make the Website accessible to the complainant will in effect require the development of a new or separate site.
- Extensive changes to infrastructure are required; there is a requirement for specialized skills which are limited and expensive; there will be possible adverse impacts upon the support and maintenance systems.
- One person working eight-hour business days would require 368 days to complete the task properly.
- $2.2 million of additional infrastructure would be required to separately host the additional designs necessary to an accessible Table of Results.

Yet the Commission, based on the testimony of expert witnesses and other findings, dismissed most of SOCOG's claims:

- The number of templates is significantly less than 1,295 and the reformatting of the templates will take considerably less than the two hours for each alleged by the respondent. A more realistic estimate for the minor changes required is ten minutes each; nor is there the need for unique manually-generated formats.
- No new infrastructure will be required because it is allegedly in place.
- A team of one experienced developer with a group of 5–10 assistants could provide an accessible site to [Web Content Accessibility Guidelines] Level A compliance in four weeks.
- Wrapping in each cell can be met by using a simple device, namely the inclusion of an invisible end-of-cell character which would indicate to a blind person the end of the text in each cell.
- The cost of making the site accessible is a modest amount.
- The number of templates has been estimated at 357 for 28 sports. Additional templates would be required for 37.

It is not clear what HREOC means by "an invisible end-of-cell character," unless they refer to `</td>`. A conversation with one of the expert witnesses previously called for the trial clarifies for this book that the initial (mistaken) assumption was that tables would have to be linearized for Maguire to understand them, which turned out not to be the case; standard accessible table HTML would suffice.

In any event, it is manifestly clear that adding accessibility tags, while more complicated in a retrofit than it would be to add them in the first place, is not qualitatively different from adding all the other tags necessary to make a large database-driven Website work. The fact that some of those tags might be reproduced six billion times during the course of the Olympics merely means that six billion pages accessible will be transmitted.

And on the topic of retrofitting...

Expert testimony

In any event, it is manifestly clear that adding accessibility tags, while more complicated in a retrofit than it would be to add them in the first place, is not qualitatively different from adding all the other tags necessary to make a large database-driven Website work.

Testimony from two expert witnesses was used: Tom Worthington, listed in his online bio as "a Visiting Fellow in the Department of Computer Science at the Australian National University and independent electronic business consultant," and Jutta Treviranus of the University of Toronto Adaptive Technology Resource Centre. (I sat in Jutta Treviranus' office and chatted with her about the case for this book.)

In Ms Treviranus' view, if accessibility had been considered by the respondent when the site was being developed it could have been totally achieved in less than one percent of the time consumed in the site's development. She has regularly visited the site and in her view it remains inaccessible in material respects. For instance in her view in some respects the situation has worsened because additional graphic material has been added without alt text.

In respect of the Schedule page, which in her view is completely inaccessible, it could be corrected by a very simple change which would take less than 1.5 hours. Mr. Worthington expressed the view that the correction would take less time than the time which was consumed in the hearing talking about it. In Ms Treviranus' view it would be unnecessary to uniquely and manually generate a new format in respect of the suggested 1,295 templates. No new infrastructure would be required; the existing team supplemented with some additional support for a short period would be sufficient. There would be no need to develop and implement a new navigation design. What the respondent suggested would take 25 business days could be effectively completed within a few hours.

Competing expert testimony

SOCOG approached the whole issue with such evident scorn and dismissiveness that it did not even train its own consultants well enough to provide an adequate defence.

> Mr. Brand and Mr. Smeal... were engaged only in the days immediately prior to the hearing commencing on 8 August 2000 [and] were required to prepare and give their evidence from positions of relative disadvantage. Their knowledge and experience with the site was necessarily very limited and the evidence of each was effectively based on the need to validate certain information and conclusions given to them by Mr. Max Judd of IBM and Dr. Ian Reinecke, the Chief Information Officer of SOCOG. Neither were able to confirm the information given to them nor were Mr. Judd nor Dr. Reinecke called to give evidence.

How's that for kneecapping yourself?

Damning conclusions

According to the Commission:

> The clear inference can be drawn from the facts and circumstances that [SOCOG] never seriously considered the issue and only when the hearing was imminent did it attempt to support its rejection of the complainant's complaint by resort to a process which was both inadequate and unconvincing.

Among other things, SOCOG engaged in delaying tactics and then used the excuse that, even if required to do so, it would not have enough time to make Olympics.com accessible. The delaying tactics included:

- Its failure/refusal to provide the information sought by the complainant in its letter dated 31 March 2000.
- Its failure to provide the statements of its witnesses as directed by the Commission.
- Its failure/refusal to reply to correspondence or to return telephone calls in the period 17 May 2000 [to] 20 June 2000.
- Its attempt to vacate the hearing dates set for 3 and 4 July 2000.
- Its stated intention to pursue an unmeritorious point in the Federal Court at the hearing on 3 July 2000 and its abandonment of the same just weeks later.
- Its failure to provide statements of its expert witnesses on 4 August 2000 – less than one week prior to the adjourned hearing.
- Its unsworn attempt to establish the truth of facts alleged by it as the basis for its claim of unjustifiable hardship on the very last date set for hearing of the matter.

We're used to corporations attempting to bulldoze impoverished litigants by outspending them, but in this case SOCOG attempted to win the case by stalling for time. It didn't work.

> [I]t is necessary to confirm the view that on the acceptable evidence of Mr. Worthington and Ms Treviranus there is no good reason to conclude that the sought-after access cannot be available to the complainant either by or during the course of the Sydney Olympic Games.

Remedy

SOCOG was ordered to engage in the following by 15 September 2000:

- Including alt text on all images and imagemap links on its Website
- Providing access to the Index of Sports from the Schedule page
- Providing access to the Results Tables to be used on the Website during the Sydney Olympic Games

SOCOG refused to comply with the order and was later ordered to pay Bruce Maguire $20,000 for its refusal to comply. According to the decision making that cash award:

> [Maguire] has persistently insisted that his disability should not be the cause of his having to accept an inferior outcome by reason of his disability. His competence at reading Braille and his application of that skill to computer technology is obviously of a high order.
>
> Accordingly, his expectations of being able to access information from [SOCOG's] Website were, not surprisingly, high – certainly as high as that which a sighted person with his skills could expect. I am satisfied that the respondent from the outset was dismissive of the complainant's concerns....
>
> This response, I am satisfied, was very hurtful for him; the suggestion that he enlist the aid of a sighted person to assist him was wholly inconsistent with his own expectations and what he himself, unaided, had been able to achieve, both at university level and in business, in spite of his disability. To dismiss him and to continue to be dismissive of him was not only hurtful, he was also made to feel, I am satisfied, various emotions including those of anger and rejection by a significant statutory agent within the community of which he himself was a part.
>
> In my view this element of dismissiveness in the respondent's original response was not relieved as the inquiry process under the DDA proceeded within the Commission. In respect of this part of the complaint it apparently persisted and his original pain was somewhat aggravated by that fact....

I am comfortably satisfied that his limited access to the Website caused him considerable feelings of hurt, humiliation and rejection. One cannot overstate the consequential effect upon him of his having to cope with the persistent need to counter what he saw as a negative, unhelpful and dismissive attitude on the part of an organization charged with the presentation of the most notable sporting event in the history of this country. This, in my view, was aggravated by his final inability to obtain the desired access to the Website in spite of his having established to the satisfaction of the Commission the fact that he had been unlawfully discriminated against.

The public statements of the respondent subsequent to 24 August 2000 were for him the final indignity. He... continued to feel the impact which the respondent's earlier dismissive attitude had had upon him. This was, no doubt, aggravated by the fact that the published statement of the respondent in justification of its noncompliance included material which had been specifically rejected by the Commission....

In the Commission's view his hurt and earlier rejection has persisted, and in spite of an apparently successful outcome he had been left with feelings of ultimate failure. It is obviously difficult for those of us not similarly disabled to share his feelings and emotions. As best one can assess, including from his presentation to the Commission, his hurtful rejection by the respondent was very considerable in his case.

Maguire stated for this book that SOCOG did indeed pay the fine, a surprising outcome – it was easy to imagine SOCOG's simply waiting until it went out of business (nearly a year after the Sydney Olympics closed) in order to avoid payment.

Conclusions

To reiterate, in the case of *Maguire vs. SOCOG*, the little person won. While the Sydney Organizing Committee for the Olympic Games acted in an arguably unprofessional and certainly a dismissive manner, the allegedly substantive reasons it advanced for denying accessibility were conclusively repudiated by Australian authorities and expert witnesses.

Curiously, IBM, SOCOG's Web contractor, maintains an accessibility Website (at IBM.com/able/) and full-time staff who do nothing but work on software, hardware, and Web accessibility. Many of those staff were helpful in writing this book. IBM has a reasonably salutary record in accessibility products, having developed IBM Home Page Reader, a screen-reader analogue specialized for surfing the Web. Yet its partnership with SOCOG gave the appearance of a corrupting influence, making IBM complicit in SOCOG's actions in denying accessibility to blind users of its Olympics.com site.

In any event, in the Maguire case we now have a firm worldwide precedent that inaccessible Websites can be and are illegal.

Section 508

During the production of this book, the U.S. government enacted the so-called Section 508 requirements, under which U.S. government agencies (with uncommon exceptions) and a limited range of nongovernmental entities and outside vendors must ensure that their Websites are accessible. (Section 508 has many other provisions that apply outside the Web.)

The Section508.gov Website tells us:

> Section 508 refers to a statutory section in the Rehabilitation Act of 1973 (found at 29 U.S.C. 794d). Congress significantly strengthened Section 508 in the Workforce Investment Act of 1998. Its primary purpose is to provide access to and use of Federal executive agencies' electronic and information technology... by individuals with disabilities.

Ohh-kaaay. Doesn't that sound like a parallel universe of accessibility requirements, one that tends to compete with the Web Content Accessibility Guidelines?

That is partly true. When it comes to Web design, Section 508 has 16 paragraphs headed as follows:

(a)   Text tags
(b)   Multimedia presentations
(c)   Colour
(d)   Readability
(e)   Server-side imagemaps
(f)   Client-side imagemaps
(g,h) Data tables
(i)   Frames
(j)   Flicker rate
(k)   Text-only alternatives
(l)   Scripts
(m)   Applets and plugins
(n)   Electronic forms
(o)   Navigation links
(p)   Time delays

Section 508 requirements are either:
- excerpted verbatim from the Web Content Accessibility Guidelines (nine of 16 items)
- identical to the WCAG save for minor variations (two)
- unique to 508 (five)

However, here is what the Access Board tells us about the differences between 508 and the WCAG:

> The final rule does not reference the WCAG 1.0. However... paragraphs (a) through (i) incorporate the exact language recommended by the WAI in its comments to the proposed rule or contain language that is not substantively different than the WCAG 1.0 and was supported in its comments.
>
> Paragraphs (j) and (k) are meant to be consistent with similar provisions in the WCAG 1.0; however, the final rule uses language which is more consistent with enforceable regulatory language. Paragraphs (l), (m), (n), (o), and (p) are different than any comparable provision in the WCAG 1.0 and generally require a higher level of access or prescribe a more specific requirement.
>
> The Board did not adopt or modify four of the WCAG 1.0 Priority 1 checkpoints....
>
> A Website required to be accessible by Section 508 would be in complete compliance if it met paragraphs (a) through (p) of these standards. It could also comply if it fully met the WCAG 1.0 Priority 1 checkpoints and paragraphs (l), (m), (n), (o), and (p) of these standards....
>
> The Board has as one of its goals to take a leadership role in the development of codes and standards for accessibility. We do this by working with model code organizations and voluntary consensus standards groups that develop and periodically revise codes and standards affecting accessibility. The Board acknowledges that the WAI has been at the forefront in developing international standards for Web accessibility and looks forward to working with them in the future on this vitally important area. However, the WCAG 1.0 were not developed within the regulatory enforcement framework.

So there you have it: Section 508 standards are different from the Web Content Accessibility Guidelines because – among other reasons not discussed here, many of them substantive and reasonable – the Guidelines just are not the way the U.S. government does things.

The general viewpoint among accessibility advocates is "As Goes the U.S. Government, So Goes the Private Sector." The assumption is that the requirements of Section 508 will become a de facto standard of accessibility for the

Websites of all vendors that sell to the U.S. government, no matter how small — or how large. The application of those standards will then spread to all parts of the Websites of such vendors (even parts unrelated to the U.S. government) and to Websites of entities that have no dealings whatsoever with the government. While this is all conjecture, it seems like plausible conjecture to me.

Further, a number of U.S. states are understood to be in the process of adopting regulations essentially or actually identical to those of Section 508, and some countries outside the U.S. are taking it upon themselves to arrive at accessibility guidelines for their own countries, though they are not necessarily based on 508.

If your company has business dealings with any of these governments, you may be required to certify not only that the work you do for their Websites meets these requirements but that your own sites meet them.

B| language codes

U**NDER THE** W**EB** C**ONTENT** A**CCESSIBILITY** G**UIDELINES**, you are required to specify changes in the "natural" or human language used in documents. You do this by adding the lang="*languagecode*" attribute to virtually any tag (like ‹p›‹/p›, ‹span›‹/span›, ‹cite›‹/cite›, or ‹hx›‹/hx›. Also, in order to specify a change in language, you must already have declared the default, base, or original language, which you do by adding lang="*languagecode*" to the ‹body&gt or (preferably) ‹html&gt tags, like so:

- body lang="en"
- html lang="fr-ca"

So just what *are* those language codes? They're two-letter abbreviations, optionally followed by a hyphen and some other qualifier. In the second example above, French is specified (fr), but of the Canadian variety (ca). The exact specification is ISO 639-1, "Codes for the Representation of Names of Languages," whose homepage resides at the Library of Congress: lcweb.loc.gov/standards/iso639-2/. (Yes, that URL says "iso639-2"; you have to hunt around at the site to find the 639-1 section, which is a bit outdated.)

Note that the companion standard, ISO 639-2, provides three-letter codes for languages – and for a vastly wider range of languages, at that. Online, however, we must stick with the two-letter codes. At least, this is my interpretation. A page at the World Wide Web Consortium Internationalization site tells us:

> According to RFC 3066, for languages with both a two-letter and a three-letter code, the two-letter code must be used. This also solves the problem of those languages that have two different three-letter codes, because all of them also have a two-letter code.

So this "solves the problem," does it? I don't see a lot of problems that are actually "solved" here. The RFC (request for comment) mentioned in this citation merely refers back to ISO 639-1 and tells us, in effect, that the only three-letter language codes we may use are those that do not have a corresponding two-letter language code. But there are somewhat complex rules in place governing when a three-letter code may be coined without creating a corresponding two-letter code.

From an accessibility perspective, this restriction will eventually have to be lifted. Textual media are not the only kind available on the Web, and as more and more video becomes available, more and more sign languages will be available, and all sign-language names exist in the three-character specification (under sgn). It is technically impossible to specify a sign language on a Website as the standards currently exist.

My recommendation? Damn the torpedoes! If you have to specify a language with a three-letter code because you cannot find a two-letter code, do it. Such a practice appears to be permitted anyway and is the only one that makes sense.

Let's start with the two-letter codes. Now, hundreds of languages have been defined, and I'm not going to list every single one of them here because the super-obscure language codes have no practical value to my audience. (It's nice to know that Faroese has its own language code, but how many readers of a book on Web accessibility will have cause to design Websites in Faroese? And won't such designers already know that Faroese's language code is fo?) Besides, the ISO 639-1 specs are all online and provide all the codes for you.

I have not found a truly reliable source for the Top Ten languages used online (after English – the Top Eleven, really). I have synthesized various lists into the following somewhat longer compilation – not quite Top Forty, but close.

Very-widely-used languages online

Japanese	ja	Dutch	nl	Korean	ko	Turkish	tr
German	de	Portuguese	pt	Polish	pl	Czech	cs
Chinese	zh	Finnish	fi	Russian	ru	Thai	th
French	fr	Swedish	sv	Hebrew	he	Arabic	ar
Spanish	es	Norwegian	no	Hungarian	hu	Icelandic	is
Italian	it	Danish	da	Greek	el		

Confusable codes

Note that country codes and language codes are often just *different enough* to get you into trouble if you're not eagle-eyed.

- Japan is jp, but Japanese is ja.
- China is cn, but Chinese is zh.

- The Netherlands is nl, and so is Dutch.
- Sweden is se, but Swedish is sv.
- Denmark is dk, but Danish is da.
- Greece is gr, but Greek is el.

Dialects

Some dialect names are standardized under ISO 639-1, while others, usually of a more fanciful nature (Cockney, Newfoundland, joual) are not. Both types are permitted; it is up to the browser or device to interpret the codes correctly.

It is possible and legal, for example, to specify all these variants of English:

- en (English: No specified variant)
- en-us (United States English)
- en-au-tas (Tasmanian English, Australia)
- en-in (Indian English)
- en-uk-Cockney-Rhyming-Slang

You must not assume, however, that browsers or devices will be able to understand or represent anything beyond the first dash.

In rather more important cases, like the two variations of Norwegian, Bokmål and Nynorsk, enough social importance is given to the dialects that they have their own codes.

- no (Norwegian: No specified variant)
- nb (Norwegian Bokmål)
- nn (Norwegian Nynorsk)

Authors writing in Norwegian will likely know which dialect they are using and can cite it appropriately. Authors who merely quote Norwegian text or make some other casual use of it may not know which is which; that's what the generic no tag is for.

If you're wondering about Chinese (no doubt you are), Mandarin and Cantonese are not the only recognized dialects, but all of them are subsumed under zh. You must use dialect codes for Mandarin (zh-guoyu) and Cantonese (zh-yue) if you wish to differentiate them. (The distinction is nearly meaningless on Websites that do not use voice given that the two dialects use the same writing system.) There is no difference in language code between Traditional and Simplified Chinese; arguably there should be.

Take my word for this as a linguist and an accessibility obsessif: This stuff is more detailed and pedantic than trainspotting, and almost as addictive to susceptible personalities. Just keep in mind that dinner-party guests are never really as interested in this topic as we are.

BiBLiOGraPHy

A bibliography of significant sources used to research this book that are not included on the book's CD-ROM follows.

Colourblindness
Brewer, Cynthia A., 1996: "Guidelines for selecting colors for diverging schemes on maps." *The Cartographic Journal* 33(2):79–86. (This, by the way, is the article documenting unconfusable color combinations and gradations.)

Brewer, Cynthia A., 1997: "Spectral schemes: Controversial color use on maps." *Cartography and Geographic Information Systems* 24(4):203–220.

Carter, Robert C., 1982: "A design tool for color displays." *Proceedings of the Human Factors Society – 26th Annual Meeting – 1982* (Norfolk, VA: Human Factors Society), 589.

Kimura, Kenji, Seiichi Sugiura, Horoaki Shinkai, and Yoshiro Nagai, 1988: "Visibility requirements for automobile CRT displays – color, contrast and luminance." *SAE Technical Papers Series* 880218 (Warrendale, PA: Society of Automotive Engineers).

Matthews, Michael L., and Karen Martins, 1987: "The influence of color on visual search and subjective discomfort using CRT displays." *Proceedings of the Human Factors Society – 31st Annual Meeting – 1987* (Norfolk, VA: Human Factors Society), 1271–1275.

Miyao, Masaru, Shinya Ishihara, Hisataka Sakakibara, Taka-aki Kondo, Shinji Yamada, Masashi Furuta, Katsumi Yamanaka, Tetsushi Yasuma, and Yasushi Toda, 1991: "Effects of color CRT display on pupil size in color-blind subjects." *Journal of Human Ergology* 20:241–247.

Olson, Judy M., and Cynthia A. Brewer, 1997: "An evaluation of color selections to accommodate map users with color-vision impairments." *Annals of the American Geographers* 87(1):103–134.

Auditory navigation

Morley, Sarah, Helen Petrie, Anne-Marie O'Neill, and Peter McNally, 1998: "Auditory navigation in hyperspace: Design and evaluation of a non-visual hypermedia system for blind users." *Proceedings of ASSETS '98, the Third Annual ACM Conference on Assistive Technologies* (Los Angeles: Association for Computing Machinery).

Raman, T.V., 1997: *Auditory user interfaces: Toward the speaking computer.* Boston: Kluwer Academic Publishers.

Ramloll, R., et al., 2001: "Using non-speech sounds to improve access to 2D tabular numerical information for visually-impaired users." http://www.dcs.gla.ac.uk/~ramesh/Online%20Publication/HCI2001Final.pdf.

COLOPHON

A *colophon* is "an inscription placed at the end of a book or manuscript usually with facts relative to its production." It's the Making Of section of a book. Not many computer books feature a colophon, but then again, *Building Accessible Websites* isn't a typical computer book, and I *am* something of an *obsessif*.

Why I wrote the book

I haven't exactly answered the question, sure to be on the tip of your tongue: "Why exactly did you write the book?" Well, I go back over twenty years in the field of what is now known generically as media access, and I've been online for over a decade. Eventually it became apparent that there was an overlap between the two worlds. I credit Geoff Freed at the WGBH Educational Foundation for putting the concept of Web accessibility on the map for me; I've known people at WGBH longer than anyone in WGBH's own Media Access Group has actually worked there, and once Geoff started working on publicly-discussed Web-accessibility projects, I began to learn whatever I could.

I got a bit tired of the high dudgeon of boy-racer designer types, who hated the entire *idea* of lifting a finger to design for accessibility. I also got fed up with the even-more-deadening hypercorrectness of accessibility advocates, who never met a beautiful Website they didn't dislike. The boy racers thought accessibility meant text-only pages and hated the prospect, while access types thought exactly the same thing and loved it.

I was, quite frankly, also tired of working Joe-jobs and was perfectly happy to earn not a whole lot of money (but in lucrative U.S. dollars, never netting me less than a 52% exchange rate) to sit around and write a book for a year (2001–2002). After having 390 journalistic articles published and many hundreds posted online, it is nice to be able to legitimately bill myself as an author.

Writing this book was a protracted and often frustrating process, and it was so painful and onerous that I have three brand-new books in the hopper. (It's only worth doing if it hurts.) Let's see if they all make it to print.

Acknowledgements

Now that I've gotten the self-aggrandizement over with, time for the requisite acknowledgements. Don't you hate the way books place acknowledgements and dedications right at the outset, forcing you to wade through streams of names of people you don't know and references to chapters and sections you haven't even read yet?

Well, I certainly hate it. Since you have presumably read the book by now (oh, I know, designer types will have *immediately* gravitated to this colophon the way teenagers head straight for the swear words in a dictionary), *now* it can exclusively be revealed who helped me out.

I salute the team at New Riders Publishing that stuck with this book from beginning to end. My "acquisitions" editor – the term always makes me think of Christian Bale in *American Psycho*: "I'm in murders and executions" – was Michael Nolan, who hates it when I refer to him as Mikey the N. You have to sit there on the phone with him for hours before he'll come out with it, but eventually it will be explained that Michael was and is a graphic designer and wrote a couple of books himself. He is, moreover, patient even with hotheaded paisans like me and has something of a radio voice. I would not have met Mikey the N were it not for the ministrations of Jeffrey "Jeffy the Z" Zeldman, the designer/author/mensch who hooked us up.

Jennifer Eberhardt was senior development editor of the book. She tends to deal with "problem" authors (my words, not hers, and certainly not New Riders') and was gracious enough to tell me I really wasn't one of those. Jennifer kills you with kindness. Michael Thurston waded through all the copy, along with Curt Cloninger, my technical editor (and a designer/author himself). Curt focused on HTML correctness, while Mark Pilgrim (Diveinto Mark.org) separately tech-edited the book for accessibility correctness.

(As the kids say today, *a big shout-out!* goes to Greg Rosmaita, who was pegged as the book's second technical editor, focusing on accessibility rather than HTML. Greg, the wryest, drollest blind man I've ever met, couldn't edit the book for reasons he will surely règale you with should you ever meet him. Try again on the second edition, Greg?)

In what passes for my Personal Life™, I benefited from the largesse of Luke Tymowski, who will simply *hate* the fact I have acknowledged him here. (Killing you with kindness, Luke. Killing you with kindness.) He hosts my various Websites and — get this — actually *lent me his PowerMac G4 Cube* when my own computer upped and croaked. (More on production in due course.) William O'Higgins came over for tea and allowed me to bore him to stupefaction.

A couple of old friends got older and stayed friends: Jeff Adams, Michel Blondeau, Colin Doyle, Bilal Halim, Brendan Kehoe.

As it turns out, Toronto is a minor hotbed of accessibility work. Jutta Treviranus at the Adaptive Technology Resource Centre at the University of Toronto actually believed in me, as did her hubby, Charles Silverman of Ryerson Polytechnic University. You know, I don't get that very often.

The reality for the author of the Web-related book is that friends are often virtual and are scattered to the four winds.

- Dean Allen, orders of magnitude more curmudgeonly even than I, worked on a design mockup, and needled me with "Done with the book, then?" over instant messaging. To answer your question, Dean: Yes.

- A lot of people in the accessibility demimonde helped me out: Bob Regan, Deneb Meketa, and Mike Williams at Macromedia; Aaron Smith at GW Micro (eyebrow-raisingly rapid and detailed responses to even the smallest questions); Charles McCathieNeville and Wendy Chisholm of the Web Accessibility Initiative (WAI). Ask Loretta Guarino Reid at Adobe about our unending, ear-cartilage-flattening telephone conversations.

- Kynn Bartlett and Charles Munat argued with me, on rare occasion even in a light-hearted and supportive way, for the better part of a year. And in fact, the habitués of the online WAI-IG (Interest Group) and -GL (Guidelines) mailing lists were always fun to spar with, including Al Gilman and, of course, Anne Pemberton.

- A certain small coterie of Webloggers were in my corner, actually: John d'Addario (Jonno.com), John Kusch (JonJonDiaries.com), Jason Schupp (Somnolent.org), Ron Yeany (LeatherEgg.com). Zeldman (again: Zeldman.com) was a supporter. I reiterate. He's a mensch.

- One lives vicariously through Trish Forcinio of Web Masters (Webmast.com) in Philadelphia, as though she were channelling Madonna in the "Deeper and Deeper" music video, a minor masterpiece despite its featuring the unsettling Udo Kier. Trish plied me with CD-Rs of the kind of disco-house "music" the klub kidz love to listen to. I add the proviso that these kidz are generally stoned out of their minds and tend to dance shirtless, the better to expose their shaven chests. Always nice to know what's happening after midnight somewhere *fabulous*. At least I can listen to the same music.

- Other correspondents: Type designer Jean-François Porchez; the very acceptable journalist Doug Robson, only the second redhead acknowledged here; Jeff Z. Klein, who got me started in sportswriting, if this can actually be believed.

- Topic experts helpfully prevented me from incurring excess embarrassment by vetting chapters on their respective topics. Joel Pokorny of the University of Chicago and Cynthia Brewer of Pennsylvania State University debugged the colourblindness chapter. Eric Meyer and Tantek Çelik spotted numerous errors in stylesheet discussions. Rudy Limeback contributed details on database integration. T.V. Raman reinforced my contention that aural cascading stylesheets are *a joke!* Meanwhile, Jukka K. Korpela read nearly the entire manuscript and pointed out my many mistakes. (That's not a problem, it's the *goal.*)
- Dana McKee, Martin Sloan, WGBH, Jeff Schriebman of CCaption.com, and others licenced their written works, research, and software.

Design parody

In a detour through hilarity, I had the brilliant idea of getting a few friends together to produce a parody commercial site – with every feature, gizmo, and doodad commercial sites tend to offer (chat! E-mail! stock tickers! Webcams!) – that would nonetheless be completely accessible. That way, whenever designers of multi-million-dollar sites complained that accessibility would cramp their precious style, we could proudly point to the parody and say, "Well, lookit. A bunch of us pikers, with no budget at all, slapped together a commercial site with all the usual 'bells and whistles,' as they are inevitably called. If we can do it, *you* can."

A good idea. Just super, really. And we even worked up a couple of prototype homepages. But interest nosedived all of a sudden, and this was not the sort of thing I could pull off by myself. Colour me disappointed, but I have half a mind to try to get it up and running after the book comes out. If that comes to be, a prominent link will be visible at my own site, joeclark.org/book/.

Production details

Now you the reader can enjoy a superexclusive, behind-the-scenes peek at Just How It Is One Writes a Computer Book. *You Are There!*

Mechanics

Can you imagine writing an entire book in HTML? Well, that's what I did.

I am actually a long-time word-processing user. (One day back in engineer school, I held up a printout of an essay I wrote. "You'll make a fine secretary someday, Joe," a fellow I had a crush on declared with icy prescience.) I specifically remember AppleWorks on the Apple IIe; every version of WordPerfect for DOS from 3 on up and for Macintosh from 2.1 on up; Word starting at version 1.0 on Macintosh. (Yes, I used the original Word. On a 128 K Mac. With my own customized bitmap font.) WordPerfect 5.1 for DOS beats everything: A better platform for pure *writing* has not been invented.

However, I am a Macintosh separatist. I actively considered running samizdat copies of 5.1 under VirtualPC, but that made as much sense as skateboards at a retirement villa. Besides, I knew that the entire text of the book had to be accessible to a blind reader, and the easiest way to do that was to write the book in validated, accessible HTML. All we'd need to do is link the files together on the book's CD-ROM.

So that's what I did. Essentially every character was typed in BBEdit, the efficient text editor. (Accept no substitutes.) I started out on my old jalopy of a computer, a PowerMac 7100/66. (With two monitors, I might add.) Then the first royalty advance cheque arrived, and I swept triumphantly out the door to buy the fairest compromise of a new machine I could stomach, an iMac 500.

A *Flower Power* iMac. The one with the pastel floral designs on the case. Yes, I'm the one – the only male owner of a Girl Power iMac, as I so cleverly call it. I wouldn't have it any other way. I have no particular fear of seeming girly, and it guarantees me an Apple collectible of the Color Classic/840AV/ Twentieth Anniversary ilk. The other available pattern, the ill-named Blue Dalmation, looked too much like desiccated vomit, showed digital-compression-like artifacts (seemingly unintended random green splotches on the case), and was *way* too butch by comparison.

By the way, my preferred screen colours in BBEdit are black text on pink. At least I'm consistent.

While writing the book, I maintained an occasional Weblog about the process at joeclark.org/bookblog/. It makes sense, really: The entire ethos of the Web centres on openness. I continue to be shocked at the dunderheaded-ness of some of my correspondents, who, despite using E-mail and surfing the Web themselves, insist that it is unwise to document the authorial process while it is happening. How very twentieth-century. These correspondents worry about making a bad impression; I suspect they never met an authority figure they didn't like.

Also, while I was writing the book, Girl Power croaked. All hard drives fail, but how many of them fail nine months into their lives? Little was lost, apart from sleep. If you've got the money, buy backup equipment.

And if you're interested, much of the writing of the book took place in a trance-like state induced by Internet radio stations, namely BassDrive and Neurofunk, that play nonstop drum & bass. The amorphousness and hook-lessness of the music made it hard to fixate on verse and chorus, eliminating a pesky distraction. Drum & bass intensifies whatever autism-like behaviours I have, forcing me to get some work done. (In the immortal words of James Lileks, "There's something calming about working in Photoshop while deafening myself with techno.") I'm sure those stations were playing the same records over and over, but really, *how could you tell?*

Graphic design

Now, then. I go back over twenty years in typography and graphic design; though I am not much of a practitioner (unless you count working as a night-shift typesetter on CompuGraphic 8600 equipment), I know my stuff cold. I was a graphic-design critic for ten years; I can name any font at ten paces and absolutely the first things I spot on any printed page are the mistakes. This book had to look superb *qua* book, with pluperfect typography and composition.

This posed a bit of a dilemma. Computer books are disposable, overlong, ill-written, and ugly, not to mention overpriced. They're disposable because the underlying technology changes; no problem there. As for length: Who needs a 600-page analysis of every nook and cranny of a topic? Especially given the dryness of so *many* of the topics? If I wanted a textbook, I'd go back to university.

Most importantly, computer-book authors are only occasionally actual writers. Typically, their métiers are computer programming (*quelle surprise*), or Web design, or systems administration. If such authors were actual writers, they wouldn't be any good at their day jobs. Yes, of course, dear reader, we can all point to exceptions, like David Pogue. But let's get real: Computer books are not so much written as assembled. Editing such books becomes a matter of language translation, transforming modern Geek into English.

Whereas I wanted to write a computer book you could sit down and read. It had to look great, and even the very oldest of oldschool typographers would be forced to mutter words of grudging respect. No guts, no glory, as they say.

But what to do about the cover? You never get a second chance to make a first impression, etc.

I'd been a fan of Matt Mahurin for a decade. He's a photographer and photoillustrator who has also directed dozens of music videos, usually in a signature chiaroscuro style: Metallica's "Unforgiven" (he's a big fan of metal and rock), "Orange Crush" by R.E.M. (like so very many of that band's videos, a fine freestanding short film), Tracy Chapman's "Fast Car." You're often able to find his disturbing photocollage illustrations in issues of the U.S. *Esquire*. (Matt desperately needs a Website. I've volunteered to work on it.)

Most memorably (some would say notoriously, but I quite disagree), Matt was the man responsible for darkening O.J. Simpson's mug shot on the June 27, 1994 cover of *Time* (while the same photo ran at the same time with much less retouching on the cover of *Newsweek*). As someone who believes that strict accuracy is not always necessary to express truth, I was right behind Matt on that one. My kinda guy.

So I E-mailed him and asked if he'd design the cover (for whatever the New Riders standard fee was). By gar, he said yes. It was a very happy day.

But how do you illustrate accessibility? It's been attempted for years, most irksomely with that ungainly and ham-fisted wheelchair logo, which consists of a white tadpole with no legs riding a wheelchair, all presented on a screaming blue backdrop.

Matt brainstormed some ideas, chief among them:

• Doorway opening out of a spiderweb. Problems: Too-literal (and English-specific) reuse of "Web" trope in illustration; evidence shows an opening door is not understood as a symbol of accessibility by real people.

• Upright portal suspended in spiderweb and seen in three-quarter view. A human figure walks through the portal, dematerializing as if the portal were made of mercury. Problem: Reuse of "Web" trope. Other than that, I loved its spookiness and abstractness. (But shouldn't the figure be walking *out* of the void?)

• Four hands, each at 90° angles, pulling open a door-shaped portal in (again) a spiderweb. (Alternatively, hands could pull toward the four corners.) Problems: "Web" trope reuse, and, as Michael Nolan pointed out, *the hands form a swastika.* (D'oh!) I liked it anyway, but I knew we'd never get anywhere with it.

The visual play on the word "Web" was too obvious for my tastes. But neither Matt nor I could come up with a smart substitution, until one day it hit me: The hands can pull open a portal from an impenetrable thicket of something. Of what, though? All I could think of were twigs and grass, as if opening up a void in the forest floor (to hunt buffalo?). It took Matt about ten seconds on the phone to suggest a thicket of *cables.* Aha!

An easy linkage to technology, with just enough abstraction to make it work. The hands (*definitely* pulling from the corners) symbolically "demystify" accessibility and open a metaphorical portal to an accessible technological future.

But what are the hands opening a portal *to*? In mockups, the portal is merely a black void. But that's where we'd set the title block. The hands, then, open a portal to the title of the book, or, by extension, to the book itself. We've got enough layers of metaphor at work here to keep Gitanes-smoking semioticians exercised for hours.

I was a tad disappointed that Matt did not photograph actual cables (power, armoured, telephone, Ethernet, fibre-optic) and create one of his combined reality/illusion illustrations, choosing instead to draw it all in

Illustrator, but who cares, really? And, in a feature not everyone noticed, there are exactly two different hands depicted, each used twice, with various artificial tints. (There was the predictable call for more racial diversity. I countered that we already had three human skin tones and one sky-blue Smurf, and you can't get more diverse than that, now, can you?)

The cover was approved, though it is apparent as I write this that Matt and I are the only people who like it. I'm not afraid of a little polarization.

Next, body copy. Out of the blue, a local graphic designer named Marc Sullivan had E-mailed me months before. We'd enjoyed a double espresso at a local high-fashion café, which on that day was thankfully free of semioticians. It turns out Marc has an unusually sharp and informed typographic sense. After a great many meandering bull sessions, punctuated by further yuppified coffee, pastries, and Clif Bars to ward off my frequent post-espresso protein crashes, Marc agreed to work up a few prototypes. (Dean Allen designed one, too – a symphony in Sabon that did not turn my crank. You win some, you lose some, Dean.)

Marc supported my criticisms of the *typography* of computer books:

- They're rarely assembled by seasoned designers with broad typographic knowledge and good taste. If that seems like an overbroad defamation of an entire profession, well, I can walk you through any bookstore and prove it.
- Typeface choices are poor. In particular, there seems to be a fondness for monospaced fonts in typesetting computer "code." The only possible reason for such usage is to line text up where such alignment actually means something, which is not always the case at all.
- Moreover, due to unsophistication, the monospaced fonts selected are tacky and either too dark or too light on the page. (Courier New, *come on down!*) The subtle and brilliant TheSans Mono series by Luc(as) de Groot, with fully 32 variations, is either ignored or overused. (A competing publisher typesets covers, headlines, code, and pretty much everything but basic body copy in TheSans Mono, for example.)

There is an assumption that people are actually going to retype all the code samples listed in a book. In practice, it is better to provide that text on a CD-ROM or online for easy copying and pasting. When typesetting the code in the book itself, design for readability.

Marc produced a few works-in-progress using candidate typefaces:

- Antiqua (actual name: TheAntiqua), coincidentally also by Luc(as) de Groot: Very regular on the page; dark typographic "colour"; very amenable to a modern technology book; nonetheless would be seen as too trendy and simplistic by typographic sophistiqués.
- Collis by Christoph Noordzij: Brand-new, and rather recherché; would also be pushing our luck in terms of bandwagon-jumping

reputation; overpriced at retail; unappealing typographic colour; bottom bowl of bicameral g doesn't quite hook up to the top, which tends to derail my reading in this font and others with the same feature, like Else and Enigma.

We settled on Joanna by Eric Gill, which dates from 1937, comfortably insulating us from accusations of trendiness. (It's hard to find an educated typographer who doesn't respect Joanna, particularly its distinctive italic, which shows much more variation from the roman than is fashionable today.) It's a face I'd enjoyed in its original Monotype hot-metal incarnations when I was a youngster. The PostScript interpretations of Joanna are too light in the body (they look rather spindly), but we are living with that.

For code samples, Marc came up with the brilliantly unexpected choice of Signa by Ole Søndergaard (2000), a nearly-monoline sans-serif face (i.e., its strokes appear almost even and consistent in thickness) with an even stranger g than Collis' that I nonetheless do not find distracting. (That's inexplicable and inconsistent of me, I know. Typography is like that.)

Signa offers just enough contrast with Joanna, and adds just enough 21st-century moxie, to create an enjoyable but unobtrusive counterpoint. Marc and I could never figure out how to pronounce the name, though: The English way (as in *signal*) or the Italian ("sinnya")? It doesn't help that the designer is Danish; we could be wrong both ways.

Much nailbiting ensued in the choice of headline fonts. We bandied about various trendy sans serifs, like Scala Sans (no, thank you) and Quadraat Sans (which I like chiefly for the chance it gives me to pronounce its name "Kvadraat," like the name of some B-movie vampire), but settled on the humanist sans serif known as Seria Sans by Martin Majoor (2000).

Marc and I decided to go to the wall in type choice for cover and chapter heads. Jeremy Tankard's demented sextet of Shire Types includes a gargoylish variant known as Warwickshire. (The others are Derbyshire, Staffordshire, Cheshire, Shropshire, and Worcestershire.) A *common case* font (mixing caps and lowercase in letters of uniform height), Warwickshire adds a bit of daring. It's just the right kind of bad taste, really. If Alexander McQueen designed type, he'd be Jeremy Tankard.

Numerals superimposed on examples used in the "Navigation" chapter are set in FF Dingbats Numbers by Johannes Erler and Olaf Stein (2000).

The worst was yet to come: I can tell you right now that HTML, with its rigid markup, actively moulds your mind and influences your fate months down the road. Just how *do* you adapt HTML elements like <code></code>, <samp></samp>, <kbd></kbd>, <var></var> (sometimes in combination: <code><var></var></code>), *and* all six of the heading elements, to the world of print typography, with its centuries of tradition? In fact, while writing the book I was crying out for *more* heading levels than a mere six, but those were hard enough to differentiate typographically. The ideal solution would have used legal numbering (1, 1.1, 1.1.1), but that's the sort of thing you want your software to handle for you automatically, and ours could not. (I am aware that it is possible to enumerate headings in HTML using stylesheets. Try getting *that* to transfer over to Quark Xpress.)

Photo credits

My thanks go out to Compu-TTY for the TTY product shot and Tieman BV for the refreshable-Braille-display product shot. Captioning and subtitling frames reflect the film *Run Lola Run* (copyright © X Filme Creative Pool 1998); captions and subtitles by Captions, Inc. Captions from online video productions are taken from the U.S. Equal Employment Opportunity Commission's series of public-service announcements and the Division of Information Technology at the University of Wisconsin's *Introduction to the Screen Reader with Neal Ewers.*

Errors and omissions

I was hell-bent to stamp out errors in the book. Some chapters were read as many as eight times, and I am sure that's *still* not enough. At my prompting, and after some reprioritizing of budget line-items, we were able to hire Moveable Inc., indisputably the best typesetting house in Canada and almost certainly the best in North America, to proof the book's final copy.

Nonetheless, I actively encourage readers to write in with corrections – any corrections at all, no matter how seemingly minor.

Readers outside Canada must reassure themselves that this book is *not* in fact rife with spelling errors. I write in Canadian English, whose orthography differs from every other kind. You can sum it up in three words: *neighbour, organize, tire* (surrounding a wheel); we use double quotation marks. (Brits and most former colonies use *neighbour, organise, tyre;* single quotes. Americans use *neighbor, organize, tire;* double quotes.) I simply cannot write consistently in American or U.K. spellings. New Riders and I decided that it was easier to live with Canadian orthography than my error-prone attempts to write in a different dialect; we would also risk too many niggly mistakes by attempting to regularize Canadian spellings into American: I expected we'd end up missing a word ending in *-our* somewhere. (And yes, from an accessibility perspective, that *does* mean that TV shows, films, and online video with American or British captions or subtitles are all misspelled as far as we're concerned.)

Further, the term *shurely* (usually written with a trailing ?!) is not a misspelling. It's an adaptation of the usage of *Private Eye* and *Frank,* the British and Canadian satirical newspapers. The original *Private Eye*–ism, attributed to the speech impediment of Lord Bill Deedes of the *Daily Telegraph,* is "shurely shome mishtake?!"

A note to accessibility advocates: Your advice may differ from mine. It ought to: This is my book, not yours. Still, I have encouraged others to write their own books, because the greater the number of accessibility books on the market, the more obvious it becomes that mine is the best. I acknowledge in advance that my recommendations are often at infuriating variance with official dogma as articulated in the WAI's Web Content Accessibility Guidelines. Dogma needs a bit of rattling now and then, and frankly, a lot of people involved with the WAI need to get out more.

Thanks for reading, and I insist you drop me a line: joeclark@joeclark.org.

index

H

n

t

u-v

w-z

VIEW CART

search ⊙

▸ Registration already a member? Log in. ▸ Book Registration

Publishing
the Voices
that Matter

OUR AUTHORS

PRESS ROOM

| web development | design | photoshop | new media | 3-D | server technologie |

EDUCATORS

ABOUT US

CONTACT US

You already know that New Riders brings you the **Voices That Matter**.

But what does that mean? It means that New Riders brings you the

Voices that challenge your assumptions, take your talents to the next

level, or simply help you better understand the complex technical world

we're all navigating.

Visit **www.newriders.com** to find:

▸ **10% discount** and **free shipping** on all book purchases

▸ Never before published chapters

▸ Sample chapters and excerpts

▸ Author bios and interviews

▸ Contests and enter-to-wins

▸ Up-to-date industry event information

▸ Book reviews

▸ Special offers from our friends and partners

▸ Info on how to join our User Group program

▸ Ways to have your Voice heard

New
Riders

WWW.NEWRIDERS.COM

VISIT OUR WEB SITE

WWW.NEWRIDERS.COM

On our web site, you'll find information about our other books, authors, tables of contents, and book errata. You will also find information about book registration and how to purchase our books, both domestically and internationally.

EMAIL US

Contact us at: **nrfeedback@newriders.com**

- If you have comments or questions about this book
- To report errors that you have found in this book
- If you have a book proposal to submit or are interested in writing for New Riders
- If you are an expert in a computer topic or technology and are interested in being a technical editor who reviews manuscripts for technical accuracy

Contact us at: **nreducation@newriders.com**

- If you are an instructor from an educational institution who wants to preview New Riders books for classroom use. Email should include your name, title, school, department, address, phone number, office days/hours, text in use, and enrollment, along with your request for desk/examination copies and/or additional information.

Contact us at: **nrmedia@newriders.com**

- If you are a member of the media who is interested in reviewing copies of New Riders books. Send your name, mailing address, and email address, along with the name of the publication or web site you work for.

BULK PURCHASES/CORPORATE SALES

The publisher offers discounts on this book when ordered in quantity for bulk purchases and special sales. For sales within the U.S., please contact: Corporate and Government Sales (800) 382-3419 or **corpsales@pearsontechgroup.com**. Outside of the U.S., please contact: International Sales (317) 581-3793 or **international@pearsontechgroup.com**.

WRITE TO US

New Riders Publishing
201 W. 103rd St.
Indianapolis, IN 46290-1097

CALL/FAX US

Toll-free (800) 571-5840
If outside U.S. (317) 581-3500
Ask for New Riders
FAX: (317) 581-4663

Solutions from experts you know and trust.

www.informit.com

OPERATING SYSTEMS

WEB DEVELOPMENT

PROGRAMMING

NETWORKING

CERTIFICATION

AND MORE...

Expert Access.
Free Content.

New Riders has partnered with **InformIT.com** to bring technical information to your desktop. Drawing on New Riders authors and reviewers to provide additional information on topics you're interested in, **InformIT.com** has free, in-depth information you won't find anywhere else.

- **Master the skills you need, when you need them**

- **Call on resources from some of the best minds in the industry**

- **Get answers when you need them, using InformIT's comprehensive library or live experts online**

- **Go above and beyond what you find in New Riders books, extending your knowledge**

As an **InformIT** partner, **New Riders** has shared the wisdom and knowledge of our authors with you online. Visit **InformIT.com** to see what you're missing.

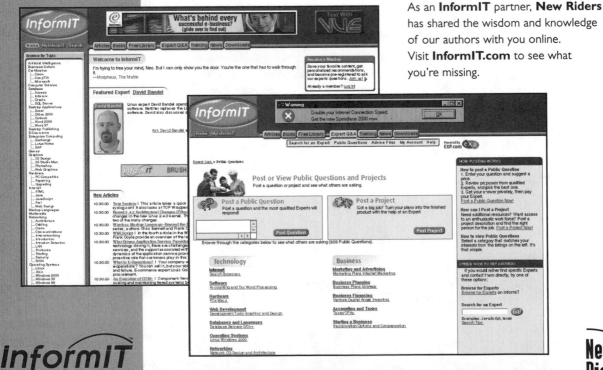

WHAT YOU'LL LEARN IN THIS BOOK

- How people with disabilities use computers

- Disability groups affected by Web accessibility, with population statistics

- Government and industry standards (like the Web Content Accessibility Guidelines and U.S. Section 508 requirements), what they get right, and what they get wrong

- HTML validation, and how to structure an accessible page

- Accessible coding of text and links, forms, and tables